D1433391

1000 Recipes

for Simple Family Food

1000 Recipes

for Simple Family Food

hamlyn

An Hachette UK Company
www.hachette.co.uk

First published in Great Britain in 2011 by
Hamlyn, a division of Octopus Publishing Group Ltd
Endeavour House, 189 Shaftesbury Avenue,
London, WC2H 8JY
www.octopusbooks.co.uk

Copyright © Octopus Publishing Group Ltd 2011

All rights reserved. No part of this work may be reproduced or
utilized in any form or by any means, electronic or mechanical,
including photocopying, recording or by any information
storage and retrieval system, without the prior written
permission of the publisher.

ISBN 978-0-600-62153-9

A CIP catalogue record for this book is available from the
British Library.

Printed and bound in China

10 9 8 7 6 5 4 3 2 1

Notes
Both metric and imperial measurements have been given in
all recipes. Use one set of measurements only, and not a
mixture of both.

Standard level spoon measurements are used in all recipes.
1 tablespoon = one 15 ml spoon
1 teaspoon = one 5 ml spoon

Ovens should be preheated to the specified temperature.
If using a fan-assisted oven, follow the manufacturer's
instructions for adjusting the time and temperature.

Fresh herbs should be used unless otherwise stated.

Eggs should be medium unless otherwise stated; choose
free-range if possible and preferably organic. The Department
of Health advises that eggs should not be consumed raw.
This book contains some dishes made with raw or lightly
cooked eggs. It is prudent for more vulnerable people, such
as pregnant and nursing mothers, invalids, the elderly, babies
and young children, to avoid uncooked or lightly cooked
dishes made with eggs.

This book includes dishes made with nuts and nut derivatives.
It is advisable for those with known allergic reactions to nuts
and nut derivatives and those who may be potentially
vulnerable to these allergies, such as pregnant and nursing
mothers, invalids, the elderly, babies and children, to avoid
dishes made with nuts and nut oils. It is also prudent to check
the labels of pre-prepared ingredients for the possible
inclusion of nut derivatives.

CONTENTS

INTRODUCTION

With today's hectic lifestyles, it is easy to see how family mealtimes are often forced to fit around many competing activities and our diets may not always be as nutritious as they could be. Time is often in such short supply that we barely have time to sit down to eat our meals, never mind plan, shop and cook them properly. Most of us would love to reduce the amount of stress in our lives and this book aims to help make mealtimes not only more interesting and healthier, but also to get the whole family involved. With 1,000 recipes to choose from you'll be able to create a variety of simple, nutritious meals whatever the occasion. Chapters are colour coded so it's easy to find the right recipe for any occasion. There are snacks for breakfasts, brunches and light dishes, a chapter on budget eats that won't break the bank, classic family favourites that are foolproof crowdpleasers, one-pot meals for a fuss-free life in the kitchen, quick meals that can be prepared and cooked in 30 minutes, inspiring vegetarian dishes, and sweets, puddings, cakes and bakes galore.

Thinking ahead

It's never been easier to shop for and prepare great food. Fresh herbs, high-quality ingredients and a good combination of flavours and textures mean that easy cooking does not mean boring eating. For example, a fantastic olive oil or organic wild salmon fillet can make the difference between a dish that is merely acceptable and one that tastes wonderful.

If you know you have a busy week ahead, try and find the time to sit down the week before to plan your meals and write a shopping list. The majority of the recipes in this book serve four as a main course, but many of the salads, soups and vegetarian options would also make great starters and will comfortably feed up to eight people. If you are cooking for two people, simply halve the quantities. If you are serving a dessert, choose one that will cook while you are eating your first course or something that can be made in advance, such as a sorbet. Using the recipes as a base, feel free to alter the quantities or experiment with the choice of ingredients.

Cooking should be fun so make sure you follow your instincts and cook to fit your mood.

Storecupboard essentials

There are certain basics that you will always need; these include staple carbohydrates such as rice and pasta (ideally the brown varieties), couscous, noodles and porridge oats. You may not always have fresh meat, but keep a bag of cashew nuts and cans of tuna, salmon and beans in the cupboard, some eggs in the fridge and a supply of frozen prawns in the freezer, and you'll have everything you need to create a nutritious protein-rich dinner in a matter of minutes. To add flavour and to help the cooking process, ensure you have chicken and vegetable stock cubes and soy sauce in the cupboard, along with olive, sesame and rapeseed oils, salt and pepper, tomato and sundried tomato paste, and key herbs and spices such as mixed herbs, mixed spice, Chinese 5-spice, ground cinnamon, coriander, cumin and nutmeg and chilli sauce or flakes.

Other ingredients that will enable you to whip up tasty sauces include flour, cornflour, canned tomatoes, passata, olives, mature chedder and some UHT dried milk. And for last-minute desserts – keep sugar, honey, maple syrup, a couple of cans of tinned fruit and some digestive biscuits in the cupboard, plus some vanilla ice cream, fruit sorbet and waffles in the freezer. Cartons of crème fraîche and plain yoghurt never go amiss in the fridge for both savoury and sweet dishes, but as these ingredients have a short shelf life, ideally they should be bought as part of your meal planning process.

Don't feel guilty about making life a little easier for yourself by using ready-made items, so stock up on jars of pesto and tapenades, cooked rice, lentils and pulses, deli-style roast vegetables. Look out, too, for jars of ready-minced garlic and ginger (widely available in supermarkets), which mean that you can add these wonderful flavours without having to spend time peeling, crushing and grating. Don't forget that you can also buy pre-cut strips of meat, such as beef or pork, which are perfect for stir-fries. Frozen pastry is essential for anyone wanting to cook easy pies or tarts: just remember to take it out of the freezer in good time to thaw before you start cooking.

Family food that's good food

Whether young or old, vegetarian or omnivore, we all need to get sufficient nutrients from our food intake to provide our bodies with energy and help to promote long-term good health. To get the complete range of nutrients our bodies need, we should be consuming carbohydrates, protein, fats, fibre and water, as well as a variety of vitamins and minerals. These nutrients not only fuel our bodies, but many of them actually help to improve our health and protect the body against disease. If we eat well, we feel well, our mood is improved and we cope better with stress, which can only be a good thing for anyone leading a busy life!

The secret is to mix up the recipes so that your family are eating as wide a variety of foods as possible – that way they will get all the benefits of improved nutrition. You may not always be able to please the whole family in one sitting, but at least if you vary the recipes, everyone will have at least one meal a week that they really love and you will not find yourself in a 'meal rut' where you eat the same foods day after day.

You will see throughout the book that recipes centre on a range of carbohydrate-based meals. Although carbs have had a bad press in recent years, good carbohydrates (otherwise known as complex carbohydrates) are vital to our health and should form the basis of every healthy diet. Complex carbohydrates include grains, bread, rice and pasta, as well as fruits and vegetables, pulses and dairy products.

Choose brown versions of pasta, bread and rice where possible as these have not had all the nutrients processed out of them and retain their fibre content. Fibre is found only in plant-based foods and plays an important role in keeping our bodies healthy – firstly because fibre keeps the gut healthy and secondly because fibrous foods help maintain our blood-sugar levels. They also take longer to digest, thereby keeping you fuller for longer and reducing the temptation to eat unhealthy snacks between meals.

Fruits and vegetables may not be every child's favourite food, but they should form the basis of most meals and should also, ideally, be your first choice for snacks. They are packed full of antioxidants which protect against disease, plus they are loaded with vitamins and minerals such as iron and calcium, which the body requires to function properly. For this reason, you will see that fruits and vegetables feature very highly in this book – in recipes such as French Toast with Blueberries on page 14, Greek Vegetable Casserole on page 233 and Minted Pea Soup on page 46. As well as providing important vitamins and minerals, they also add wonderful flavour, texture and colour to your meals.

Pulses are also an excellent source of fibre and feature in a variety of tasty recipes within our 'One Pot' meals and 'Vegetarian' chapters. Introducing your family to pulses is a great idea. Not only are they good sources of protein, but they are also full of B vitamins, calcium and iron, are low in saturated fat and are cholesterol-free!

If your children are anything like the norm, getting them to eat protein should not be a problem. Many of the meaty treats such as Lamb Hotpot with Dumplings on page 103 are real family classics – and who could resist Fast Chicken Curry on page 189 or Meatballs with Tomato Sauce on page 141 – they are absolute winners with adults and children alike! Getting younger children to eat fish and seafood may be a little more tricky, but try the Tuna Melts on page 274 or the Salmon Pasta Bake on page 287, and watch the whole family wolf down their fish and come back for more.

Get cooking!

A successful meal takes a little planning and time, good ingredients, a dash of inspiration and some gentle encouragement. If cooking for your family has been a disappointing or time-consuming experience in the past, this book should provide you with plenty of inspiration to turn the tide on those mealtime blues.

SIMPLE SNACKS & LIGHT BITES

CRUNCHY HONEY YOGURT

Serves **6**
Preparation time **10 minutes**
Cooking time **5 minutes**

500 g (1 lb) **Greek yogurt**
125 g (4 oz) **strawberries**, quartered

Topping
50 g (2 oz) **flaked almonds**
50 g (2 oz) **pumpkin seeds**
50 g (2 oz) **sunflower seeds**
3 tablespoons **sesame seeds**
50 g (2 oz) **oats**
6 tablespoons **golden caster sugar**
4 tablespoons **clear honey**, plus extra to drizzle
 (optional)

Mix the almonds, seeds, oats and sugar in a large bowl. Line a large baking sheet with nonstick baking paper, then pour the nut and seed mixture over. Lightly shake the baking sheet to level the ingredients.

Drizzle the honey in thin streams over the top, then place under a preheated medium grill for 3–4 minutes until the sugar begins to caramelize and the nuts and seeds turn golden brown. Remove from the grill and set aside to cool and harden. Place the hardened nuts and seeds in a polythene bag and bash with a rolling pin to crush into a crunchy topping.

Spoon the yogurt into a bowl and fold in the strawberries. Divide between 6 serving bowls and sprinkle with the topping. (Store any leftover topping in an airtight container for up to 2 weeks.) Drizzle with more honey, if liked.

For yogurt-coated cereal topping, melt 125 g (4 oz) white chocolate in a heatproof bowl set over a pan of gently simmering water. Remove from the heat and add 2 tablespoons of natural yogurt. Crunch up 50 g (2 oz) cornflakes and 2 whole shredded wheat bicuits on to a baking parchment-lined baking sheet and scatter over 25 g (1 oz) rice puffs. Drizzle over the warm white chocolate and yogurt coating and refrigerate for 1 hour until set. Once set, transfer the paper to a chopping board and roughly chop the cereals to form a rough and chunky topping.

10

LATE GREAT BREAKFAST

Serves **4**
Preparation time **15 minutes**
Cooking time **15–20 minutes**

400 g (13 oz) sheet
 ready-rolled **puff pastry**
1 **red pepper**, cored, deseeded and roughly chopped
2 **tomatoes**, cut into wedges
125 g (4 oz) **button mushrooms**, cut in half
2 tablespoons **olive oil**
6 **eggs**
8 thin-cut rindless rashers **streaky** or **back bacon**
15 g (½ oz) **butter**, plus extra for greasing

Unroll the pastry and cut out four 12 x 10 cm (5 x 4 inch) rectangles. Using the tip of a small knife, make a shallow cut about 1 cm (½ inch) in from the edges of each rectangle, making sure you don't cut right through to the base. Place the pastry rectangles on a greased baking sheet.

Arrange the pepper, tomatoes and mushrooms on the pastry cases, keeping them away from the marked rims. Drizzle with 1 tablespoon of the oil and bake in a preheated oven, 220°C (425°F), Gas Mark 7, for 15–20 minutes until the pastry is well risen and golden.

While the pastry cases are baking, beat the eggs in a bowl. Heat the remaining oil in a frying pan and gently fry the bacon for about 2 minutes on each side until crisp, turning the rashers with a fish slice or wooden spatula. Melt the butter in a large saucepan. Tip in the beaten eggs and cook over a gentle heat, stirring continuously until scrambled.

Remove the baking sheet from the oven and transfer the pastries to serving plates. Spoon some scrambled eggs on to the centre of each and top with the bacon rashers. Serve while still hot.

For sausage & tomato pasties, place 8 good-quality chipolata sausages under a hot grill and cook, turning, for 8–10 minutes until golden and cooked, adding 8 halved, small tomatoes to the grill pan cut side up for the final 5 minutes of cooking. Halve the sausages and toss with the tomatoes and 1 tablespoon chopped parsley and use to fill the pastries, as above.

MORNING MUFFINS & TOMATO KETCHUP

Serves **4**
Preparation time **15 minutes**
Cooking time **20–25 minutes**

500 g (1 lb) good-quality **sausages**
1 tablespoon chopped **rosemary**
3 tablespoons chopped **parsley**
1 tablespoon **thick honey**
1 teaspoon **vinegar**
4 **eggs**
2 **English muffins**, halved

Ketchup
400 g (13 oz) can **chopped tomatoes**
2 tablespoons **maple syrup**
1 tablespoon **soft brown sugar**
3 tablespoons **red wine vinegar**

Place all the ketchup ingredients into a heavy-based frying pan and bring to the boil. Reduce the heat and gently simmer for 5–7 minutes, uncovered, stirring occasionally until the sauce is thick and pulpy. Whiz in a food processor until smooth, then place in a jar and cool.

Cut along the length of each sausage, ease the skin off and discard it. Place the sausagemeat in a bowl with the herbs and honey and mix well. Using damp hands, shape into 8 small patties, then cook under a preheated medium grill for 10–12 minutes, turning once, until golden.

Meanwhile, bring a frying pan half-filled with water, with the vinegar added, to the boil. Reduce the heat to a simmer, then immediately break the eggs, well spaced apart, into the water and cook for 1 minute until the white is opaque. Remove from the water using a slotted spoon and keep warm.

Toast the muffin halves until golden and lightly crisp. Place a warm muffin half on to each of 4 serving plates and top with 2 sausage patties, a poached egg and a spoonful of ketchup.

For tomato & mushroom muffins, heat 1 tablespoon olive oil in a heavy-based frying pan and cook 250 g (8 oz) halved chestnut mushrooms and 4 halved plum tomatoes over a moderate heat for 4–5 minutes until soft and golden, turning occasionally. Poach the eggs and toast the muffins as above. Serve the muffins with the warm tomatoes, mushrooms and eggs on top with a drizzle of ketchup.

PANCAKE STACK WITH MAPLE SYRUP

Serves **4**
Preparation time **10 minutes**
Cooking time **6 minutes**

1 **egg**
100 g (3½ oz) **strong plain flour**
125 ml (4 fl oz) **milk**
2½ tablespoons **vegetable oil**
1 tablespoon **caster sugar**
bottled **maple syrup**, to drizzle
8 scoops of **vanilla ice cream**

Put the egg, flour, milk, oil and sugar in a food processor or blender and whiz until smooth and creamy.

Heat a large frying pan over a medium heat and put in 4 half-ladlefuls of the batter to make 4 pancakes.

After about 1 minute the tops of the pancakes will start to set and air bubbles will rise to the top and burst. Use a spatula to turn the pancakes over and cook on the other side for 1 minute.

Repeat twice more until you have used all the batter and made 12 small pancakes in all.

Bring the pancakes to the table as a stack, drizzled with maple syrup, and serve 3 pancakes to each person, with scoops of ice cream.

For orange-flavoured pancakes, make a batter from 125 g (4 oz) plain flour, 2 teaspoons each caster sugar and grated orange rind, 1 teaspoon each cream of tartar and golden syrup, ½ teaspoon each salt and bicarbonate of soda, 1 egg, 125 ml (4 fl oz) warm milk and a few drops of orange essence. Cook the pancakes as above.

FRENCH TOAST WITH BLUEBERRIES

Serves **4**
Preparation time **5 minutes**
Cooking time **10 minutes**

2 **eggs**
25 g (1 oz) **caster sugar**
½ teaspoon **ground cinnamon**
4 tablespoons **milk**
25 g (1 oz) **butter**
4 thick slices **brioche**
100 g (3½ oz) **blueberries**
8 tablespoons thick **Greek yogurt**
4 teaspoons **honey**, to drizzle

Beat the eggs in a bowl with the sugar, cinnamon and milk. Heat the butter in a large, heavy-based frying pan. Dip the brioche slices, 2 at a time, into the egg mixture on both sides, then lift into the hot pan and fry for 1–2 minutes on each side until golden.

Repeat with the remaining brioche slices. Mix half the blueberries into the yogurt.

Serve the warm French toasts with spoonfuls of the yogurt on top, the remaining blueberries scattered over and a thin drizzle of honey on top.

For sugar & cinnamon French toast, make the French toasts as above and place on serving plates once cooked and warm. Mix 50 g (2 oz) demerara sugar with ½ teaspoon ground cinnamon. Dredge each of the warm French toasts with the cinnamon sugar and serve.

BREAKFAST SMOOTHIES

Serves **2**
Preparation time **5 minutes**

2 bananas
300 ml (½ pt) **milk**
4 tablespoons natural **fromage frais**
3 tablespoons **maple syrup**
50 g (2 oz) **hot oat cereal**

To serve
banana slices
malt loaf, cut into chunks

Place the bananas in a food processor with the milk, fromage frais and maple syrup and blend until smooth. Add the oat cereal and whiz again to thicken. Pour into 2 large glasses.

Arrange banana slices and chunks of malt loaf on 2 cocktail sticks and balance them across the top of the glasses, to serve.

For peanut-butter smoothies, replace the banana slices with 4 tablespoons crunchy peanut butter, and change the maple syrup to honey. Make as above, whizzing until smooth.

MELTING MUSHROOMS

Serves **4**
Preparation time **10 minutes**
Cooking time **9–12 minutes**

2 tablespoon **olive oil**
4 large flat **mushrooms**
4 small fresh **tomatoes**, roughly chopped
1 tablespoon **tomato purée**
4 tablespoons canned **cannellini beans**, drained
  and rinsed
1 tablespoon **clear honey**
1 tablespoon chopped **parsley**
50 g (2 oz) **Gruyère** or **Edam cheese**, thinly sliced
1 tablespoon freshly grated **Parmesan cheese**
4 slices **wholemeal toast**, to serve

Heat the oil in a large, heavy-based frying pan and cook the mushrooms over a moderate heat for 2–3 minutes, turning once, until they are softened. Place the mushrooms, stalk side up, on a foil-lined grill rack.

Add the tomatoes to the pan juices, and cook, stirring occasionally, for 4–5 minutes until the tomatoes are thick and pulpy. Add the tomato purée, beans and honey and continue to cook for a further 1 minute. Remove from the heat and stir in the parsley.

Divide the mixture between the mushrooms and arrange the slices of Gruyère or Edam over the top. Sprinkle the mushrooms with the Parmesan and place under a preheated hot grill for 2–3 minutes until golden and bubbling. Serve with slices of hot buttered wholemeal toast.

For egg-topped melting mushrooms, follow the recipe as above. Towards the end, poach 4 eggs in a frying pan half-filled with boiling water with 1 teaspoon vinegar for 1–2 minutes, then remove from the water using a slotted spoon and place on the mushrooms.

SMOKED SALMON CONES

Serves **4**
Preparation time **15 minutes**

2 **small cucumbers**, halved lengthways, deseeded and
  cut into thin strips
1 teaspoon prepared **English mustard**
1 tablespoon **white wine vinegar**
½ teaspoon **caster sugar**
1 tablespoon finely chopped **dill**
2 **flour tortillas**
4 tablespoons **crème fraîche**
125 g (4 oz) **smoked salmon trimmings**, any larger
  pieces cut into wide strips
salt and **pepper**

Put the cucumber strips in a shallow glass or ceramic bowl. In a small bowl, mix together the mustard, vinegar, sugar and dill. Season well with salt and pepper, then pour over the cucumbers. Leave to stand for 5 minutes.

Cut the tortillas in half and lay on a board or work surface. Spread 1 tablespoon crème fraîche over each tortilla half.

Divide the smoked salmon pieces between the tortillas and top with the cucumber mixture. Add a little salt and pepper, if liked, and roll up each tortilla to form a cone around the filling. Secure each cone with a cocktail stick, if liked.

For chicken & mango cones, put 125 g (4 oz) diced, cooked chicken breast meat, 1 large peeled, stoned and diced mango and 1 tablespoon chopped coriander leaves in a bowl. Add 4 tablespoons mayonnaise, a squeeze of lime juice, and salt and pepper to taste. Toss gently to combine, then divide between the tortilla halves and roll up, as above.

CHICKEN CLUB SANDWICH

Serves **4**
Preparation time **15 minutes**
Cooking time **10 minutes**

4 small boneless, skinless **chicken breasts**,
   thinly sliced
8 rashers **smoked streaky bacon**
1 tablespoon **sunflower oil**
12 slices **bread**
4 tablespoons **light mayonnaise**
125 g (4 oz) **dolcelatte or bleu d'Auvergne cheese**,
   thinly sliced
4 **tomatoes**, thinly sliced
40 g (1½ oz) **watercress**

Fry the chicken and bacon in the oil for 6–8 minutes, turning once or twice until golden and the chicken is cooked through.

Toast the bread on both sides, then spread with the mayonnaise. Divide the chicken and bacon between four slices of toast, then top with the sliced cheese. Cover the cheese with 4 more slices of toast, then add the tomato slices and watercress. Complete the sandwich stacks with the final slices of toast.

Press the sandwiches together, then cut each stack into 4 small triangles. Secure with cocktail sticks, if needed, and serve immediately.

For deli deluxe chicken sandwich, fry the chicken in the oil as above, omitting the bacon. Split and toast the cut sides of a ciabatta loaf, spread the lower half with 4 teaspoons of black-olive tapenade, then top with 2 tablespoons of mayonnaise. Add the chicken to the tapenade toast, cover with 125 g (4 oz) sliced brie cheese, then 75 g (3 oz) sun-dried tomatoes and 40 g (1½ oz) rocket leaves. Top with the remaining toast, then cut into 4 thick slices. Serve warm.

AUBERGINE, TOMATO & FETA ROLLS

Serves **4**
Preparation time **15 minutes**
Cooking time **about 6 minutes**

2 **aubergines**
3 tablespoons **olive oil**
125 g (4 oz) **feta cheese**, roughly diced
12 **sun-dried tomatoes in oil**, drained
15–20 **basil leaves**
salt and **pepper**

Trim the ends of the aubergines, then cut a thin slice lengthways from either side of each; discard these slices, which should be mainly skin. Cut each aubergine lengthways into 4 slices. Heat the grill on the hottest setting or heat a griddle pan until very hot.

Brush both sides of the aubergine slices with the oil, then cook under the grill or in the griddle pan for 3 minutes on each side or until browned and softened.

Lay the aubergine slices on a board and divide the feta, tomatoes and basil leaves between them. Season well with salt and pepper. Roll up each slice from a short end and secure with a cocktail stick. Arrange on serving plates and serve immediately, or cover and set aside in a cool place, but not the refrigerator, and serve at room temperature when required.

For courgette & mozzarella rolls, use 3–4 large courgettes, then trim the ends and sides as for the aubergines. Cut each courgette lengthways into 3 slices, depending on their thickness, brush with oil and cook under the grill or in a griddle pan as for the aubergines until browned and softened. Spread the courgette slices with red pesto, then top with 125 g (4 oz) diced mozzarella cheese and the basil leaves. Roll up and serve as above.

PRAWN TOASTS

Serves **4**
Preparation time **15 minutes**
Cooking time **about 5 minutes**

175 g (6 oz) **prawns**
2.5 cm (1 inch) piece fresh **root ginger**, peeled
 and finely grated
1 **spring onion**, finely chopped
1 **egg white**, beaten
1 tablespoon **cornflour**
1 teaspoon **sesame oil**
1 teaspoon **dark soy sauce**, plus extra to serve
4 medium-cut slices **'best of both' bread**
4 tablespoons **sesame seeds**
6 tablespoons **vegetable oil**

Place the prawns in a food processor with the ginger, spring onion, egg white, cornflour, sesame oil and soy sauce and whiz to form a thick paste.

Spread the mixture on each of the slices of bread. Place the sesame seeds on a large plate and press the prawn toast, prawn side down, in the seeds to lightly cover.

Heat 2 tablespoons of the oil in a large, heavy-based frying pan. Cook 2 of the prawn toasts, prawn side down first for 1–2 minutes until golden; then turn over and cook the other side for 1 minute until golden. Repeat the process wiping out the pan with kitchen paper and heating the remaining oil first. Drain on kitchen paper, then cut into triangles.

Serve the toasts with plenty of cucumber and sweetcorn salsa (see below), if liked.

For cucumber & sweetcorn salsa to serve as an accompaniment, finely chop ¼ cucumber and place in a bowl with 4 tablespoons chopped fresh coriander and a 200 g (7 oz) can sweetcorn, drained. Finely chop ½ red pepper and add to the mix, then add 1 tablespoon sweet chilli sauce and mix together. Spoon on to the sesame prawn toasts to serve.

18

SIMPLE SNACKS & LIGHT BITES

ITALIAN PESTO CHICKEN BURGERS

Serves **4**
Preparation time **15 minutes**, plus chilling
Cooking time **10–13 minutes**

500 g (1 lb) **minced chicken**
2 **garlic cloves**, finely chopped
4 **spring onions**, finely chopped
2 teaspoons **pesto**
1 **egg yolk**
1 tablespoon **sunflower oil**
4 **ciabatta rolls**
2 tablespoons **mayonnaise**
40 g (1½ oz) **rocket, watercress and spinach salad**
50 g (2 oz) **sun-dried tomatoes in oil**, drained, sliced
salt and **pepper**

Put the chicken, garlic, spring onions, pesto and egg yolk in a bowl, add seasoning, then mix together well. Divide into 4, then shape into thick burgers. Chill for 1 hour.

Heat the oil in a nonstick frying pan, add the burgers and fry for about 10–13 minutes, turning once or twice until they are golden brown and cooked through.

Split the ciabatta rolls in half and lightly toast the cut sides. Spread with mayonnaise, then add the salad and tomatoes to the lower half of each roll. Top with the burgers and the other half of each roll, and serve with oven chips.

For curried chicken burgers, mix 2 teaspoons hot curry paste and 2 tablespoons chopped coriander into the chicken mixture instead of the pesto. Fry as above, then serve in warmed round naan breads with salad and mango chutney.

CHEESY TWISTS

Makes **about 15**
Preparation time **15 minutes**
Cooking time **8–12 minutes**

50 g (2 oz) **Cheddar cheese**, grated
75 g (3 oz) **self-raising flour**, plus extra for dusting
½ teaspoon **mustard powder**
50 g (2 oz) chilled **butter**, cut into cubes
1 **egg yolk**

Put the Cheddar into a mixing bowl, then sift the flour and mustard powder into the bowl. Add the butter, then rub the cheese, butter and flour together until the butter is broken up and covered in flour and the mixture looks like fine breadcrumbs. Add the egg yolk to the mixture and stir with a wooden spoon until you have a stiff dough.

Roll out the dough on a well-floured surface until it is about 5 mm (¼ inch) thick. Take a sharp knife and cut the dough into about 15 long strips, about 1 cm (½ inch) thick. Pick up each strip carefully and twist it gently before laying it on a baking sheet lined with nonstick baking paper.

Bake the twists in a preheated oven, 220°C (425°F), Gas Mark 7, for 8–12 minutes until golden brown, then remove them from the oven and allow to cool on the baking sheet.

For spinach & Parmesan twists, place the flour in a food processor with a handful of spinach leaves and whiz until fine and green in colour. Add the remaining ingredients, replacing the Cheddar with freshly grated Parmesan, then continue as above.

CHOCOLATE-TOFFEE POPCORN

Makes about **175 g (6 oz)**
Preparation time **15 minutes**
Cooking time **about 10 minutes**

about 50 g (2 oz) **milk chocolate**, broken into pieces
50 g (2 oz) **firm toffees**
4 tablespoons **milk**
1 tablespoon **vegetable oil**
75 g (3 oz) **popcorn kernels**

Place the chocolate pieces in a small heatproof bowl. Microwave on medium power for 1 minute. Leave to stand for 2 minutes, then microwave again for 30 seconds at a time until melted, stirring frequently to avoid lumps. (Alternatively, melt the chocolate carefully in a small heatproof bowl over a small saucepan of gently simmering water.)

Unwrap the toffees and put them in a polythene bag. Place on a chopping board and tap firmly with a rolling pin until the toffees have broken into small pieces. Tip the pieces into a small saucepan and add the milk. Cook on the lowest possible heat until the toffee has melted (this will take several minutes, depending on the firmness of the toffee). Remove from the heat.

Put the oil in a large saucepan with a tight-fitting lid and heat for 1 minute. Add the popcorn kernels and cover with the lid. Cook until the popping sound stops, then tip the corn out on to a large baking sheet or roasting tin and leave for 5 minutes.

Using a teaspoon, drizzle lines of the toffee sauce over the corn until lightly coated. Drizzle with lines of chocolate in the same way.

For golden-nugget popcorn, cook the popcorn kernels as above, but replace the remaining ingredients with 4 tablespoons golden syrup heated in a small pan with 25 g (1 oz) butter until melted, then add 50 g (2 oz) roughly chopped roasted cashews. Cool slightly then toss with the popcorn to coat lightly.

CHEESY RED DIP WITH BREADSTICKS

Serves **4**
Preparation time **45 minutes**, plus resting
Cooking time **30–40 minutes**

500 g (1 lb) **plain flour**
½ teaspoon **salt**
1 teaspoon **sugar**
5 g (¼ oz) fast-action
   dried yeast
300 ml (½ pint) **warm water**
6 tablespoons **olive oil**
2 tablespoons **sesame seeds**
1 tablespoon **poppy seeds**

Dip
2 **red peppers**, cored, deseeded and quartered
2 **tomatoes**
1 tablespoon **olive oil**
1 tablespoon **balsamic vinegar**
200 g (7 oz) **soft cheese**
1 tablespoon chopped **thyme** (optional)

Sift the flour and salt into a large bowl and add the sugar and yeast. Stir in the measured warm water and 3 tablespoons of the oil. Mix well to form a smooth dough, then turn out on to a well-floured surface and knead for 10 minutes until smooth and elastic. Cover and allow to rest for 15 minutes before kneading again for a further 10 minutes. Return to the bowl, cover with clingfilm and allow to stand for 30 minutes.

Knead the dough again to knock out the air, then cut into 4 pieces. Cut each quarter into 4 pieces, then stretch and roll each piece to make a long breadstick shape. Brush a baking sheet with the remaining oil. Roll the breadsticks in the oil, then sprinkle half with the sesame seeds and half with the poppy seeds. Bake in a preheated oven, 180°C (350°F), Gas Mark 4, for 30 minutes until golden and crisp. Remove from the oven and allow to cool.

Meanwhile, place the peppers on a baking sheet with the tomatoes and drizzle with the oil. Roast for 30 minutes in the oven with the breadsticks. Remove and place in a polythene bag and allow to cool. Remove from the bag and peel away the skins and discard. Place in a food processor with all the cooking juices, vinegar, cheese and thyme, if using and whiz until well blended and rough-textured. Transfer to a serving bowl and serve with the breadsticks.

For creamy avocado dip, place 1 large quartered avocado in a food processor with the finely grated rind and juice of 1 lime, 100 g (4 oz) soft cheese and 2 tablespoons sweet chilli sauce and whiz until smooth. Serve with the breadsticks.

SALTED PRETZELS

Makes **35–40 pretzels**
Time **1½–2½ hours**, depending on machine, plus shaping, proving and baking

Dough
275 ml (9 fl oz) **milk**
1 teaspoon **salt**
300 g (10 oz) **strong white bread flour**
75 g (3 oz) **rye flour**
1 tablespoon **caster sugar**
1 teaspoon **fast-action dried yeast**

To finish
4 teaspoons **sea salt**
2 teaspoons **caster sugar**

Lift the bread pan out of the machine and fit the blade. Put the dough ingredients in the pan, following the order specified in the manual. Fit the pan into the machine and close the lid. Set to the dough programme.

Put 2 teaspoons sea salt in a small saucepan with the sugar and 3 tablespoons water. Heat until the salt and sugar dissolve, then turn into a small bowl. Grease 2 baking sheets.

At the end of the programme turn the dough out on to a floured surface and roll it out to a rectangle, about 35 x 25 cm (14 x 10 inches). Cover loosely with a clean, dry tea towel and leave to stand for 20 minutes. Cut the rectangle across at 1 cm (½ inch) intervals. Take a piece of dough and bend the ends around to meet, twisting the ends together. Press the ends down on to the curved side of the rope to shape the pretzel. Use the remaining dough to make more pretzels and place them on 2 large, greased baking sheets. Cover loosely with oiled clingfilm and leave for a further 20 minutes.

Bake in a preheated oven, 220°C (425°F), Gas Mark 7, for 8 minutes until golden. Brush with the salt glaze and sprinkle with more salt. Cool on a wire rack.

For garlic & rosemary twigs, make the dough as above, adding 1 crushed garlic clove and 1 tablespoon finely chopped rosemary with the milk. Roll out the dough and cut into 25 cm (10 inch) strips, then through the centre into shorter sticks. Brush with 1 egg yolk, mixed with 2 teaspoons water and 1 teaspoon sugar. Place on greased baking sheets, sprinkle with salt and bake as above.

ONION & MUSHROOM QUESADILLAS

Serves **4**
Preparation time **10 minutes**
Cooking time **about 30 minutes**

3 tablespoons **olive oil**
2 **red onions**, thinly sliced
1 teaspoon **caster sugar**
8 **flour tortillas**
200 g (7 oz) **button mushrooms**, sliced
150 g (5 oz) **Cheddar cheese**, grated
a small handful of **parsley**, chopped
salt and **pepper**

Heat 2 tablespoons of the oil in a large frying pan, add the onions and cook until soft. Add the sugar and cook for 3 minutes or until caramelized. Remove the onions with a slotted spoon and set aside. Heat the remaining oil in the pan, add the mushrooms and cook for 3 minutes or until golden brown. Set aside.

Heat a nonstick frying pan and add 1 tortilla. Scatter over a quarter of the red onions, mushrooms, Cheddar and parsley. Season to taste with salt and pepper. Cover with another tortilla and cook until browned on the underside. Turn over and cook until browned on the other side. Remove from the pan and keep warm.

Repeat with the remaining tortillas and ingredients. Cut into wedges and serve with a salad.

For spinach & Brie quesadillas, replace the mushrooms with 200 g (7 oz) cooked, chopped spinach leaves and use 150 g (5 oz) Brie, cut into slices, instead of the Cheddar. Cook and serve as above.

SMOKED TROUT BRUSCHETTA

Serves **4**
Preparation time **5 minutes**
Cooking time **5 minutes**

12 thick slices of **French bread**
2 **large garlic cloves**, halved
2 tablespoons **extra virgin olive oil**, plus extra for drizzling
250 g (8 oz) **tzatziki**
250 g (8 oz) **hot smoked trout**, flaked
chopped **dill**, to garnish
pepper

Toast the bread in a preheated griddle pan or under a preheated grill.

While still hot, rub the toast all over with the garlic halves and sprinkle with the oil. Top each piece with a large spoonful of tzatziki and pile on the trout. Season to taste with pepper and serve garnished with chopped dill and drizzled with extra oil.

For homemade tzatziki, coarsely grate 1 large cucumber and squeeze out all the liquid, then put the flesh in a bowl. Add 4–5 tablespoons thick Greek yogurt, season well with salt and pepper and mix together.

MIXED BEAN SALSA WITH TORTILLA CHIPS

Serves **4**
Preparation time **10 minutes**, plus standing

2 x 400 g (13 oz) cans **mixed beans**, drained and rinsed
3 **tomatoes**, chopped
1 **red pepper**, cored, deseeded and finely diced
6 **spring onions**, sliced
1 teaspoon finely chopped **red chilli**
2 tablespoons **olive oil**
1 tablespoon **white wine vinegar**
chopped **coriander**, to garnish
salt and **pepper**

To serve
tortilla chips
soured cream

Put the beans, tomatoes, red pepper and spring onions in a food processor and blend until fairly smooth.

In a small bowl, whisk together the chilli, oil and vinegar, pour over the bean mixture and toss to coat. Season to taste with salt and pepper and garnish with coriander. Cover and leave to stand at room temperature for about 30 minutes to allow the flavours to mingle.

Serve the salsa with tortilla chips and soured cream.

For mixed bean pilau, which will work as a substantial starter or side dish, add 375 g (12 oz) basmati rice to a pan, cover with 600 ml (1 pint) water and bring to the boil. Reduce the heat, cover and simmer for 12 minutes without removing the lid. Remove from the heat, toss in the mixed bean salsa (see above) and stir in 3 tablespoons chopped coriander leaves. Replace the lid and return to a very low heat for 5 minutes. Serve hot.

24

CAMEMBERT 'FONDUE'

Serves **4**
Preparation time **10 minutes**
Cooking time **5–10 minutes**

1 whole **Camembert cheese**, 250 g (8 oz) in weight
2 tablespoons **olive oil**
leaves stripped from 2 **rosemary sprigs**
crusty **French bread**
50 g (2 oz) **walnuts**, roughly chopped and toasted
2 tablespoons **clear honey**

Put the Camembert in an ovenproof dish. Make a few cuts in the top, then drizzle with the oil and sprinkle with the rosemary leaves.

Cover with foil and bake in a preheated oven, 200°C (400°F), Gas Mark 6, for 5–10 minutes until gooey.

Cut the bread into chunky pieces and lightly toast until golden brown.

Sprinkle the walnuts over the cooked Camembert, drizzle with the honey and serve immediately with the toasted chunks of bread.

For Brie & hazelnut 'fondue', use a 250 g (8 oz) round of Brie instead of the Camembert and sprinkle 50 g (2 oz) chopped, toasted hazelnuts over the baked cheese in place of the walnuts.

BEEF & ASPARAGUS BAGELS

Serves **2**
Preparation time **5 minutes**
Cooking time **2 minutes**

4 **asparagus spears**, each cut into three
40 g (1½ oz) **watercress**
1 tablespoon **low-fat mayonnaise**
1 teaspoon **Dijon mustard** (optional)
2 **multigrain bagels**
100 g (3½ oz) **cooked beef**, very thinly sliced

Put a pan of lightly salted water on to boil. Boil the asparagus, if fresh, briefly, for 30 seconds or so, then drain well and set aside. (Asparagus in jars does not need cooking.)

Remove the larger stalks from the watercress and chop it. Place the mayonnaise and mustard, if using, in a bowl and stir in the watercress.

Split the bagels in half and toast under a preheated grill. Spread the halves with the flavoured mayonnaise. Top with the beef and asparagus spears and wrap securely. The bagels can be refrigerated for 1–2 days.

For smoked salmon & asparagus bagels, replace the cooked beef with 125 g (4 oz) smoked salmon and replace the watercress used to flavour the mayonnaise with 1 teaspoon finely grated lemon zest. Toast the bagels as above and fill with the salmon, lemon mayonnaise and asparagus.

LIGHTLY SPICED CHICKEN NUGGETS

Serves **4**
Preparation time **15 minutes**
Cooking time **15–20 minutes**

50 g (2 oz) **plain flour**
4 x 150 g (5 oz) boneless, skinless **chicken breasts**,
    cut into bite-sized chunks
1 **egg**, beaten
150 g (5 oz) **fine wholemeal breadcrumbs**
1 teaspoon **Cajun spice**
2 tablespoons chopped **parsley**
Tomato ketchup (see page 12), to dip

Place the flour on a plate and toss the chicken in it.

Pour the beaten egg on to a plate. Mix the breadcrumbs with the Cajun spice and parsley on a separate plate. Dip each of the chicken pieces in the beaten egg, then toss in the seasoned breadcrumbs and place on a large baking sheet.

Bake the chicken nuggets in a preheated oven, 200°C (400°F), Gas Mark 6, for 15–20 minutes until golden and cooked through.

Serve hot with tomato ketchup to dip, if liked.

For salmon goujons, replace the chicken with salmon fillets. Cut the fillets into chunks or strips and toss in breadcrumbs seasoned with the finely grated zest of 1 lemon, instead of Cajun spice, and the parsley as above. Bake for 10–15 minutes and serve with mayonnaise flavoured with the juice from the lemon.

MULTICOLOURED ROOT CHIPS

Serves **4**
Preparation time **15 minutes**
Cooking time **25–30 minutes**

2 **sweet potatoes**, cut into slim wedges with skin on
1 large **baking potato**, cut into slim wedges with
   skin on
2 **parsnips**, cut into long wedges
3 tablespoons **olive oil**
1 teaspoon **Cajun seasoning**
3 tablespoons chopped **parsley**

Mayonnaise
1 **egg**
150 ml (¼ pint) **olive oil**
½ teaspoon **mustard powder**
1 tablespoon **white wine vinegar**
1 tablespoon chopped **parsley**

Put the sweet potato, baking potato and parsnip wedges in a bowl and drizzle with the olive oil, tossing well to coat lightly. Sprinkle with the Cajun seasoning and toss again to coat. Transfer to a large baking sheet and roast in a preheated oven, 200°C (400°F), Gas Mark 6, for 25–30 minutes, until the vegetables are crisp and golden.

Meanwhile, make the mayonnaise. Place all the ingredients except the parsley in a small measuring jug, and using an electric blender whiz until a thick mayonnaise is formed. Stir in the parsley.

Serve the chips tossed with the parsley, with a tub of the mayonnaise, to dip.

For cheese & chive mayonnaise to serve as an alternative accompaniment, make the mayonnaise as above and stir in 2 tablespoons soured cream, 1 tablespoon freshly grated Parmesan cheese and 2 tablespoons fresh snipped chives. Serve with the root chips, to dip.

PAN-FRIED CHICKEN WRAPS

Serves **4**
Preparation time **15 minutes**
Cooking time **5 minutes**

2 tablespoons **olive oil**
3 boneless, skinless **chicken breasts**, about 150 g
  (5 oz) each, thinly sliced into strips
3 tablespoons **clear honey**
1 teaspoon **wholegrain mustard**
4 **soft flour tortillas**

Coleslaw
¼ small **white cabbage**, finely shredded
1 large **carrot**, grated
3 tablespoons **olive oil**
2 tablespoons **red wine vinegar**
1 teaspoon **Dijon mustard**
2 tablespoons chopped **parsley**

Make the coleslaw. Put the white cabbage in a large mixing bowl with the carrot and toss together well. In a small jug whisk together the oil, vinegar and mustard. Pour over the cabbage and carrot and toss well to coat. Add the parsley and toss again. Set aside.

Heat the oil in a large nonstick frying pan and cook the chicken strips over a high heat for 4–5 minutes until golden and cooked through. Remove from the heat and add the honey and mustard. Toss well to coat.

Warm the tortillas in a microwave for 10 seconds on high (or in a warm oven), then spread each with the coleslaw and top with the chicken pieces. Wrap each tightly, then cut in half to serve.

For maple-glazed gammon wraps, omit the chicken and cut 3 x 175 g (6 oz) gammon steaks into strips. Heat the oil and cook the gammon over a high heat for 3–4 minutes until golden and cooked through. Remove from the heat and toss with 3 tablespoons maple syrup (instead of the honey) and the mustard. Assemble the wraps as above.

BUTTER BEAN & ANCHOVY PÂTÉ

Serves **2–3**
Preparation time **5 minutes**

425 g (14 oz) can **butter beans**, drained and rinsed
50 g (2 oz) can **anchovy fillets** in oil
2 **spring onions**, finely chopped
2 tablespoons **lemon juice**
1 tablespoon **olive oil**
4 tablespoons chopped **coriander**
salt and **pepper**

To serve
lemon wedges
4–6 slices **rye bread**, toasted

Put all the ingredients except the coriander in a food processor or blender and process until well mixed but not smooth. Alternatively, mash the beans with a fork, finely chop the anchovies and mix the ingredients together by hand.

Stir in the coriander and season well. Serve with lemon wedges and accompanied with toasted rye bread.

For butter bean & mushroom pâté, replace the anchovies with 250 g (8 oz) sliced mushrooms. Cook these in 2 tablespoons olive oil with 1 finely chopped garlic clove until greatly reduced and all juices have evaporated. Cool. Purée the mushrooms in a food processor or blender, or mash with a fork, and add the butter beans, processing or mixing as above.

THAI CHICKEN SHELLS WITH CORIANDER

Serves **4**
Preparation time **10 minutes**
Cooking time **15 minutes**

1 teaspoon **vegetable oil**
2 **chicken breasts**, about
    150 g (5 oz) each, sliced
1 tablespoon red or green **Thai curry paste**
400 ml (14 fl oz) can **coconut milk**
250 g (8 oz) **basmati rice**
3 tablespoons chopped fresh **coriander**
3 **spring onions**, sliced
4 **Little Gem lettuces**, separated into individual leaves
2 **limes**, cut into wedges

Heat the oil in a nonstick frying pan, add the chicken and fry for 2 minutes.

Add the curry paste and continue to fry for 1 minute, then add half the coconut milk, bring to the boil and simmer gently for 10 minutes.

Meanwhile, put the rice in a saucepan with the remaining coconut milk and 100 ml (3½ fl oz) water. Bring to the boil, then reduce the heat, cover and simmer for 10–12 minutes until the liquid is absorbed, adding a little extra water if necessary. Turn the heat off and stir in the coriander.

Put chicken and spring onion slices and some rice on a lettuce leaf and squeeze the lime wedges over the filled shells before eating.

For quick Chinese-style stir-fry, cook 300 g (10 oz) chicken strips for 1 minute in 50 ml (2 fl oz) vegetable oil with 1 tablespoon chopped garlic. Add 150 g (5 oz) sliced green pepper and 5 deseeded and sliced red chillies and cook for a minute, then stir in 75 g (3 oz) sliced onion, 1 tablespoon oyster sauce, 1 teaspoon fish sauce, ½ tablespoon light soy sauce and ¼ teaspoon dark soy sauce. Stir-fry until the chicken is cooked through then serve.

ORANGE & AVOCADO SALAD

Serves **4**
Preparation time **15 minutes**

4 large juicy **oranges**
2 small ripe **avocados**, peeled and stoned
2 teaspoons **cardamom pods**
3 tablespoons **light olive oil**
1 tablespoon **clear honey**
pinch of **ground allspice**
2 teaspoons **lemon juice**
salt and **pepper**
sprigs of **watercress**,
    to garnish

Cut the skin and the white membrane off the oranges. Working over a bowl to catch the juice, cut between the membranes to remove the segments. Slice the avocados and toss gently with the orange segments. Pile on to serving plates.

Reserve a few whole cardamom pods for garnishing. Crush the remainder using a mortar and pestle to extract the seeds or place them in a small bowl and crush with the end of a rolling pin. Pick out and discard the pods.

Mix the seeds with the oil, honey, allspice and lemon juice. Season to taste and stir in the reserved orange juice. Garnish the salads with sprigs of watercress and the reserved cardamom pods and serve with the dressing spooned over the top.

For orange & walnut salad, separate the segments from 2 large oranges as above and mix them with 1 crushed garlic clove, 75 g (3 oz) chopped walnut halves and 4 thinly sliced heads of chicory. Stir in 3 tablespoons walnut oil and $1/2$ teaspoon caster sugar. Decorate with whole walnuts and serve.

HALOUMI WITH CUCUMBER SALAD

Serves **4**
Preparation time **10 minutes**
Cooking time **5–6 minutes**

1 **cucumber**, sliced into long, thin ribbons
20 Greek-style pitted **black olives**
2 tablespoons chopped **parsley**
2 tablespoons chopped **mint**
1 **green pepper**, cored, deseeded and diced
8 **radishes**, sliced into thin batons
2 **spring onions**, thinly sliced (optional)
4 tablespoons **olive oil**
2 tablespoons **lemon juice**
8 thick slices of **country-style bread**
250 g (8 oz) **haloumi cheese**, sliced
1 tablespoon finely grated **lemon rind**
pepper

Combine the cucumber, olives, herbs, green pepper, radishes and spring onions (if used) with 3 tablespoons of the oil and the lemon juice. Season with pepper and set aside.

Heat a frying pan or griddle pan to medium-hot and toast the bread for 1–2 minutes on each side until golden and slightly charred. Toss the cheese in the remaining oil and lemon rind and season with pepper, add to the pan and cook for 3–4 minutes, turning once, until golden.

Put a cheese slice on top of each piece of toast and serve with the salad.

For tomato, mint & avocado salad, roughly chop 4 ripe plum tomatoes, very finely slice $1/2$ red onion and roughly dice 1 ripe but firm avocado. Gently toss all the ingredients in 2 tablespoons olive oil, with 2 tablespoons chopped fresh mint and the juice of $1/2$ lemon.

THAI CHICKEN NOODLE SALAD

Serves **4**
Preparation time **10 minutes**
Cooking time **10 minutes**

250 g (8 oz) **thin rice noodles**
6 tablespoons **Thai sweet chilli sauce**
2 tablespoons **Thai fish sauce**
juice of 2 **limes**
2 **cooked boneless, skinless chicken breasts**
1 **cucumber**, cut into ribbons
1 **red chilli**, finely chopped
1 small handful of **coriander leaves**

Put the noodles in a large heatproof bowl and pour boiling water over to cover. Leave for 6–8 minutes until tender, then drain and rinse well under cold running water.

Whisk together the sweet chilli sauce, fish sauce and lime juice in a bowl. Shred the chicken and toss with the dressing to coat.

Add the noodles, cucumber and chilli to the chicken mixture and toss gently to combine. Scatter over the coriander leaves and serve the salad immediately.

For seafood noodle salad, replace the chicken with 500 g (1 lb) cooked peeled prawns and 200 g (7 oz) cooked shelled mussels, and scatter over a small handful of basil leaves instead of coriander leaves.

PAN-FRIED LIVER & BACON SALAD

Serves **4**
Preparation time **10 minutes**
Cooking time **8–12 minutes**

6 tablespoons **olive oil**
375 g (12 oz) **calves' liver**, dusted with **seasoned flour**
250 g (8 oz) cooked **new potatoes**, sliced
200 g (7 oz) **streaky bacon**, sliced
3 **shallots**, sliced
2 tablespoons **raspberry vinegar**
1 tablespoon **wholegrain mustard**
1 head **frisée**, leaves separated
salt and **pepper**

Heat 2 tablespoons of the oil in a frying pan. Fry the floured liver for 1–2 minutes on each side. Lift on to kitchen paper and keep warm.

Add 1 tablespoon of the oil to the pan and fry the potato slices, turning occasionally, for 4–5 minutes or until crisp and golden. Lift on to kitchen paper and keep warm with the liver.

Add 1 tablespoon of the oil to the pan and fry the bacon for 2–3 minutes before adding the shallots. Cook until soft and golden.

Mix together the raspberry vinegar, mustard and remaining oil.

Arrange the salad leaves on serving plates and pile on the potatoes, bacon and shallots. Slice the liver thinly before arranging on each salad, drizzle over the dressing and serve.

For chicken liver, mushroom & bacon salad, omit the calves' livers and start by frying the potatoes, as above. When adding the shallots to the bacon, also add 100 g (3½ oz) button mushrooms. Lastly, fry 375 g (12 oz) diced chicken livers. Arrange as above.

GREEK-STYLE FETA SALAD

Serves **4**

Preparation time **15 minutes**

4 **tomatoes**, cut into wedges

½ **cucumber**, cut into bite-sized cubes

1 **green pepper**, cored, deseeded and cut into rings
   or thinly sliced

1 **red onion**, thinly sliced

200 g (7 oz) **feta cheese**, cubed

100 g (3½ oz) **pitted black olives**

4 tablespoons **olive oil**

2 tablespoons **white wine vinegar**

2–3 teaspoons finely chopped **oregano**

salt and **pepper**

Arrange the tomatoes, cucumber, green pepper and red onion in a serving dish.

Top the salad ingredients with the feta and olives. Season well with salt and pepper and drizzle with the oil and vinegar. Serve sprinkled with the oregano.

For watermelon, feta & sunflower seed salad, add 200 g (7 oz) cubed watermelon to the salad ingredients used above. Toast 2 tablespoons sunflower seeds and sprinkle over the salad before serving.

CHORIZO, EGG & CIABATTA SALAD

Serves **4**
Preparation time **10 minutes**
Cooking time **10 minutes**

½ **ciabatta loaf**, cut into chunks
6 tablespoons **olive oil**
2 tablespoons **red wine vinegar**
2 teaspoons **wholegrain mustard**
4 **eggs**
200 g (7 oz) **chorizo**, thickly sliced
4 handfuls of **young spinach leaves**
salt and **pepper**

Toss the ciabatta chunks in 2 tablespoons of the oil, spread out on a baking sheet and bake in a preheated oven, 200°C (400°F), Gas Mark 6, for 10 minutes or until golden brown.

Meanwhile, in a small bowl, whisk together the remaining oil, the vinegar and wholegrain mustard to make the dressing.

Poach the eggs in a large saucepan of barely simmering water for 5 minutes. Fry the chorizo in a dry frying pan over a medium heat for 3–4 minutes or until crisp and cooked through.

Toss the spinach and chorizo in a bowl with a little of the dressing. Divide between 4 plates, scatter over the ciabatta croûtons and top each salad with a poached egg. Drizzle with the remaining dressing, season to taste with salt and pepper and serve immediately.

For fatoush pitta salad, another classic salad that features pieces of bread, in this case pitta bread, combine 2 cored, deseeded and diced green peppers, ½ diced cucumber, 4 diced ripe tomatoes, 1 finely chopped red onion, 2 crushed garlic cloves, 2 tablespoons chopped parsley and 1 tablespoon each of chopped mint and coriander in a large bowl. Toss with the Lemon Dressing on page 78. Toast 2 pitta breads in a preheated griddle pan or under a preheated grill, then tear into bite-sized pieces and stir into the salad. Cover and leave to stand at room temperature for about 30 minutes to allow the flavours to mingle.

CREAMY COURGETTES WITH WALNUTS

Serves **4**
Preparation time **10 minutes**
Cooking time **10–15 minutes**

3 tablespoons **olive oil**
1 **onion**, chopped
4 **courgettes**, cut into matchsticks
2 **celery sticks**, cut into matchsticks
250 g (8 oz) **soft cheese with garlic**
100 g (3½ oz) **walnut pieces**
salt and **pepper**

Heat the oil in a large frying pan, add the onion and cook for 5 minutes until soft. Add the courgettes and celery and cook for 4–5 minutes until soft and starting to brown.

Add the cheese and cook for 2–3 minutes until melted. Stir in the walnuts, season to taste with salt and pepper and serve immediately.

For curried courgettes, cook the onion as above, then add 2 small, quartered potatoes and cook for 2–3 minutes. Stir in the courgettes, sliced, with ½ teaspoon chilli powder, ½ teaspoon turmeric, 1 teaspoon ground coriander and ½ teaspoon salt. Add 150 ml (¼ pint) water, cover and cook over a low heat for 8–10 minutes until the potatoes are tender.

STRAWBERRY & CUCUMBER SALAD

Serves **4–6**
Preparation time **10 minutes**, plus chilling

1 large **cucumber**, halved lengthways, deseeded and thinly sliced
250 g (8 oz) **strawberries**, halved or quartered if large

For the balsamic dressing
1 tablespoon **balsamic vinegar**
1 teaspoon **wholegrain mustard**
1 teaspoon **clear honey**
3 tablespoons **olive oil**
salt and **pepper**

Put the cucumber slices and strawberry halves or quarters in a shallow bowl.

Put all the dressing ingredients in a screw-top jar, season to taste with salt and pepper, and shake well.

Pour the dressing over the cucumber and strawberries. Toss gently, then cover and chill for 5–10 minutes before serving.

For cucumber & dill salad, prepare the cucumber as specified above, then put the slices in a colander set over a plate or in the sink. Sprinkle with 2 teaspoons salt and leave to stand for 20–30 minutes, to allow the excess moisture to drain away. Rinse under cold running water, then drain thoroughly and transfer to a shallow serving dish. In a bowl, mix together 4 tablespoons thick Greek yogurt, 1 teaspoon white wine vinegar and 2 tablespoons chopped dill. Season well with pepper. Pour over the cucumber, toss gently to combine and serve garnished with dill sprigs.

CHICKPEA & CHILLI SALAD

Serves **4**
Preparation time **10 minutes**, plus standing

2 x 400 g (13 oz) cans **chickpeas**, drained and rinsed
2 **plum tomatoes**, roughly chopped
4 **spring onions**, thinly sliced
1 **red chilli**, deseeded and thinly sliced
4 tablespoons roughly chopped **coriander leaves**
grilled pitta bread, cut into thin fingers, to serve

For the lemon dressing
2 tablespoons **lemon juice**
1 **garlic clove**, crushed
2 tablespoons **olive oil**
salt and **pepper**

Combine all the salad ingredients in a shallow bowl.

Put all the dressing ingredients in a screw-top jar, season to taste with salt and pepper, and shake well. Pour over the salad and toss well to coat all the ingredients.

Cover the salad and leave to stand at room temperature for about 10 minutes to allow the flavours to mingle. Serve with grilled pitta bread fingers.

For white bean & sun-dried tomato salad, combine 2 x 400 g (13 oz) cans cannellini beans, drained and rinsed, 125 g (4 oz) sun-dried tomatoes in oil, drained and roughly chopped, 1 tablespoon chopped and pitted black olives, 2 teaspoons drained and rinsed capers and 2 teaspoons chopped thyme leaves. Toss in the lemon dressing and leave to stand as above, then serve with toasted slices of ciabatta bread.

AUBERGINE & COURGETTE SALAD

Serves **4**
Preparation time **15 minutes**
Cooking time **4–6 minutes**

2 **aubergines**, thinly sliced
2 **courgettes**, thinly sliced
3 tablespoons **olive oil**
125 g (4 oz) **feta cheese**

For the honey-mint dressing
50 g (2 oz) **mint leaves**, roughly chopped, plus
    extra leaves to garnish
1 tablespoon **clear honey**
1 teaspoon prepared **English mustard**
2 tablespoons **lime juice**
salt and **pepper**

Brush the aubergine and courgette slices with the oil. Heat the grill on the hottest setting. Cook the vegetables under the grill for 2–3 minutes on each side until lightly cooked.

Arrange the grilled vegetables in a shallow dish. Crumble the feta and sprinkle it over the vegetables.

Whisk all the dressing ingredients together in a small bowl, seasoning to taste with salt and pepper. Pour the dressing over the salad and toss to coat. Scatter with mint leaves to garnish and serve with toasted flat breads or crusty baguette.

For tahini dressing, as an alternative to the honey-mint dressing, put 2 tablespoons tahini paste in a bowl. Slowly beat in 4 tablespoons natural yogurt and 1–2 tablespoons cold water as necessary to make a drizzling consistency. Stir in 2 tablespoons chopped parsley and 1 crushed garlic clove. Season to taste with salt and pepper. Pour over the salad and toss to coat.

CELERY, RED ONION & POTATO SALAD

Serves **4**
Preparation time **10 minutes**
Cooking time **10–15 minutes**

500 g (1 lb) **new potatoes**, halved
1 **small fennel bulb**, halved, cored and finely sliced
2 **celery sticks**, thinly sliced
1 **red onion**, halved and thinly sliced
celery leaves or **dill sprigs**, to garnish (optional)

For the mayonnaise dressing
150 ml (¼ pint) **mayonnaise**
2 teaspoons **wholegrain mustard**
2 tablespoons finely chopped **dill**
salt and **pepper**

Cook the potatoes in a large saucepan of salted boiling water for 10–15 minutes or until tender.

Meanwhile, combine the fennel, celery and onion in a large, shallow bowl. To make the dressing, mix all the ingredients together in a small bowl and season to taste with salt and pepper.

Drain the potatoes, rinse under cold running water, then drain again. Add the potatoes to the salad. Add the dressing and toss until well coated. Garnish with celery leaves or dill sprigs, if liked, before serving.

For herbed vinaigrette dressing, as a fresh, fragrant alternative to the mayonnaise dressing above, put 4 tablespoons olive oil, 1 tablespoon chopped parsley, 1 tablespoon chopped basil, 1 teaspoon grated lemon rind and 1 tablespoon white wine vinegar in a screw-top jar with salt and pepper to taste and shake well. Toss with the vegetables as directed above, and garnish with a few torn basil leaves.

GADO GADO SALAD

Serves **4**
Preparation time **15 minutes**
Cooking time **10 minutes**

For the salad
4 **eggs**
1 **iceberg lettuce**, finely shredded
2 **carrots**, peeled and cut into matchsticks
½ **cucumber**, peeled and cut into matchsticks
½ **red pepper**, cored, deseeded and cut into matchsticks

For the peanut dressing
4 tablespoons **crunchy peanut butter**
juice of 1 **lime**
1 tablespoon **clear honey**
1 tablespoon **soy sauce**
½ teaspoon finely chopped **red chilli**

Put the eggs in a saucepan of cold water and bring to the boil. Cook for 10 minutes, then plunge into cold water to cool. Shell the eggs, then cut them in half lengthways.

Combine all the remaining salad ingredients in a bowl, then add the egg halves.

Put all the dressing ingredients in a saucepan and heat gently, stirring, until combined. Drizzle the dressing over the salad and serve immediately or serve the dressing as a dipping sauce for the salad.

For gado gado with noodles & tofu to serve as an impressive main course, cook 300 g (10 oz) dried fine egg noodles in a saucepan of boiling water for 4 minutes or until just tender while the eggs are cooking as in step 1 above. Drain and refresh the noodles under cold running water. Spread over the base of a shallow serving platter. Pat 125 g (4 oz) firm tofu dry with kitchen paper, then cut into bite-sized cubes. Heat a shallow depth of groundnut oil in a frying pan, add the tofu cubes and cook over a high heat until crisp and browned all over. Remove with a slotted spoon and drain on kitchen paper. Assemble the salad as above, spoon on top of the noodles and scatter with the tofu. Drizzle over the dressing and serve warm.

THAI BEEF SALAD

Serves **4**
Preparation time **15 minutes**, plus standing
Cooking time **6–8 minutes**

2 lean rump or sirloin **steaks**, about 150 g (5 oz) each,
   trimmed
150 g (5 oz) **baby sweetcorn**
1 large **cucumber**
1 small **red onion**, finely chopped
3 tablespoons chopped **coriander**
4 tablespoons **rice wine vinegar**
4 tablespoons **sweet chilli dipping sauce**
2 tablespoons **sesame seeds**, lightly toasted, to
   garnish

Put the steaks in a preheated hot griddle pan and cook for 3–4 minutes on each side. Allow to rest for 10–15 minutes, then slice the meat thinly.

Meanwhile, cook the sweetcorn in boiling water for 3–4 minutes or until tender. Refresh under cold water and drain well.

Slice the cucumber in half lengthways, then scoop out and discard the seeds. Cut the cucumber into 5 mm (1/4 inch) slices.

Put the beef, sweetcorn, cucumber, onion and chopped coriander in a large bowl. Stir in the vinegar and chilli sauce and mix well. Garnish the salad with sesame seeds and serve.

For Thai tofu salad, omit the steaks and cube 500 g (1 lb) firm tofu. Griddle for 2–3 minutes on each side until hot and golden. Mix with the other ingredients and garnish, as above.

SOFT BOILED EGG & BACON SALAD

Serves **4**
Preparation time **10 minutes**
Cooking time **10 minutes**

4 thick slices of **day-old bread**
6 tablespoons **olive oil**
4 **eggs**
1 tablespoon **Dijon mustard**
juice of ½ **lemon**
100 g (3½ oz) **streaky bacon**, cut into bite-sized
   pieces
100 g (3½ oz) **rocket leaves**
salt and **pepper**

Cut the bread into small bite-sized pieces and toss in 2 tablespoons of the oil. Spread out on a baking sheet and bake in a preheated oven, 200°C (400°F), Gas Mark 6, for 10 minutes or until golden brown.

Meanwhile, cook the eggs in a saucepan of boiling water for 4 minutes. Drain, then cool under cold running water for 1 minute.

Whisk together the remaining oil, mustard and lemon juice in a small bowl.

Heat a nonstick frying pan, add the bacon and cook over a medium heat for 5 minutes until crisp and golden. Put into a bowl with the rocket.

Shell the eggs, then roughly break in half and add to the bacon and rocket. Scatter over the croûtons, then drizzle over the dressing, season to taste with salt and pepper and serve immediately.

For creamy yogurt dressing, to drizzle over the salad instead of the mustard dressing, whisk together 4 tablespoons olive oil, the juice of 1 lemon, 6 tablespoons natural yogurt, 1 crushed garlic clove, 1 teaspoon clear honey and 1 teaspoon dried oregano.

MALAY BEEF WITH PEANUT SAUCE

Serves **4**
Preparation time **10 minutes**
Cooking time **15 minutes**

500 g (1 lb) sirloin or rump **steak**, thinly sliced
1 tablespoon **vegetable oil**

Marinade
$\frac{1}{2}$ teaspoon **turmeric**
1 teaspoon **ground cumin**
$\frac{1}{2}$ teaspoon **fennel seeds**
1 **bay leaf**, finely shredded
$\frac{1}{2}$ teaspoon **ground cinnamon**
75 ml (3 fl oz) **coconut cream**

Rice
250 g (8 oz) **Thai jasmine rice**
200 ml (7 fl oz) **coconut milk**
$\frac{1}{2}$ teaspoon **salt**

Peanut sauce
2 tablespoons **crunchy peanut butter**
$\frac{1}{4}$ teaspoon **cayenne pepper**
1 tablespoon **light soy sauce**
125 ml (4 fl oz) **coconut cream**
$\frac{1}{2}$ teaspoon **caster sugar**

Make the marinade by mixing together all the ingredients in a non-metallic bowl. Add the beef, mix thoroughly, then thread the beef on to skewers and set aside to marinate.

Put the rice, coconut milk, salt and 250 ml (8 fl oz) water in a rice cooker or a covered saucepan over a low heat. Cook for about 15 minutes until the rice is cooked and the liquid has been absorbed.

Meanwhile, add the ingredients for the peanut sauce to a small saucepan with 3 tablespoons water and heat gently, stirring.

Heat the oil in a large frying pan and cook the beef skewers for about 5 minutes, turning so that each side is browned evenly. Serve immediately with the rice and peanut sauce.

For bean sprout & carrot salad to serve as an accompaniment, coarsely grate 4 carrots, roughly chop 4 spring onions and combine with 200 g (7 oz) bean sprouts.

42

HOT & SOUR SOUP

Serves **4**
Preparation time **10 minutes**
Cooking time **10 minutes**

600 ml (1 pint) **fish stock**
4 kaffir lime leaves
4 slices of **fresh root ginger**
1 **red chilli**, deseeded and sliced
1 **lemon grass stalk**
125 g (4 oz) **mushrooms**, sliced
100 g (3$\frac{1}{2}$ oz) **dried rice noodles**
75 g (3 oz) **baby spinach**
125 g (4 oz) **cooked peeled tiger prawns**
2 tablespoons **lemon juice**
pepper

Put the stock, lime leaves, ginger, chilli and lemon grass in a large saucepan. Cover and bring to the boil. Add the mushrooms, reduce the heat and simmer for 2 minutes.

Break the noodles into short lengths, drop into the soup and simmer for 3 minutes. Add the spinach and prawns and simmer for 2 minutes until the prawns are heated through. Add the lemon juice. Remove and discard the lemon grass stalk and season with pepper before serving.

For wholemeal soda bread to serve as an accompaniment, stir 250 g (8 oz) plain white flour, 1 teaspoon bicarbonate of soda, 2 teaspoons cream of tartar and 2 teaspoons salt into a large bowl. Stir in 375 g (12 oz) wholemeal flour, 300 ml ($\frac{1}{2}$ pint) milk and 4 tablespoons water and mix to a soft dough. Turn out on to a floured surface, knead lightly, then shape into a large round about 5 cm (2 inches) thick. Put on a floured baking sheet, cut a deep cross in the top and sprinkle with flour. Bake in a preheated oven, 220°C (425°F), Gas Mark 7, for 25–30 minutes.

SEAFOOD HOTPOT

Serves **4**
Preparation time **25 minutes**
Cooking time **15 minutes**

1 teaspoon **sesame oil**
1 tablespoon **vegetable oil**
3 **shallots**, chopped
3 **garlic cloves**, crushed
1 **onion**, sliced
150 ml (¼ pint) **coconut milk**
150 ml (¼ pint) **water**
3 tablespoons **rice wine vinegar**
1 **lemon grass stalk**, chopped
4 **kaffir lime leaves**
1 **red chilli**, chopped
300 ml (½ pint) **fish stock** or **water**
1 tablespoon **caster sugar**
2 **tomatoes**, quartered
4 tablespoons **fish sauce**
1 teaspoon **tomato purée**
375 g (12 oz) **straight-to-wok rice noodles**
375 g (12 oz) **tiger prawns**, heads removed and peeled
125 g (4 oz) **squid**, cleaned and cut into rings
175 g (6 oz) **clams**, scrubbed
400 g (13 oz) can **straw mushrooms**, drained
20 **basil leaves**

Heat the sesame and vegetable oils together in a large pan, add the shallots and garlic and fry gently for 2 minutes or until softened but not browned.

Add the onion, coconut milk, measurement water, vinegar, lemon grass, lime leaves, chilli, stock or water and sugar to the pan, bring to the boil and boil for 2 minutes. Reduce the heat and add the tomatoes, fish sauce and tomato purée and cook for 5 minutes. Stir in the rice noodles.

Add the prawns, squid rings, clams and mushrooms to the hotpot and simmer gently for 5–6 minutes or until the seafood is cooked. Stir in the basil leaves. Serve the hotpot immediately.

For nuoc mam dipping sauce to serve as an accompaniment, mix the following ingredients together: 6 tablespoons fish sauce, 2 teaspoons caster sugar, 1 tablespoon rice wine vinegar, 3 finely chopped hot red chillies, 2 finely chopped hot green chillies. Leave to stand for 1 hour.

THAI PRAWN SOUP

Serves **4**
Preparation time **20 minutes**
Cooking time **20 minutes**

Soup base
5 cm (2 inch) piece of **galangal** or **fresh root ginger**, cut into very thin slices
500 ml (1 pint) **coconut milk**
250 ml (8 fl oz) **chicken stock** or **vegetable stock**
2 tablespoons **fish sauce**
6 **kaffir lime leaves**
1–2 tablespoons **green curry paste**

Soup
½ bunch **spring onions**, chopped
150 g (5 oz) **cup mushrooms**, sliced
250 g (8 oz) **broccoli**, finely chopped
300 g (10 oz) **raw peeled prawns**
1 tablespoon freshly squeezed **lime juice**
4 tablespoons roughly chopped **fresh coriander**

To make the soup base, combine the galangal or ginger, coconut milk, stock, fish sauce, lime leaves and curry paste in a saucepan and bring to the boil, then simmer for 10 minutes, stirring occasionally.

Add the spring onions, mushrooms and broccoli to the hot soup base, then simmer for 5–6 minutes until the vegetables are cooked but still crunchy.

Add the prawns and simmer for 3–5 minutes until they are pink and cooked through. Stir in the lime juice and fresh coriander and serve.

For homemade green curry paste, toast 1 tablespoon coriander seeds and 2 teaspoons cumin seeds in a dry pan over a medium heat for 2–3 minutes, shaking constantly. Grind the roasted seeds and 1 teaspoon black peppercorns using a pestle and mortar until finely ground. Put the ground spices in a food processor and blend for 5 minutes. Add 8 roughly chopped large green chillies, 20 chopped shallots, a 5 cm (2 inch) piece fresh root ginger, chopped, 12 chopped small garlic cloves, 75 g (3 oz) chopped fresh coriander leaves, 6 shredded kaffir lime leaves, 3 finely chopped lemon grass stalks, 2 teaspoons grated lime rind, 2 teaspoons salt and 2 tablespoons olive oil. Blend for 10 seconds at a time until you have a smooth paste. Store in the refrigerator for up to 2 weeks.

NOODLE SOUP WITH CHICKEN

Serves **4–6**
Preparation time **20 minutes**
Cooking time **30 minutes**

300 g (10 oz) skinned and boned **chicken breasts**
1 teaspoon **ground turmeric**
2 teaspoons **salt**
2 **lemon grass stalks**
3 tablespoons skinned and roasted **peanuts**
3 tablespoons **white long-grain rice**
2 tablespoons **vegetable oil**
1 **onion**, chopped
3 **garlic cloves**, crushed
5 cm (2 inch) piece of **fresh root ginger**, peeled and
  finely chopped
¼ teaspoon **ground paprika**
1 hot **red bird chilli**, chopped
2 tablespoons **fish sauce**
900 ml (1½ pints) **water**
250 g (8 oz) **straight-to-wok wheat noodles** (somen)

To garnish
3 **hard-boiled eggs**, halved
2 tablespoons chopped **fresh coriander**
handful **spring onions**, shredded

Cut the chicken breasts into 1.5 cm (³/4 inch) cubes. Mix the turmeric with the salt, rub into the cubes of chicken and leave to stand for 30 minutes.

Bruise the lemon grass with the side of a rolling pin to release the flavour. Finely crush the roasted peanuts in a food processor or using a pestle and mortar. Heat a dry frying pan and toast the rice until golden brown, then finely crush to a powder in a food processor or spice grinder.

Heat the oil in a large pan and fry the onion until just softened. Add the chicken together with the garlic, ginger, lemon grass, paprika and chilli. Add the fish sauce and measurement water and bring to the boil.

Reduce the heat to a simmer. Mix together the crushed peanuts and ground rice and add to the pan. Simmer for about 10–15 minutes or until the chicken has cooked through and the broth thickened slightly.

Stir the noodles into the pan and heat for 1 minute.

Ladle the chicken soup into bowls and serve garnished with the hard-boiled eggs, chopped coriander and shredded spring onions. Add an extra splash of fish sauce, to taste.

For prawn and coconut noodle soup, use 400 g (13 oz) raw peeled prawns instead of the chicken and add to the pan with the noodles, cooking gently until they turn pink. Replace the wheat noodles with rice noodles and omit the hard-boiled eggs.

TOMATO RISONI SOUP

Serves **4**
Preparation time **10 minutes**
Cooking time **18 minutes**

2 tablespoons **olive oil**, plus extra for drizzling
1 large **onion**, finely chopped
2 **celery sticks**, finely chopped
4 **large tomatoes**
1.5 litres (2½ pints) **vegetable stock**
150 g (5 oz) **dried risoni or orzo** or any tiny shaped
  dried pasta
6 tablespoons finely chopped **flat leaf parsley**
salt and **pepper**

Heat the oil in a large saucepan over a medium heat, add the onion and celery and cook until soft.

Meanwhile, score a cross in the base of each tomato, then put in a heatproof bowl of boiling water for 1 minute. Plunge into cold water, then peel the skin away from the cross. Halve the tomatoes, then scoop out the seeds and discard. Roughly chop the flesh.

Add the tomatoes, stock, onions and celery to the pan and bring to the boil. Add the pasta and cook for 10 minutes or until al dente. Season to taste with salt and pepper and stir in the parsley.

Remove from the heat, ladle into warmed bowls and drizzle with oil before serving.

For homemade vegetable stock, put 625 g (1¼ lb) mixed vegetables (excluding potatoes, parsnips and other starchy root vegetables), 2 peeled garlic cloves, 8 peppercorns and 1 bouquet garni in a large saucepan, add 1.8 litres (3 pints) water and bring to the boil. Reduce the heat and simmer gently for 40 minutes, skimming any scum that rises to the surface. Strain through a muslin-lined sieve. If not using straight away, leave to cool before covering and refrigerating.

BUTTER BEAN & BACON SOUP

Serves **4**
Preparation time **15 minutes**
Cooking time **24 minutes**

2 tablespoons **olive oil**
175 g (6 oz) **smoked bacon**, chopped
25 g (1 oz) **butter**
1 **onion**, chopped
2 **garlic cloves**, roughly chopped
2 **celery sticks**, chopped
1 **leek**, roughly chopped
750 ml (1¼ pints) hot **ham** or **vegetable stock**
400 g (13 oz) can **butter beans**, drained and rinsed
2 large sprigs of **parsley**
3 sprigs of **thyme**
2 **bay leaves**
100 ml (3½ fl oz) **double cream**
salt and **pepper**

Heat 1 tablespoon of the oil in a large pan and fry the bacon until it is crisp and golden. Remove with a slotted spoon and set aside to drain on kitchen paper.

Melt the butter and remaining oil in the pan over a medium heat and cook the onion, garlic, celery and leek, stirring frequently, for about 10 minutes or until soft and golden.

Add the stock and butter beans with the herbs and season to taste. Bring to the boil, then turn the heat down and simmer gently for about 10 minutes before removing from the heat. Remove the herbs and blend until smooth.

Stir in the cream, season to taste and serve in large bowls, scattered with crispy bacon.

For smoked sausage & borlotti bean soup, replace the smoked bacon with 250 g (8 oz) smoked pork sausage and use a 400 g (13 oz) can of borlotti beans instead of the butter beans. Omit the cream.

MINTED PEA SOUP

Serves **4**
Preparation time **10 minutes**
Cooking time **20 minutes**

1 tablespoon **butter**
1 **onion**, finely chopped
1 **potato**, finely chopped
1 litre (1¾ pints) **vegetable stock**
400 g (13 oz) **frozen peas**
6 tablespoons finely chopped **mint leaves**
salt and **pepper**
crème fraîche (optional)

Melt the butter in a saucepan, add the onion and potato and cook for 5 minutes. Add the stock and bring to the boil, then reduce heat and simmer gently for 10 minutes or until the potato is tender.

Add the peas to the pan and cook for a further 3–4 minutes. Season well with salt and pepper, remove from the heat and stir in the mint. Purée in a food processor or blender until smooth. Ladle into warmed bowls and top each with a dollop of crème fraîche, if liked.

For chunky pea & ham soup, cook 1 chopped carrot and 1 chopped turnip with the onion and potato, then add 1 litre (1¾ pints) ham or chicken stock. Once the root vegetables are tender, add 300 g (10 oz) chopped cooked ham, 4 finely chopped spring onions and 2 tablespoons chopped parsley with the peas and cook for 3–4 minutes. Do not blend the soup, but ladle into warmed bowls and serve with crusty bread.

FRIED GOATS' CHEESE

Serves **4**
Preparation time **15 minutes**
Cooking time **10 minutes**

4 individual **goats' cheeses**, about 65 g (2½ oz) each
2 **eggs**, beaten
4 tablespoons **fresh white breadcrumbs**
about 200 ml (7 fl oz) **vegetable oil**, for deep-frying
125 g (4 oz) **rocket leaves**
2 tablespoons **olive oil**
salt and **pepper**

For red onion marmalade
1 tablespoon **olive oil**
2 **red onions**, thinly sliced
125 ml (4 fl oz) **red wine**
3 tablespoons **red wine vinegar**
50 g (2 oz) **caster sugar**

Dip the cheeses in the beaten egg and then coat evenly with the breadcrumbs. Cover and chill while you prepare the onion marmalade.

Heat the olive oil in a small saucepan, add the onions and cook for 2 minutes. Stir in the wine, vinegar and sugar, then cook for 5 minutes or until the onions are translucent. Remove with a slotted spoon and set aside, reserving the juices in the pan.

Heat the vegetable oil in a nonstick frying pan to 180–190°C (350–375°F) or until a cube of bread browns in 30 seconds. (Take care not to overfill the frying pan. If necessary, use a saucepan or deep frying pan.) Add the goats' cheeses and cook for 2 minutes or until golden. Remove with a slotted spoon and drain well on kitchen paper.

Divide the rocket between 4 plates and drizzle the olive oil and reserved juices from the onions over the top. Season to taste with salt and pepper. Place the goats' cheeses on the rocket and top with the onion marmalade. Serve immediately.

For fried Camembert & tomato-chilli sauce, cut a 250 g (8 oz) Camembert into wedges, coat and chill as above. Bring a 400 g (13 oz) can chopped tomatoes, 2–3 finely chopped red chillies, 2 crushed garlic cloves, 125 g (4 oz) soft light brown sugar, 4 tablespoons white wine vinegar, 1 tablespoon Worcestershire sauce and ½ teaspoon salt to the boil in a saucepan. Reduce the heat and simmer gently for 30 minutes or until thick. Cook the Camembert as above and serve with the sauce.

GOATS' CHEESE & TOMATO TARTS

Serves **4**
Preparation time **15 minutes**
Cooking time **10–12 minutes**

4 sheets of **filo pastry**, about 25 cm (10 inches)
  square each
1 tablespoon **olive oil**
20 **cherry tomatoes**, halved
200 g (7 oz) **firm goats' cheese**, cut into 1 cm
  (½ inch) cubes
20 g (¾ oz) **pine nuts**
2 teaspoons **thyme leaves**
salt and **pepper**

Lightly oil 4 individual tartlet tins, each about 10 cm (4 inches) in diameter. Brush a sheet of filo pastry with a little of the oil. Cut in half, then across into 4 equal-sized squares and use to line one of the tins. Repeat with the remaining pastry sheets. Brush any remaining oil over the pastry in the tins.

Put 5 tomato halves in the bottom of each tartlet. Top with the goats' cheese, then add the remaining tomato halves and pine nuts. Sprinkle with the thyme leaves and season well with salt and pepper.

Bake the tartlets in a preheated oven, 200°C (400°F), Gas Mark 6, for 10–12 minutes or until the pastry is crisp and golden. Serve hot with a leafy green salad.

For feta & pepper tarts, roll out 175 g (6 oz) puff pastry on a lightly floured work surface and use to line the tartlet tins. Core and deseed 1 yellow and 1 orange pepper, then slice into thin strips and toss in a little olive oil. Cut 200 g (7 oz) feta cheese into 1 cm (½ inch) cubes. Divide half the pepper strips between the tartlets, top with the cheese, then add the remaining pepper strips, and scatter over the pine nuts, as above. Sprinkle with 2 teaspoons dried oregano and season well with salt and pepper. Bake at the same temperature as specified above for about 15 minutes or until the pastry is golden.

CIABATTA

Makes **2 loaves**

Time **2–3 hours**, depending on machine, plus standing, shaping, proving and baking

Starter

150 ml (¼ pint) warm **water**

125 g (4 oz) **strong white bread flour**

¼ teaspoon **caster sugar**

¼ teaspoon **fast-action dried yeast**

To finish

225 ml (7½ fl oz) **water**

2 tablespoons **olive oil**

1½ teaspoons **salt**

375 g (12 oz) **strong white bread flour**, plus extra for dusting

1½ teaspoons **caster sugar**

1 teaspoon **fast-action dried yeast**

Lift the bread pan out of the machine and fit the blade. Put the starter ingredients in the pan, following the order specified in the manual.

Fit the pan into the machine and close the lid. Set to the dough programme. Turn off the machine before the second kneading cycle and leave the dough to stand for at least 4 hours.

Lift the bread pan out of the machine and add the remaining ingredients. Return to the machine and set to the dough programme.

At the end of the programme turn the dough out on to a floured surface and cut it in half. (The dough will be very sticky.) Using well-floured hands, gently pull the dough into 2 loaves, each about 28 cm (11 inches) long. Place them on a greased and floured baking sheet. Leave in a warm place, uncovered, for about 30 minutes or until it is about half as big again.

Bake in a preheated oven, 220°C (425°F), Gas Mark 7, for about 20 minutes until golden and the loaves sound hollow when tapped with the fingertips. Transfer to a wire rack to cool. Dust with flour.

For sun-dried tomato & herb ciabatta, drain and thinly slice 75 g (3 oz) sun-dried tomatoes in olive oil. Roughly chop 15 g (½ oz) fresh mixed herbs (such as basil, parsley, oregano and thyme). Make the dough in the machine as above using olive oil from the tomato jar and adding the sliced tomatoes and herbs when the machine beeps. Turn out on to a floured surface and finish as above.

PITTA BREAD

Makes **8 breads**

Time 1½–2½ **hours**, depending on machine, plus shaping, proving and baking

250 ml (8 fl oz) **water**
1 tablespoon **olive oil**
1 teaspoon **salt**
½ teaspoon **ground cumin**
375 g (12 oz) **strong white bread flour**
1 teaspoon **caster sugar**
1 teaspoon **fast-action dried yeast**

Lift the bread pan out of the machine and fit the blade. Put the ingredients in the pan, following the order specified in the manual.

Fit the pan into the machine and close the lid. Set to the dough programme.

At the end of the programme turn the dough out on to a floured surface and cut it into 8 equal-sized pieces. Roll out each piece to an oval about 15 cm (6 inches) long. Arrange in a single layer on a well-floured clean, dry tea towel. Cover loosely with a second clean, dry tea towel and leave to rise in a warm place for 30 minutes.

Put a floured baking sheet in a preheated oven, 230°C (450°F), Gas Mark 8, and leave to heat up for 5 minutes. Transfer half the breads to the baking sheet and cook for 5–6 minutes until just beginning to colour. Remove from the oven and leave to cool on a wire rack while you cook the remainder. Wrap the still warm pittas in a clean, dry tea towel to keep them soft until ready to serve. If they are left to go cold, warm the pittas through in a hot oven before serving.

For olive & herb mini pittas, make the dough as above, but add 50 g (2 oz) pitted and chopped black olives and a large handful of chopped parsley and mint to the dough when the machine beeps. At the end of the programme turn the dough out on to a floured surface and cut it into 16 pieces. Thinly roll out each piece to an oval 10–12 cm (4–5 inches) long. Prove and bake as above.

CHORIZO & MANCHEGO BUNS

Makes **12 buns**

Time **1½–2½ hours**, depending on machine, plus shaping, proving and baking

225 ml (7½ fl oz) **water**
3 tablespoons **olive oil**
100 g (3½ oz) **Manchego cheese**, grated
1 teaspoon **salt**
1 teaspoon ground **hot paprika**
450 g (14½ oz) **strong white bread flour**
2 teaspoons **caster sugar**
1¼ teaspoons **fast-action dried yeast**
125 g (4 oz) **chorizo sausage**, diced

Lift the bread pan out of the machine and fit the blade. Put the ingredients, except the chorizo, in the pan, following the order specified in the manual.

Fit the pan into the machine and close the lid. Set to the dough programme, adding the chorizo when the machine beeps.

At the end of the programme turn the dough out on to a floured surface and divide it into 12 equal pieces. Shape each piece into a ball. Cut 12 x 15 cm (6 inch) squares of baking parchment. Push a parchment square down into the section of a muffin or Yorkshire pudding tray and drop a ball of dough into it. Repeat with the remainder. Cover loosely with a clean, dry tea towel and leave in a warm place for 30 minutes until risen.

Use a pair of kitchen scissors to snip across the top of each bun. Bake in a preheated oven, 220°C (425°F), Gas Mark 7, for 20 minutes until risen and golden. Transfer to a wire rack to cool.

For prosciutto & Parmesan crown, fry 100 g (3½ oz) chopped prosciutto in 1 tablespoon olive oil until lightly browned. Make the dough as above, using 75 g (3 oz) grated Parmesan cheese instead of the Manchego and adding the prosciutto when the machine beeps. Once the dough is shaped into balls, fit them into a greased 20 cm (8 inch) round cake tin. Leave to rise and bake as above, but increasing the cooking time to 25—30 minutes. After baking, transfer to a wire rack to cool and serve, torn into individual buns.

PROVENÇAL-STYLE PICNIC SLICE

Makes **10 thick slices**

Time **1½–2½ hours**, depending on machine, plus shaping, proving and baking

Dough
2 tablespoons **olive oil**
4 tablespoons chopped **herbs**, such as thyme, oregano and rosemary
75 g (3 oz) **Parmesan cheese**, grated
250 ml (8 fl oz) **milk**
1 teaspoon **salt**
350 g (11½ oz) **strong white bread flour**
1 tablespoon **caster sugar**
1 teaspoon **fast-action dried yeast**

To finish
5 tablespoons **sun-dried tomato paste**
350 g (11½ oz) **mixed roasted vegetables**, such as peppers, courgettes and red onions
2 tablespoons **olive oil**
milk, to brush
25 g (1 oz) **Parmesan cheese**, grated, for sprinkling
salt and **black pepper**

Lift the bread pan out of the machine and fit the blade. Put the dough ingredients in the pan, following the order specified in the manual. Add the herbs and cheese with the milk.

Fit the pan into the machine and close the lid. Set to the dough programme.

At the end of the programme turn the dough out on to a floured surface and roll it out to a 28 cm (11 inch) square. Spread with the tomato paste and scatter with the roasted vegetables. Drizzle with the oil and a little salt and pepper.

Roll up the dough so the filling is enclosed and cut it into 10 thick slices. Arrange the slices in a staggered line on a large, greased baking sheet, resting each slice against the one behind so the filling is revealed. Cover with oiled clingfilm and leave to rise in a warm place for about 40 minutes or until almost doubled in size.

Brush the dough with milk and sprinkle with cheese. Bake in a preheated oven, 200°C (400°F), Gas Mark 6, for 25 minutes until risen and golden. Serve warm, broken into slices.

For leek & Stilton picnic loaf, make the dough as above but reducing the Parmesan to 40 g (1½ oz). Thinly slice 350 g (11½ oz) leeks and sauté them in 25 g (1 oz) butter until soft. Leave to cool. Roll out the dough as above and scatter with the leeks, 150 g (5 oz) crumbled, creamy Stilton cheese and plenty of black pepper. Roll up the dough and finish as above.

HOT CROSS BUNS

Makes **12 buns**
Time **1½–2½ hours**, depending on machine, plus shaping, proving and baking

Dough
1 **egg**, beaten
275 ml (9 fl oz) **milk**
40 g (1½ oz) **unsalted butter**, softened
½ teaspoon **salt**
2 teaspoons **ground mixed spice**
500 g (1 lb) **strong white bread flour**
3 tablespoons **light muscovado sugar**
1½ teaspoons **fast-action dried yeast**
100g (3½ oz) **raisins**

To finish
50 g (2 oz) **plain flour**
4 tablespoons **milk**
2 tablespoons **caster sugar**

Lift the bread pan out of the machine and fit the blade. Add the dough ingredients, except the raisins, to the pan, following the order specified in the manual.

Fit the pan into the machine and close the lid. Set to the dough programme, adding the raisins when the machine beeps.

At the end of the programme turn the dough out on to a floured surface and divide it into 12 pieces. Shape each into a ball and space 5 cm (2 inches) apart on a greased baking sheet. Cover loosely with oiled clingfilm and leave to rise in a warm place for 30 minutes.

Make the crosses. Beat 4–5 tablespoons water into the flour to make a paste. Put it in a greaseproof piping bag (or spoon it into the corner of a small polythene bag) and snip off the tip. Pipe crosses over the buns.

Bake in a preheated oven, 220°C (425°F), Gas Mark 7, for 15 minutes until risen and golden. Heat the milk and sugar in a pan until the sugar dissolves. Bring to the boil and brush over the buns. Cool on a wire rack.

For hot cross bun loaf, put 275 ml (9 fl oz) milk, 25 g (1 oz) soft butter, ½ teaspoon salt, grated rind of 1 lemon, 2 teaspoons ground mixed spice, 450 g (14½ oz) white bread flour, 50 g (2 oz) light muscovado sugar and 1½ teaspoons fast-action dried yeast in the bread pan, following the order specified in the manual. Set to a 750g (1½ lb) loaf size on the sweet programme, adding 225 g (7½ oz) luxury mixed dried fruit when the machine beeps. Halfway through baking, pipe a cross on the surface using the mixture above. After baking brush with the glaze.

FRUITED TEACAKES

Makes **8 teacakes**
Time **1½–2½ hours**, depending on machine, plus shaping, proving and baking

Dough
300 ml (½ pint) **milk**
50 g (2 oz) **unsalted butter**, softened
½ teaspoon **salt**
1 teaspoon **ground mixed spice**
2 teaspoons **vanilla bean paste** or **vanilla extract**
450 g (14½ oz) **strong white bread flour**
75 g (3 oz) **light muscovado sugar**
1¼ teaspoons **fast-action dried yeast**
150 g (5 oz) **mixed dried fruit**, to glaze

To finish
beaten **egg**, to glaze
caster sugar, for sprinkling

Lift the bread pan out of the machine and fit the blade. Put the dough ingredients, except the dried fruit, in the pan, following the order specified in the manual.

Fit the pan into the machine and close the lid. Set to the dough programme, adding the dried fruit when the machine beeps.

At the end of the programme turn the dough out on to a floured surface and cut it into 8 equal pieces. Shape each piece into a ball and space them, about 3 cm (1¼ inches) apart, on a large, greased baking sheet. Cover loosely with oiled clingfilm and leave to rise in a warm place for about 30 minutes or until almost doubled in size.

Brush with beaten egg to glaze and bake in a preheated oven, 220°C (425°F), Gas Mark 7, for 15–20 minutes until risen and golden. Transfer to a wire rack to cool and sprinkle with the caster sugar. Serve split and buttered.

For iced finger buns, beat 2 eggs and make up to 300 ml (½ pint) with milk. Continue to make the dough as above, omitting the mixed spice and dried fruit, and using the milk and egg mixture to replace the 300 ml (½ pint) milk. Turn the dough out on to a floured surface and cut it into 8 equal pieces. Shape each into finger roll shapes and place on a greased baking sheet, spacing them about 4 cm (1½ inches) apart. Leave the buns to rise and bake as above. Once cooled, spread the tops with glacé icing, made by mixing together 100 g (3½ oz) icing sugar with 2–3 teaspoons lemon or orange juice.

QUICK
MID-WEEK
MEALS

MUSSELS IN TARRAGON CREAM SAUCE

Serves **4**
Preparation time **20 minutes**
Cooking time **15 minutes**

1 kg (2 lb) **fresh mussels**
50 g (2 oz) **butter**
2 **shallots**, finely chopped
2 **garlic cloves**, crushed
1 teaspoon **ground coriander**
2 teaspoons chopped **lemon thyme**
1 tablespoon **plain flour**
1 glass **white wine**, about
    150 ml (¼ pint)
2 tablespoons chopped **tarragon**
150 ml (¼ pint) **double cream**
salt and **pepper**
crusty bread (optional)

Scrub the mussels, scraping off any barnacles and pulling away the beards. Discard any damaged shells or any open ones that don't close when tapped firmly with a knife or against the edge of the sink.

Melt the butter in a large saucepan. Add the shallots, garlic, coriander and thyme and fry very gently for 2 minutes. Remove from the heat and stir in the flour to make a thin paste. Gradually beat in the wine, using a whisk or wooden spoon, until smooth.

Return to the heat and cook, stirring, until the sauce is thick and smooth. Stir in the tarragon. Tip in the mussels and cover with a lid. Cook for about 5 minutes, shaking the pan frequently, until the shells have opened.

Drain the mussels to warmed bowls, discarding any that remain closed.

Stir the cream into the sauce and bring to the boil. Season to taste and ladle the sauce over the mussels. Serve with warm, crusty bread, if liked.

For steamed mussels in white wine sauce, prepare the mussels as in the first step. Melt 25 g (1 oz) butter in a large saucepan and fry 1 small onion chopped, 1–2 garlic cloves finely chopped and 1 small leek finely sliced until soft. Add the mussels, 300 ml (½ pint) dry white wine and 150 ml (¼ pint) water, cover and bring to the boil. Cook for 2–5 minutes until the mussels open, then divide into serving bowls. Mix 25 g (1 oz) butter with 15 g (½ oz) plain flour to form a paste. Gradually add to the juices in the pan, stirring to thicken. Bring to the boil, stir in 2 tablespoons chopped parsley, season and pour over the mussels.

HADDOCK & SHELLFISH SOUP

Serves **4**
Preparation time **15 minutes**
Cooking time **20 minutes**

500 g (1 lb) **undyed smoked haddock**
25 g (1 oz) **butter**
1 large **leek**, chopped
2 teaspoons **medium curry paste**
1 litre (1¾ pints) **fish stock**
50g/2 oz **creamed coconut**, chopped
3 **bay leaves**
150 g (5 oz) **French beans**, cut into 1 cm
    (½ inch) lengths
3 small **courgettes**, chopped
250 g (8 oz) **cooked mixed seafood**, e.g. **prawns,**
    mussels, squid rings, thawed if frozen
100 ml (3½ fl oz) **single cream**
4 tablespoons finely chopped **parsley**
salt and **pepper**

Cut the haddock into small pieces, discarding the skin and any bones.

Melt the butter in a large saucepan and gently fry the leek for 3 minutes to soften. Add the curry paste, stock and creamed coconut and bring almost to the boil. Reduce the heat and simmer gently, covered, for 10 minutes until the leek is soft.

Stir in the bay leaves, beans and courgettes and cook for 2 minutes to soften slightly. Add the smoked haddock and mixed seafood, 3 tablespoons of the cream and the parsley and cook very gently for 5 minutes until the haddock flakes easily.

Season to taste and spoon into serving bowls. Serve swirled with the remaining cream.

For smoked salmon and mangetout soup, replace the haddock with 500 g (1 lb) lightly smoked salmon and cook as above. Replace the French beans with the same quantity of mangetout.

SALMON FILLETS WITH SAGE & QUINOA

Serves **4**
Preparation time **5 minutes**
Cooking time **15 minutes**

200 g (7 oz) **quinoa**
100 g (3½ oz) **butter**, at room temperature
8 **sage leaves**, chopped
small bunch of **chives**
grated rind and juice of **1 lemon**
4 **salmon fillet steaks**, about 125 g (4 oz) each
1 tablespoon **olive oil**
salt and **pepper**

Cook the quinoa in unsalted boiling water for about 15 minutes or until cooked but firm.

Meanwhile, mix the butter with the sage, chives and lemon rind and add salt and pepper to taste.

Rub the salmon steaks with the oil, season with pepper and cook in a preheated hot griddle pan for about 6 minutes, turning carefully once. Remove and set aside to rest.

Drain the quinoa, stir in the lemon juice and season to taste. Spoon on to serving plates and top with the salmon, topping each piece with a knob of sage butter.

For salmon with tarragon & couscous, replace the sage leaves with 4 sprigs of tarragon and the quinoa with 250 g (8 oz) couscous. Soak the couscous in 400 ml (14 fl oz) just-boiled water for 5–8 minutes until the grains are soft. Fluff the couscous with a fork and season. Dress with a little lemon juice and olive oil and serve with the salmon, as above.

BUTTERY LOBSTER TAILS WITH AÏOLI

Serves **4**
Preparation time **20 minutes**
Cooking time **7–8 minutes**

4 raw **lobster tails**
50 g (2 oz) **butter**
2 tablespoons **garlic-infused oil**
finely grated rind of 1 **lemon**
2 tablespoons chopped **chervil**, plus extra sprigs
   to garnish
cucumber ribbons, to serve

Aïoli
1 large **egg yolk**
3–4 **garlic cloves**, crushed
1 tablespoon **lemon juice**
175 ml (6 fl oz) **olive oil**
1 tablespoon snipped **chives**
salt and **pepper**

Make the aïoli. With all the ingredients at room temperature, beat the egg yolk in a bowl with the garlic, lemon juice and a large pinch of salt and pepper, either by hand or with an electric whisk. Gradually add the oil, drop by drop, beating constantly until it is all completely incorporated and you have a thick, smooth emulsion. Stir in the chives.

Dot the lobster tails with the butter and drizzle with the garlic oil. Cook the lobster tails, flesh-side up, under a preheated grill for 7–8 minutes until cooked through. Sprinkle with the lemon rind and chopped chervil and serve immediately with cucumber ribbons and the aïoli in small bowls.

For lobster tails with sun-dried tomato sauce, combine 2 tablespoons each of sun-dried tomato paste, mascarpone and pesto with 2 teaspoons finely grated lemon rind and 2 teaspoons lemon juice. Season well.

SCALLOPS WITH PANCETTA

Serves **4**
Preparation time **10 minutes**, plus cooling time
Cooking time **15 minutes**

8 small vine-ripened **tomatoes**, halved
2 **garlic cloves**, finely chopped
8 **basil leaves**
2 tablespoons **olive oil**
2 tablespoons **balsamic vinegar**
8 thin slices of **pancetta**
16–20 **king scallops**, corals and muscles removed
8 canned **artichoke hearts in oil**, drained and halved
125 g (4 oz) **lamb's lettuce**, trimmed
salt and **pepper**

Arrange the tomatoes close together, cut side up, in a roasting tin. Scatter over the chopped garlic and basil, drizzle with 1 tablespoon each of the oil and balsamic vinegar and season well with salt and pepper. Cook in a preheated oven, 220°C (425°F), Gas Mark 7, for 15 minutes.

Meanwhile, cook the pancetta slices in a preheated hot griddle pan for about 2 minutes, turning once, until crisp and golden. Transfer to a plate lined with kitchen paper until needed.

Quickly sear the scallops for 1 minute in the hot griddle, then turn them over and cook for a further minute on the other side until cooked and starting to caramelize. Remove, cover with foil and leave to rest for 2 minutes.

Meanwhile, cook the artichoke hearts for about 2 minutes until hot and charred.

Toss the lamb's lettuce with the remaining oil and balsamic vinegar and arrange on serving plates. Top with the artichokes, tomatoes, crispy pancetta and scallops. Serve immediately.

For salmon & pancetta salad, omit the tomatoes and cook the pancetta, as above. Instead of the scallops, use a chunky 450 g (14 1/2 oz) fresh salmon fillet. Brush the salmon lightly with olive oil before searing on a hot griddle for 2–3 minutes until golden, turning once. Cook the artichoke hearts as above. Substitute the lamb's lettuce with rocket and shredded Little Gem hearts. Toss and arrange as above.

CRUNCHY SWORDFISH WITH PUY LENTILS

Serves **4**
Preparation time **12 minutes**
Cooking time **15 minutes**

4 skinless **swordfish fillets**, about 175 g (6 oz) each
2 tablespoons **olive oil**
500 g (1 lb) cooked **Puy lentils**, heated
8 **sun-blushed tomatoes**, roughly chopped
small bunch of **basil**, shredded
1 tablespoon **capers in brine**, drained and rinsed
4 **spring onions**, finely sliced
8 pitted **black olives**, roughly chopped
2 tablespoons **olive oil**
salt and **pepper**
2 **lemons**, halved, to serve

Crust
75 g (3 oz) **breadcrumbs**
grated rind of 1 **lemon**
1 teaspoon finely chopped **rosemary**
2 tablespoons finely chopped **parsley**

Mix together the ingredients for the crust and add some salt and pepper. Rub the fish fillets in the oil and then press them into the crust mixture to coat.

Transfer the fish to a nonstick baking sheet and carefully tip over the remaining crust. Cook in a preheated oven, 220°C (425°F), Gas Mark 7, for 15 minutes until the fish is flaky and the crust is golden and crunchy.

Put the hot lentils in a bowl and stir in the remaining ingredients. Serve immediately with the fish fillets and lemon halves.

For crunchy hake with Mediterranean potatoes, replace the swordfish with 4 x 200 g (7 oz) hake steaks and prepare as above. Instead of the lentils, peel and halve 700 g (1 lb 7 oz) red new potatoes, boil them for 10–15 minutes, drain, then toss with the other ingredients.

COCONUT & CORIANDER MUSSELS

Serves **4**
Preparation time **10 minutes**
Cooking time **15 minutes**

1 tablespoon **vegetable oil**
4 **spring onions**, finely chopped
2½ cm (1 inch) length **galangal** or **fresh root ginger**, shredded
1 **green chilli**, finely chopped
200 ml (7 fl oz) can **coconut milk**
large bunch of **coriander**, chopped, plus extra to garnish
1 tablespoon chopped **Thai basil** (optional)
200 ml (7 fl oz) **fish stock**
2 tablespoons **Thai fish sauce**
2 tablespoons **lime juice**
1 tablespoon **soy sauce**
1 tablespoon **soft brown sugar**
3–4 **lime leaves**, shredded (optional)
1 kg (2 lb) **mussels**, scrubbed and debearded
desiccated coconut, toasted, to garnish (optional)

Heat the oil in a large saucepan and cook the spring onions, galangal or ginger and chilli for 2 minutes until soft. Add the remaining ingredients except the mussels and warm gently until the sugar has dissolved. Turn up the heat and bring up to boiling point, then reduce the heat and simmer gently for 5 minutes to allow the flavours to develop.

Tip the mussels into the coconut sauce and cover with a tight-fitting lid. Cook for 3–4 minutes or until the mussels have opened – discard any that have not.

Spoon into serving bowls with plenty of the juices and sprinkle with extra coriander leaves and desiccated coconut, if using. Serve immediately with steamed jasmine rice or butternut squash.

For coconut & coriander seafood with lime rice, replace the mussels with 500 g (1 lb) fresh or frozen prepared seafood mix and cook as above, but omitting the lime leaves. Cook 250 g (8 oz) rice with the grated rind of 1 lime. Serve the rice in bowls and ladle over the seafood. Serve with prawn crackers.

MUSSEL & LEMON CURRY

Serves **4**
Preparation time **15 minutes**
Cooking time **15 minutes**

1 kg (2 lb) **mussels**, scrubbed and debearded
125 ml (4 fl oz) **lager**
125 g (4 oz) **unsalted butter**
1 **onion**, chopped
1 **garlic clove**, crushed
2.5 cm (1 inch) **fresh root ginger**, peeled and grated
1 tablespoon medium **curry powder**
150 ml (¼ pint) **single cream**
2 tablespoons **lemon juice**
salt and **pepper**
chopped **parsley**, to garnish

Discard any mussels that are broken or do not close immediately when sharply tapped with a knife. Put them in a large saucepan with the lager, cover and cook, shaking the pan frequently, for 4 minutes until all the shells have opened. Discard any that remain closed. Strain, reserve the cooking liquid and keep it warm.

Meanwhile, melt the butter in a large saucepan and fry the onion, garlic, ginger and curry powder, stirring frequently, for 5 minutes. Strain in the reserved mussel liquid and bring to a boil. Boil until reduced by half, whisk in the cream and lemon juice and simmer gently.

Stir in the mussels, warm through and season to taste. Garnish with chopped parsley and serve with crusty bread, if liked.

For prawn & lemon curry with warm lemon naan, substitute the mussels with shelled raw prawns. You will need about 10 prawns per person, cut almost in half down the centre to allow the flavours to penetrate the flesh. Cook in the same way as the mussels for 3–4 minutes until the flesh turns pink. Serve with 4 warm naan breads brushed with lemon butter, made by mixing the rind of 1 lemon with 50 g (2 oz) melted butter.

SQUID WITH LEMON MAYONNAISE

Serves **4**
Preparation time **30 minutes**
Cooking time **9 minutes**

500 g (1 lb) prepared **squid**
50 g (2 oz) **plain flour**
1 tablespoon **paprika**
pinch of **cayenne pepper**
olive oil, for deep-frying
salt and **pepper**

Lemon and herb mayonnaise
2 **egg yolks**
½ teaspoon **wholegrain mustard**
1 tablespoon **lemon juice**, plus extra to taste
200 ml (7 fl oz) **light olive oil**
1 tablespoon chopped **flat leaf parsley**, plus extra
  to garnish
1 tablespoon chopped **chervil**
1 tablespoon chopped **chives**
2 tablespoons chopped **watercress**
finely grated rind of 1 **lemon**
1 small **garlic clove**, crushed
lemon wedges, to serve

Make the mayonnaise. Beat the egg yolks in a bowl with the mustard and lemon juice. Add the oil, drop by drop, beating constantly until it is incorporated and you have a thick, smooth emulsion. Season and stir in the herbs, watercress, lemon rind and garlic, adding extra lemon juice to taste. Cover and chill until required.

Wash the squid and pat dry with kitchen paper. Cut the bodies into rings about 2 cm (¾ inch) thick. Mix together the flour, paprika and cayenne and season well. Put the flour in a plastic bag, add the squid rings and tentacles and shake until they are coated.

Heat the oil in a large frying pan or deep-fat fryer to 180°C (350°F) or until a cube of bread browns in 20 seconds. Remove about one-third of the squid from the bag and shake off the excess flour. Carefully drop the squid into the oil and fry for 2–3 minutes until golden and crispy, then remove with a slotted spoon. Drain on kitchen paper and keep them warm.

Transfer the squid to 4 serving plates, sprinkle with parsley and serve immediately with lemon wedges and Lemon and herb mayonnaise.

For stir-fried squid, prepare and season the squid as above. Stir-fry in 6 tablespoons olive oil. Remove, drain and keep warm while you cook 1 sliced onion, 1 sliced green pepper, 2 crushed garlic cloves, 1 bay leaf, 450 g (14½ oz) chopped tomatoes and 50 g (2 oz) pitted black olives. Return the squid to the pan, sprinkle over 4 tablespoons chopped parsley and serve.

BREAM WITH NEW POTATOES

Serves **4**
Preparation time **5 minutes**
Cooking time **20 minutes**

500 g (1 lb) baby **new potatoes**
3–4 tablespoons **olive oil**
6 tablespoons fresh **mayonnaise**
1 tablespoon chopped **chervil**
½ **garlic clove**, crushed
4 boned **sea bream fillets**
2 tablespoons **lemon juice**
sea salt and **pepper**

Put the new potatoes in a large saucepan with 1–2 tablespoons of the oil. Place over a medium-low heat and cover with a tight-fitting lid. Cook for about 20 minutes, shaking the pan frequently to move the potatoes around. When done, the potatoes should be cooked and crispy golden. Remove from the pan and sprinkle with sea salt.

Meanwhile, mix together the mayonnaise with the chervil and garlic.

Heat the remaining oil in a large frying pan over a medium-high heat. Season the fish with salt and pepper and cook, flesh-side down, for 1 minute before turning carefully and frying for a further 2–3 minutes until the skin is crispy. Squeeze over the lemon juice and serve immediately with the crispy potatoes and garlicky mayonnaise.

For mackerel with horseradish soured cream, replace the chervil and garlic with 2 tablespoons horseradish sauce and the mayonnaise with thick soured cream. Substitute the bream with 4 mackerel fillets, seasoned with salt and pepper and a pinch of chilli powder. Cook in the same way as the bream and serve with new potatoes, as above.

SCALLOPS WITH CITRUS DRESSING

Serves **4**
Preparation time **10 minutes**
Cooking time **7–9 minutes**

16 large **raw prawns**, heads removed
24 fresh **scallops**, roe removed
1 large ripe but firm **mango**, peeled, stoned and
    cut into chunks
125 g (4 oz) mixed **salad leaves**

Citrus dressing
juice of ½ **pink grapefruit**
finely grated rind and juice of 1 **lime**
1 teaspoon **clear honey**
1 tablespoon **raspberry vinegar**
75 ml (3 fl oz) **lemon oil**

Make the citrus dressing by mixing together all the ingredients in a small bowl.

Poach the prawns in simmering water for 2 minutes and drain.

Put the scallops, mango and prawns in a bowl and pour over 3 tablespoons of the dressing. Mix well to coat before threading them alternately on skewers.

Heat the oil in a large frying pan over a medium heat and fry the skewers for about 5–7 minutes, turning and basting occasionally until golden brown and cooked.

Arrange the skewers on plates with salad leaves and serve with the remaining dressing.

For haloumi & mango kebabs with citrus dressing, replace the scallops and prawns with 450–500 g (14½ oz–1 lb) haloumi, cut into cubes. Coat with the dressing, skewer with the mango and fry, as above. Alternatively, cook on a barbecue for the same amount of time until slightly charred.

TERIYAKI SALMON WITH NOODLES

Serves **4**
Preparation time **12 minutes**
Cooking time **15 minutes**

4 boneless, skinless **salmon fillets**, about 150 g
    (5 oz) each
2 teaspoons **sesame oil**
4 **spring onions**, thinly sliced
350 ml (12 fl oz) hot **vegetable stock**
2 tablespoons **light soy sauce**
50 g (2 oz) **miso paste**
1 tablespoon **mirin** or
    1 teaspoon **brown sugar**
300 g (10 oz) ready-cooked **udon noodles**
4 baby heads **pak choi**, halved lengthways

Teriyaki sauce
3 tablespoons **sake**
1 teaspoon **dark soy sauce**
3 tablespoons **light soy sauce**
2 tablespoons **caster sugar**
1 tablespoon **clear honey**
2 tablespoons **mirin** or extra **sugar**

Make the teriyaki sauce. Put all the ingredients in a small saucepan and stir over a medium heat until the sugar has dissolved. Increase the heat a little and simmer for 5 minutes until thickened. Set aside to cool.

Meanwhile, rub the teriyaki sauce over the salmon fillets and arrange them in an ovenproof dish. Cook under a preheated grill for 4–5 minutes on each side, basting occasionally. Remove and set aside.

Heat the sesame oil in a frying pan and stir-fry the spring onions for 2 minutes. Add the stock, soy sauce, miso paste and mirin or sugar, stirring to dissolve. Simmer gently and add the noodles and pak choi and cook for 2 minutes until the leaves have wilted.

Serve immediately topped with the grilled salmon.

For herb-crusted salmon with grilled asparagus, cook 250 g (8 oz) trimmed asparagus spears in boiling water for 5 minutes. Brush one side of each salmon fillet with olive oil. Chop about 25 g (1 oz) parsley and use to coat the salmon, then griddle or fry in olive oil for about 3 minutes on each side. Serve the salmon topped with the asparagus spears and with some crusty bread.

GARGANELLI WITH RED MULLET

Serves **4**
Preparation time **10 minutes**
Cooking time **12 minutes**

400 g (13 oz) **dried garganelli**
125 g (4 oz) **unsalted butter**
4 slices of **Parma ham**, cut into 2.5 cm (1 inch) strips
300 g (10 oz) **red mullet fillets**, cut into 2.5 cm
  (1 inch) pieces
10 **sage leaves**, roughly chopped
salt and **black pepper**

Cook the pasta in a large saucepan of salted boiling water according to the packet instructions until al dente.

Meanwhile, melt the butter in a large frying pan over a medium heat. When the butter starts to foam, add the Parma ham and cook, stirring, for 2–3 minutes. Season the red mullet with salt and pepper and add to the pan, skin-side down. Scatter with the sage and cook for 2–3 minutes until the fish is opaque all the way through. If the butter begins to colour too much, reduce the heat slightly.

Drain the pasta, reserving a ladleful of the cooking water, and toss into the frying pan with the fish. Stir gently to combine, then add the reserved pasta cooking water and stir over a medium heat until the pasta is well coated and looks silky. Serve immediately.

For lemon sole garganelli, use 300 g (10 oz) lemon sole instead of the mullet and replace the sage with 4 sprigs tarragon. Toss 50 g (2 oz) roughly chopped pitted black olives into the pasta at the last minute.

KING PRAWN & COURGETTE LINGUINE

Serves **4**

Preparation time **10 minutes**

Cooking time **10–12 minutes**

400 g (13 oz) **dried linguine**
3 tablespoons **olive oil**
200 g (7 oz) peeled **raw king prawns**
2 **garlic cloves**, crushed
finely grated **rind of 1 unwaxed lemon**
1 **fresh red chilli**, deseeded and finely chopped
400 g (13 oz) **courgettes**, coarsely grated
50 g (2 oz) **unsalted butter**, cut into cubes
salt

Cook the pasta in a large saucepan of salted boiling water according to the packet instructions until al dente. Drain.

Meanwhile, heat the oil in a large frying pan over a high heat until the surface of the oil seems to shimmer slightly. Add the prawns, garlic, lemon rind and chilli, season with salt and cook, stirring, for 2 minutes until the prawns turn pink. Add the courgettes and butter, season with a little more salt and stir well. Cook, stirring, for 30 seconds.

Toss in the pasta and stir until the butter has melted and all the ingredients are well combined. Serve immediately.

For squid & pumpkin sauce, replace the prawns with 200 g (7 oz) prepared squid rings and the courgette with 400 g (13 oz) coarsely grated pumpkin, and cook as described above.

PRAWNS WITH SESAME NOODLES

Serves **4**
Preparation time **8 minutes**
Cooking time **6 minutes**

250 g (8 oz) **egg noodles**
1 tablespoon **sesame oil**, plus extra to serve
1 tablespoon **vegetable oil**
1 **yellow pepper**, cored, deseeded and sliced
1 **red pepper**, cored, deseeded and sliced
75 g (3 oz) **shiitake** or **chestnut mushrooms**, trimmed
  and thinly sliced
1 large **carrot**, peeled and cut into thin sticks
2 **spring onions**, thinly sliced lengthways
1 **red chilli**, finely chopped
300 g (10 oz) **large cooked peeled prawns**
1 tablespoon **sesame seeds**, lightly toasted

Cook the noodles in a large saucepan of unsalted water for 4 minutes or according to the instructions on the packet.

Meanwhile, heat a large wok over a high heat until smoking. Add the oils and stir-fry the peppers for 1–2 minutes. Add the mushrooms, cook for 1 minute, then add the carrot and cook for a further minute. Add the spring onions, chilli and prawns and stir-fry for 2 minutes.

Drain the noodles and add them to the wok. Mix to combine, heat through, then scatter with the sesame seeds and serve immediately.

For teriyaki prawns with vegetables on soba, substitute the egg noodles for soba noodles (made with buckwheat flour). Prepare the vegetables and noodles as above but cook the prawns separately, adding 1 sliced garlic clove and 4 tablespoons ready-made teriyaki sauce. Serve the prawns on the soba noodles and sprinkle with coriander instead of sesame seeds.

QUICK TUNA STEAK WITH GREEN SALSA

Serves **4**
Preparation time **14 minutes**, plus marinating
Cooking time **2–4 minutes**

2 tablespoons **olive oil**
grated rind of 1 **lemon**
2 teaspoons chopped **parsley**
½ teaspoon crushed **coriander seeds**
4 fresh **tuna steaks**, about 150 g (5 oz) each
salt and **pepper**
dressed **lettuce salad**, to serve

Salsa
2 tablespoons **capers**, chopped
2 tablespoons chopped **cornichons**
1 tablespoon finely chopped **parsley**
2 teaspoons chopped **chives**
2 teaspoons finely chopped **chervil**
30 g (1½ oz) pitted **green olives**, chopped
1 **shallot**, finely chopped (optional)
2 tablespoons **lemon juice**
2 tablespoons **olive oil**

Mix together the oil, lemon rind, parsley and coriander seeds with plenty of pepper in a bowl. Rub the tuna steaks with the mixture.

Combine the ingredients for the salsa, season to taste and set aside.

Heat a griddle or frying pan until hot and cook the tuna steaks for 1–2 minutes on each side to cook partially. The tuna should be well seared but rare. Remove and allow to rest for a couple of minutes.

Serve the tuna steaks with a spoonful of salsa, a dressed salad and plenty of fresh crusty bread.

For yellow pepper & mustard salsa, combine the following: 2 yellow peppers, finely chopped; 1 tablespoon Dijon mustard; 2 tablespoons each finely chopped chives, parsley and dill; 1 teaspoon sugar; 1 tablespoon cider vinegar and 2 tablespoons olive oil.

KING PRAWNS WITH JAPANESE SALAD

Serves **4**
Preparation time **10 minutes, plus cooling**
Cooking time **3 minutes**

400 g (13 oz) **raw, peeled king prawns**
200 g (7 oz) **bean sprouts**
125 g (4 oz) **mangetout**, shredded
100 g (3½ oz) **water chestnuts**, thinly sliced
½ **iceberg lettuce**, shredded
12 **radishes**, thinly sliced
1 tablespoon **sesame seeds**, lightly toasted

Dressing
2 tablespoons **rice vinegar**
125 ml (4 fl oz) **sunflower oil**
1 teaspoon **five spice powder** (optional)
2 tablespoons **mirin**

Set a steamer over a pan of simmering water and steam the king prawns for 2–3 minutes until cooked and pink. Set aside and leave to cool.

Make the dressing by mixing together all the ingredients in a small bowl.

Toss together the bean sprouts, mangetout, water chestnuts, lettuce and radishes and scatter over the prawns and sesame seeds. Drizzle over the dressing and serve immediately.

For chilli sauce to serve as an accompaniment, combine 1 finely chopped garlic clove, ½ teaspoon finely grated fresh root ginger, 2 teaspoons light soy sauce, 1 tablespoon sweet chilli sauce and ½ tablespoon tomato ketchup. Mix well.

BROCCOLI & SAUSAGE ORECCHIETTE

Serves **4**

Preparation time **5 minutes**

Cooking time **15 minutes**

2 tablespoons **olive oil**

1 **onion**, finely chopped

200 g (7 oz) **Italian pork sausage**

large pinch of **crushed dried chillies**

300 g (10 oz) **dried orecchiette**

200 g (7 oz) **broccoli**, broken into florets

40 g (1¼ oz) **pecorino cheese**, freshly grated, plus
   extra to serve

salt

Heat the oil in a frying pan over a low heat, add the onion and cook, stirring occasionally, for 6–7 minutes until softened. Split the sausage open and break up the sausagemeat with a fork. Add the sausagemeat chunks and chillies to the pan and increase the heat to medium. Cook, stirring, for 4–5 minutes until the sausagemeat is golden brown.

Meanwhile, cook the pasta and broccoli in a large saucepan of salted boiling water according to the pasta packet instructions until the pasta is al dente. Don't be alarmed if the broccoli starts to break up – it needs to be very tender.

Drain the pasta and broccoli and toss into the frying pan with the sausagemeat. Stir in the pecorino and serve immediately with a bowl of extra grated pecorino on the side.

For cauliflower & chorizo sauce, replace the Italian pork sausage with 200 g (7 oz) sliced chorizo. Cut 250 g (8 oz) cauliflower into small florets and cook with the pasta as above.

69

SWEET & SOUR PORK NOODLES

Serves **4**
Preparation time **15 minutes**
Cooking time **12–16 minutes**

8 tablespoons **tomato ketchup**
3 tablespoons **soft brown sugar**
2 tablespoons **white wine vinegar**
175 g (6 oz) medium **egg noodles**
2 tablespoons **sesame oil**
375 g (12 oz) lean **pork**, cut into strips
2.5 cm (1 inch) piece fresh **root ginger**, peeled
   and chopped
1 **garlic clove**, crushed
125 g (4 oz) **mangetouts**, halved in length
1 large **carrot**, cut into strips
175 g (6 oz) **bean sprouts**
200 g (7 oz) can **bamboo shoots**, drained

Place the ketchup, sugar and vinegar in a small saucepan and heat gently for 2–3 minutes until the sugar has dissolved, then set aside.

Cook the egg noodles for 3–5 minutes or according to packet instructions until tender, then drain and set aside.

Heat the oil in a wok or large, heavy-based frying pan and cook the pork strips over a high heat for 2–3 minutes until beginning to turn golden, then add the ginger, garlic, mangetouts and carrot. Stir-fry for a further 2 minutes, then add the bean sprouts and bamboo shoots and stir-fry for 1 minute until all the ingredients are piping hot.

Add the warm, drained noodles and sauce and toss over the heat, using 2 spoons to mix really well and heat through. Serve in warmed serving bowls.

For prawn stir-fry with a thickened soy sauce, heat the oil and cook the ginger, garlic, mangetouts and carrot for 2–3 minutes, then add the bean sprouts and bamboo shoots and 250 g (8 oz) prawns and stir-fry for 1–2 minutes. Replace the sauce ingredients with 150 ml (¼ pint) soy sauce, gently heated in a small pan. Add 1 tablespoon cornflour blended with 2 tablespoons water and ½ teaspoon Chinese 5-spice powder. Stir until warmed and thickened, then remove from the heat. Add to the stir-fry, toss and serve.

CHORIZO CARBONARA

Serves **4**
Preparation time **5 minutes**
Cooking time **18–20 minutes**

125 g (4 oz) **chorizo sausage**, sliced
1 tablespoon **olive oil**
375 g (12 oz) **dried penne**
4 **eggs**
50 g (2 oz) **Parmesan cheese**, freshly grated,
   plus extra to serve
salt and **black pepper**

Put the chorizo and oil in a frying pan over a very low heat and cook, turning occasionally, until crisp. The melted fat released by the chorizo will be an essential part of your sauce.

Cook the pasta in a large saucepan of salted boiling water according to the packet instructions until it is al dente.

Meanwhile, crack the eggs into a bowl, add the Parmesan and season with salt and a generous grinding of pepper. Mix together with a fork.

Just before the pasta is ready, increase the heat under the frying pan so that the oil and melted chorizo fat start to sizzle. Drain the pasta thoroughly, return to the pan and immediately stir in the egg mixture and the sizzling-hot contents of the frying pan. Stir vigorously so that the eggs cook evenly. Serve immediately with a scattering of grated Parmesan.

For spicy chorizo & leek carbonara, fry 1 finely sliced leek in 2 tablespoons olive oil for 6–8 minutes until soft, then add the chorizo and cook as above. Add ½ teaspoon hot paprika to the egg mixture and complete the recipe as above.

SPECK, SPINACH & TALEGGIO FUSILLI

Serves **4**
Preparation time **5 minutes**
Cooking time **15 minutes**

375 g (12 oz) **dried fusilli**
100 g (3½ oz) **speck slices**
150 g (5 oz) **Taleggio cheese**, cut into small cubes
150 ml (½ pint) **double cream**
125 g (4 oz) **baby spinach**, roughly chopped
salt and **black pepper**
freshly grated **Parmesan cheese** (optional)

Cook the pasta in a large saucepan of salted boiling water according to the packet instructions until it is al dente.

Meanwhile, cut the speck into wide strips.

Drain the pasta, return to the pan and place over a low heat. Add the speck, Taleggio, cream and spinach and stir until most of the cheese has melted. Season with a generous grinding of pepper and serve immediately with a scattering of grated Parmesan, if liked.

For mozzarella & ham fusilli, use 150 g (5 oz) mozzarella instead of the Taleggio and replace the speck with 100 g (3½ oz) Black Forest ham. Mozzarella will give a milder flavour than Taleggio.

QUICK PASTA CARBONARA

Serves **4**
Preparation time **10 minutes**
Cooking time **10 minutes**

400 g (13 oz) **dried spaghetti** or **other long thin pasta**
2 tablespoons **olive oil**
200 g (7 oz) **pancetta**, cut into cubes
3 **eggs**
4 tablespoons freshly grated **Parmesan cheese**
3 tablespoons chopped **flat leaf parsley**
3 tablespoons **single cream**
salt and **black pepper**

Cook the pasta in a large saucepan of boiling salted water according to the packet instructions until al dente.

Meanwhile, heat the oil in a large, nonstick frying pan over a medium heat, add the pancetta and cook, stirring frequently, for 4–5 minutes until crisp.

Beat the eggs with the Parmesan, parsley and cream in a bowl. Season with salt and pepper and set aside.

Drain the pasta and add to the pancetta mixture. Stir over a low heat until combined, then pour in the egg mixture. Stir and remove the pan from the heat. Continue stirring for a few seconds until the eggs are lightly cooked and creamy. Serve immediately.

For mushroom carbonara, add 100 g (3½ oz) sliced mushrooms with the pancetta and cook as above.

ASPARAGUS & BACON FARFALLE

Serves **4**
Preparation time **10 minutes**
Cooking time **15 minutes**

400 g (13 oz) **asparagus**, trimmed
1 large **garlic clove**, crushed
4 tablespoons **olive oil**
50 g (2 oz) **Parmesan cheese**, freshly grated
8 **streaky bacon** or **pancetta rashers**
400 g (13 oz) **dried farfalle**
salt and **black pepper**
fresh **Parmesan cheese shavings**, to serve

Cut the tips off the asparagus and reserve. Cut the stalks into 2.5 cm (1 inch) pieces and blanch in a saucepan of boiling water for 3–4 minutes until very tender. Drain and put in a food processor with the garlic, oil and Parmesan. Process to make a smooth paste. Season with salt and pepper.

Arrange the bacon rashers in a single layer on a baking sheet and cook under a preheated hot grill for 5–6 minutes until crisp and golden. Break into 2.5 cm (1 inch) lengths.

Meanwhile, cook the pasta in a large saucepan of salted boiling water according to the packet instructions until al dente, adding the reserved asparagus tips to the pan 3 minutes before the end of the cooking time.

Drain the pasta and stir into a bowl with the asparagus sauce. Scatter with the crispy bacon and Parmesan shavings and serve immediately.

For creamy courgette & bacon farfalle, omit the asparagus tips and instead pan-fry 250 g (8 oz) sliced small courgettes in 25 g (1 oz) butter while the pasta is cooking and the bacon grilling. When cooked, toss the pasta with the courgette and the bacon and 4 tablespoons single cream.

TORTELLINI WITH CREAMY HAM & PEAS

Serves **4**
Preparation time **2 minutes**
Cooking time **8–12 minutes**

15 g (½ oz) **unsalted butter**
150 g (5 oz) shelled **peas**, defrosted if frozen
75 g (3 oz) **ham**, cut into strips
300 g (10 oz) **crème fraîche**
large pinch of freshly grated **nutmeg**
500 g (1 lb) **fresh spinach and ricotta** or **meat tortellini**
40 g (1½ oz) **Parmesan cheese**, freshly grated, plus extra to serve

Melt the butter in a large frying pan over a medium heat until it begins to sizzle. Add the peas and ham and cook, stirring, for 3–4 minutes if using fresh peas, or just 1 minute if using defrosted frozen peas.

Stir in the crème fraîche, add the nutmeg and season with salt and pepper. Bring to the boil and boil for 2 minutes until slightly thickened.

Cook the tortellini in a large saucepan of salted boiling water according to the packet instructions until it is al dente. Drain and toss into the creamy sauce with the Parmesan. Gently stir to combine and serve at once with a scattering of Parmesan.

For bacon & courgette tortellini, replace the ham with the same quantity of bacon strips, frying them for 4 minutes. Then add 200 g (7 oz) chopped courgette in place of the peas, and proceed as above.

PORK WITH AUBERGINE & NOODLES

Serves **4**
Preparation time **15 minutes**
Cooking time **15 minutes**

500 g (1 lb) **minced pork**
250 g (8 oz) **thick, flat rice noodles**
about 3 tablespoons **vegetable** or **groundnut oil**
1 large **aubergine**, cut into 1 cm (½ inch) dice
2 tablespoons **coriander leaves**, plus extra to garnish

Marinade

1 tablespoon **dark soy sauce**
3 tablespoons **light soy sauce**, plus extra to serve
  (optional)
1 tablespoon **cornflour**
1 teaspoon **clear honey**
1 tablespoon **chilli paste**
2 teaspoons finely chopped **garlic**
1 tablespoon finely chopped **root ginger**

Make the marinade by mixing together all the ingredients in a non-metallic bowl. Add the pork and combine thoroughly until the liquid has been absorbed. Set aside.

Cook the noodles in boiling water for 2–3 minutes or according to the instructions on the packet. Drain.

Heat the oil until smoking in a large wok or frying pan. Carefully stir-fry the aubergine until golden and soft. Remove with a slotted spoon and leave to drain on kitchen paper.

Add more oil to the pan if necessary and stir-fry the pork until browned and cooked through. Pour in 75 ml (3 fl oz) water and allow to gently bubble. Return the aubergine to the wok and heat through, then add the coriander leaves.

Serve the pork and aubergine piled on top of the noodles and with a scattering of coriander leaves and some extra light soy sauce, if liked.

For minced steak with okra & rice, cook 250 g (8 oz) rice instead of noodles and substitute the minced pork with the same quantity of minced steak. Replace the aubergine with 200 g (7 oz) okra, sliced into 1 cm (½ inch) pieces and fry for 5 minutes. Serve as above.

PORK & PEPPERCORN TAGLIATELLE

Serves **4**
Preparation time **10 minutes**
Cooking time **20 minutes**

350 g (11½ oz) dried **tagliatelle verde** or similar
2 tablespoons **olive oil**
500 g (1 lb) **pork tenderloin fillet**, sliced
1 **onion**, finely chopped
1 large **garlic clove**, chopped
2 tablespoons **brandy**
75 ml (3 fl oz) **white wine**
2 tablespoons **raisins** soaked in 50 ml (2 fl oz) warm
  apple juice
1 teaspoon chopped **rosemary**
1½ tablespoons **green peppercorns in brine**, drained
  and chopped
3 **juniper berries** (optional)
250 ml (8 fl oz) **single cream**
salt and **pepper**

Cook the pasta in lightly salted boiling water according to the instructions on the packet.

Meanwhile, heat the oil in a large frying pan and brown the pork slices for 2 minutes, turning once. Remove with a slotted spoon and set aside. Add the onion to the pan and cook for about 5 minutes before adding the garlic. Cook for a further minute until softened.

Pour in the brandy, wine, raisins and apple juice, rosemary, green peppercorns and juniper berries (if used), bring to the boil and bubble over high heat for 1–2 minutes. Reduce the heat, stir in the cream and simmer gently for 5 minutes.

Return the pork to the pan and stir for 3–5 minutes, or until cooked through and tender. Turn the heat off. Toss through the prepared pasta and serve.

For pork & sun-dried tomato tagliatelle, replace the raisins with chopped sun-dried tomatoes. There is no need to soak them in the apple juice, but don't omit it altogether: just add it at the same time as the tomatoes.

PORK FILLET WITH MUSHROOMS

Serves **4**
Preparation time **15 minutes**
Cooking time **15–17 minutes**

4 tablespoons **olive oil**
500 g (1 lb) **pork tenderloin**, sliced into 5 mm
(¼ inch) discs
300 g (10 oz) **mushrooms**, trimmed and cut
into chunks
1 **lemon**
300 ml (½ pint) **crème fraîche**
2 sprigs of **tarragon**, leaves stripped
salt and **pepper**

Heat 2 tablespoons of the oil in the pan over a medium-high heat and fry the pork slices for 3–4 minutes, turning once so that they are browned on both sides. Remove with a slotted spoon.

Add the remaining oil to the pan, tip in the mushrooms and cook for 3–4 minutes, stirring occasionally, until softened and golden.

Cut half of the lemon into slices and add to the pan to brown a little on each side, then remove and set aside.

Return the pork to the pan, add the crème fraîche and tarragon and pour in the juice from the remaining lemon. Season well, bring to the boil, then reduce the heat and leave to bubble gently for 5 minutes. Add the prepared lemon slices at the last minute and gently stir through.

Serve the pork with white rice or crispy potato wedges.

For couscous with petit pois to serve as an accompaniment, soak 250 g (8 oz) couscous in 400 ml (14 fl oz) just-boiled water or vegetable stock and leave for 5–8 minutes until soft. Fluff up the couscous with a fork and season. Boil 150 g (5 oz) frozen petit pois for 3 minutes, drain, then mix them with the couscous. Before serving, add a handful of chopped chives, a few knobs of butter and season with black pepper.

PORK IN CIDER WITH PAPPARDELLE

Serves **4**
Preparation time **8 minutes**
Cooking time **20 minutes**

15 g (½ oz) **dried wild mushrooms**
3 tablespoons **olive oil**
400 g (13 oz) boneless **pork loin steaks**
150 g (5 oz) **smoked bacon**, sliced
8 **shallots**, quartered
300 ml (½ pint) **dry cider**
125 ml (4 fl oz) **cider vinegar**
2 sprigs of **thyme**
1 **bay leaf**, torn
400 g (13 oz) fresh **pappardelle** or thick ribbon pasta
200 ml (7 fl oz) **crème fraîche**
salt and **pepper**

Soak the dried mushrooms for 5–10 minutes in 6 tablespoons boiling water.

Meanwhile, heat the oil in a large frying pan over a medium heat and fry the pork and bacon for approximately 3 minutes until browned. Add the shallots and continue frying for a further 2–3 minutes until golden and beginning to soften.

Pour in the dry cider and cider vinegar and add the mushrooms and soaking liquid. Stir in the herbs and season well. Bring to the boil, then reduce the heat, cover and leave to bubble gently for 10–12 minutes until the shallots are soft.

Meanwhile, cook the pasta in lightly salted boiling water for 3 minutes or according to the instructions on the packet. Drain and transfer to serving dishes.

Stir the crème fraîche into the pork, increase the heat briefly and then place the meat on the pasta and spoon over the sauce. Serve immediately.

For venison in red wine, substitute the pork for 4 venison steaks cut into strips and replace the cider with red wine. Omit the cider vinegar. Serve as above.

CRISPY PARMA HAM PARCELS

Serves **4**
Preparation time **10 minutes**
Cooking time **4 minutes**

8 slices of **Parma ham** or **prosciutto**
100 g (3½ oz) creamy **blue cheese**, such as Roquefort,
   St Agur, dolcelatte or Gorgonzola, thinly sliced
1 teaspoon chopped **thyme leaves**
1 **pear**, peeled, cored and diced
25 g (1 oz) **walnuts**, chopped

To serve
watercress leaves tossed in **olive oil** and **balsamic**
   vinegar
1 **pear**, peeled, cored and sliced

Put a slice of Parma ham on a chopping board and then put a second slice across it to form a cross shape.

Arrange one quarter of the cheese slices in the centre, scatter over some thyme and top with one quarter of the diced pear.

Add one quarter of the walnuts, then fold over the sides of the ham to form a neat parcel. Repeat this process to make 4 parcels.

Transfer the parcels to a foil-lined grill pan and cook under a preheated hot grill for about 2 minutes on each side until the ham is crisp and the cheese is beginning to ooze out of the sides.

Serve the parcels immediately with the dressed watercress leaves and slices of pear.

For figs with Parma ham, quarter 8 fresh figs, leaving them attached at the base. Mix 1 teaspoon Dijon mustard with 125 g (4 oz) ricotta cheese, season to taste and spoon over the figs. Divide 85 g (3¼ oz) Parma ham, cut into strips, among them and drizzle over 2 tablespoons balsamic vinegar.

GREEN BEAN & BACON FRITTATA

Serves **4**
Preparation time **10 minutes**
Cooking time **about 10 minutes**

175 g (6 oz) **fine green beans**
6 **back bacon** rashers
100 g (4 oz) frozen **peas**, defrosted
6 **eggs**
1 teaspoon **wholegrain mustard**
½ teaspoon **ground paprika**
2 tablespoons **vegetable oil**
4 tablespoons freshly grated **Parmesan cheese**

Cook the green beans in boiling water for 5 minutes. Drain and refresh with cold water to stop them from cooking further, then roughly chop and set aside. Meanwhile, place the bacon under a preheated medium grill for 3–4 minutes until golden and cooked. Cool slightly, then snip roughly with scissors. Toss the green beans and bacon with the peas.

Beat the eggs with the mustard and paprika. Heat the oil in a medium nonstick frying pan with a metal handle, then pour in the eggs. Working quickly, scatter over the beans, peas and bacon. Cook over a gentle heat until the base has set.

Sprinkle over the Parmesan and place the pan under the grill for 2–3 minutes until the frittata is set and golden.

Cut the frittata into wedges. If not serving immediately, wrap it in foil to keep warm.

For mushroom & bacon frittata, omit the beans and peas. Heat 1 tablespoon olive oil in a frying pan and cook 250 g (8 oz) quartered chestnut mushrooms for 4–5 minutes until soft and golden. Pour into the egg mixture in the pan and cook as above, with the Parmesan sprinkled over before grilling. Serve cut into wedges, either warm or cold.

PROSCIUTTO & PORCINI PAPPARDELLE

Serves **4**
Preparation time **10 minutes**
Cooking time **6–10 minutes**

400 g (13 oz) **dried pappardelle** or **homemade pappardelle**
2 tablespoons **olive oil**
1 **garlic clove**, crushed
250 g (8 oz) **fresh porcini mushrooms**, sliced
250 g (8 oz) **prosciutto slices**
150 ml (¼ pint) **whipping cream**
handful of **flat leaf parsley**, chopped
75 g (3 oz) **Parmesan cheese**, freshly grated
salt and **black pepper**

Cook the pasta in a large saucepan of salted boiling water until it is al dente: according to the packet instructions for dried pasta or for 2–3 minutes if using fresh pasta.

Meanwhile, heat the oil in a saucepan over a medium heat, add the garlic and porcini and cook, stirring frequently, for 4 minutes. Cut the prosciutto into strips, trying to keep them separate. Add to the porcini mixture with the cream and parsley and season with salt and pepper. Bring to the boil, then reduce the heat and simmer for 1 minute.

Drain the pasta, add to the sauce and toss well, using 2 spoons to mix evenly. Scatter with the Parmesan, toss well and serve immediately.

For spaghetti with dried porcini & pine nuts, soak 125 g (4 oz) dried porcini in enough hot water to cover them for 15 minutes, to rehydrate them. Drain, reserving the water, pat dry with kitchen paper and fry as above. Once the porcini has been fried, as above, add the reserved soaking water to the pan and boil until the liquid has almost evaporated. Stir in the prosciutto and cream as above. Briefly toast 2 tablespoons pine nuts in the oven and add to the sauce before combining with the cooked spaghetti.

PASTA WITH PANCETTA & SCALLOPS

Serves **4**
Preparation time **15 minutes**
Cooking time **15–20 minutes**

5 tablespoons **extra virgin olive oil**
125 g (4 oz) **pancetta**, cut into cubes
1 **fresh red chilli**, deseeded and finely chopped
2 **garlic cloves**, thinly sliced
250 g (8 oz) **raw shelled scallops**
400 g (13 oz) **dried linguine**
100 ml (3½ fl oz) **dry white wine**
2 tablespoons roughly chopped **flat leaf parsley**
salt

Heat the oil in a large frying pan over a medium heat, add the pancetta and cook, stirring occasionally, for 4–5 minutes until golden and crisp. Remove from the heat and stir in the chilli and garlic. Leave the flavours to infuse while you prepare the scallops and start cooking the pasta.

If you have bought scallops with the orange roe, carefully separate the roe from the main body of the scallops. Using a small, sharp knife, slice once across the thickness of each scallop to make thinner discs. Set aside.

Cook the pasta in a large saucepan of salted boiling water according to packet instructions until al dente.

When the pasta is almost ready, heat the frying pan with the pancetta over a high heat. When the oil starts to sizzle, season the scallops and roes with salt, add to the pan and cook, stirring gently, for 2 minutes. Pour in the wine and boil rapidly for 2 minutes.

Drain the pasta and stir into the frying pan with the parsley. Toss the pasta over the heat for 30 seconds, to combine all the flavours. Serve immediately.

For pasta with asparagus, scallops & pancetta, simply add 150 g (5 oz) asparagus tips to the pasta cooking water for the last 3 minutes of the cooking time and complete the recipe as above.

79 QUICK MID-WEEK MEALS

STIR-FRIED BEEF WITH VEGETABLES

Serves **4**
Preparation time **15 minutes**
Cooking time **5 minutes**

3 tablespoons **rice wine vinegar**
4 tablespoons **clear honey**
4 tablespoons **light soy sauce**
3 tablespoons **mirin**
½ **cucumber**
1 **fennel bulb**, quartered
1 bunch **radishes**, trimmed
500 g (1 lb) **lean rump** or **sirloin steak**
1 tablespoon **cornflour**
5 tablespoons **stir-fry** or **wok oil**
1 **medium red chilli**, deseeded and thinly sliced
25 g (1 oz) **fresh root ginger**, chopped
1 bunch **spring onions**, thinly sliced
300 g (10 oz) **straight-to-wok noodles**
25 g (1 oz) chopped **fresh coriander**

Mix together the vinegar, honey, soy sauce and mirin in a small bowl.

Halve the cucumber lengthways and scoop out the seeds. Push the cucumber, fennel and radishes through a food processor fitted with a slicing attachment. (Alternatively, slice as thinly as possible by hand.)

Trim any fat from the beef and slice very thinly. Dust with the cornflour.

Heat 2 tablespoons of the oil in a wok or large frying pan. Add the chilli, ginger and beef and stir-fry quickly for 1 minute. Drain to a large plate. Add the spring onions to the pan and stir-fry quickly for a further minute. Drain to the plate.

Heat a little more oil and stir-fry half the shredded vegetables for about 30 seconds. Drain to the plate. Stir-fry the remainder and drain to the plate.

Pour the remaining oil into the pan and add the noodles and coriander. Cook, stirring, for a few seconds to heat through and break up the noodles, then tip the beef and vegetables back into the pan. Add the vinegar mixture and cook for about 30 seconds until heated through. Serve immediately.

For stir-fried beef with Chinese vegetables, omit the cucumber, fennel and radishes. Thinly slice 200 g (7 oz) sugarsnap peas, 2 courgettes and 2 sweet peppers and stir-fry in 2 batches with a 200 g (8 oz) can water chestnuts, halved, as in the fifth step.

INDIVIDUAL ITALIAN FILLET STEAK PARCELS

Serves **4**
Preparation time **10 minutes**
Cooking time **20 minutes**

1 tablespoon **olive oil**
4 **fillet steaks**, about 150 g (5 oz) each
8 large squares of **filo pastry**
150 g (5 oz) **butter**, melted
125 g (4 oz) **buffalo mozzarella cheese**, cut into 4 slices
2 teaspoons chopped **marjoram**
2 teaspoons chopped **oregano**
4 **sun-blushed tomatoes**, shredded
2 tablespoons finely grated **Parmesan cheese**
salt and **pepper**

Salad
150 g (5 oz) **rocket**
125 g (4 oz) **buffalo mozzarella cheese**, cubed
½ **red onion**, finely sliced (optional)
2 ripe **plum tomatoes**, sliced

Heat the oil in a hot frying pan and sear the steaks for 2 minutes on each side (they will continue cooking in the oven). Remove and set aside.

Brush each sheet of pastry with melted butter and arrange 2 sheets on a work surface. Place a steak in the centre of the pastry, followed by a slice of mozzarella, one-quarter of the herbs and sun-blushed tomato shreds. Season and bring up the sides of the pastry. Scrunch it together at the top to seal the steak into a parcel. Sprinkle over one-quarter of the grated Parmesan. Repeat with the remaining steaks.

Cook in a preheated oven, 220°C (425°F), Gas Mark 7, for 15 minutes until the pastry is crisp and golden brown. Remove and leave to rest for 2–3 minutes.

Toss the salad ingredients together, season and serve with the parcels.

For summertime chicken parcels, use 4 chicken breasts instead of the steaks – you will need to fry them for about 5 minutes on each side. For a stronger flavour, replace the toppings with either 125 g (4 oz) sliced Gorgonzola, 25 g (1 oz) roughly chopped walnuts and 2 tablespoons roughly chopped chives or 125 g (4 oz) sliced firm goats' cheese, 25 g (1 oz) black pitted olives and 2 tablespoons shredded basil.

FETA & WATERMELON SALAD

Serves **4**
Preparation time **10 minutes**
Cooking time **2 minutes**

1 tablespoon **black sesame seeds**
500 g (1 lb) **watermelon**, peeled, deseeded and diced
175 g (6 oz) **feta cheese**, diced
875 g (1¾ lb) **rocket**
sprigs of **mint**, **parsley** and **coriander**
6 tablespoons **olive oil**
1 tablespoon **orange flower water**
1½ tablespoons **lemon juice**
1 teaspoon **pomegranate syrup** (optional)
½ teaspoon **caster sugar**
salt and **pepper**

Heat a frying pan and dry-fry the sesame seeds for 2 minutes until aromatic, then set aside.

Arrange the watermelon and feta on a large plate with the rocket and herbs.

Whisk together the oil, orange flower water, lemon juice, pomegranate syrup (if used) and sugar. Season to taste with salt and pepper, then drizzle over the salad. Scatter over the sesame seeds and serve with toasted pitta bread.

For quick feta & tomato salad, mix 500 g (1 lb) skinned and chopped tomatoes with 250 g (8 oz) cubed feta and 50 g (2 oz) pitted black olives. Drizzle over a mixture of 3 tablespoons olive oil, 2 chopped garlic cloves and ½ teaspoon caster sugar. Season with plenty of black pepper and serve.

QUICK ONE-POT RATATOUILLE

Serves **4**
Preparation time **10 minutes**
Cooking time **20 minutes**

100 ml (3½ fl oz) **olive oil**
2 **onions**, chopped
1 medium **aubergine**, cut into bite-sized cubes
2 **large courgettes**, cut into bite-sized pieces
1 **red pepper**, cored, deseeded and cut into bite-sized pieces
1 **yellow pepper**, cored, deseeded and cut into bite-sized pieces
2 **garlic cloves**, crushed
400 g (13 oz) can **chopped tomatoes**
4 tablespoons chopped **parsley** or **basil**
salt and **pepper**

Heat the oil in a large saucepan until very hot, add the onions, aubergine, courgettes, peppers and garlic and cook, stirring constantly, for a few minutes until softened. Add the tomatoes, season to taste with salt and pepper and stir well.

Reduce the heat, cover the pan tightly and simmer for 15 minutes until all the vegetables are cooked. Remove from the heat and stir in the chopped parsley or basil before serving.

For Mediterranean vegetable pie, spoon the cooked vegetable mixture into a medium-sized ovenproof dish. Cook 800 g (1 lb 10 oz) quartered potatoes in a large saucepan of salted boiling water for 12–15 minutes or until tender, then drain and roughly mash with 200 g (7 oz) finely grated Cheddar cheese. Spread over the vegetable mixture, then bake in a preheated oven, 180°C (350°F), Gas Mark 4, for 20 minutes or until lightly golden on top.

FRAGRANT LAMB CUTLETS

Serves **4**
Preparation time **5 minutes**, plus marinating
Cooking time **15 minutes**

12 **lamb cutlets**
4 **sweet potatoes**, baked in their skins
salt and **pepper**
rocket leaves, to serve

Marinade
finely grated rind and juice of ½ **lemon**
2 **garlic cloves**, crushed
2 tablespoons **olive oil**, plus extra for brushing
4 sprigs of **rosemary**, finely chopped
4 **anchovy fillets in olive oil**, drained and finely
   chopped
2 tablespoons **lemon cordial**

Mix together all the marinade ingredients in a non-metallic bowl, then add the lamb cutlets. Season to taste with salt and pepper, turn the cutlets to coat and set aside for 15 minutes to marinate.

Cook the cutlets under a preheated hot grill for 3–5 minutes on each side or until slightly charred and cooked through. Keep warm and allow to rest.

Meanwhile, cut the baked sweet potatoes into quarters, scoop out some of the flesh and brush the skins with oil. Season to taste with salt and pepper and cook for about 15 minutes under the grill until crisp. Serve with the lamb cutlets and rocket leaves.

For pork patties with sweet potato slices,

mix 500 g (1 lb) minced pork with the marinade ingredients, omitting the anchovies. Using your hands, form the mince mixture into little patties and cook under a hot grill for 5–6 minutes on each side until browned and cooked through. Serve with sweet potato skins and rocket leaves, as above.

CRISPY LAMB MOROCCAN ROLLS

Serves **2**
Preparation time **15 minutes**
Cooking time **10 minutes**

250 g (8 oz) **lamb mince**
1 teaspoon **ground cinnamon**
3 tablespoons **pine nuts**
2 **naan breads**, warmed
200 g (7 oz) **hummus**
2 tablespoons **mint leaves**
1 **Little Gem lettuce**, finely shredded (optional)

Fry the mince in a large, nonstick frying pan for 8–10 minutes until it becomes golden brown. Add the cinnamon and pine nuts and cook again for 1 minute. Remove from the heat.

Place the warm naan breads on a chopping board and, using a rolling pin, firmly roll to flatten.

Mix the hummus with half the mint leaves, then spread in a thick layer over the warmed naans. Spoon over the crispy lamb, then scatter over the shredded lettuce, if using, and the remaining mint leaves. Tightly roll up and secure with cocktail sticks. Serve immediately, or wrap tightly in foil to transport.

For lamb kofta, mix the raw mince with 4 finely chopped spring onions, 1 teaspoon ground cinnamon, a very finely chopped tomato and 1 egg yolk until blended together. Form into a very large, thin patty shape, and grill or cook in a large, heavy-based frying pan on one side for 3 minutes, then on the other side for 2 minutes, until golden. Spread 1 warm naan with 2 tablespoons Greek yogurt, scatter with the mint leaves and shredded lettuce, if using and slip the large flattened kofta on top. Roll tightly and secure with cocktail sticks. Cut the kofta in half to serve 2.

TAVERNA-STYLE GRILLED LAMB WITH FETA

Serves **4**
Preparation time **8 minutes**
Cooking time **6–8 minutes**

500 g (1 lb) leg or **shoulder of lamb**, diced

Marinade
2 tablespoons chopped **oregano**
1 tablespoon chopped **rosemary**
grated rind of 1 **lemon**
2 tablespoons **olive oil**
salt and **pepper**

Feta salad
200 g (7 oz) **feta cheese**, sliced
1 tablespoon chopped **oregano**
2 tablespoons chopped **parsley**
grated rind and juice of 1 **lemon**
½ small **red onion**, finely sliced
3 tablespoons **olive oil**

Mix together the marinade ingredients in a non-metallic bowl, add the lamb and mix to coat thoroughly. Thread the meat on to 4 skewers.

Arrange the sliced feta on a large serving dish and sprinkle over the herbs, lemon rind and sliced onion. Drizzle over the lemon juice and oil and season with salt and pepper.

Cook the lamb skewers under a preheated hot grill or in a griddle pan for about 6–8 minutes, turning frequently until browned and almost cooked through. Remove from heat and leave to rest for 1–2 minutes.

Serve the lamb, with any pan juices poured over, with the salad and accompanied with plenty of crusty bread, if liked.

For pork with red cabbage, replace the lamb with the same quantity of lean, boneless pork. Marinate and cook the pork as above. Replace the feta with 250 g (8 oz) finely chopped red cabbage. Omit the oregano and swap the lemon for an orange. Mix the ingredients together and marinate for 5 minutes before serving.

THAI SESAME CHICKEN PATTIES

Serves **4**
Preparation time **15 minutes**, plus chilling
Cooking time **10 minutes**

4 spring onions
15 g (½ oz) **fresh coriander**, plus extra to garnish
500 g (1 lb) **minced chicken**
3 tablespoons **sesame seeds**, toasted
1 tablespoon **light soy sauce**
3.5 cm (1½ inch) piece **root ginger**, finely grated
1 **egg white**
1 tablespoon **sesame oil**
1 tablespoon **sunflower oil**
Thai sweet chilli dipping sauce, to serve
spring onion curls (optional)

Finely chop the spring onions and coriander in a food processor or with a knife. Mix with the chicken, sesame seeds, soy sauce, ginger and egg white.

Divide the mixture into 20 mounds on a chopping board, then shape into slightly flattened rounds with wetted hands. Chill for 1 hour (or longer if you have time).

Heat the sesame and sunflower oils in a large frying pan, add the patties and fry for 10 minutes, turning once or twice until golden and cooked through to the centre. Arrange on a serving plate with a small bowl of chilli dipping sauce in the centre. Garnish with extra coriander leaves and spring onion curls, if liked.

For baby leaf stir-fry with chilli to serve as an accompaniment, heat 2 teaspoons sesame oil in the finished pattie pan, add a 250 g (8 oz) pack of ready-prepared baby leaf and baby vegetable stir-fry ingredients and stir-fry for 2–3 minutes until the vegetables are hot. Mix in 2 tablespoons light soy sauce and 1 tablespoon Thai sweet chilli dipping sauce. Serve in a side bowl with the chicken patties.

CHICKEN & VEGETABLE SKEWERS

Serves **4**
Preparation time **10 minutes**
Cooking time **15 minutes**

4 **chicken thighs**, skinned and boned
2 tablespoons **clear honey**
2 tablespoons **mild wholegrain mustard**
1 **courgette**, cut into 8 large pieces
1 **carrot**, cut into 8 large pieces

Cut the chicken thighs into bite-sized pieces and toss in the honey and mustard. Arrange the chicken pieces on a baking sheet and bake in a preheated oven, 180°C (350°F), Gas Mark 4, for 15 minutes until cooked through and lightly golden. Set aside and leave to cool.

Take 8 bamboo skewers and thread with the cooked chicken pieces and the raw vegetables.

Serve with the honey and mustard mixture for dipping. The skewers can also be refrigerated for adding to the following day's lunchbox.

For sticky chicken with honey & garlic, mix together 2 tablespoons tomato ketchup, 2 teaspoons runny honey, 2 finely chopped cloves of garlic and 1 tablespoon of sunflower oil. Dip the chicken into the ketchup mixture then cook as above. Thread on to skewers with 1 red pepper, deseeded, cored and cut into chunks and 8 cherry tomatoes.

CHICKEN WITH SPRING HERBS

Serves **4**
Preparation time **15 minutes**
Cooking time **20 minutes**

250 g (8 oz) **mascarpone cheese**
1 handful of **chervil**, finely chopped
½ bunch of **parsley**, finely chopped
2 tablespoons chopped **mint leaves**
4 **boneless chicken breasts**, skin on
200 ml (7 fl oz) **white wine**
25 g (1 oz) **butter**
salt and **pepper**

Mix together the mascarpone and herbs in a bowl and season well with salt and pepper.

Lift the skin away from each chicken breast and spread a quarter of the mascarpone mixture on each breast. Replace the skin and smooth carefully over the mascarpone mixture. Season to taste with salt and pepper.

Place the chicken in a baking dish and pour the wine around it. Dot the butter over the chicken.

Roast in a preheated oven, 180°C (350°F), Gas Mark 4, for 20 minutes until the chicken is golden and crisp. Remove from the oven and serve with garlic bread.

For baby glazed carrots as an alternative accompaniment to garlic bread, melt 25 g (1 oz) butter in a saucepan, add 500 g (1 lb) young carrots, quartered lengthways, a pinch of sugar, and salt and pepper to taste. Pour over just enough water to cover and simmer gently for 15–20 minutes until the carrots are tender and the liquid has evaporated, adding 2 tablespoons orange juice towards the end of the cooking time. Serve with the chicken garnished with chopped parsley.

CHICKEN WITH SPINACH & RICOTTA

Serves **4**
Preparation time **5 minutes**
Cooking time **25 minutes**

4 boneless, skinless **chicken breasts**, 125 g
 (4 oz) each
125 g (4 oz) **ricotta cheese**
125 g (4 oz) cooked **spinach**, squeezed dry
¼ teaspoon grated **nutmeg**
8 slices **Parma ham**
2 tablespoons **olive oil**, plus extra for drizzling
salt and **pepper**

To serve
lemon wedges
rocket leaves

Make a long horizontal slit through the thickest part of each chicken breast without cutting right through.

Crumble the ricotta into a bowl. Chop the spinach and mix into the ricotta with the nutmeg. Season with salt and pepper.

Divide the stuffing between the slits in the chicken breasts and wrap each one in 2 pieces of Parma ham, winding it around the chicken to cover the meat totally.

Heat the oil in a shallow ovenproof pan, add the chicken breasts and sauté for 4 minutes on each side or until the ham starts to brown. Transfer to a preheated oven, 200°C (400°F), Gas Mark 6, and cook for 15 minutes. Serve with lemon wedges and rocket leaves drizzled with olive oil.

For chicken with mozzarella & sun-dried tomatoes, instead of the ricotta, spinach and nutmeg, stuff each chicken breast with a thick slice of mozzarella and a sun-dried tomato piece, drained of its olive oil. Season well with black pepper and continue as in the main recipe.

SZECHUAN CHICKEN

Serves **4**
Preparation time **5 minutes**, plus marinating
Cooking time **16–20 minutes**

3 tablespoons **soy sauce**
2 tablespoons **dry sherry**
1 teaspoon **rice vinegar**
3 cm (1¼ inch) piece **root ginger**, peeled and finely
 chopped
1 **garlic clove**, crushed
1 tablespoon **Chinese chilli paste**
½ teaspoon **Szechuan peppercorns**, ground
1 tablespoon **dark sesame oil**
4 x 125 g (4 oz) boneless, skinless **chicken breasts**
fresh coriander leaves, chopped, to garnish

Mix together all the ingredients except the chicken in a shallow dish to make the marinade. Add the chicken breasts, coat well with the marinade and leave to marinate at room temperature for 2 hours.

Heat a griddle pan (or ordinary frying pan). Cook the chicken for 8–10 minutes on each side and garnish with coriander. Serve with soba noodles and stir-fried oyster mushrooms.

For sesame greens with black bean sauce, to accompany the chicken, fry 2 tablespoons sesame seeds in 1 teaspoon sunflower oil until lightly browned. Add 1 tablespoon soy sauce, cover with a lid and take off the heat. When the bubbling subsides, scoop the seeds into a dish. Rinse 400 g (13 oz) spring greens and thickly slice, stir fry in 1 tablespoon oil with 2 cloves finely chopped garlic until just wilted. Mix in 3 tablespoons ready-made black bean sauce. Serve sprinkled with the seeds.

CHICKEN & SPINACH MASALA

Serves **4**
Preparation time **15 minutes**
Cooking time **13–16 minutes**

2 tablespoons **oil**
1 **onion**, thinly sliced
2 **garlic cloves**, crushed
1 **green chilli**, deseeded and thinly sliced
1 teaspoon finely grated **fresh root ginger**
1 teaspoon **ground coriander**
1 teaspoon **ground cumin**
200 g (7 oz) can **tomatoes**
750 g (1½ lb) **chicken thighs**, skinned, boned and cut
  into bite-sized chunks
200 ml (7 fl oz) **crème fraîche**
300 g (10 oz) **spinach**, roughly chopped
2 tablespoons chopped **fresh coriander**
salt and **pepper**
flat breads (optional)

Heat the oil in a large, heavy-based saucepan. Add the onion, garlic, chilli and ginger. Stir-fry for 2–3 minutes and then add the ground coriander and cumin. Stir and cook for a further 1 minute.

Pour in the tomatoes and cook gently for 3 minutes. Increase the heat and add the chicken. Cook, stirring, until the outside of the chicken is sealed. Stir in the crème fraîche and spinach.

Cover the pan and cook the chicken mixture gently for 6–8 minutes, stirring occasionally. Stir in the chopped coriander with seasoning to taste. Serve with toasted flat breads, if liked

For spiced lemon rice to serve as an accompaniment, place 200 g (7 oz) basmati rice in a sieve and wash thoroughly under cold running water. Drain and set aside. Heat 1 tablespoon olive oil in a nonstick saucepan and when hot add 12–14 curry leaves, 1 dried red chilli, ½ cinnamon stick, 2–3 cloves, 4–6 cardamom pods, 2 teaspoons cumin seeds and ¼ teaspoon ground turmeric. Stir-fry for 20-30 seconds, then add the rice. Stir-fry for 2 minutes, then add the juice of 1 large lemon and 450 ml (¾ pint) boiling water. Bring to the boil, cover the pan and reduce the heat to low. Cook for 10–12 minutes, remove from heat and allow to stand for 10 minutes, then fluff up with a fork before serving.

NOODLES & SEVEN-SPICE CHICKEN

Serves **4**
Preparation time **15 minutes**
Cooking time **12 minutes**

3 pieces of **stem ginger** from a jar, plus 3 tablespoons
of the syrup

2 tablespoons **rice wine vinegar**

3 tablespoons **light soy sauce**

4 skinned and boned **chicken breasts**, about 150 g
(5 oz)–175 g (6 oz) each

1 tablespoon **Thai seven-spice seasoning**

3 tablespoons **stir-fry** or **wok oil**

3 **shallots**, thinly sliced

125 g (4 oz) **baby corn**, halved

300 g (10 oz) **straight-to-wok medium** or **thread
noodles**

300 g (10 oz) **baby spinach**

200 g (7 oz) **bean sprouts**

Finely shred the pieces of stem ginger. Mix the ginger syrup with the vinegar and soy sauce and reserve.

Halve each chicken breast horizontally and then cut widthways into thin strips. Toss with the seven-spice seasoning.

Heat the oil in a large frying pan or wok and stir-fry the chicken pieces over a gentle heat for 5 minutes until beginning to brown.

Add the shallots and fry for 2 minutes. Stir in the baby corn and fry for 1 minute. Add the noodles and spinach and scatter with the shredded stem ginger. Stir-fry, mixing the ingredients together, until the spinach starts to wilt.

Add the bean sprouts and soy sauce mixture and cook, stirring, for a further 1 minute or until heated through. Serve immediately.

For noodles with seven-spice prawn, replace the chicken with 400 g (13 oz) peeled and deveined raw prawns, toss with the seven-spice seasoning and cook as above. Replace the spinach with 200 g (7 oz) roughly chopped pak choi.

CHICKEN WITH PEANUT SAUCE

Serves **4**
Preparation time **5 minutes**
Cooking time **16–20 minutes**

4 x 125 g (4 oz) boneless, skinless **chicken breasts**
1 tablespoon **soy sauce**
2 tablespoons **crunchy or smooth peanut butter**
4 tablespoons **lemon juice**
4 tablespoons **water**
pepper

To garnish
coriander leaves
peanuts, fried, chopped (optional)

Heat a griddle pan (or ordinary frying pan). Place the chicken breasts in the pan and cook for 8–10 minutes on each side.

Meanwhile, place the soy sauce, peanut butter, lemon juice, water and a little pepper in a small saucepan. Mix well and heat gently, adjusting the consistency of the sauce with a little more water if necessary, so that it is slightly runny but coats the back of a spoon.

When the chicken is cooked, serve with the peanut sauce drizzled over the top, garnished with coriander and chopped fried peanuts, if liked. Serve with mixed vegetable noodles.

For egg fried rice, to serve as an alternative accompaniment, add 250 g (8 oz) long rice to a saucepan of boiling water. Simmer for 8 minutes, then add 150 g (5 oz) frozen peas and cook for 2 minutes before draining. Heat 1 teaspoon sunflower oil in a frying pan, add 2 beaten eggs and make a thin omelette. Roll the omelette up, shred and mix with the cooked rice.

SPICED CHICKEN & MANGO SALAD

Serves **4**
Preparation time **15 minutes**
Cooking time **5–6 minutes**

4 small boneless, skinless **chicken breasts**
6 teaspoons **mild curry paste**
Juice of 1 **lemon**
150 g (5 oz) **low-fat natural yogurt**
1 **mango**
50 g (2 oz) **watercress**
½ **cucumber**, diced
½ **red onion**, chopped
½ **iceberg lettuce**

Cut the chicken breasts into long, thin slices. Put 4 teaspoons of the curry paste in a plastic bag with the lemon juice and mix together by squeezing the bag. Add the chicken and toss together.

Half-fill the base of a steamer with water and bring to the boil. Place the chicken in the top of the steamer in a single layer, cover and steam for 5–6 minutes until thoroughly cooked. Test the chicken.

Meanwhile, mix the remaining curry paste in a bowl with the yogurt.

Cut a thick slice off either side of the mango to reveal the large, flat stone. Trim the flesh away from the stone, then remove the peel and cut the flesh into bite-sized chunks.

Rinse the watercress with cold water and tear it into bite-sized pieces. Add to the yogurt dressing with the cucumber, red onion and mango and toss together gently.

Tear the lettuce into pieces, divide it among 4 plates, spoon the mango mixture on top and complete with the warm chicken strips.

For coronation chicken, mix the curry paste and yogurt with 4 tablespoons mayonnaise. Stir in 500 g (1 lb) cold cooked diced chicken and 40 g (1½ oz) sultanas. Sprinkle with 25 g (1 oz) toasted flaked almonds and serve on a bed of mixed salad and herb leaves.

CHICKEN WITH SAGE & LEMON

Serves **4**
Preparation time **15 minutes**, plus marinating
Cooking time **20 minutes**

4 boneless, skinless **chicken breasts**, about 150 g
  (5 oz) each
5 tablespoons **olive oil**
3 tablespoons **lemon juice**
28 small **sage leaves**
3 tablespoons **unsalted butter**
cooked puy lentils (optional)
salt and **pepper**

Place the chicken breasts in a single layer in a non-metallic dish. Pour over 3 tablespoons of the oil, and the lemon juice. Scatter over the sage leaves, turn the chicken so that the breasts are evenly coated, then cover and leave to marinate for about 30 minutes.

Lift the chicken breasts from the marinade and reserve the sage leaves separately. Pat the breasts dry. Strain the marinade into a small bowl.

Heat the butter and the remaining oil in a frying pan, add the chicken, and cook for about 10 minutes over a moderate heat until browned. Turn the chicken breasts over, season with salt and pepper, and tuck the sage leaves around them. Cook for a further 10 minutes until the underside is brown and the chicken is cooked through. Transfer the chicken to a warmed serving plate, cover and keep warm.

Tilt the pan and pour off the fat. Place the pan back on the heat and stir in the reserved marinade, scraping up any brown bits from the bottom of the pan. Boil until reduced to a brown glaze. Serve the chicken in slices, on a bed of puy lentils, if liked. Pour the remaining marinade over the chicken and garnish with the sage leaves.

For garlic & lemon mash, as an alternative to the lentil accompaniment, boil 750 g (1 1/2 lb) potatoes until tender. Drain and mash with 50 g (2 oz) butter, the grated rind and juice of 1/2 lemon and 3 cloves of finely chopped garlic.

ASIAN CITRUS CHICKEN SKEWERS

Serves **4**
Preparation time **5 minutes**, plus marinating
Cooking time **20 minutes**

500 g (1 lb) boneless, skinless **chicken breasts**, cubed
grated rind and juice of 1 **lemon**
2 teaspoons **Chinese 5-spice powder**
1 tablespoon **dark soy sauce**
mixed vegetables (carrots, spring onions, radishes),
  cut into strips (optional)

Place the chicken, lemon rind and juice, 5-spice powder and soy sauce in a bowl. Stir to combine, cover, then leave to marinate in the refrigerator for at least 1 hour or overnight.

Thread the chicken pieces on to 4 presoaked wooden skewers, pushing them tightly together. Grill for 10 minutes under a preheated moderate grill. Turn the skewers, baste with any remaining marinade, and grill for a further 10 minutes. Serve on a bed of vegetables, if liked.

For piri piri chicken skewers, mix the grated lemon rind and juice with 2 tablespoons olive oil then add 2 teaspoons piri piri seasoning, 2 teaspoons tomato purée and 2 cloves of finely chopped garlic. Add the chicken, marinade then grill as above.

CHICKEN & AVOCADO SALAD

Serves **4**
Preparation time **15 minutes**

125 g (4 oz) **light mayonnaise**
2 tablespoons **mango chutney**
grated rind and juice of 1 **lime**
2 **avocados**, halved, stoned, peeled, diced
4 **spring onions**, thinly sliced
¼ **cucumber**, diced
125–150 g (4–5 oz) **cooked chicken**, diced
2 **Little Gem lettuces**
40 g (1½ oz) **mixed salad leaves**
small bunch **fresh coriander**, optional

Mix the mayonnaise, mango chutney and lime rind together in a large bowl. Toss the lime juice with the avocados, then add to the dressing. Add the spring onions, cucumber and chicken and fold the mixture together lightly so that it is semi-mixed.

Divide the lettuce leaves between 4 serving plates and top with the other salad leaves. Spoon over the chicken salad and garnish with torn coriander leaves, if liked. Serve immediately.

For chicken Waldorf salad, mix the same quantity of mayonnaise with the grated rind of ½ lemon, tossing the juice with 2 cored and diced dessert apples. Add the apples to the dressing along with 40 g (1½ oz) sultanas, 4 stems celery, thickly sliced, and 125–150 g (4–5 oz) diced cooked chicken. Serve on salad leaves as above, omitting the coriander.

HOT DUCK & COCONUT NOODLES

Serves **4**
Preparation time **10 minutes**
Cooking time **15 minutes**

4 **confit duck legs**
250 ml (8 fl oz) **coconut milk**
200 ml (7 fl oz) **chicken stock**
2 tablespoons **Thai fish sauce**
3 whole **star anise**
1 teaspoon **chilli flakes**
25 g (1 oz) **fresh root ginger**, thinly sliced
1 small bunch of **coriander**, chopped
juice of 2 **limes**
250 g (8 oz) **flat rice noodles**
4 tablespoons **coconut shavings**, toasted
50 g (2 oz) **cashew nuts**, toasted

Heat a large frying pan and put the duck legs and their fat, skin-side down, in the pan. Cook over a medium heat for 10 minutes until the skins turn golden and crispy. Turn and cook for a further 2–3 minutes until the legs are heated through. Drain on kitchen paper, then tear the meat into small pieces and discard the bones.

Meanwhile, pour the coconut milk into a pan with the stock, fish sauce, star anise, chilli flakes, ginger and half the chopped coriander and bring to simmering point. Leave to bubble gently for 10 minutes to allow the flavours to infuse. Stir in the lime juice.

Cook the noodles in unsalted boiling water for about 3 minutes or according to the instructions on the packet, then drain and heap into serving bowls.

Scatter over the duck meat and pour over the hot coconut broth. Sprinkle with the coconut shavings, cashews and remaining coriander. Serve immediately.

For spiced prawn stir-fry, omit the duck and instead mix 400 g (13 oz) raw prawns with 25 g (1 oz) freshly grated ginger, 1 crushed garlic clove, 1 freshly chopped red chilli and 1 tablespoon vegetable oil. Heat a wok until smoking, add another tablespoon vegetable oil and stir-fry the prawns for 2–3 minutes until pink and cooked through. Serve with the noodles and a ladle of the hot coconut broth, finishing as before with cashews and coriander.

SMOKED DUCK SALAD

Serves **4**
Preparation time **15 minutes**

150 g (5 oz) **lamb's lettuce**
1½ **oranges** or **blood oranges**, cut into segments
100 g (3½ oz) **smoked duck breast**, thinly sliced
seeds of 1 **pomegranate**
50 g (2 oz) **shelled pistachios**

Dressing

juice of ½ **blood orange**
1 small **shallot**, finely chopped
1 tablespoon **red wine vinegar**
1 teaspoon **wholegrain mustard**
4 tablespoons **olive oil**

Arrange the lamb's lettuce on 4 large serving plates, add the orange segments and slices of duck. Scatter over the pomegranate seeds and pistachios.

Make the dressing by putting the ingredients in a screw-top jar and shaking well to combine. Drizzle the dressing over each salad, and serve immediately.

For duck & watercress salad with cranberries & pecans, replace the lamb's lettuce with watercress and the pomegranate seeds and pistachios with 4 tablespoons dried cranberries and 50 g (2 oz) chopped pecans.

CHICKEN ALLA MILANESE

Serves **4**
Preparation time **12 minutes**
Cooking time **20 minutes**

1 kg (2 lb) **floury potatoes**, peeled and cut in half
4 boneless, skinless **chicken breasts**, about 150 g (5 oz) each
2 small **eggs**, beaten
3 tablespoons **olive oil**
150 g (5 oz) **butter**
4 ripe **tomatoes**, roughly chopped
2 tablespoons **capers in brine**, drained and rinsed
4 tablespoons **white wine**
4 tablespoons **lemon juice**
100 g (3½ oz) **rocket**
salt and **pepper**

Crust

2 teaspoons **dried oregano**
100 g (3½ oz) **breadcrumbs**
½ teaspoon **garlic powder**
finely grated rind of 1 **lemon**
50 g (2 oz) **Parmesan cheese**, finely grated

Cook the potatoes in lightly salted boiling water for about 20 minutes or until soft.

Meanwhile, mix together the ingredients for the crust and tip the mixture on to a plate. Put the chicken breasts between 2 sheets of clingfilm or greaseproof paper and batter with a rolling pin or mallet until flat. Dip the chicken into the beaten egg, then press into the crust mixture to coat.

Heat the oil in a large frying pan and cook the chicken for 3 minutes on each side or until cooked through and golden. Set aside and keep warm.

Add half the butter to the pan and stir in the tomatoes, capers and white wine. Season and allow to bubble for 2–3 minutes.

Drain and mash the potatoes with the lemon juice, the remaining butter and plenty of seasoning. Spoon on to serving plates with the crispy chicken. Quickly stir the rocket into the tomatoes and pile a little on to each piece of chicken. Serve immediately.

For spinach with raisins & pine nuts to serve as an accompaniment, put 1 chopped onion, 4 tablespoons raisins and 50 g (2 oz) butter in a large pan. Add 1 kg (2 lb) spinach and 3 tablespoons water. Cover and cook for 3–5 minutes, shaking the pan occasionally, until the spinach has wilted. Mix well and serve.

ASIAN STEAMED-CHICKEN SALAD

Serves **4**
Preparation time **10 minutes, plus cooling**
Cooking time **8–10 minutes**

4 boneless, skinless **chicken breasts**, about 150 g
  (5 oz) each
½ small **Chinese cabbage**, finely shredded
1 large **carrot**, grated
200 g (7 oz) **bean sprouts**
small bunch of **coriander**, finely chopped
small bunch of **mint**, finely chopped
1 **red chilli**, deseeded and finely sliced (optional)

Dressing
125 ml (4 fl oz) **sunflower oil**
juice of 2 **limes**
1½ tablespoons **Thai fish sauce**
3 tablespoons **light soy sauce**
1 tablespoon finely chopped fresh **root ginger**

Put the chicken breasts in a bamboo or other steamer set over a large pan of simmering water. Cover and leave to steam for about 8 minutes or until the chicken is cooked through. Alternatively, poach the chicken for 8–10 minutes until the meat is cooked and tender.

Meanwhile, make the dressing by mixing together the ingredients in a bowl.

When the chicken is cool enough to handle, cut or tear it into strips and mix the pieces with 2 tablespoons of the dressing. Leave to cool.

Toss all the vegetables and herbs together and arrange in serving dishes. Scatter over the cold chicken and serve immediately with the remaining dressing.

For Asian steamed-prawn salad with peanuts, use 450 g (14½ oz) medium-sized raw, peeled prawns steamed in the same way as the chicken for 2–3 minutes until pink and firm. Finish with a couple of tablespoons of crushed unsalted peanuts.

TURKEY & PUMPKIN SEED SALAD

Serves **4**
Preparation time **12 minutes**
Cooking time **6 minutes**

3 tablespoons **sunflower oil**
400 g (13 oz) minced **turkey**
1 tablespoon **preserved jalapeño peppers**, sliced
200 g (7 oz) can **sweetcorn**, drained
1 ripe **avocado**, peeled, stoned and cut into chunks
2 ripe **tomatoes**, chopped
1 small **red onion**, finely diced
small bunch of **coriander**, chopped
salt and **pepper**

Dressing
juice of 2 **limes**
1 teaspoon **clear honey**
4 tablespoons **pumpkin
  seed oil**

To serve
½ small **red cabbage**, shredded
250 g (8 oz) **buffalo mozzarella cheese**, cubed
4 **taco shells**
3 tablespoons **pumpkin seeds**, to sprinkle

Make the dressing by mixing together the ingredients in a small bowl. Season to taste and set aside.

Heat the oil in a large frying pan and fry the turkey for 5–6 minutes until cooked and beginning to colour. Scrape into a bowl, mix with half the dressing and set aside to cool.

Make a chunky salsa by combining the peppers, sweetcorn, avocado, tomatoes, red onion and coriander. Mix with the remaining dressing.

When the turkey is cool, mix it with the salsa and serve with the cabbage, mozzarella and taco shells with the pumpkin seeds scattered over.

For turkey with white cabbage & sunflower seed salad, replace the pumpkin-seed oil in the dressing with olive oil and the red cabbage with white cabbage. Substitute the mozzarella with finely diced Gruyère or Gouda and the pumpkin seeds with sunflower seeds. Omit the tacos, serving the salad as a base with the turkey mix on top.

FAST FAMILY
FAVOURITES

FISH & CHIPS IN PAPER CONES

Serves **4**

Preparation time **20 minutes**

Cooking time **30–40 minutes**

750 g (1½ lb) **baking potatoes**, cut into thick chips

2 tablespoons **olive oil**

125 g (4 oz) **wholemeal breadcrumbs**

finely grated rind of 1 **lemon**

3 tablespoons chopped **parsley**

4 x 150 g (5 oz) chunky **white fish fillets**, each cut into 4 chunky pieces or goujons

50 g (2 oz) **plain flour**

1 **egg**, beaten

Tomato Ketchup (see page 12), to serve

Toss the potato chips with the oil, then roast in a preheated oven, 200°C (400°F), Gas Mark 6, for 30–40 minutes, turning occasionally until golden and crisp.

Meanwhile, toss the breadcrumbs with the lemon rind and parsley on a plate. Lightly coat the fish goujons in the flour, then the beaten egg, and finally the breadcrumbs. Place on a baking sheet and roast in a preheated oven, 200°C (400°F), Gas Mark 6, for the final 20 minutes of the chips' cooking time, until the fish is opaque and cooked through.

Roll 4 sheets of A5 paper into cones and seal with tape. Place in a bottle holder to help load each with chips, and place 4 goujons on top. Allow the kids to eat these healthy fish and chips with their fingers, dipping them into the ketchup for good measure!

For lemony mayonnaise dip to serve as an alternative accompaniment, place 1 egg, 150 ml (¼ pint) olive oil and 1 tablespoon white wine vinegar in a jug and whiz with a hand blender until a thick mayonnaise is formed. Fold in the grated rind of 1 small lemon and 2 tablespoons of the juice, along with 2 tablespoons chopped parsley.

FISH PIE

Serves **4**

Preparation time **15 minutes**

Cooking time **1 hour 10 minutes**

300 g (10 oz) **raw peeled prawns**

2 teaspoons **cornflour**

300 g (10 oz) **skinned white fish**, e.g. **haddock**, cut into small pieces

2 teaspoons **green peppercorns in brine**, rinsed and drained

1 small **fennel bulb**, roughly chopped

1 small **leek**, roughly chopped

15 g (½ oz) **fresh dill**

15 g (½ oz) **fresh parsley**

100 g (3½ oz) **fresh** or **frozen peas**

350 g (12 oz) **ready-made** or **homemade cheese sauce**

750 g (1½ lb) **baking potatoes**, thinly sliced

75 g (3 oz) **Cheddar cheese**, grated

salt and **pepper**

Dry the prawns, if frozen and thawed, by patting between sheets of kitchen paper. Season the cornflour and use to coat the prawns and white fish. Lightly crush the peppercorns using a pestle and mortar.

Put the peppercorns in a food processor with the fennel, leek, dill, parsley and a little salt and blend until very finely chopped, scraping the mixture down from the sides of the bowl if necessary. Tip into a shallow, ovenproof dish.

Scatter the prawns and fish over the fennel mixture and mix together a little. Scatter the peas on top.

Spoon half the cheese sauce over the filling and spread roughly with the back of a spoon. Layer up the potatoes on top, seasoning each layer as you go. Spoon the remaining sauce over the top, spreading it in a thin layer. Sprinkle with the cheese.

Bake in a preheated oven, 220°C (425°F), Gas Mark 7, for 30 minutes until the surface has turned pale golden. Reduce the oven temperature to 180°C (350°F), Gas Mark 4, and cook for a further 30–40 minutes until the potatoes are completely tender. Serve with a tomato salad.

For smoked fish and caper pie, use 625 g (1¼ lb) smoked pollack, skinned and cut into small chunks in place of the prawns and white fish. Use 2 tablespoons capers instead of the green peppercorns.

HERBY CHICKPEA CRAB CAKES

Serves **4**
Preparation time **10 minutes**
Cooking time **7 minutes**

400 g (13 oz) can **chickpeas**, rinsed and drained
2 **spring onions**, thinly sliced
3 tablespoons chopped **parsley**
2 tablespoons chopped **chives**
1 **egg yolk**
1 teaspoon **piri piri sauce**
1 teaspoon **Worcestershire sauce**
2 tablespoons **mayonnaise**
150 g (5 oz) coarse dry **breadcrumbs**
300 g (10 oz) **white crab meat**
2 tablespoons **olive oil**

To serve
125 g (4 oz) **rocket leaves**
4 tablespoons **Aïoli** (see page 57)

Put the chickpeas, spring onions, herbs, egg yolk, piri piri sauce, Worcestershire sauce, mayonnaise and 50 g (2 oz) of the breadcrumbs in a food processor and process briefly. Add the crab meat and pulse quickly to combine, adding more breadcrumbs if the mixture is too wet.

Transfer the mixture to a bowl and form it into 4 large or 8 small patties. Press them into the remaining breadcrumbs until well coated.

Heat the oil in a large frying pan and fry the crab cakes for about 5 minutes, turning carefully once, until crisp and golden. Drain on kitchen paper and serve immediately with rocket leaves and a dollop of aïoli.

For avocado & watercress sauce to serve instead of the aïoli, chop 1 tablespoon capers and 100 g (3½ oz) watercress and mash 1 avocado. Mix together with 200 ml (7 fl oz) Greek yogurt.

COD FILLET WITH TOMATOES & ROCKET

Serves **4**
Preparation time **5 minutes**
Cooking time **12–15 minutes**

4 chunky **cod fillets**, about 150 g (5 oz) each
3 tablespoons **olive oil**
2 **garlic cloves**, chopped
300 g (10 oz) **cherry tomatoes on the vine**
2 tablespoons **balsamic vinegar**
4 tablespoons shredded **basil**
125 g (4 oz) **rocket leaves**
salt and **pepper**

Rub the cod fillets all over with 1 tablespoon of the oil and season well. Scatter over the garlic and put the fish in a roasting tray. Arrange the cherry tomatoes alongside and drizzle with the remaining oil, the balsamic vinegar and basil. Season to taste.

Transfer the tray to a preheated oven, 220°C (425°F), Gas Mark 7, and cook for 12–15 minutes until the fish is flaky and the tomatoes roasted.

Serve the cod with the tomatoes and rocket leaves.

For cod with Italian-style salsa, fry the cod fillets for 5–6 minutes until cooked and golden brown. To make the salsa, combine 8 finely chopped sun-dried tomatoes, 2 tablespoons roughly chopped basil leaves, 1 tablespoon drained capers, 1 tablespoon lightly crushed toasted pine nuts and 2 tablespoons olive oil. Serve with a rocket salad.

BLACKENED COD WITH CITRUS SALSA

Serves **4**
Preparation time **15 minutes**
Cooking time **15 minutes**

1 large **orange**
1 **garlic clove**, crushed
2 large **tomatoes**, deseeded and diced
2 tablespoons chopped **basil**, plus extra to garnish
75 g (3 oz) pitted **black olives**, chopped
5 tablespoons **olive oil**
4 **cod fillets**, about 175 g (6 oz) each
1 tablespoon **jerk seasoning**
salt and **pepper**

Cut the skin and the white membrane off the orange. Working over a bowl to catch the juice, cut between the membranes to remove the segments. Halve the segments and mix them with the reserved juice and the garlic, tomatoes, basil, olives and 4 tablespoons of the oil. Season to taste with salt and pepper and set aside to infuse.

Brush the cod with the remaining oil and coat with the jerk seasoning. Heat a large, heavy-based frying pan and cook the cod, skin-side down, for 5 minutes. Turn the fish over and cook for a further 3 minutes. Transfer to a preheated oven, 150°C (300°F), Gas Mark 2, to rest for about 5 minutes. Garnish the fish with basil and serve with the salsa and a green salad.

For quick crumbed cod, mix together 3 tablespoons each breadcrumbs, torn basil leaves and grated Parmesan cheese, 2 pieces drained and chopped sun-dried tomato, 1 tablespoon olive oil and the grated rind of 1 lemon. Press the mixture over 4 pieces of cod, each 175 g (6 oz), and cook in a preheated oven, 190°C (375°F), Gas Mark 5, for 20 minutes.

CREAMY SMOKED FISH GRATIN

Serves **4**
Preparation time **10 minutes**
Cooking time **20 minutes**

4 **plum tomatoes**, chopped
250 g (8 oz) boneless **smoked trout fillets**, skin removed
400 g (13 oz) boneless **smoked haddock fillets**, skin removed
75 g (3 oz) grated **Gruyère** or **Emmental cheese**
2 tablespoons freshly grated **Parmesan cheese**
2 tablespoons chopped **chives**
200 ml (7 oz) **double cream**
salt and **pepper**
500 g (1 lb) **new potatoes**, steamed (optional)

Arrange the tomatoes over the bottom of 4 lightly buttered individual ovenproof dishes or 1 large ovenproof dish. Cut the fish into chunks and scatter them over the tomatoes. Top with the grated cheeses and chopped chives.

Pour over the cream, place on a baking sheet and cook in a preheated oven, 220°C (425°F), Gas Mark 7, for about 20 minutes until the gratin is bubbling and golden and the fish is cooked.

Serve immediately with steamed new potatoes, if liked.

For creamy cod with prawns, replace the trout and haddock with 450 g (14½ oz) skinless and boneless cod, cut into chunks, and 250 g (8 oz) peeled and cooked prawns. Replace the chives with about 25 g (1 oz) chopped parsley. Finish as above and serve with mashed potatoes with chopped dill added.

PAN-FRIED HADDOCK FILLETS

Serves **4**
Preparation time **15 minutes**
Cooking time **20 minutes**

1 kg (2 lb) **floury potatoes**, peeled
75 ml (3 fl oz) **full-fat milk**
150 g (5 oz) **butter**
4 **haddock fillets**, about 150 g (5 oz) each, skin on
2 tablespoons **capers in brine**, drained and rinsed
4 tablespoons **lemon juice**
salt and **pepper**

Cook the potatoes in lightly salted boiling water for about 20 minutes. Mash until smooth with the milk and 50 g (2 oz) of the butter. Season well.

Meanwhile, melt the remaining butter in a large frying pan, add the haddock fillets, skin-side down, and cook for about 3 minutes until golden and crispy. Carefully turn over the fillets and cook for a further 1–2 minutes.

Remove the fillets and transfer to serving plates with the mashed potato.

Return the pan to the hob. Increase the heat until the butter turns nut-brown in colour, then add the capers and lemon juice. Bubble for a minute and then spoon over the fish and potatoes. Serve immediately.

For trout fillets with almonds, replace the haddock fillets with trout fillets and fry as above, finishing with almonds instead of capers.

SIMPLE SEAFOOD CURRY

Serves **4**
Preparation time **20 minutes**
Cooking time **35 minutes**

40 g (1½ oz) **fresh root ginger**, grated
1 teaspoon **ground turmeric**
2 **garlic cloves**, crushed
2 teaspoons **medium curry paste**
150 ml (¼ pint) **natural yogurt**
625 g (1¼ lb) **white fish fillets**, skinned
2 tablespoons **oil**
1 large **onion**, sliced
1 **cinnamon stick**, halved
2 teaspoons **dark muscovado sugar**
2 **bay leaves**
400 g (13 oz) can **chopped tomatoes**
300 ml (½ pint) **fish stock** or **vegetable stock**
500 g (1 lb) **waxy potatoes**, cut into small chunks
25 g (1 oz) chopped **fresh coriander**
salt and **pepper**

Mix together the ginger, turmeric, garlic and curry paste in a bowl. Stir in the yogurt until combined. Cut the fish into large pieces and add to the bowl, stirring until coated in the spice mixture.

Heat the oil in a large saucepan and gently fry the onion, cinnamon, sugar and bay leaves until the onion is soft. Add the tomatoes, stock and potatoes and bring to the boil. Cook, uncovered, for about 20 minutes until the potatoes are tender and the sauce has thickened.

Tip in the fish and spicy yogurt and reduce the heat to its lowest setting. Cook gently for about 10 minutes or until the fish is cooked through. Check the seasoning and stir in the coriander to serve.

For homemade fish stock, melt a knob of butter in a large saucepan and gently fry off 2 roughly chopped shallots, 1 small, roughly chopped leek and 1 roughly chopped celery stick or fennel bulb. Add 1 kg (2 lb) white fish or shellfish bones, heads and trimmings, several sprigs of parsley, ½ lemon and 1 teaspoon peppercorns. Cover with cold water and bring to a simmer. Cook, uncovered, on the lowest setting for 30 minutes. Strain through a sieve and leave to cool.

LAMB CHOPS WITH OLIVE COUSCOUS

Serves **4**
Preparation time **25 minutes**, plus marinating
Cooking time **10–12 minutes**

6 **anchovy fillets in olive oil**, drained and chopped
2 tablespoons **black olive tapenade**
2–3 sprigs of **thyme**, leaves stripped and chopped
1 sprig of **rosemary**, leaves stripped and chopped
2 **bay leaves**, torn
2–3 **garlic cloves**, crushed
finely grated rind of 1 **lemon**
4 tablespoons **white wine**
125 ml (4 fl oz) **olive oil**
4 **lamb loin chops**, about 150 g (5 oz) each
300 g (10 oz) **medium-grain couscous**
2 tablespoons **salted capers** or **capers in brine**,
  drained and rinsed
100 g (3½ oz) **spicy-marinated green olives**, chopped
75 g (3 oz) **wild rocket leaves**, plus extra for serving
4 tablespoons **lemon juice**, plus extra for serving
salt and **pepper**

Mash the anchovies with a fork and stir them into a bowl with the tapenade. Add the herbs, garlic and lemon rind, then pour in the wine and 4 tablespoons of the oil. Stir thoroughly, then rub the mixture into the lamb chops. Cover and leave at room temperature for about 1 hour.

Put the couscous into a heatproof bowl and stir in 2 tablespoons of the oil so that the grains are covered. Season with salt and pour over 400 ml (14 fl oz) boiling water. Leave to stand for 5–8 minutes until the grains are soft.

Season the lamb chops with pepper and cook them for about 2 minutes in a preheated hot griddle pan. Sprinkle with a little salt, then cook the other side for a further 2 minutes. Transfer to a warm dish, cover with foil and leave to rest for 5 minutes.

Fluff up the couscous with a fork and gently fold in the capers, olives and rocket. Sprinkle over the lemon juice, then heap the couscous on to warm plates. Arrange a lamb chop on each heap and spoon over the juices. Sprinkle with rocket leaves, drizzle with the remaining oil and an extra squeeze of lemon juice and serve immediately with lemon wedges.

For stir-fried lamb, heat 1½ tablespoons vegetable oil in a wok and cook 250 g (8 oz) fillet of lamb, thinly sliced, for a few minutes. Add 1 tablespoon each oyster sauce and Thai fish sauce, 1 crushed garlic clove and 1 tablespoon finely sliced red chilli and cook for a further 2 minutes. Garnish with mint leaves.

LAMB HOTPOT WITH DUMPLINGS

Serves **4**
Preparation time **30 minutes**
Cooking time **about 1 hour**

1 tablespoon **vegetable oil**
1 small **onion**, chopped
375 g (12 oz) boneless **lamb**, cubed
1 **leek**, chopped
75 g (3 oz) ready-to-eat **dried apricots**, chopped
375 g (12 oz) **new potatoes**, halved
1 tablespoon **thyme leaves**
2 tablespoons **plain flour**
600 ml (1 pint) **rich lamb stock**

Dumplings
125 g (4 oz) **plain flour**
½ teaspoon **salt**
1 teaspoon **thyme leaves**
50 g (2 oz) **vegetable suet**
about 4 tablespoons cold **water**

Heat the oil in a large, heavy-based saucepan and cook the onion and lamb over a moderate heat for 4–5 minutes until golden and soft. Add the leek, apricots and new potatoes and cook for 2 minutes, then add the thyme and flour and stir well to coat lightly. Pour in the stock, then bring to the boil and cover and simmer gently for 35 minutes, stirring occasionally.

Meanwhile, make the dumplings. Place the flour and salt in a bowl with the thyme leaves and suet and mix well. Mix in enough water to make an elastic dough. Divide into 12 and shape into small walnut-sized balls using lightly floured hands. Stir the hotpot and top up with a little water if necessary, then drop the dumplings into the stock and cover and simmer for 15 minutes until the dumplings have almost doubled in size.

Serve the hotpot ladled into warm serving bowls with the dumplings.

For vegetable hotpot with cheesy dumplings, omit the lamb and replace with 2 chopped carrots, 1 roughly chopped red pepper and 1 chopped courgette. Also replace the lamb stock with vegetable stock, and cook as above. Add 3 tablespoons raisins with the apricots. Add 25 g (1 oz) finely grated Cheddar cheese to the plain flour when making the dumplings and cook as above.

SPICED LAMB WITH BEAN PURÉE

Serves **2–3**
Preparation time **20 minutes, plus resting**
Cooking time **50 minutes**

2 large **baking potatoes**, cut into 1.5 cm
  (¾ inch) pieces
4 tablespoons **olive oil**
40 g (1½ oz) **breadcrumbs**
1 **garlic clove**, crushed
2 tablespoons chopped **fresh coriander**
1 teaspoon **ground coriander**
1 teaspoon **ground cumin**
1 **egg yolk**
1 **rack of lamb**, chined and trimmed
4 large **flat mushrooms**
150 g (5 oz) **frozen baby broad beans**
1 tablespoon chopped **mint**
100 ml (3½ fl oz) **white wine**
salt and **pepper**

Toss the potatoes with 2 tablespoons of the oil and salt and pepper in a small, sturdy roasting pan. Roast in a preheated oven, 200°C (400°F), Gas Mark 6, for 15 minutes.

Mix together the breadcrumbs, garlic, fresh coriander, spices and seasoning. Cut away any thick areas of fat from the skinned side of the lamb. Brush the lamb with the egg yolk and spoon the breadcrumb mixture over, pressing down gently with the back of the spoon. Brush the mushrooms with the remaining oil and a little seasoning.

Turn the potatoes in the pan and add the lamb, crusted-side uppermost. Return to the oven for 30 minutes. (The cutlets will still be slightly pink in the middle after this time, so cook for a little longer if you prefer them well done.) After 15 minutes of the cooking time, turn the potatoes in the oil and add the mushrooms. Return to the oven for the remaining cooking time.

Drain the meat to a board. Cover with foil and leave to rest for 15 minutes. Transfer the potatoes and mushrooms to a warmed serving dish.

Add the broad beans, mint and wine to the roasting pan and cook over a gentle heat for 5 minutes until the beans are tender. Tip into a blender or food processor and blend until smooth. Check the seasoning and spoon on to warmed serving plates. Carve the lamb into cutlets and add to the plates with the mushrooms and potatoes.

TASTY TEATIME PASTIES

Makes **6**
Preparation time **25 minutes**, plus chilling
Cooking time **25 minutes**

375 g (12 oz) **plain flour**
½ teaspoon **salt**
175 g (6 oz) **butter**, cubed
2–3 tablespoons cold **water**
1 tablespoon **vegetable oil**
½ small **onion**, chopped
175 g (6 oz) lean **lamb**, finely sliced
1 small **potato** or 2 **baby new potatoes**, peeled
  and diced
300 ml (½ pint) hot **lamb stock**
1 teaspoon **Dijon mustard**, optional
2 tablespoons finely chopped **mint**
beaten **egg**

Sift the flour and salt into a large mixing bowl and add the butter. Rub the butter into the flour until the mixture resembles fine breadcrumbs. Add the measured water and mix to form a rough dough. Turn on to a lightly floured work surface and knead until smooth. Place in a food bag and refrigerate for 30 minutes.

Meanwhile, heat the oil in a frying pan and cook the onion and lamb over a moderate heat for 5 minutes, stirring occasionally, until beginning to brown. Add the potato, reduce the heat and cook for a further 2 minutes, stirring occasionally until beginning to brown.

Mix the lamb stock with the mustard and pour into the pan. Cover with a tight-fitting lid and simmer gently for 15 minutes, stirring occasionally until the potatoes are soft yet still retaining their shape, and the meat is tender. Stir in the mint and set aside to cool.

Roll out the pastry to 5 mm (¼ inch) thick, and using a 15 cm (6 inch) saucer as a template, cut out 6 rounds. Lightly brush the edges of each of the circles with a little water and place 2 tablespoons of the mixture in the centre of each. Fold up to enclose the filling and pinch and gently twist the edges to seal. Place on a baking sheet and lightly glaze each one with the beaten egg. Bake in a preheated oven, 200°C (400°F), Gas Mark 6, for 20–25 minutes until the pastry is golden and crisp. Wrap loosely in foil to keep warm.

ASIAN LAMB BURGERS

Serves **4**
Preparation time **20 minutes**
Cooking time **30 minutes**

2 **garlic cloves**, crushed
1 **lemon grass stalk**, finely chopped
25 g (1 oz) **fresh root ginger**, grated
large handful of **fresh coriander**, roughly chopped
1 **hot red chilli**, deseeded and thinly sliced
500 g (1 lb) **lean minced lamb**
2 tablespoons **oil**
1 small **cucumber**
1 bunch **spring onions**
200 g (7 oz) **pak choi**
3 tablespoons **light muscovado sugar**
finely grated **rind** of 2 **limes**, plus 4 tablespoons **juice**
2 tablespoon **fish sauce**
50 g (2 oz) **roasted peanuts**
salt

Blend the garlic, lemon grass, ginger, coriander, chilli and a little salt in a food processor to make a thick paste. Add the lamb and blend until mixed. Tip out on to the work surface and divide the mixture into 4 pieces. Roll each into a ball and flatten into a burger shape.

Heat the oil in a sturdy roasting pan and fry the burgers on both sides to sear. Transfer to a preheated oven, 200°C (400°F), Gas Mark 6, and cook, uncovered, for 25 minutes until the burgers are cooked through.

Meanwhile, peel the cucumber and cut in half lengthways. Scoop out the seeds with a teaspoon and discard. Cut the cucumber into thin, diagonal slices. Slice the spring onions diagonally. Roughly shred the pak choi, keeping the white parts separate from the green.

Using a large metal spoon, drain off all but about 2 tablespoons fat from the roasting pan. Arrange all the vegetables except the green parts of the pak choi around the meat and toss them gently in the pan juices. Return to the oven, uncovered, for 5 minutes.

Mix together the sugar, lime rind and juice and fish sauce. Scatter the pak choi greens and peanuts into the roasting pan and drizzle with half the dressing. Toss the salad ingredients together gently. Transfer the lamb and salad to serving plates and drizzle with the remaining dressing.

For chicken burgers, use minced chicken instead of the lamb. Replace the pak choi with shredded spring greens and peanuts with salted cashews.

LAMB WITH ROSEMARY OIL

Serves **4**
Preparation time **10 minutes**
Cooking time **10–20 minutes**

about 750 g (1 ½ lb) **lamb loin roast**, trimmed of fat
4 **garlic cloves**, cut into slivers
a few small sprigs of **rosemary**
2 **red onions**, quartered
50 ml (2 fl oz) **olive oil**
1 tablespoon chopped **rosemary**
salt and **pepper**

Make small incisions all over the lamb loin and insert the garlic slivers and rosemary sprigs.

Place the meat in a preheated hot griddle pan and cook, turning occasionally, until seared all over for about 10 minutes for rare or about 20 minutes for well done.

Add the onions half-way through the cooking time and char on the outside. Let the lamb rest for 5 minutes, then carve into slices.

Meanwhile, put the oil and rosemary in a mortar and crush with a pestle to release the flavours. Season with salt and pepper.

Spoon the rosemary oil over the lamb slices and serve at once with the fried onions.

Serve with fresh pasta, lightly tossed in oil, and Parmesan shavings.

For lamb chops with garlic & herbs, cut 4 garlic cloves into slivers and insert into incisions in 8 lamb chops. Place each chop on a square of foil and divide 50 g (2 oz) butter, 3 tablespoons lemon juice and 1 tablespoon each dried oregano and dried mint among them. Season and fold the foil to encase the meat. Cook in a preheated oven, 180°C (350°F), Gas Mark 4, for 1 ½–2 hours.

SRI LANKAN-STYLE LAMB CURRY

Serves **4**
Preparation time **10 minutes**
Cooking time **28–33 minutes**

500 g (1 lb) **shoulder** or **leg of lamb**, diced
2 **potatoes**, peeled and cut into large chunks
4 tablespoons **olive oil**
400 g (13 oz) can **chopped tomatoes**
salt and **pepper**

Curry paste
1 **onion**, grated
1 tablespoon finely chopped fresh **root ginger**
1 teaspoon finely chopped **garlic**
½ teaspoon **turmeric**
1 teaspoon **ground coriander**
½ teaspoon **ground cumin**
½ teaspoon **fennel seeds**
½ teaspoon **cumin seeds**
3 **cardamom pods**, lightly crushed
2 **green chillies**, finely chopped
5 cm (2 inch) **cinnamon stick**
2 **lemon grass stalks**, finely sliced

Make the curry paste by mixing together all the ingredients in a large bowl – for a milder curry remove the seeds from the chillies before chopping them finely. Add the lamb and potatoes and combine well.

Heat the oil in a heavy-based pan or casserole and tip in the meat and potatoes. Use a wooden spoon to stir-fry for 6–8 minutes. Pour in the chopped tomatoes and 150 ml (¼ pint) water, bring to the boil and season well then allow to bubble gently for 20–25 minutes until the potatoes are cooked and the lamb is tender.

Serve accompanied with toasted naan bread and a bowl of Greek yogurt, if liked.

For beef & potato curry, use 500 g (1 lb) diced rump steak instead of the lamb. Prepare it in the same way as the lamb, then serve it with a generous sprinkling of chopped coriander.

MEDITERRANEAN ROAST LAMB

Serves **6**
Preparation time **20 minutes, plus resting**
Cooking time **1 hour 20 minutes–1 hour 40 minutes**

1 tablespoon **chopped rosemary**
2 teaspoons **mild paprika**
1.5 kg (3 lb) **leg of lamb**
3 tablespoons **olive oil**
2 tablespoons **sun-dried tomato paste**
2 **garlic cloves**, crushed
2 **red onions**, cut into wedges
1 **fennel bulb**, cut into wedges
2 **red peppers**, deseeded and cut into chunks
2 **orange** or **yellow peppers**, deseeded and cut into chunks
3 **courgettes**, thickly sliced
50 g (2 oz) **pine nuts**
300 ml (½ pint) **red** or **white wine**
salt and **pepper**

Mix the rosemary and paprika with a little salt and rub all over the surface of the lamb. Put in a large roasting pan and roast in a preheated oven, 220°C (425°F), Gas Mark 7, for 15 minutes.

Meanwhile, mix the oil with the tomato paste and garlic. Put all the vegetables in a bowl, add the oil mixture and toss the ingredients together until coated.

Reduce the oven temperature to 180°C (350°F), Gas Mark 4. Tip the vegetables into the pan around the lamb and scatter with the pine nuts and a little salt. Return to the oven for a further 1 hour. (The lamb will still be pink in the centre. If you prefer it well done, cook for an extra 20 minutes, draining the vegetables to a serving plate if they start to become too browned.)

Drain the lamb to a serving plate or board, ready to carve. Cover with foil and leave to rest for 15 minutes. Using a slotted spoon, drain the vegetables to a serving dish and keep warm.

Pour the wine into the roasting pan and bring to the boil on the hob, scraping up the residue from the base. Boil for a few minutes until slightly reduced and serve.

For fruited bulgar wheat to serve as an accompaniment, put 375 g (12 oz) bulgar wheat into a heatproof bowl with ¼ teaspoon each ground cinnamon and nutmeg. Add 400 ml (14 fl oz) boiling water or stock, cover and leave to rest in a warm place for 20 minutes. Stir in 75 g (3 oz) each chopped dates and seedless sultanas and serve.

GREEK LAMB WITH TZATZIKI TOASTS

Serves **4**
Preparation time **15 minutes**
Cooking time **1½ hours**

750 g (1½ lb) **lamb chump chops**
2 teaspoons **dried oregano**
3 **garlic cloves**, crushed
4 tablespoons **olive oil**
1 medium **aubergine**, about 300 g (10 oz), diced
2 **red onions**, sliced
200 ml (7 fl oz) **white** or **red wine**
400 g (13 oz) can **chopped tomatoes**
2 tablespoons **clear honey**
8 **kalamata olives**
8 thin slices **French stick**
200 g (7 oz) **tzatziki**
salt and **pepper**

Cut the lamb into large pieces, discarding any excess fat. Mix the oregano with the garlic and a little seasoning and rub into the lamb.

Heat half the oil in a large saucepan or sauté pan and fry the lamb in batches until browned. Drain to a plate.

Add the aubergine to the pan with the onions and remaining oil and cook very gently, stirring frequently, for about 10 minutes until softened and lightly browned. Return the meat to the pan with the wine, tomatoes, honey, olives and seasoning. Cover with a lid and cook on the lowest setting for about 1¼ hours or until the lamb is very tender. Lightly toast the bread and spoon the tzatziki on top.

Check the stew for seasoning and turn into shallow bowls. Serve with the toasts on the side.

For homemade tzatziki, coarsely grate a 5 cm (2 inch) piece peeled cucumber and pat dry between several sheets of kitchen paper. In a bowl, mix with 200 g (7 oz) natural yogurt, 1 tablespoon finely chopped mint, 1 crushed garlic clove and seasoning.

BAKED TURKEY BURRITO

Serves **4**
Preparation time **12 minutes**
Cooking time **30–33 minutes**

4 tablespoons **vegetable oil**
500 g (1 lb) **turkey breast**, thinly sliced
1 large **onion**, sliced
1 **red pepper**, cored, deseeded and sliced
1 **yellow pepper**, cored, deseeded and sliced
150 g (5 oz) can **red kidney beans**, rinsed and drained
150 g (5 oz) **cooked rice**
juice of 1 **lime**
8 medium-sized **plain flour tortillas**
6 tablespoons medium-hot ready-made **salsa**
2 tablespoons sliced, **preserved jalapeño peppers** (optional)
250 g (8 oz) **Cheddar cheese**, grated
salt and **pepper**

To serve
guacamole
½ **iceberg lettuce**, shredded

Heat 2 tablespoons of the oil in a large frying pan and stir-fry the sliced turkey for 3–4 minutes until it is beginning to colour, then remove it with a slotted spoon. Increase the heat, add the remaining oil and fry the onion and peppers for 5–6 minutes, stirring only occasionally so that they colour quickly without softening too much.

Reduce the heat, return the turkey to the pan and stir in the beans and cooked rice. Season well, squeeze over the lime juice and remove from the heat. Spoon the filling on to the tortillas, roll them up and arrange them in a rectangular ovenproof dish.

Pour the salsa over the tortillas and scatter over the jalapeño peppers (if used) and Cheddar. Cook in a preheated oven, 200°C (400°F), Gas Mark 6, for about 20 minutes, until hot and the cheese has melted. Serve immediately with guacamole and shredded lettuce on the side.

For hot tomato salsa to serve as an accompaniment, chop 500 g (1 lb) tomatoes, 1 hot red chilli, 1 garlic clove and 1 small onion. Add 2 tablespoons tomato purée, 2 tablespoons red wine vinegar and 2 tablespoons sugar. Mix well. Alternatively, blend all the ingredients in a food processor until finely chopped.

BIRYANI

Serves **4**
Preparation time **25 minutes**
Cooking time **40 minutes**

3 **onions**
2 **garlic cloves**, chopped
25 g (1 oz) **fresh root ginger**, roughly chopped
2 teaspoons **ground turmeric**
¼ teaspoon **ground cloves**
½ teaspoon **dried chilli flakes**
¼ teaspoon **ground cinnamon**
2 teaspoons **medium curry paste**
1 tablespoon **lemon juice**
2 teaspoons **caster sugar**
300 g (10 oz) lean **chicken, turkey breast** or **lamb fillet**, cut into small pieces
6 tablespoons **oil**
1 small **cauliflower**, cut into small florets
2 **bay leaves**
300 g (10 oz) **basmati rice**
750 ml (1¼ pints) **chicken** or **vegetable stock**
1 tablespoon **black onion seeds**
salt and **pepper**
2 tablespoons toasted flaked **almonds**, to garnish

Roughly chop 1 onion and put in a food processor with the garlic, ginger, turmeric, cloves, chilli flakes, cinnamon, curry paste, lemon juice, sugar and salt and pepper. Blend to a thick paste and turn into a bowl. Add the meat to the bowl and mix together well.

Thinly slice the second onion. Heat 5 tablespoons of the oil in a large frying pan and fry the onion slices until deep golden and crisp. Drain on kitchen paper.

Chop the third onion. Add the cauliflower to the frying pan and fry gently for 5 minutes. Add the chopped onion and fry gently, stirring, for about 5 minutes until the cauliflower is softened and golden. Drain.

Heat the remaining oil in the pan. Tip in the meat and marinade and fry gently for 5 minutes, stirring.

Stir in the bay leaves, rice and stock and bring to the boil. Reduce the heat and simmer very gently, stirring occasionally, for 10–12 minutes until the rice is tender and the stock absorbed, adding a little water to the pan if the mixture is dry before the rice is cooked. Stir in the black onion seeds. Return the cauliflower to the pan and heat through.

Pile on to serving plates and serve scattered with the crisp onion and toasted almonds. Serve with a cucumber raita (see below), if you like.

For cucumber and mint raita, gently mix together the following in a bowl: 175 g (6 oz) natural yogurt, 75 g (3 oz) cucumber, deseeded and coarsely grated, 2 tablespoons chopped mint, 1 pinch ground cumin and lemon juice and salt to taste. Stand for 30 minutes.

112

THAI CHICKEN POT ROAST

Serves **3–4**
Preparation time **15 minutes**
Cooking time **1 hour 35 minutes**

1.25 kg (2½ lb) **chicken**
1 tablespoon **Thai seven-spice seasoning**
2 tablespoons **oil**
3 **garlic cloves**, crushed
1 **hot red chilli**, deseeded and sliced
40 g (1½ oz) **fresh root ginger**, finely chopped
200 ml (7 fl oz) **chicken stock**
2 **lemon grass stalks**, chopped
1 tablespoon **fish sauce**
1 tablespoon **caster sugar**
2 tablespoons **lime juice**
50 g (2 oz) **fresh coriander**, plus extra to sprinkle
1 bunch **spring onions**
½ teaspoon **ground turmeric**
400 ml (14 fl oz) can **coconut milk**
200 g (7 oz) **baby spinach**
300 g (10 oz) **straight-to-wok rice noodles**

Rub the chicken skin with the seven-spice seasoning. Heat the oil in a flameproof casserole and fry the chicken on all sides until lightly browned. Scatter in the garlic, chilli and ginger and fry for 1 minute.

Add the stock and bring to the boil. Cover and place in a preheated oven, 180°C (350°F), Gas Mark 4, for 45 minutes.

Put the lemon grass, fish sauce, sugar and lime juice in a food processor. Roughly chop the coriander and spring onions and add to the processor with the turmeric. Blend until finely chopped. Add the coconut milk and blend until smooth.

Pour the spicy milk over the chicken and return to the oven for a further 45 minutes until the chicken is very tender.

Remove from the oven and stir the spinach and rice noodles into the sauce around the chicken. Leave to rest for 10 minutes, then serve.

For homemade chicken stock, put a chicken carcass, trimmings such as the giblets and the scrapings left in the pan after a roast in a large saucepan. Add 1 large, unpeeled and halved onion, 1 chopped carrot, 1 celery stick, roughly chopped, several bay leaves and 1 teaspoon of peppercorns. Cover with cold water and heat until simmering. Cook on the lowest setting, uncovered, for 1½ hours. Strain through a sieve and leave to cool.

ROAST CHICKEN WITH SPICE RUB

Serves **4**
Preparation time **20 minutes**
Cooking time **1 hour 20 minutes–1 hour 30 minutes**

1.5 kg (3 lb) **whole chicken**
3 tablespoons **olive oil**
1 teaspoon **fennel seeds**, roughly crushed
1 teaspoon **cumin seeds**, roughly crushed
1 teaspoon crushed **dried red chillies**
1 teaspoon **dried oregano**
½ teaspoon **ground cinnamon**
625 g (1¼ lb) **baby new potatoes**
2 **shallots**, finely chopped
2 **garlic cloves**, finely chopped (optional)
150 g (5 oz) **fine green beans**
juice of **1 lemon**
200 ml (7 fl oz) **chicken stock**
small bunch **fresh coriander** or **flat leaf parsley**, or
   mix of the two, roughly chopped
salt and **pepper**

Put the chicken into a large roasting tin and drizzle with 2 tablespoons of the oil. Mix the crushed seeds, chillies, oregano and cinnamon with some salt and pepper, then sprinkle half over the chicken.

Cover the chicken loosely with foil, then roast in a preheated oven, 190°C (375°F), Gas Mark 5, for 40 minutes. Remove the foil and baste with the pan juices. Add the potatoes to the tin, toss in the juices, then cook uncovered for 40–50 minutes, basting and turning the potatoes once or twice until golden brown. Re-cover the chicken with foil if the spice rub begins to overbrown.

Meanwhile, heat the remaining oil in a small saucepan, add the shallots and garlic, if liked, and fry for 5 minutes until softened. Stir in the remaining spice rub and cook for 1 minute. Cook the green beans in a saucepan of boiling water for 5 minutes, then drain and toss in the shallot mixture with the lemon juice.

When the chicken is cooked, add the green-bean mixture to the potatoes. Mix together, then add the stock and bring to the boil on the hob. Sprinkle with the herbs, carve the chicken and serve.

For roast chicken with herbes de Provence, roughly chop the leaves from 3 stems of rosemary, 3 stems of thyme and 2 lavender flowers. Mix with 1 teaspoon coarse salt and ¼ teaspoon roughly crushed coloured peppercorns. Sprinkle half over the chicken and the rest over the potatoes. Continue as above.

SWEET-GLAZED CHICKEN

Serves **4**
Preparation time **10 minutes**
Cooking time **45 minutes**

2 tablespoons **olive oil**
4 skinned and boned **chicken breasts**, about 150 g
   (5 oz) each
8 **fresh apricots**, halved and stoned
2 **pears**, peeled, quartered and cored
500 g (1 lb) **new potatoes**
1 **onion**, cut into wedges
grated **rind** and juice of 2 **oranges**
a few **thyme sprigs**, chopped
1 tablespoon **wholegrain mustard**
1 tablespoon **clear honey**
4 tablespoons **crème fraîche**
pepper

Heat the oil in a flameproof casserole, season the chicken with salt and pepper and add to the pan. Fry for 2–3 minutes on each side until golden, then add the apricots, pears, potatoes and onion.

Mix together the orange rind and juice, thyme, mustard and honey and pour over the chicken. Cover the dish with foil and bake in a preheated oven, 180°C (350°F), Gas Mark 4, for 40 minutes, removing the foil halfway through the cooking time.

When the chicken is cooked, stir the crème fraîche into the sauce before serving.

For wilted spinach with pine nuts and raisins to serve as an accompaniment, place 65 g (2½ oz) raisins in a small heatproof bowl, cover with boiling water and leave for 5 minutes. Meanwhile, heat 3 tablespoons olive oil in a frying pan and fry 50 g (2 oz) pine nuts until pale golden. Stir in 2 crushed garlic cloves. Drain the raisins and add to the pan with 625 g (1¼ lb) baby spinach. Cook for 1 minute, turning until the spinach has wilted. Add grated lemon rind and salt and pepper to taste.

CLASSIC COQ AU VIN

Serves **4**
Preparation time **25 minutes**
Cooking time **1 hour
20 minutes**

25 g (1 oz) **plain flour**
8 mixed **chicken thigh** and **drumstick joints**
2 tablespoons **olive oil**
375 g (12 oz) **shallots**, halved if large
125 g (4 oz) **smoked streaky bacon**
2 **garlic cloves**, finely chopped
4 tablespoons **brandy** or **cognac**
300 ml (½ pint) **cheap burgundy red wine**
200 ml (7 fl oz) **chicken stock**
2 teaspoons **tomato purée**
fresh or dried **bouquet garni**
salt and **pepper**

For the garlic croûtons
25 g (1 oz) **butter**
1 tablespoon **olive oil**
1 **garlic clove**, finely chopped
½ stick **French bread**, thinly sliced

Mix the flour on a plate with a little seasoning, then use to coat the chicken joints. Heat the oil in a large shallow flameproof casserole (or frying pan and transfer chicken to a casserole dish later), add the chicken and cook over a high heat until golden on all sides. Lift out on to a plate.

Fry the shallots and bacon until golden, then stir in the garlic and return the chicken to the casserole. Pour over the brandy or cognac and when bubbling flame with a long taper. As soon as the flames subside, pour in the red wine and stock, then mix in the tomato purée and bouquet garni. Season, then cover the casserole and transfer to a preheated oven, 180°C (350°F), Gas Mark 4, and cook for 1¼ hours until tender.

When the chicken is cooked, pour the liquid from the casserole into a saucepan and boil for 5 minutes to reduce and thicken slightly, if liked. Return the liquid to the casserole.

Heat the butter and oil in a frying pan for the croûtons, add the garlic and cook for 1 minute, then add the bread slices in a single layer. Fry on both sides until golden. Serve the coq au vin in shallow bowls topped with the croûtons.

For flamed chicken with calvados & apple, fry the chicken as above, adding 4 tablespoons calvados instead of the brandy. Pour in 300 ml (½ pint) cider in place of the red wine and omit the tomato purée. Transfer to a casserole dish and add 1 cored and thickly sliced Granny Smith dessert apple. Continue as above.

HONEY-SPICED CHICKEN BREASTS

Serves **4**
Preparation time **8 minutes**
Cooking time **20–25 minutes**

4 boneless **chicken breasts**, with skins, about 150 g (5 oz) each

Spiced honey
2 tablespoons **mango chutney**
1 tablespoon **clear honey**
2 teaspoons **Worcestershire sauce**
1 teaspoon **garlic powder**
1 teaspoon **piri piri sauce**
2 tablespoons **red wine vinegar**
2 teaspoons **wholegrain mustard**
salt and **pepper**

Slash the chicken breasts 3–4 times with a sharp knife, then place in a baking dish.

Mix together all the ingredients for the spiced honey and spoon over the chicken. Toss until well coated.

Put the chicken in a preheated oven, 220°C (425°F), Gas Mark 7, for 20–25 minutes or until the meat is cooked through and the skin is crispy.

Leave the chicken to rest for a few minutes before serving with chunky potato chips, if liked.

For herbed honey chicken with sweet potato chips, replace the spiced honey with a herbed honey sauce, as follows. Mix 2 tablespoons of honey and 2 tablespoons cider vinegar with 1 tablespoon each of chopped thyme, tarragon and sage. Spoon over the chicken, as above, and serve with chunky sweet potato chips, if liked.

CHICKEN KIEVS

Serves **4**
Preparation time **40 minutes**, plus freezing and chilling
Cooking time **20 minutes**

125 g (4 oz) **butter**, at room temperature
2 tablespoons chopped **chives**
1 tablespoon chopped **parsley**
2 teaspoons chopped **tarragon** (optional)
1 **garlic clove**, finely chopped
2 teaspoons **lemon juice**
4 boneless, skinless **chicken breasts**, each about
   100 g (5 oz)
2 tablespoons **plain flour**
125 g (4 oz) **fresh breadcrumbs**
2 **eggs**
3 tablespoons **sunflower oil**
pepper

Beat the butter with the herbs, garlic, lemon juice and a little pepper. Spoon into a line about 25 cm (10 inches) long on a sheet of clingfilm or foil, then roll up into a neat log shape. Freeze for 15 minutes.

Meanwhile, put one of the chicken breasts between two large sheets of clingfilm and beat with a rolling pin until it forms a rectangle about 3 mm (1/8 inch) thick, being careful not to make any holes in the chicken. Repeat with the other chicken breasts.

Cut the herb butter into 4 pieces and put one on each chicken breast. Fold in the sides, then the top and bottom, to make a tight parcel.

Put the flour on a plate and the breadcrumbs on a second plate, and beat the eggs in a shallow dish. Roll the kievs in the flour, then coat in the egg and roll in the breadcrumbs. Put back on to the empty flour plate and chill for 1 hour (longer if you have time).

Heat the oil in a large frying pan, add the kievs and cook over a medium heat for 5 minutes, turning until evenly browned. Transfer to a baking sheet, then complete cooking in a preheated oven, 200°C (400°F), Gas Mark 6, for 15 minutes or until the chicken is cooked through. Serve with braised red cabbage.

For chicken, garlic & sun-dried tomato kievs, chop 50 g (2 oz) drained sun-dried tomatoes in oil and stir into 150 g (5 oz) garlic and herb cream cheese. Divide between the flattened chicken breasts, then shape, chill and cook as above.

STOVED CHICKEN WITH BLACK PUDDING

Serves **4**

Preparation time **20 minutes**

Cooking time **2 hours
5 minutes**

4 **chicken thigh** and **drumstick joints**

2 tablespoons **plain flour**

1 tablespoon **sunflower oil**

2 **onions**, thinly sliced

50 g (2 oz) **butter**

1 kg (2 lb) **potatoes**, thinly sliced

1 **dessert apple**, cored, diced

125 g (4 oz) **black pudding**, peeled, diced

450 ml (¾ pint) **chicken stock**

salt and **pepper**

Coat the chicken in the flour and seasoning.

Heat the oil in a large frying pan, add the onions and fry for 5 minutes until pale golden. Mix in any remaining flour, then scoop the onions out of the pan and set aside.

Heat half the butter in the frying pan, add the chicken and fry on both sides until golden. Arrange a thin layer of potatoes in the base of an ovenproof casserole dish, top with half the onions, then the chicken pieces. Add the apple and black pudding, then spoon over the remaining onions. Arrange the remaining potatoes in an overlapping layer on the top. Pour the stock over the top, then season the potatoes.

Cover the dish tightly and cook in a preheated oven, 180°C (350°F), Gas Mark 4, for 1½ hours. Remove the lid, dot the potatoes with the remaining butter and cook for 30 minutes more until golden brown. Serve in shallow bowls.

For stoved chicken with bacon & sage, omit the black pudding and apple and add 125 g (4 oz) diced smoked streaky bacon when frying the onions. Add 2–3 stems sage, depending on size, to the casserole dish along with the fried chicken.

ROAST CHICKEN WITH LEMON BASTE

Serves **4–5**
Preparation time **35 minutes**
Cooking time **1 hour 30 minutes**

1.75 kg (3½ lb) **whole chicken**
100 g (3½ oz) **full-fat cream cheese**
3 tablespoons **olive oil**
25 g (1 oz) **preserved lemon**, well drained, deseeded, finely chopped
25 g (1 oz) mixed fresh **basil** and **parsley**, finely chopped
3 **garlic cloves**, finely chopped
675 g (1 lb 6 oz) small **new potatoes**, scrubbed
250 g (8 oz) **chantenay carrots**, scrubbed
125 g (4 oz) **baby corn**
200 g (7 oz) **fine asparagus**, trimmed
200 ml (7 fl oz) **dry white wine**
200 ml (7 fl oz) **chicken stock**
salt and **cayenne pepper**

Remove the trussing elastic from the chicken and set aside. Insert a small sharp knife between the skin and the flesh at the top of one of the breasts, then enlarge to make a small slit. Slide a finger into the slit and gently move the finger to lift the skin away from the chicken breast and make a pocket, being careful not to tear the skin. Do the same from the base of the breast until the skin is completely loosened, then continue over the top of the leg. Repeat on the other chicken breast and leg.

Mix the cream cheese with 1 tablespoon of the oil, and add the lemon, herbs, garlic, salt and cayenne pepper. Lift small amounts of the cheese mix at a time on to a round-bladed knife and insert into the pocket beneath the chicken skin until it has all been added. Ease it into an even layer by pressing the outside of the skin.

Transfer the chicken to a roasting tin and reshape it by twisting the trussing elastic around the legs and parson's nose. Cover with oiled foil and roast in a preheated oven, 190°C (375°F), Gas Mark 5, for 50 minutes. Baste the chicken with the pan juices, then re-cover. Add the potatoes, carrots and remaining oil (but do not cover these with foil) and roast for 30 minutes, turning once. Remove the foil from the chicken, baste and add the corn and asparagus. Roast for 10 minutes until the asparagus is just tender and the chicken cooked when tested.

Transfer to a serving plate, add the wine and stock to the roasting tin and bring to the boil on the hob, scraping up the residue in the tin and seasoning to taste. Strain into a jug and serve with the chicken.

CHICKEN, LEMON & OLIVE STEW

Serves **4**
Preparation time **20 minutes**
Cooking time **1 hour**

1.5 kg (3 lb) **chicken**
about 4 tablespoons **olive oil**
12 **baby onions**, peeled but left whole
2 **garlic cloves**, crushed
1 teaspoon each **ground cumin, ginger** and **turmeric**
½ teaspoon **ground cinnamon**
450 ml (¾ pint) **chicken stock**
125 g (4 oz) **kalamata olives**
1 **preserved lemon**, pulp and skin discarded, chopped
2 tablespoons chopped **fresh coriander**
salt and **pepper**

Joint the chicken into 8 pieces (or ask your butcher to do this for you). Heat the oil in a flameproof casserole and brown the chicken on all sides. Remove the pieces with a slotted spoon and set aside.

Add the onions, garlic and spices and sauté over a low heat for 10 minutes until just golden. Return the chicken to the pan, stir in the stock and bring to the boil. Cover and simmer gently for 30 minutes.

Add the olives, preserved lemon and coriander and cook for a further 15–20 minutes until the chicken is really tender. Taste and adjust the seasoning, if necessary.

For green couscous to serve as an accompaniment, shake together 150 ml (¼ pint) olive oil and 50 ml (2 fl oz) lemon juice until well combined. Season with salt and pepper. Tip 250 g (8 oz) cooked couscous, into a warmed serving dish and stir in 1 bunch chopped spring onions, 50 g (2 oz) chopped rocket and ½ cucumber, halved, deseeded and chopped. Stir in the lemon juice dressing and serve.

ROAST POUSSINS WITH OREGANO

Serves **4**
Preparation time **10 minutes**, plus resting
Cooking time **55 minutes**

50 g (2 oz) **butter**
finely grated rind of 1 **lemon**
2 tablespoons **oregano**, chopped
1 large **garlic clove**, crushed
2 **poussins**, about 500 g (1 lb) each
150 g (5 oz) **peppery mixed salad leaves**
salt and **pepper**

Mash together the butter, lemon rind, oregano, garlic and seasoning. Lift the skin from the poussins and slide the flavoured butter between the flesh and skin, or, if you prefer, smear the butter over the skin.

Put the poussins side by side in a roasting tin and cook in a preheated oven, 220°C (425°F), Gas Mark 7, for about 55 minutes, basting occasionally, until golden and crispy and the juices run clear. Remove from the oven and leave to rest for 5 minutes.

Transfer the poussins to a chopping board and use a long, sharp knife to cut each one carefully in half lengthways. Serve immediately with the salad leaves.

For classic potato gratin, to serve as an accompaniment and which can be cooked in the oven at the same time as the poussins, use 750 g (1½ lb) peeled and thinly sliced potatoes, blanched for a minute or two in boiling, salted water. Drain the potatoes and tip them into a large, oven-proof dish. Scatter over 2 finely chopped garlic cloves and season. Pour over 350 ml (12 fl oz) double cream and sprinkle with a little grated nutmeg. Dot with 50 g (2 oz) butter, then put the dish in the oven for around 45 minutes or until soft when pieced with a knife.

SPICED TURKEY & PEPPER WRAPS

Serves **4**
Preparation time **15 minutes**
Cooking time **40 minutes**

1 teaspoon **mild chilli powder**
½ teaspoon **ground cumin**
1 teaspoon chopped **thyme**
625 g (1¼ lb) lean **turkey breast fillet**, cut into small chunks
4 **mixed peppers**, deseeded and cut into large chunks
2 **red onions**, sliced
4 tablespoons **olive oil**
2 large **courgettes**, cut into chip-sized pieces
1 teaspoon **cornflour**
2 tablespoons **red** or **white wine vinegar**
2 tablespoons **clear honey**
2 tablespoons **sun-dried tomato paste**
few drops **Tabasco sauce**
4 tablespoons **water**
50 g (2 oz) **dried pineapple**, sliced
4 **flour tortillas**, warmed
salt

Mix the chilli powder with the cumin, thyme and a little salt and use to coat the turkey. Scatter in a large roasting pan with the peppers and onions.

Drizzle with the oil and toss the ingredients lightly together. Place the pan in a preheated oven, 220°C (425°F), Gas Mark 7, for 15 minutes. Add the courgettes to the pan, mixing them into the pan juices, and return to the oven for a further 20 minutes until the turkey is cooked through and the vegetables are tender.

Mix together the cornflour and vinegar to make a smooth paste. Add the honey, tomato paste, Tabasco and a little salt and add to the roasting pan with the measurement water. Stir together well. Scatter with the pineapple and return to the oven for a further 2–3 minutes until the glaze has slightly thickened to coat the meat and vegetables. Divide between the warmed tortillas, roll up and serve.

For spiced sweet potato wraps, omit the turkey and use 625 g (1¼ lb) sweet potatoes, thinly sliced and coated in the chilli mixture as above. Replace the onions with 2 bunches spring onions, chopped, and the courgettes with 1 small aubergine, thinly sliced. Add the aubergines with the peppers and spring onions after 15 minutes of the cooking time.

CHICKEN & SEAFOOD PAELLA

Serves **4**
Preparation time **25 minutes**
Cooking time **45 minutes**

150 ml (¼ pint) **olive oil**
150 g (5 oz) **chorizo**, cut into small pieces
4 boned **chicken thighs**, cut into pieces
300 g (10 oz) **squid rings**
8 large **raw prawns**
1 **red pepper**, deseeded and chopped
4 **garlic cloves**, crushed
1 **onion**, chopped
250 g (8 oz) **paella rice**
1 teaspoon **saffron threads**
450 ml (¾ pint) **chicken stock** or **fish stock**
100 g (3½ oz) **peas** or **broad beans**
300 g (10 oz) **fresh mussels**
salt and **pepper**
lemon or **lime wedges**, to garnish

Heat half the oil in a large paella, sauté or frying pan and gently fry the chorizo for 5 minutes, turning it in the oil. Drain to a plate. Add the chicken thighs to the pan and fry for about 5 minutes until cooked through. Drain to the plate. Cook the squid rings and prawns in the oil, turning the prawns once, until pink. Drain to the plate while cooking the rice.

Add the red pepper, garlic and onion to the pan and fry gently for 5 minutes until softened. Stir in the rice, turning it in the oil for 1 minute. Add the saffron and stock to the pan and bring to the boil. Reduce the heat, cover with a lid or foil and cook gently for about 20 minutes until the rice is cooked through.

Scrub the mussels, scraping off any barnacles and pulling away the beards. Discard any damaged shells or any open ones that don't close when tapped gently with a knife.

Return the chorizo, chicken, squid and prawns to the pan with the peas or beans and mix thoroughly. Scatter the mussels over the top, pushing them down slightly into the rice. Cover and cook for a further 5 minutes or until the mussels have opened. Discard any shells that remain closed. Check the seasoning and serve garnished with lemon or lime wedges.

For pork paella, replace the chicken with 400 g (13 oz) lean belly pork, diced and cooked as above. Replace the squid with 8 fresh scallops with roes and the mussels with the same quantity of small clams.

SPICY BASQUE-STYLE CHICKEN

Serves **4**
Preparation time **12 minutes**
Cooking time **45–47 minutes**

1 kg (2 lb) **chicken pieces** (thighs, drumsticks, etc.)
1 heaped tablespoon **seasoned flour**
3 tablespoons **olive oil**
1 **onion**, sliced
1 **red pepper**, cored, deseeded and sliced
1 **green pepper**, cored, deseeded and sliced
2 **garlic cloves**, crushed
1 teaspoon **paprika**
1 teaspoon **hot smoked paprika**
100 g (3½ oz) **prosciutto**, torn into pieces
75 ml (3 fl oz) **Marsala**
150 ml (¼ pint) **white wine**
400 g (13 oz) can **chopped tomatoes**
1 teaspoon **dried thyme**
salt and **pepper**

Dust the chicken in the seasoned flour. Heat the oil in a large, heavy-based casserole over a medium-high heat and fry the chicken until golden brown. Remove and set aside.

Reduce the heat, add the onion and peppers and cook, stirring frequently, for 4–5 minutes until softened and golden. Stir in the garlic, paprikas and prosciutto and fry for a further 1–2 minutes.

Return the chicken to the pan, pour in the Marsala, wine, 100 ml (3½ fl oz) water and the tomatoes. Stir in the thyme and season to taste. Bring to the boil, then reduce the heat to a simmer, cover the pan and leave for 30–35 minutes until the chicken is cooked and the sauce is rich and thick.

Serve the chicken in bowls with lots of sauce.

For pan-fried polenta with olives to serve as an accompaniment, cut 2 x 500 g (1 lb) packets of ready-made polenta into 2.5 cm (1 inch) slices. Fry the slices in olive oil and sprinkle with 2 tablespoons chopped black olives and 1 teaspoon chopped fresh parsley. Add 1 crushed garlic clove and fry quickly. Serve as above.

LEMON CHILLI CHICKEN

Serves **4**
Preparation time **25 minutes**, plus marinating
Cooking time **45 minutes**

1.75 kg (3½ lb) **chicken**, cut into 8 pieces
8 **garlic cloves**
4 juicy **lemons**, squeezed, skins reserved
1 small **red chilli**, deseeded and chopped
2 tablespoons **orange flower honey**
4 tablespoons chopped **parsley**, plus sprigs
    to garnish
salt and **pepper**

Arrange the chicken pieces in a shallow flameproof dish. Peel and crush 2 of the garlic cloves and add them to the lemon juice with the chilli and honey. Stir well, then pour this mixture over the chicken. Tuck the lemon skins around the meat, cover and leave to marinate in the refrigerator for at least 2 hours or overnight, turning once or twice.

Turn the chicken pieces so they are skin side up, scatter over the remaining whole garlic cloves and put the lemon skins, cut sides down, on top.

Cook the chicken in a preheated oven, 200°C (400°F), Gas Mark 6, for 45 minutes or until golden brown and tender. Stir in the parsley, season to taste and serve garnished with parsley sprigs.

For coriander rice & peas to serve as an accompaniment, boil 250 g (8 oz) frozen peas for about 3 minutes, drain them and toss them in 50 g (2 oz) melted butter with 2 chopped spring onions and a handful of chopped fresh coriander. Fork the peas into the rice and serve.

LIME, GINGER & CORIANDER CHICKEN

Serves **4**
Preparation time
    5–10 minutes
Cooking time **50 minutes**

3 **limes**
1 cm (½ inch) cube **fresh root ginger**, peeled and finely
    grated
4 tablespoons finely chopped **coriander**, plus extra
    leaves to serve
2 teaspoons **vegetable oil**
4 **chicken legs**
300 g (10 oz) **Thai jasmine rice**
salt

Finely grate the rind of 2 of the limes and halve these limes. Mix the rind with the ginger and coriander in a non-metallic bowl and stir in 1 teaspoon of the oil to make a rough paste.

Carefully lift the skin from the chicken legs and push under the ginger paste. Pull the skin back into place, then cut 3–4 slashes in the thickest parts of the legs and brush with the remaining oil.

Put the legs in a roasting tin, flesh-side down, with the halved limes and cook in a preheated oven, 220°C (425°F), Gas Mark 7, for 45–50 minutes, basting occasionally. The legs are cooked when the meat comes away from the bone and the juices run clear.

Meanwhile, put the rice in a pan with 400 ml (14 fl oz) cold water, cover with a tight-fitting lid and cook over a medium-low heat for 10 minutes until the water has been absorbed and the rice is almost cooked. Set aside somewhere warm until the chicken has finished cooking.

Spoon the rice into small bowls to mould, then turn it on to serving plates. Add the chicken legs, squeeze over the roasted lime and scatter with coriander leaves. Serve immediately with the remaining lime, cut into wedges.

For Mediterranean chicken, replace the ginger paste with a red pesto made by blending 6 sun-dried tomatoes, 1 tablespoon pine nuts, ½ clove chopped garlic, 1 tablespoon chopped basil, 1 teaspoon grated lemon rind, 1 tablespoon lemon juice, 3 tablespoons olive oil and 1 tablespoon grated Parmesan cheese.

CRISPY DUCK WITH GINGER & ORANGE

Serves **4**
Preparation time **10 minutes**
Cooking time **24–26 minutes**

1 teaspoon **vegetable oil**
4 **duck breasts**, skin slashed
350 g (11½ oz) **spring greens**, shredded
1 tablespoon **balsamic vinegar**
1 piece **conserved ginger in syrup**, chopped
50 ml (2 fl oz) strong **orange and cinnamon tea**
  infusion (or other citrus tea)
½ teaspoon **mixed peppercorns**, crushed
salt

Heat the oil in a frying pan over a medium heat and fry the duck breasts, skin-side down, for about 15 minutes until the skin is really crispy. Drain off the excess fat, turn the duck over and fry for a further 5 minutes. Remove and keep warm.

Put the spring greens in a steamer over a pan of boiling water and steam for 2–3 minutes or until wilted.

Add the remaining ingredients to the frying pan and season with salt to taste, then stir to mix and allow to bubble for 2–3 minutes.

Serve the duck breasts with the sauce poured over and with the steamed spring greens.

For duck with sherry-lime marmalade, omit the vinegar, ginger and tea and instead make a sauce with 4 tablespoons dry sherry and 4 tablespoons lime marmalade. Sprinkle a handful of chopped mint on to the spring greens before serving.

CHICKEN WITH SPRING VEGETABLES

Serves **4**
Preparation time **10 minutes**, plus resting
Cooking time **about 1¼ hours**

1.5 kg (3 lb) **chicken**
about 1.5 litres (2½ pints) hot **chicken stock**
2 **shallots**, halved
2 **garlic cloves**
2 sprigs of **parsley**
2 sprigs of **marjoram**
2 sprigs of **lemon thyme**
2 **carrots**, halved
1 **leek**, trimmed and sliced
200 g (7 oz) **tenderstem broccoli**
250 g (8 oz) **asparagus**, trimmed
½ **Savoy cabbage**, shredded

Put the chicken in a large saucepan and pour over enough stock just to cover the chicken. Push the shallots, garlic, herbs, carrots and leek into the pan and place over a medium-high heat. Bring to the boil, then reduce the heat and simmer gently for 1 hour or until the chicken is falling away from the bones.

Add the remaining vegetables to the pan and simmer for a further 6–8 minutes or until the vegetables are cooked.

Turn off the heat and leave to rest for 5–10 minutes before serving the chicken and vegetables in deep bowls with spoonfuls of the broth. Remove the skin, if preferred, and serve with plenty of crusty bread.

For Chinese chicken soup, use the same amount of stock and but omit all the vegetables and herbs. Instead, use a sliced 8 cm (3 inch) length of fresh root ginger, 2 garlic cloves, sliced, 1 teaspoon Chinese five spice powder, 4–5 whole star anise and 100 ml (3½ fl oz) dark soy sauce. Add baby corn and mangetout instead of the spring vegetables and cook as above.

GARLIC BUTTER-STUFFED CHICKEN

Serves **4**

Preparation time **25 minutes**

Cooking time **40 minutes**

50 g (2 oz) coarse **breadcrumbs**

3 tablespoons **olive oil**

4 large skinned **chicken breast fillets**

25 g (1 oz) **butter**, softened

50 g (2 oz) **cream cheese**

2 **garlic cloves**, crushed

finely grated rind of 1 **lemon**

4 tablespoons chopped **parsley**

150 g (5 oz) **French beans**, diagonally sliced into
    3.5 cm (1½ inch) lengths

400 g (13 oz) can **flageolet beans**, drained

200 ml (7 fl oz) **white wine**

salt and **pepper**

Put the breadcrumbs in a flameproof casserole with 1 tablespoon of the oil and heat gently until the breadcrumbs begin to brown and crisp. Drain to a plate.

Using a small knife, make a horizontal cut in each chicken breast to create a pocket for stuffing. Beat the butter with the cream cheese, garlic, lemon rind, 1 tablespoon of the parsley and salt and pepper. Pack the stuffing into the chicken breasts and seal the openings with wooden cocktail sticks.

Heat the remaining oil in the casserole and fry the chicken on both sides until lightly browned. Drain. Scatter the French beans and flageolet beans into the casserole and add the wine and a little seasoning. Arrange the chicken on top.

Cover and place in a preheated oven, 190°C (375°F), Gas Mark 5, for 20 minutes. Remove the lid and sprinkle the chicken pieces with the breadcrumbs. Return to the oven, uncovered, for a further 10 minutes until the chicken is cooked through. Transfer the chicken to plates. Stir the remaining parsley into the beans, then spoon around the chicken.

For roast potatoes with garlic to serve as an accompaniment, heat 50 ml (2 fl oz) olive oil in a roasting pan in a preheated oven, 230°C (450°F), Gas Mark 8. Quarter 750 g (1½ lb) potatoes, then add with 2 tablespoons chopped rosemary to the hot oil, tossing to coat. Roast for 20 minutes. Remove, turn the potatoes, scatter with 4 sliced garlic cloves and return to the oven for a further 10–20 minutes.

124

ALL-IN-ONE CHICKEN PIE

Serves **4**
Preparation time **20 minutes**
Cooking time **45–50 minutes**

250 g (8 oz) **broccoli florets**
1 tablespoon **olive oil**
375 g (12 oz) boneless, skinless **chicken breasts**,
    cubed
6 **streaky bacon** rashers, chopped
2 small **carrots**, chopped
25 g (1 oz) **butter**
25 g (1 oz) **plain flour**
300 ml (½ pint) **milk**
1 tablespoon **white wine vinegar**
1 teaspoon **Dijon mustard**
200 ml (7 fl oz) **crème fraîche**
2 tablespoons chopped **tarragon** or **parsley**
500 g (1 lb) packet **shortcrust pastry**
beaten **egg**, for glazing

Cook the broccoli for 5 minutes until tender. Drain and refresh with cold water, then set aside. Heat the oil in a nonstick frying pan and cook the chicken and bacon over a moderate heat for 7–8 minutes. Add the carrots and cook for a further 3–4 minutes until golden all over. Remove from the heat.

Heat the butter in a medium saucepan and add the flour. Cook over a gentle heat for a few seconds, then remove from the heat and gradually add the milk until well mixed. Add the vinegar and mustard and mix well. Return to the heat and stir continuously until boiled and thickened. Add the crème fraîche and herbs. Add the chicken and vegetables and stir well to coat, then transfer to a round pie dish.

Roll out the pastry on a floured surface to just larger than the dish. Moisten the rim of the dish with a little water, then place the pastry over the top, trim the edges and decorate with any remaining pastry trimmings if liked. Glaze lightly with the beaten egg. Bake in a preheated oven, 180°C (350°F), Gas Mark 4, for 25–30 minutes until crisp and golden.

For creamy chunky gammon pie, replace the chicken and bacon with a 500 g (1 lb) gammon joint. Half fill a large pan with water, then add 3 peppercorns and a bay leaf. Lower the gammon into the pan, then bring to the boil and cook for 1½ hours. Drain and set aside to cool. Cook the carrots with the broccoli, then cut the gammon into chunks and add the vegetables and gammon to the sauce. Continue as above.

GRIDDLED CHICKEN FAJITAS

Serves **4**
Preparation time **20 minutes**, plus marinating
Cooking time **16–20 minutes**

4 x 125 g (4 oz) boneless, skinless **chicken breasts**
4 large **soft flour tortillas**
150 ml (¼ pint) **soured cream**
4 **tomatoes**, skinned and sliced
1 **avocado**, sliced
4 **spring onions**, sliced
½ **red onion**, finely chopped
tortilla chips (optional)
salt and **pepper**

For the marinade
2 tablespoons **soy sauce**
3 cm (1¼ inch) piece **root ginger**, finely chopped
2 **garlic cloves**, finely chopped
2 tablespoons **olive oil**
1 bunch **fresh coriander**, chopped
1 **chilli**, chopped
2 tablespoons **lime juice**

Combine all the ingredients for the marinade in a shallow dish. Add the chicken breasts and leave to marinate at room temperature for 2 hours, or in the refrigerator for 24 hours.

Heat a griddle pan (or ordinary frying pan). Place the marinated chicken breasts in the pan to cook for 8–10 minutes on each side. When cooked, remove the chicken from the pan and slice it into long strips.

Place the tortillas under a preheated grill and cook for 30 seconds on each side. Spread over one side of each tortilla a spoonful of soured cream, a little tomato, avocado and a sprinkling of spring onions and red onion.

Add the pieces of griddled chicken and season. Roll up each tortilla tightly and cut in half across each one. Serve with tortilla chips, if liked.

For guacamole, to accompany the fajitas, halve and stone 2 ripe avocados. Scoop out the flesh then mash with a fork. Mix with the juice of 1 lime, 3 tablespoons chopped fresh coriander, 1 skinned and finely diced tomato and if liked, 1 finely chopped jalapeno chilli. Spoon on to the tortillas instead of soured cream.

126

CHICKEN THATCH

Serves **4**
Preparation time **25 minutes**
Cooking time **35 minutes**

1 tablespoon **sunflower oil**
4 boneless, skinless **chicken thighs**, diced
1 **onion**, chopped
2 tablespoons **plain flour**
450 ml (¾ pint) **chicken stock**
2 teaspoons **Dijon mustard**
1 large **carrot**, diced
750 g (1½ lb) **potatoes**, quartered
150 g (5 oz) **courgettes**, diced
75 g (3 oz) **sugar snap peas**, halved
75 g (3 oz) **frozen peas**
40 g (1½ oz) **butter**
3 tablespoons **milk**
75 g (3 oz) **mature Cheddar cheese**, grated
salt and **pepper**

Heat the oil in a saucepan, add the chicken and onion and fry for 5 minutes, stirring until browned. Stir in the flour, then gradually mix in the stock. Bring to the boil, then add the mustard, carrot and a little seasoning. Cover and simmer for 30 minutes.

Meanwhile, cook the potatoes in a saucepan of boiling water until tender. Add the courgettes, sugar snap peas and frozen peas to a smaller saucepan of boiling water and cook for 3 minutes. Drain and set aside.

Drain the potatoes and mash with two-thirds of the butter and all the milk. Season and stir in two-thirds of the cheese.

Spoon the chicken mixture into a 1.3 litre (2¼ pint) pie dish or 4 individual dishes, add the just-cooked green vegetables, then spoon the mash on top. Dot with the remaining butter and sprinkle with the remaining cheese. Grill until golden, then serve immediately. (For an oven-baked chicken thatch, chill the dish once the grated cheese has been sprinkled on top, then bake when needed, in a preheated oven, 190°C (375°F), Gas Mark 5, for 35 minutes until piping hot or 25 minutes for smaller dishes.)

For chicken & bacon thatch, add 4 chopped rashers of smoked back bacon when frying the chicken and onion. Omit the courgettes, sugar snaps and peas and cook 125 g (4 oz) frozen sweetcorn instead. Drain and add to the chicken. Finish as above.

CHICKEN WITH PRESERVED LEMONS

Serves **4–5**
Preparation time **20 minutes**
Cooking time **1 hour
45 minutes**

2 tablespoons **olive oil**
1 **onion**, finely chopped
3 **garlic cloves**
1 teaspoon **ground ginger**
1½ teaspoons **ground cinnamon**
large pinch **saffron threads**, toasted, crushed
1.75 kg (3½ lb) **whole chicken**
750 ml (1¼ pints) **chicken stock** or water
150 g (5 oz) large **black olives**, rinsed, soaked
  (optional)
1 **preserved lemon**, chopped
large bunch **coriander**, finely chopped
large bunch **parsley**, finely chopped
salt and **pepper**

Heat the oil in a frying pan, add the onion and fry gently, stirring frequently until softened and golden.

Meanwhile, using a pestle and mortar, crush the garlic with a pinch of salt, then work in the ginger, cinnamon, saffron and a little pepper. Stir into the onions, cook until fragrant, then remove from the pan and spread over the chicken.

Put the chicken into a heavy saucepan or flameproof casserole that it just fits, heat gently and brown the chicken for about 2–3 minutes, turning often. Add the stock or water, and bring to just simmering point. Cover and simmer gently for about 1¼ hours, turning the chicken over 2–3 times.

Add the olives, preserved lemon, coriander and parsley to the pan. Cover and cook for about 15 minutes until the chicken is very tender. Taste the sauce – if the flavour needs to be more concentrated, transfer the chicken to a warmed serving dish, cover and keep warm, and boil the cooking juices to a rich sauce. Tilt the pan and skim off any surplus fat, then pour over the chicken. Serve with couscous, if liked.

For chicken & tomato tagine, reduce the stock or water to 450 ml (¾ pint) and add a 400 ml (13 oz) can of chopped tomatoes. Cover and simmer as above. Omit the olives and lemon instead adding 75 g (3 oz) thickly sliced okra and the coriander and parsley as above for the last 5 minutes of cooking. Serve with rice or warmed Arab flat breads.

CHICKEN & MUSHROOM LASAGNE

Serves **4–6**
Preparation time **45 minutes**
Cooking time **1 hour 25 minutes**

8 **chicken thighs**
150 ml (¼ pint) **dry white wine**
300 ml (½ pint) **chicken stock**
few stems **thyme**
2 tablespoons **olive oil**
2 **onions**, thinly sliced
2 **garlic cloves**, finely chopped
100 g (3½ oz) **exotic mushrooms**
125 g (4 oz) **shiitake mushrooms**, sliced
50 g (2 oz) **butter**
50 g (2 oz) **plain flour**
200 ml (7 fl oz) **double cream**
250 g (8 oz) pack of 6 **fresh lasagne sheets**
40 g (1½ oz) **Parmesan cheese**, freshly grated
salt and **pepper**

Pack the chicken thighs into the base of a saucepan, add the wine, stock, thyme and a little seasoning. Bring to the boil, then cover and simmer for 45 minutes until tender.

Meanwhile, heat the oil in a frying pan, add the onions and fry for 5 minutes until just turning golden. Mix in the garlic and cook for 2–3 minutes, stir in the mushrooms and fry for 2–3 minutes until golden.

Lift the chicken out of the pan, drain and set aside. Pour the stock into a measuring jug. Make up to 600 ml (1 pint) with water if needed. Wash and dry the pan, then melt the butter in it. Stir in the flour, then gradually whisk in the stock and bring to the boil, stirring until thickened and smooth. Stir in the cream and adjust the seasoning, if needed.

Soak the lasagne sheets in boiling water for 5 minutes. Cut the skin and bones away from the chicken and dice the meat. Drain the lasagne sheets.

Pour a thin layer of sauce into the base of a 20 x 28 x 5 cm (8 x 11 x 2 inch) ovenproof dish or roasting tin, then cover with 2 sheets of the lasagne. Spoon over half the mushroom mixture and half the chicken, then cover with a thin layer of sauce. Repeat the layers, then cover with the remaining lasagne and sauce. Sprinkle with the Parmesan and set aside until required.

Cook in a preheated oven, 190°C (375°F), Gas Mark 5, for 40 minutes until piping hot and the top is golden. Serve with salad and garlic bread.

TURKEY & WILD MUSHROOM PASTIES

Serves **4**
Preparation time **8 minutes**, plus soaking
Cooking time **29–32 minutes**

25 g (1 oz) **dried wild mushrooms**
4 tablespoons **olive oil**
450 g (14½ oz) **turkey breast**, sliced
100 g (3½ oz) **prosciutto**, torn into pieces
200 g (7 oz) **field** or **portabello mushrooms**, trimmed
  and sliced
100 ml (3½ fl oz) **red wine**
1 teaspoon chopped **thyme**
250 g (8 oz) **mascarpone cheese**
500 g (1 lb) **puff pastry** (thawed if frozen)
1 **egg**, beaten
salt and **pepper**
watercress, to garnish

Soak the mushrooms in 4 tablespoons boiling water for 5–10 minutes. Heat 2 tablespoons of the oil in a frying pan and fry the turkey for 2–3 minutes until golden. Add the prosciutto and cook for 2 minutes before adding the fresh and dried mushrooms. Fry for 3–4 minutes until the mushrooms are soft and golden.

Pour the wine into the pan, then add the thyme. Allow the liquid to bubble for 2–3 minutes until evaporated. Remove from the heat, stir in the mascarpone and season to taste.

Roll out the pastry into a rectangular shape until it forms a thin layer and cut into four. Spoon one-quarter of the mixture on to the centre of each quarter of pastry. Brush a little beaten egg around the edges, fold over the pastry and press firmly to seal.

Brush the remaining egg over the closed pasties, score the tops with a knife, if liked, and cook in a preheated oven, 200°C (400°F), Gas Mark 6, for 20 minutes until golden and crispy.

For turkey & mushroom pie, increase the wine to 300 ml (½ pint) and simmer for 5 minutes. Finish the filling as above. Replace the puff pastry with shortcrust. Roll it out into a thick layer to cover a 22 cm (9 inch) pie dish with an overlap of 5 cm (2 inches). Cut a strip of pastry 1 cm (½ inch) wide and put it round the rim of the dish. Add the filling and cover with the remaining pastry. Glaze with egg and bake in a preheated oven, 200°C (400°F), Gas Mark 6, for 20 minutes then lower the heat to 180°C (350°F), Gas Mark 4 for a further 10–15 minutes.

CHICKEN WITH SPINACH CHERMOULA

Serves **4**
Preparation time **12 minutes**
Cooking time **25 minutes**

4 boneless, skinless **chicken breasts**, about 175 g
  (6 oz) each, cut into large pieces
2 tablespoons **olive oil**
1 large **red onion**, sliced
400 g (13 oz) can **chickpeas**, rinsed and drained
8 ready-to-eat **dried apricots**, sliced
pinch of **saffron**
200 g (7 oz) **spinach leaves**, stalks removed
½ small **preserved lemon**, finely diced (optional)
small bunch of **coriander**, roughly chopped
small bunch of **flat leaf parsley**, roughly chopped

Chermoula
3 tablespoons ready-made **chermoula mix**
1 teaspoon **harissa paste**
juice of 1 **lemon**
100 ml (3½ fl oz) **olive oil**

Make the chermoula by putting all the ingredients in a screw-top jar and shaking to combine. Mix half the paste with the chicken and set aside.

Heat the oil in a large frying pan over a medium heat and fry the onion for about 8 minutes until soft and golden. Increase the heat a little, tip in the coated chicken and cook for about 12 minutes, stirring frequently. Stir in the chickpeas, apricots, saffron and the remaining chermoula paste and cook for a further 3–4 minutes. The chicken and spices should be cooked through.

Stir in the spinach and cook until just wilted, then add the preserved lemon (if used) and herbs. Serve immediately on warm pitta or flat breads.

For homemade chermoula, instead of the ready-made chermoula mix, stir together 2 teaspoons ground cumin, 2 teaspoons ground coriander, 1 teaspoon turmeric, 1 teaspoon salt and 1 teaspoon ground black pepper.

SOUTHERN FRIED CHICKEN

Serves 4
Preparation time **25 minutes**
Cooking time **35–40 minutes**

500 g (1 lb) **sweet potatoes**, peeled
500 g (1 lb) **baking potatoes**, scrubbed
6 tablespoons **sunflower oil**
1½ teaspoons **smoked paprika**
1½ teaspoons **dried oregano**
1 teaspoon **dried mustard powder**
1 teaspoon **dried crushed red chillies**
4 tablespoons **plain flour**
2 **eggs**
2 tablespoons **water**
125 g (4 oz) **fresh breadcrumbs**
4 **chicken thigh** and **drumstick joints**
salt and **pepper**

Thickly slice the sweet and baking potatoes, then cut into thick wedges. Mix 3 tablespoons of the oil with 1 teaspoon paprika, 1 teaspoon oregano, ½ teaspoon mustard, ½ teaspoon chilli seeds and some salt in a large plastic bag or bowl. Add the potatoes and toss in the oil mixture.

Mix the remaining paprika, oregano, mustard, chilli seeds and seasoning with the flour on a large plate. Beat the eggs and measured water in a shallow dish and put the breadcrumbs on a second large plate.

Coat the chicken pieces in the flour mixture, then the beaten egg, then the breadcrumbs, until completely covered.

Heat a large roasting tin in the oven, 200°C (400°F), Gas Mark 6, for 5 minutes. Meanwhile, heat the remaining oil in a large frying pan, add the chicken and fry until pale golden. Transfer the chicken to the hot roasting tin, add the potatoes and roast for 30–35 minutes until the chicken is cooked through and the potatoes crisp and golden. Transfer to serving plates and serve with mayonnaise and salad.

For cheesy fried chicken escalopes, make up the vegetables as above, then mix the remaining paprika, chilli seeds and a little salt and pepper with the flour. Coat 4 skinless, boneless chicken breasts, each cut into thin flat slices, in the flour mixture, then in the beaten egg, then in 100 g (3½ oz) fresh breadcrumbs mixed with 2 tablespoons grated Parmesan cheese. Fry in the oil for 10–12 minutes until golden and cooked through.

CHEESE & BACON PASTRIES

Serves 6
Preparation time **15 minutes**
Cooking time **20–25 minutes**

500 g (1 lb oz) packet **puff pastry**
flour, for dusting
2 teaspoon **Dijon mustard** (optional)
50 g (2 oz) **Gruyère cheese**, thinly sliced
50 g (2 oz) **Cheddar cheese**, thinly sliced
3 tablespoons chopped **parsley**
6 **back bacon** rashers, thinly sliced
beaten **egg**

Roll out the pastry on a lightly floured surface to a rectangle measuring 30 x 45 cm (12 x 18 inches). Cut the pastry into 6 x 15 cm (6 inch) squares.

Spread the pastry all over with a thin layer of mustard. Arrange the Gruyère and Cheddar slices on each of the pastry squares in a diagonal line. Sprinkle with the parsley, then ruffle the bacon across the top. Lightly brush the pastry edges with a little warm water, then fold each of the opposite corners up and over the filling to meet, then press to seal with a fork. Place on a baking sheet.

Lightly brush the pastries with beaten egg and bake in a preheated oven, 200°C (400°F), Gas Mark 6, for 20–25 minutes until golden. Serve warm.

For haloumi & tomato pastries, replace the bacon and cheeses with 175 g (6 oz) haloumi cheese, thinly sliced, and 125 g (4 oz) halved cherry tomatoes. Arrange on top of the mustard-spread pastry and sprinkle with the parsley. Bake as above until golden.

SAUSAGE & SWEET POTATO HASH

Serves **4**
Preparation time **15 minutes**
Cooking time **45 minutes**

3 tablespoons **olive oil**
8 **pork sausages**
3 large **red onions**, thinly sliced
1 teaspoon **caster sugar**
500 g (1 lb) **sweet potatoes**, scrubbed and cut
    into small chunks
8 **sage leaves**
2 tablespoons **balsamic vinegar**
salt and **pepper**

Heat the oil in a large frying pan or flameproof casserole and fry the sausages turning frequently, for about 10 minutes, until browned. Drain to a plate.

Add the onions and sugar to the pan and cook gently, stirring frequently, until lightly browned. Return the sausages to the pan with the sweet potatoes, sage leaves and a little seasoning.

Cover the pan with a lid or foil and cook over a very gentle heat for about 25 minutes until the potatoes are tender.

Drizzle with the vinegar and check the seasoning before serving.

For wilted watercress with garlic and nutmeg to serve as an accompaniment, heat 4 tablespoons olive oil in a large saucepan, add 1 crushed garlic clove and cook for 30–60 seconds until soft. Add 750 g (1¼ lb) watercress and stir-fry over a high heat for 1–2 minutes until wilted. Season with salt and pepper and add grated nutmeg to taste.

POT-ROASTED PORK WITH PRUNES

Serves **5–6**
Preparation time **20 minutes, plus resting**
Cooking time **2 hours**

1 kg (2 lb) skinned, boned and rolled **loin of pork**
25 g (1 oz) **butter**
1 tablespoon **olive oil**
3 tablespoons **mustard seeds**
2 **onions**, sliced
4 **garlic cloves**, crushed
2 **celery sticks**, sliced
1 tablespoon **plain flour**
1 tablespoon chopped **thyme**
300 ml (½ pint) **white wine**
150 g (5 oz) **pitted prunes**, halved
500 g (1 lb) small **new potatoes**, e.g. **Jersey Royals**
2 tablespoons chopped **mint**
salt and **pepper**

Rub the pork with salt and pepper. Melt the butter with the oil in a large, flameproof casserole and sear the pork on all sides. Drain to a plate.

Add the mustard seeds and onions and fry for about 5 minutes until beginning to colour. Stir in the garlic and celery and cook for 2 minutes. Add the flour and cook, stirring for 1 minute.

Stir in the thyme, wine and seasoning and let the mixture bubble up. Return the pork to the pan and cover with a lid. Transfer to a preheated oven, 160°C (325°F), Gas Mark 3, for 45 minutes.

Stir the prunes, potatoes and mint into the cooking juices around the pork and return to the oven for a further 1 hour until the potatoes are very tender. Leave to rest for 15 minutes before serving.

For pot-roasted pork with shallots and peaches, use 4 shallots instead of the onions in the second step. Omit the prunes and add 2 sliced fresh peaches and 1 tablespoon clear honey for the final 20 minutes of cooking time.

TARTIFLETTE-STYLE PIZZA

Serves **4**
Preparation time **20 minutes**, plus resting
Cooking time **23–25 minutes**

290 g (9½ oz) **pizza base mix**
25 g (1 oz) **butter**
1 tablespoon **olive oil**
200 g (7 oz) **smoked bacon lardons** or **smoky bacon bits**
2 **onions**, sliced
1 **garlic clove**, chopped
200 ml (7 fl oz) **crème fraîche**
250 g (8 oz) cooked **potatoes**, thinly sliced
250 g (8 oz) **Reblochon cheese**, sliced

Make the pizza base according to the instructions on the packet. Form the dough into 4 balls and roll them out into ovals. Cover lightly with oiled clingfilm and leave in a warm place.

Melt the butter and olive oil in a large frying pan and fry the bacon for 3–4 minutes or until cooked. Add the onions and garlic and fry gently for 5–6 minutes or until soft and golden.

Spread 1 tablespoon of the crème fraîche over each pizza base. Top with slices of potato, some of the bacon and onion mixture and 2–3 slices of Reblochon. Cook in a preheated oven, 220°C (425°F), Gas Mark 7, for 15 minutes until bubbling and golden.

Serve immediately with an extra dollop of the remaining crème fraîche on top, if liked.

For artichoke heart & dolcelatte pizza, replace the potatoes with 2 x 475 g (15 oz) cans of artichoke hearts, drained and halved. Top with sliced dolcelatte.

POTATO & BACON CAKES

Serves **4**
Preparation time **15 minutes**, plus chilling
Cooking time **about 45 minutes**

1 kg (2 lb) **potatoes**, cut into chunks
vegetable oil, for shallow-frying
6 **spring onions**, sliced
200 g (7 oz) **back bacon**, chopped
2 tablespoons chopped **flat leaf parsley**
plain flour, for coating
25 g (1 oz) **butter**
salt and **pepper**

For the tomato sauce
200 ml (7 fl oz) **crème fraîche**
2 tablespoons chopped **basil**
2 tablespoons chopped **tomatoes**

Cook the potatoes in a large saucepan of salted boiling water for 15–20 minutes until tender. Drain well, return to the pan and mash.

Heat a little oil in a frying pan, add the spring onions and cook for 2–3 minutes, then add the bacon and cook until browned. Add to the mash with the parsley. Season well with salt and pepper. Form the potato mixture into 8 cakes, then cover and chill in the refrigerator until firm.

Lightly coat the cakes in flour. Melt the butter in a nonstick frying pan, add the cakes, in batches, and cook over a medium heat for 4–5 minutes on each side until browned and heated through.

Meanwhile, to make the sauce, put the crème fraîche in a bowl and mix in the basil and tomatoes. Season well with salt and pepper.

Serve the cakes hot with the sauce.

For salmon fishcakes with soured cream & mushroom sauce, use a 200 g (7 oz) can red salmon instead of the bacon. Drain and flake the salmon into the mashed potato mixture. Form into cakes and cook as above. Meanwhile, melt 25 g (1 oz) butter in a saucepan, add 100 g (3½ oz) sliced button mushrooms and cook for 1 minute. Stir in 200 ml (7 fl oz) soured cream and ¼ teaspoon paprika and season to taste with salt and pepper. Heat through gently and serve with the fishcakes.

ONE POT ROAST PORK

Serves **4**
Preparation time **25 minutes**
Cooking time 1½ **hours**

4 boneless **pork steaks**, e.g. **leg** or **loin**, each about
   2.5 cm (1 inch) thick
50 g (2 oz) **toasted hazelnuts**
1 **garlic clove**, crushed
3 **spring onions**, finely chopped
4 plump, ready-to-eat **dried apricots**, finely chopped
4 tablespoons **oil**
625 g (1¼ lb) **baking potatoes**, cut into small chunks
1 **red onion**, cut into wedges
1 **dessert apple**, peeled, cored and cut into wedges
2 **red chicory hearts**, cut into wedges
2 teaspoons **plain flour**
300 ml (½ pint) **medium cider**
salt and **pepper**

Using a sharp knife, make deep horizontal cuts in each of the pork steaks to make cavities for the stuffing.

Whizz the hazelnuts in the food processor. Add the garlic, spring onions, apricots and a little seasoning and blend until combined. Pack the mixture into the pork steaks and flatten with the palms of your hands. Season the steaks with salt and pepper.

Heat 1 tablespoon of the oil in a large, sturdy roasting pan and brown the pork on both sides. Drain.

Add the potatoes and onion to the roasting pan with the remaining oil and toss together until coated. Roast in a preheated oven, 200°C (400°F), Gas Mark 6, for 40 minutes until pale golden, turning once. Add the pork to the pan and roast for 15 minutes. Add the apple and chicory wedges, brushing them with a little oil from the pan, and roast for a further 20 minutes or until the pork is cooked through. Drain the meat and vegetables to warmed serving plates.

Stir the flour into the pan juices, scraping up any residue around the edges of the pan. Gradually blend in the cider and cook, stirring, until thickened and bubbling. Season to taste and serve with the roast.

For roast pork with spicy prunes, mix 25 g (1 oz) breadcrumbs with 4 chopped plump prunes, 1 thin-cut streaky bacon rasher, finely chopped, 1 crushed garlic clove, 1 teaspoon grated fresh root ginger and seasoning. Use to stuff the pork and continue as above.

134

CHORIZO & SMOKED PAPRIKA PENNE

Serves **4**
Preparation time **15 minutes**
Cooking time **26 minutes**

1 tablespoon **olive oil**
200 g (7 oz) **chorizo sausage**, diced
1 **onion**, chopped
2 **garlic cloves**, chopped
1 teaspoon **hot smoked paprika**
1 tablespoon **capers**
1 teaspoon **dried oregano**
1 teaspoon finely grated **lemon rind**
pinch of **caster sugar**
150 g (5 oz) **roasted red pepper**, sliced
800 g (1 lb 10 oz) can **chopped tomatoes**
350 g (11½ oz) dried **penne**
salt and **pepper**

To serve
chilli oil (optional)
4 tablespoons grated **Parmesan cheese**

Heat the oil in a large pan and fry the chorizo for 2 minutes until golden. Add the onion and garlic and cook for about 5 minutes or until soft and golden.

Stir in the paprika and cook for a further minute, then add the capers, oregano, lemon rind, sugar, red pepper and tomatoes. Bring to the boil, then reduce the heat and simmer gently for 15 minutes.

Meanwhile, cook the penne in lightly salted boiling water according to the instructions on the packet.

Drain the pasta and stir it into the chorizo sauce. Serve immediately with a drizzle of chilli oil (if used) and the freshly grated Parmesan.

For garlic, oregano & Parmesan toasts, to serve as an accompaniment, split a ciabatta loaf in half lengthways and then cut each length in half. Mix 1 crushed garlic clove with 1 teaspoon dried oregano and 2 tablespoons olive oil. Drizzle over the ciabatta and scatter each piece with 1 teaspoon finely grated Parmesan. Place under a hot grill for 3–4 minutes until toasted and golden.

PORK CHOPS WITH LEMON & THYME

Serves **4**
Preparation time **20 minutes**
Cooking time **28–30 minutes**

finely grated rind of 1 **lemon**
1 tablespoon chopped **thyme**
2 tablespoons **olive oil**
2 **garlic cloves**, crushed
4 **pork chops**, about 200 g (7 oz) each
1 kg (2 lb) **floury potatoes**, peeled and quartered
200 ml (7 fl oz) **double cream**
50 g (2 oz) **butter**
salt and **pepper**
thyme, leaves or flowers, to garnish

Mix together the lemon rind, thyme, oil, garlic and plenty of pepper and rub the mixture over the pork chops. Set aside.

Meanwhile, cook the potatoes in lightly salted boiling water for about 20 minutes or until soft. Drain, return to the pan and mash. Add the cream, butter and seasoning and use a electric hand-held whisk to beat until smooth.

Heat a dry frying pan over a medium-high heat and cook the pork chops for 4–5 minutes on each side, depending on their thickness, until cooked and golden.

Remove the pork from the heat and leave to rest for 1–2 minutes before serving garnished with a few thyme leaves or flowers and accompanied by the fluffy mash.

For spinach & Parmesan mash instead of plain mash, cook, drain and chop 500 g (1 lb) spinach. Mash the potatoes with butter and milk (omit the cream) and stir in the spinach and 50 g (2 oz) freshly grated Parmesan.

MEATY BOSTON BEANS

Serves **4–6**
Preparation time **15 minutes, plus overnight soaking**
Cooking time **2 hours**

300 g (10 oz) **haricot beans**
15 g (½ oz) **butter**
200 g (7 oz) **smoked bacon lardons**
375 g (12 oz) **lean diced pork**
1 **onion**, chopped
1 tablespoon chopped **thyme** or **rosemary**
400 g (13 oz) can **chopped tomatoes**
3 tablespoons **black treacle**
2 tablespoons **tomato purée**
2 tablespoons **grainy mustard**
1 tablespoon **Worcestershire sauce**
salt and **pepper**

Put the beans in a bowl, cover with cold water and leave to soak overnight.

Drain the beans and put in a flameproof casserole. Cover with water and bring to the boil. Reduce the heat and simmer gently for 15–20 minutes or until the beans have softened slightly. Test by removing a few on a fork and squeezing them gently – they should give a little. Drain the beans.

Wipe out the dish and melt the butter. Add the bacon and pork and fry gently for 10 minutes until beginning to brown. Add the onion and cook for a further 5 minutes.

Stir in the drained beans, thyme or rosemary and tomatoes. Add enough water to just cover the ingredients and bring to the boil. Cover with a lid and transfer to a preheated oven, 150°C (300°F), Gas Mark 2. Cook for about 1 hour or until the beans are very tender.

Mix together the treacle, tomato purée, mustard, Worcestershire sauce and seasoning. Stir into the beans and return to the oven for a further 30 minutes.

For veggie Boston beans, replace the haricot beans with the same quantity of butter beans and soak and drain as above. Replace the bacon and pork with 12 vegetarian sausages and fry off before the onion in the third step until lightly browned. Remove from the pan and set aside. Add the onion and continue as above. Add the veggie sausages in the final stage before the sauce and cook for 30 minutes.

PORK & BEETROOT GOULASH

Serves **4**
Preparation time **30 minutes**
Cooking time **2½ hours**

2 tablespoons **olive oil**
450 g (14½ oz) **lean pork**, diced
2 **onions**, sliced
1 teaspoon **hot smoked paprika**
1 teaspoon **caraway seeds**
750 g (1½ lb) piece of **smoked bacon knuckle**
3 **bay leaves**
1.2 litres (2 pints) **water**
300 g (10 oz) **beetroot**, diced
300 g (10 oz) **red cabbage**, finely sliced
3 tablespoons **tomato purée**

Heat the oil in a large saucepan and fry the diced pork until browned. Add the onions, paprika and caraway and fry gently for a further 5 minutes until the onions are browned.

Add the piece of bacon knuckle, the bay leaves and measurement water. Bring to the boil, cover with a lid and reduce the heat to the lowest setting. Cook very gently for about 2 hours until the bacon knuckle is very tender and the meat falls easily from the bone.

Drain the knuckle to a plate and leave until cool enough to handle. Pull the meat from the bone and shred it back into the pan, discarding the skin and bone.

Add the beetroot, cabbage and tomato purée to the pan and cook gently, covered, for about 15 minutes until the beetroot and cabbage are tender. Check the seasoning and serve.

For swede and carrot mash to serve as an accompaniment, cook 500 g (1 lb) carrots in boiling water for 10 minutes. Add 1 kg (2 lb) swede, peeled and cut into chunks. Cook until tender. Drain thoroughly and return to the pan. Mash with 1 teaspoon chopped thyme and 3 tablespoons olive oil.

SPICY SAUSAGE CASSOULET

Serves **2**
Preparation time **15 minutes**
Cooking time **35 minutes**

3 tablespoons **olive oil**
1 **red onion**, finely chopped
1 **garlic clove**, crushed
1 **red pepper**, deseeded and roughly chopped
2 **celery sticks**, roughly chopped
200 g (7 oz) can **chopped tomatoes**
125 ml (4 fl oz) **chicken stock**
2 teaspoons **dark soy sauce**
1 teaspoon **Dijon mustard**
400 g (13 oz) can **black-eyed beans**, rinsed and drained
125 g (4 oz) **smoked pork sausage**, roughly chopped
50 g (2 oz) **fresh breadcrumbs**
25 g (1 oz) freshly grated **Parmesan cheese**
2 tablespoons chopped **parsley**

Heat 1 tablespoon of the oil in a frying pan or small sauté pan. Add the onion, garlic, red pepper and celery and cook over a low heat, stirring occasionally, for 3–4 minutes.

Add the tomatoes, stock and soy sauce. Bring to the boil, then reduce the heat and simmer for about 15 minutes, or until the sauce begins to thicken. Add the mustard, beans and sausage and continue to cook for a further 10 minutes.

Mix the breadcrumbs, Parmesan and parsley together and sprinkle over the sausage mixture. Drizzle with the remaining oil. Place under a preheated moderate–hot grill for 2–3 minutes or until golden brown.

For mixed leaf and pomegranate salad to serve as an accompaniment, put 1½ tablespoons raspberry vinegar and 1 tablespoon olive oil with a little salt and pepper in a salad bowl and mix lightly. Cut ½ pomegranate into large pieces and flex the skin so that the small seeds fall out. Add the seeds to the salad bowl. Break 50 g (2 oz) mixed salad leaves into bite-sized pieces and add to the salad bowl, tossing all the ingredients in the salad dressing.

SALT BEEF WITH SPRING VEGETABLES

Serves **6**
Preparation time **10 minutes, plus resting**
Cooking time **2½ hours**

1.75 kg (3½ lb) piece of **salted** and **rolled brisket**
 or **silverside of beef**
1 **onion**
15 **whole cloves**
300 g (10 oz) **baby onions** or **shallots**, peeled but
 left whole
3 **bay leaves**
plenty of **thyme** and **parsley sprigs**
½ teaspoon **ground allspice**
300 g (10 oz) small **carrots**
1 small **swede**, cut into small chunks
500 g (1 lb) **floury potatoes**, cut into chunks
pepper
chopped **parsley**, to garnish

Put the beef in a flameproof casserole in which it fits quite snugly. Stud the onion with the cloves and add to the casserole with the baby onions or shallots, bay leaves, herbs, allspice and plenty of pepper.

Add just enough water to cover the beef and bring slowly to the boil. Cover with a lid and place in a preheated oven, 120°C (250°F), Gas Mark ½, for 2½ hours or until the meat is tender, adding the carrots, swede and potatoes to the casserole after 1 hour of the cooking time. Leave to rest for 15 minutes before carving.

Drain the meat to a plate or board. Cut into thin slices and serve on warmed plates with the vegetables. Sprinkle with parsley and serve with a jug of the cooking juices for pouring over.

For herb dumplings to serve as an accompaniment, rub 50 g (2 oz) diced butter into 125 g (4 oz) self-raising flour until the mixture resembles fine breadcrumbs. Add 2 tablespoons finely chopped flat leaf parsley and ½ teaspoon dried thyme; season with salt and pepper. Mix with 1 lightly beaten egg and add a little water to make a sticky dough. Using a tablespoon, form into small balls and add to the casserole once cooked. Let the casserole bubble up on the hob, cover and cook for 15–20 minutes until the dumplings have risen.

BEEF WITH WALNUT PESTO

Serves **6**
Preparation time **20 minutes, plus resting**
Cooking time **1 hour 40 minutes**

150 g (5 oz) **walnut pieces**
2 **garlic cloves**, roughly chopped
50 g (2 oz) can **anchovies**
2 tablespoons **hot horseradish sauce**
25 g (1 oz) chopped **parsley**
2 tablespoons **olive oil**
1.5 kg (3 lb) **rolled topside** or **top rump of beef**
1 large **onion**, finely chopped
2 **celery sticks**, chopped
300 ml (½ pint) **red wine**
150 ml (¼ pint) **beef stock**
4 **carrots**, cut into chunky slices
300 g (10 oz) **baby turnips**
500 g (1 lb) **new potatoes**
200 g (7 oz) **French beans**
salt and **pepper**
chopped **parsley**, to garnish

Put the walnuts in a food processor or blender with the garlic, anchovies and their oil, horseradish, parsley, 1 tablespoon of the oil and plenty of black pepper and blend to a thick paste, scraping the mixture down from the sides of the bowl.

Untie the beef and open it out slightly. If there is already a split through the flesh, make the cut deeper so that it will take the stuffing. If it is a perfectly rounded piece of beef, make a deep cut so that you can pack in the stuffing. Once the stuffing is in place, reshape the meat into a roll. Tie with string, securing at 2.5 cm (1 inch) intervals. Pat the meat dry with kitchen paper and season with salt and pepper.

Heat the remaining oil in a flameproof casserole and fry the meat on all sides to brown. Drain to a plate.

Add the onion and celery to the pan and fry gently for 5 minutes. Return the meat to the pan and pour the wine and stock over it. Add the carrots and turnips. Bring just to the boil, cover with a lid and place in preheated oven, 160°C (325°F), Gas Mark 3. Cook for 30 minutes.

Tuck the potatoes around the beef and sprinkle with salt. Return to the oven for a further 40 minutes until the potatoes are tender. Stir in the beans and return to the oven for 20 minutes until the beans have softened. Leave to rest for 15 minutes before carving the meat.

For beef with hazelnut pesto, omit the walnuts and use the same quantity of hazelnuts. Replace the anchovies with 4 tablespoons capers and the turnips with the same quantity of swede, cut into chunks.

CHILLI CON CARNE

Serves **2**
Preparation time **15 minutes**
Cooking time **45 minutes**

2 tablespoon **olive oil**
1 **red onion**, finely chopped
3 **garlic cloves**, finely chopped
250 g (8 oz) **lean minced beef**
½ teaspoon **ground cumin**
1 small **red pepper**, deseeded and diced
400 g (13 oz) can **chopped tomatoes**
1 tablespoon **tomato purée**
2 teaspoons **mild chilli powder**
200 ml (7 fl oz) **beef stock**
400 g (13 oz) can **red kidney beans**, rinsed
   and drained
salt and **pepper**

Heat the oil in a saucepan. Add the onion and garlic and cook for 5 minutes or until beginning to soften. Add the mince and cumin and cook for a further 5–6 minutes or until browned all over.

Stir in the red pepper, tomatoes, tomato purée, chilli powder and stock and bring to the boil. Reduce the heat and simmer gently for 30 minutes.

Add the beans and cook for a further 5 minutes. Season to taste and serve with brown rice, cooked according to the packet instructions.

For homemade beef stock, put 750g (1½ lb) raw or cooked beef bones in a large, heavy-based saucepan with a large, unpeeled and halved onion, 2 carrots and 2 celery sticks, roughly chopped, 1 teaspoon peppercorns and several bay leaves and thyme sprigs. Cover with cold water and heat until simmering. Reduce the heat to its lowest setting and cook very gently, uncovered, for 3–4 hours. Strain through a sieve and leave to cool. Store for up to a week in the refrigerator or freezer.

QUICK BEEF STROGANOFF

Serves **4**
Preparation time **10 minutes**
Cooking time **15 minutes**

2 tablespoons **paprika**
1 tablespoon **plain flour**
450 g (14½ oz) sliced **beef sirloin**
300 g (10 oz) **long grain white rice**
25 g (1 oz) **butter**
4 tablespoons **vegetable** or **sunflower oil**
1 large **onion**, thinly sliced
250 g (8 oz) **chestnut mushrooms**, trimmed and sliced
300 ml (½ pint) **soured cream**
salt and **pepper**
1 tablespoon chopped **curly parsley**, to garnish

Mix together the paprika and flour in a large bowl, add the beef and turn to coat.

Cook the rice in lightly salted boiling water for 13 minutes until cooked but firm. Drain, set aside and keep warm.

Meanwhile, melt the butter and 2 tablespoons of the oil in a large frying pan and cook the onion for about 6 minutes or until soft. Add the mushrooms and cook for a further 5 minutes or until soft. Remove with a slotted spoon and set aside.

Add the remaining oil to the pan, increase the heat to high and add the beef. Fry until browned all over, then reduce the heat. Return the onion mixture to the pan along with the soured cream; bring to the boil, then reduce the heat and allow to bubble gently for 1–2 minutes. Season well.

Serve immediately with the cooked rice and a sprinkling of chopped parsley.

For mushroom & red pepper Stroganoff, omit the beef, increase the quantity of chestnut mushrooms to 500 g (1 lb) and add 2 thinly sliced red peppers. Cook the mushrooms with the onion until they have reduced and the onion is soft. Remove the mixture from the pan. Cook the peppers until tender. Return the onion mixture to the pan, as above. Sprinkle with pine nuts to serve.

MEATBALLS WITH TOMATO SAUCE

Serves **4**
Preparation time **25 minutes**
Cooking time **30 minutes**

500 g (1 lb) **lean minced beef**
3 **garlic cloves**, crushed
2 **small onions**, finely chopped
25 g (1 oz) **breadcrumbs**
40 g (1½ oz) freshly grated **Parmesan cheese**
6 tablespoons **olive oil**
100 ml (3½ fl oz) **red wine**
2 x 400 g (13 oz) cans **chopped tomatoes**
1 teaspoon **caster sugar**
3 tablespoons **sun-dried tomato paste**
75 g (3 oz) **pitted Italian black olives**, roughly chopped
4 tablespoons roughly chopped **oregano**
125 g (4 oz) **mozzarella cheese**, thinly sliced
salt and **pepper**

Put the beef in a bowl with half the crushed garlic and half the onion, the breadcrumbs and 25 g (1 oz) of the Parmesan. Season and use your hands to thoroughly blend the ingredients together. Shape into small balls, about 2.5 cm (1 inch) in diameter.

Heat half the oil in a large frying pan or sauté pan and fry the meatballs, shaking the pan frequently, for about 10 minutes until browned. Drain.

Add the remaining oil and onion to the pan and fry until softened. Add the wine and let the mixture bubble until the wine has almost evaporated. Stir in the remaining garlic, the tomatoes, sugar, tomato paste and a little seasoning. Bring to the boil and let the mixture bubble until slightly thickened.

Stir in the olives, all but 1 tablespoon of the oregano and the meatballs. Cook gently for a further 5 minutes.

Arrange the mozzarella slices over the top and scatter with the remaining oregano and Parmesan. Season with black pepper and cook under the grill until the cheese starts to melt. Serve in shallow bowls with warmed, crusty bread.

For Greek-style meatballs, use 500 g (1 lb) lean minced lamb instead of the beef. Replace the olives with 50 g (2 oz) pine nuts. Before adding them to the pan in the fourth step, dry-fry in a small frying pan over a medium heat for 3–5 minutes until lightly browned, shaking constantly.

OXTAIL STEW

Serves **4**
Preparation time **20 minutes**
Cooking time **3¾ hours**

2 tablespoons **plain flour**
1 tablespoon **mustard powder**
1 teaspoon **celery salt**
2 kg (4 lb) **oxtail**
50 g (2 oz) **butter**
2 tablespoons **oil**
2 **onions**, sliced
3 **large carrots**, sliced
3 **bay leaves**
100 g (3½ oz) **tomato purée**
100 ml (3½ fl oz) **dry sherry**
1 litre (1¾ pints) **beef stock** or **vegetable stock**
salt and **pepper**

Mix together the flour, mustard powder and celery salt on a large plate and use to coat the oxtail pieces. Melt half the butter with 1 tablespoon of the oil in a large, flameproof casserole. Brown the oxtail, half at a time, and drain to a plate.

Add the onions and carrots to the pan with the remaining butter and oil. Fry until beginning to brown. Return the oxtail to the pan with the bay leaves and any remaining flour left on the plate.

Mix together the tomato purée, sherry and stock and add to the dish. Bring to the boil, then reduce the heat and cover with a lid.

Place in a preheated oven, 150°C (300°F), Gas Mark 2, for about 3½ hours or until the meat is meltingly tender and falling from the bone. Check the seasoning and serve with plenty of warmed bread.

For oxtail, herb and red wine stew, add 1 parsnip cut into small chunks, with the onions and carrots in the second step. When returning the oxtail to the pan, add 1 teaspoon each finely chopped rosemary and thyme with the bay leaves. Replace the sherry with the same quantity of red wine.

ONE POT,
FEED THE LOT

SEA BASS & SPICY POTATOES

Serves **2**
Preparation time **15 minutes**
Cooking time **1 hour**

500 g (1 lb) **baking potatoes**
3 tablespoons **olive oil**
2 tablespoons **sun-dried tomato tapenade**
½ teaspoon **mild chilli powder**
2 small whole **sea bass**, scaled and gutted
2 tablespoons mixed chopped **herbs**, e.g. **thyme**,
   parsley, **chervil**, **tarragon**
1 **garlic clove**, crushed
2 **bay leaves**
½ **lemon**, sliced
handful of **pitted black olives**
salt and **pepper**

Cut the potatoes into 1 cm (½ inch) thick slices – you can peel them first if you wish to, but this isn't necessary. Cut into chunky chips. Mix 2 tablespoons of the oil with the tapenade, chilli powder and plenty of salt. Toss in a bowl with the potatoes until evenly coated.

Tip the potatoes into a shallow ovenproof dish or roasting pan and bake in a preheated oven, 200°C (400°F), Gas Mark 6, for 30 minutes until pale golden, turning the potatoes once or twice during cooking.

Meanwhile, score the fish several times on each side. Mix the remaining oil with 1 tablespoon of the herbs, the garlic and a little salt and pepper. Pack the bay leaves, lemon slices and remaining herbs into the fish cavities and lay the fish over the potatoes in the dish, pushing the potatoes to the edges of the dish.

Brush the garlic and herb oil over the fish and scatter the olives over the potatoes. Return to the oven for a further 30 minutes until the fish is cooked through. Test by piercing the thick end of the fish with a knife; the flesh should be cooked through to the bone.

For tomato salad to serve as an accompaniment, slice 2 large tomatoes and arrange on a platter. Slice ½ small red onion and place on top of the tomatoes. Mix the following dressing ingredients together thoroughly: 6 tablespoons olive oil, 2 tablespoons cider vinegar, 1 garlic clove crushed, ½ teaspoon Dijon mustard and salt and pepper. Drizzle over the tomatoes and sprinkle over a little chopped parsley.

144

POT-ROASTED TUNA WITH LENTILS

Serves **4**
Preparation time **15 minutes**
Cooking time **50 minutes–1 hour 5 minutes**

½ teaspoon **celery salt**
750 g (1½ lb) **tuna**, in one slender piece
1 **fennel bulb**
3 tablespoons **olive oil**
250 g (8 oz) **black lentils**, rinsed
1 glass **white wine**, about 150 ml (¼ pint)
250 ml (8 fl oz) **fish stock** or **vegetable stock**
4 tablespoons chopped **fennel leaves** or **dill**
2 tablespoons **capers**, rinsed and drained
400 g (13 oz) can **chopped tomatoes**
salt and **pepper**

Mix the celery salt with a little pepper and rub all over the tuna. Cut the fennel bulb in half, then into thin slices.

Heat the oil in a flameproof casserole and fry the tuna on all sides until browned. Drain. Add the sliced fennel to the pan and fry gently until softened.

Add the lentils and wine and bring to the boil. Boil until the wine has reduced by about half. Stir in the stock, fennel leaves or dill, capers and tomatoes and return to the boil. Cover with a lid and transfer to a preheated oven, 180°C (350°F), Gas Mark 4, for 15 minutes.

Return the tuna to the casserole and cook gently for a further 20 minutes until the lentils are completely tender. The tuna should still be slightly pink in the centre. If you prefer it well done, return to the oven for a further 15–20 minutes. Check the seasoning and serve.

For pot-roasted lamb with lentils, replace the tuna with a 625 g (1¼ lb) piece of rolled loin of lamb. Fry off the lamb as above in the second step. Omit the fennel bulb and use the same quantity of chicken stock instead of the fish or vegetable stock. Replace the fennel or dill with the same quantity of rosemary or oregano. Continue as above, cooking for 30 minutes instead of 20. If you prefer your lamb well done, return to the oven for a further 20 minutes.

PLAICE WITH SAMBAL

Serves **4**
Preparation time **30 minutes**
Cooking time **30 minutes**

1 small **lemon grass stalk**
2 **garlic cloves**, crushed
6 tablespoons grated **fresh coconut**
2 **green chillies**, deseeded
  and finely chopped
4 small whole **plaice**, scaled
  and gutted
4 tablespoons **oil**

Coconut and tamarind sambal
1 **onion**, finely chopped
1 **garlic clove**, crushed
1 tablespoon **oil**
2 tablespoons grated **fresh coconut**
1 **red chilli**, deseeded and
  finely chopped
150 ml (¼ pint) **boiling water**
2 tablespoons **dried tamarind pulp**
2 teaspoons **caster sugar**
1 tablespoon **white wine vinegar**
1 tablespoon chopped **fresh coriander**

Finely chop the lemon grass stalk and mix with the garlic, coconut and green chillies. Smear this dry mixture over each plaice, then cover and leave to marinate in the refrigerator for 2 hours or overnight.

Make the coconut and tamarind sambal by gently frying the onion and garlic in the oil in a large frying pan until softened. Add the coconut with the red chilli, stir to coat in the oil and cook for 2–3 minutes. Pour the measurement water over the tamarind pulp in a heatproof bowl and stand for 10 minutes to dissolve.

Strain the juice from the tamarind pulp, mashing as much of the pulp through the sieve as possible. Add this juice to the pan with the sugar and simmer gently for 5 minutes. Add the vinegar, remove from the heat and leave to cool. When cold, stir in the chopped coriander. Turn into a bowl and wipe the pan clean.

Heat the oil in the pan and gently fry the plaice 2 at a time in the hot oil, turning once. After 6–8 minutes, when they are golden brown and cooked, remove from the oil and drain on kitchen paper. Keep warm while cooking the remaining fish. Serve the fish piping hot with the coconut and tamarind sambal.

For perfumed rice to serve as an accompaniment, cook 325 g (11 oz) fragrant long-grain rice in boiling water until tender. Fry 1 bunch spring onions, thinly sliced, in 2 teaspoons oil for 30 seconds. Add the finely grated rind of 1 lime and 4–6 shredded kaffir lime leaves. Stir in the drained rice and a little salt.

DILL & MUSTARD BAKED SALMON

Serves **4**
Preparation time **20 minutes**
Cooking time **55 minutes**

3 tablespoons chopped **dill**
2 tablespoons **grainy mustard**
2 tablespoons **lime juice**
1 tablespoon **caster sugar**
150 ml (¼ pint) **double cream**
2 small **fennel bulbs**, thinly sliced
2 tablespoons **olive oil**
750 g (1½ lb) **salmon fillet**, skinned
4 **hard-boiled eggs**, quartered
250 g (8 oz) **puff pastry**
beaten **egg yolk**, to glaze
salt and **pepper**

Mix together the dill, mustard, lime juice and sugar in a bowl. Stir in the cream and a little seasoning.

Put the fennel in a 2 litre (3½ pint) shallow, ovenproof dish or pie dish. Drizzle with the oil and bake in a preheated oven, 200°C (400°F), Gas Mark 6, for 20 minutes, turning once or twice during cooking, until softened.

Cut the salmon into 8 chunky pieces and add to the dish with the egg quarters, tucking them between the fennel slices so that all the ingredients are evenly mixed. Spoon the cream mixture over and return to the oven for 15 minutes.

Roll out the pastry on a lightly floured surface and cut out 8 x 6 cm (2½ inch) squares. Brush the tops with egg yolk to glaze and make diagonal markings over the surface of the pastry with the tip of a sharp knife. Sprinkle with pepper.

Place a double thickness of greaseproof paper over the dish of salmon and put the pastry squares on the paper. Bake for 10–15 minutes until the pastry is risen and golden. Slide the pastry squares on to the salmon and serve with a herb salad.

For dill, mustard and salmon pie, replace the lime juice with lemon juice and scatter the salmon with 1 tablespoon capers. Replace the puff pastry with 6 sheets of filo pastry. Place on top of the salmon dish in layers, brushing each layer with melted butter and crumpling slightly. Bake for 20–25 minutes.

SPICED FISH TAGINE

Serves **4**
Preparation time **15 minutes**
Cooking time **35 minutes**

625 g (1¼ lb) **halibut steaks**
1 teaspoon **cumin seeds**
1 teaspoon **coriander seeds**
4 tablespoons **olive oil**
1 large **onion**, sliced
3 pared strips of **orange rind**, plus 2 tablespoons
   juice
3 **garlic cloves**, sliced
½ teaspoon **saffron threads**
150 ml (¼ pint) **fish stock**
50 g (2 oz) **dates**, sliced
25 g (1 oz) **flaked almonds**, lightly toasted
salt and **pepper**

Cut the halibut into chunky pieces, discarding the skin and any bones. Season lightly. Crush the cumin and coriander seeds using a pestle and mortar.

Heat the oil in a large frying pan or sauté pan and gently fry the onion and orange rind for 5 minutes. Add the garlic and crushed spices and fry, stirring, for a further 2–3 minutes.

Add the fish, turning the pieces to coat in the spices. Crumble in the saffron and pour in the stock and orange juice. Scatter with the dates and almonds.

Cover with a lid or foil and cook very gently for 20–25 minutes or until the fish is cooked through. Check the seasoning and serve with steamed couscous.

For spicy swordfish tagine, replace the halibut with the same quantity of swordfish steaks cut into chunks. Add a mild or medium red chilli, deseeded and chopped, with the crushed spices. Use 25 g (1 oz) dried figs and 25 g (1 oz) dried apricots instead of the dates.

RICH FISH STEW

Serves **4**
Preparation time **25 minutes**
Cooking time **40 minutes**

4 tablespoons **olive oil**
1 **onion**, chopped
1 small **leek**, chopped
4 **garlic cloves**, crushed
1 teaspoon **saffron threads**
400 g (13 oz) can **chopped tomatoes**
4 tablespoons **sun-dried tomato paste**
1 litre (1¾ pints) **fish stock**
3 **bay leaves**
several **thyme sprigs**
750 g (1½ lb) **mixed fish**, e.g. **haddock**, **bream**,
   halibut, **bass**, skinned, boned and cut into
   chunky pieces
250 g (8 oz) **raw peeled prawns**
salt and **pepper**
8 tablespoons **aïoli** (see page 57) and baguette slices,
   to garnish

Heat the oil in a large saucepan and gently fry the onion and leek for 5 minutes. Add the garlic and fry for a further 1 minute.

Stir in the saffron, tomatoes, tomato paste, stock, bay leaves and thyme. Bring to the boil, then reduce the heat and simmer gently for 25 minutes.

Gently stir in the mixed fish and cook very gently for 5 minutes. Stir in the prawns and cook for a further 2–3 minutes until the prawns have turned pink and the fish flakes easily when pierced with a knife.

Check the seasoning and ladle the stew into shallow bowls. To garnish, spoon some aïoli on to baguette slices and rest them over the stew.

For homemade aïoli, combine the following ingredients in a food processor or blender and blend until creamy: 2 egg yolks, 1 crushed garlic clove, ½ teaspoon sea salt and 1 tablespoon white wine vinegar. Season with pepper. With the motor running, gradually pour 300 ml (½ pint) olive oil through the funnel until the mixture is thick and glossy. Add a little boiling water if it becomes too thick. Transfer to a bowl, cover and refrigerate until required.

CLAM & POTATO CHOWDER

Serves **4**
Preparation time **15 minutes**
Cooking time **30 minutes**

1 kg (2 lb) small **fresh clams**
25 g (1 oz) **butter**
2 **onions**, chopped
150 ml (¼ pint) **white wine**
1.2 litres (2 pints) **fish stock** or **chicken stock**
½ teaspoon **medium curry paste**
¼ teaspoon **ground turmeric**
500 g (1 lb) **floury potatoes**, diced
150 g (5 oz) **watercress**, tough stalks removed
plenty of freshly grated **nutmeg**
squeeze of **lemon juice**
salt and **pepper**

Rinse and check over the clams, discarding any damaged shells or any open ones that don't close when tapped with a knife. Transfer to a bowl.

Melt the butter in a large saucepan and gently fry the onions for 6–8 minutes until soft. Add the wine and bring to the boil. Tip in the clams and cover with a lid. Cook for about 5 minutes until the clams have opened, shaking the pan several times during cooking.

Once the shells are all opened, remove from the heat and tip into a colander set over a large bowl to catch the juices. When cool enough to handle, remove the clams from the shells and discard the shells. Reserve the clams and tip the cooking juices back into the pan.

Add the stock, curry paste, turmeric and potatoes to the saucepan and bring to the boil. Reduce the heat, cover and simmer for 10–15 minutes until the potatoes are tender.

Return the clams to the pan with the watercress, nutmeg and lemon juice and heat through gently for 2 minutes. Use a stick blender to lightly blend the chowder without completely puréeing it. Season with salt and pepper to taste.

For mussel, spinach and potato chowder, replace the clams with the same quantity of mussels and prepare as above. Replace the watercress with the same quantity of baby spinach.

MEDITERRANEAN ROASTED FISH

Serves **4**
Preparation time **15 minutes**
Cooking time **40 minutes**

5 tablespoons **olive oil**
2 **shallots**, thinly sliced
75 g (3 oz) **pancetta**, chopped
50 g (2 oz) **pine nuts**
2 teaspoons chopped **rosemary**, plus several extra sprigs
1 thick slice **white bread**, made into breadcrumbs
50 g (2 oz) can **anchovies**, drained and chopped
2 **red onions**, thinly sliced
6 **tomatoes**, cut into wedges
2 **haddock fillets**, each about 300 g (10 oz), skinned
salt and **pepper**

Heat 2 tablespoons of the oil in a large roasting pan and fry the shallots and pancetta, stirring frequently, until beginning to colour. Add the pine nuts and chopped rosemary with a little pepper and fry for a further 2 minutes. Drain to a bowl, add the breadcrumbs and anchovies and mix well.

Add the onions to the pan and fry for 5 minutes until slightly softened. Stir in the tomato wedges and remove from the heat. Push to the edges of the pan to leave a space for the fish in the centre.

Check the fish for any stray bones and place one fillet in the pan. Pack the stuffing mixture on top, pressing it firmly on to the fish with your hands. Lay the second fillet on top, skinned-side down, and season with a little salt and pepper.

Drizzle with the remaining oil and place in a preheated oven, 180°C (350°F), Gas Mark 4, for 30 minutes until the fish is cooked through. Test by piercing a thick area with a knife.

For spinach and walnut salad to serve as an accompaniment, heat 1 tablespoon clear honey in a small frying pan, add 125 g (4 oz) walnuts and stir-fry over a medium heat for 2–3 minutes until glazed. Meanwhile, blanch 250 g (8 oz) green beans in lightly salted boiling water for 3 minutes and drain. Place in a large bowl with 200 g (7 oz) baby spinach. Whisk the following dressing ingredients together and season with salt and pepper: 4 tablespoons walnut oil, 2 tablespoons olive oil and 1–2 tablespoons sherry vinegar. Pour over the leaves and scatter the walnuts.

SPICY PRAWN & POTATO SAUTÉ

Serves **2**
Preparation time **15 minutes**
Cooking time **25 minutes**

3 tablespoons smooth **mango chutney**
½ teaspoon **hot smoked paprika**
1 tablespoon **lemon** or **lime juice**
4 tablespoons **oil**
400 g (13 oz) **raw peeled prawns**
500 g (1 lb) **baking potatoes**, cut into 1.5 cm
   (¾ inch) dice
2 **garlic cloves**, crushed
400 g (13 oz) can **chopped tomatoes**
50 g (2 oz) **creamed coconut**, chopped into
   small pieces
salt and **pepper**
mustard and cress or **snipped chives**, to garnish

Mix together the mango chutney, paprika and lemon or lime juice in a small bowl.

Heat half the oil in a frying pan or sauté pan and fry the prawns for about 3 minutes, turning once, until pink, then immediately drain them from the pan.

Add the potatoes to the pan with the remaining oil and fry very gently for about 10 minutes, turning frequently, until the potatoes are golden and cooked through. Add the garlic and cook for a further 1 minute.

Add the tomatoes and bring to the boil. Reduce the heat and cook gently until the sauce turns pulpy. Stir in the creamed coconut and mango mixture and cook gently until the coconut has dissolved into the sauce.

Stir in the prawns for a few seconds to heat through. Check the seasoning and serve scattered with mustard and cress or chives.

For curried prawn and sweet potato sauté, replace the paprika with 1–2 teaspoons medium curry paste. Replace the potatoes with the same quantity of sweet potatoes, scrubbed or peeled.

MONKFISH WITH COCONUT RICE

Serves **4**
Preparation time **20 minutes**
Cooking time **25 minutes**

625 g (1¼ lb) **monkfish fillets**
4 long, slender **lemon grass stalks**
1 bunch **spring onions**
3 tablespoons **stir-fry** or **wok oil**
½ teaspoon **crushed dried chillies**
2 **garlic cloves**, sliced
300 g (10 oz) **Thai fragrant rice**
400 g (13 oz) can **coconut milk**
50 g (2 oz) **creamed coconut**, chopped
200 ml (7 fl oz) **hot water**
2 tablespoons **rice wine vinegar**
150 g (5 oz) **baby spinach**
salt and **pepper**

Cut the monkfish into 3 cm (1¼ inch) cubes. Using a large knife, slice each lemon grass stalk in half lengthways. (If the stalks are very thick, pull off the outer layers, finely chop them and add to the oil with the chilli flakes.) Cut the thin ends of each stalk to a point and thread the monkfish on to the skewers. If it is difficult to thread the fish, pierce each piece with a small knife first to make threading easier.

Finely chop the spring onions, keeping the white and green parts separate.

Heat the oil in a large frying pan with the chilli flakes, garlic and white parts of the spring onions. Add the monkfish skewers and fry gently for about 5 minutes, turning once, until cooked through. Drain to a plate.

Add the rice, coconut milk and creamed coconut to the frying pan and bring to the boil. Reduce the heat, cover with a lid or foil and cook gently for 6–8 minutes, stirring frequently, until the rice is almost tender and the milk absorbed. Add the measurement water and cook, covered, for a further 10 minutes until the rice is completely tender, adding a little more water if the mixture boils dry before the rice is tender.

Stir in the vinegar, remaining spring onions and then the spinach, turning it in the rice until wilted. Arrange the skewers over the rice. Cover and cook gently for 3 minutes, then serve immediately.

FETA-STUFFED PLAICE

Serves **4**
Preparation time **20 minutes**
Cooking time **40 minutes**

2 tablespoons chopped **mint**
2 tablespoons chopped **oregano**
25 g (1 oz) **Parma ham**, finely chopped
2 **garlic cloves**, crushed
4 **spring onions**, finely chopped
200 g (7 oz) **feta cheese**
8 **plaice fillets**, skinned
300 g (10 oz) **courgettes**, sliced
4 tablespoons **garlic-infused olive oil**
8 **flat mushrooms**
150 g (5 oz) **baby plum tomatoes**, halved
1 tablespoon **capers**, rinsed and drained
salt and **pepper**

Put the mint, oregano, ham, garlic and spring onions in a bowl. Crumble in the feta cheese, season with plenty of pepper and mix together well.

Put the fish fillets skinned-side up on the work surface and press the feta mixture down the centres. Roll up loosely and secure with wooden cocktail sticks.

Scatter the courgettes into a shallow, ovenproof dish and drizzle with 1 tablespoon of the oil. Place in a preheated oven, 190°C (375°F), Gas Mark 5, for 15 minutes. Remove from the oven and add the plaice fillets to the dish. Tuck the mushrooms, tomatoes and capers around the fish and season lightly. Drizzle with the remaining oil.

Return to the oven for a further 25 minutes or until the fish is cooked through.

For tomato and garlic bread to serve as an accompaniment, mix together 75 g (3 oz) softened butter, 2 crushed garlic cloves, 3 tablespoons sun-dried tomato paste and a little salt and pepper. Make vertical cuts 2.5 cm (1 inch) apart through a ciabatta loaf, cutting not quite through the base. Push the garlic and tomato paste mixture into the cuts. Wrap in foil and bake in the oven under the fish for 15 minutes. Unwrap the top of the bread and return to the oven for 10 minutes.

CRAYFISH RISOTTO

Serves **4**
Preparation time **10 minutes**
Cooking time **30 minutes**

50 g (2 oz) **butter**
2 **shallots**, finely chopped
1 **mild red chilli**, thinly sliced
1 teaspoon **mild paprika**
1 **garlic clove**, crushed
300 g (10 oz) **risotto rice**
1 glass **dry white wine**, about 150 ml (¼ pint)
a few **lemon thyme sprigs**
about 1.2 litres (2 pints) hot **fish stock** or **chicken stock**
3 tablespoons roughly chopped **tarragon**
300 g (10 oz) **crayfish tails** in brine, drained
salt
freshly grated **Parmesan cheese**, to garnish

Melt half the butter in a large saucepan or deep-sided sauté pan and gently fry the shallots until softened. Add the chilli, paprika and garlic and fry gently for 30 seconds, without browning the garlic.

Sprinkle in the rice and fry gently for 1 minute, stirring. Add the wine and let it bubble until almost evaporated.

Add the thyme and a ladleful of the stock and cook, stirring, until the rice has almost absorbed the stock. Continue cooking, adding the stock a ladleful at a time, and letting the rice absorb most of the stock before adding more. Once the rice is tender but retaining a little bite, the risotto is ready – this will take about 25 minutes. You may not need all the stock.

Stir in the tarragon, crayfish and remaining butter and heat through gently for 1 minute. Add a little extra salt if necessary and serve immediately, garnished with Parmesan and with a watercress salad, if you like.

For prawn risotto, cook 350 g (11½ oz) raw peeled prawns in the butter, as in the first step. Cook until pink, drain, then return to the pan in the fourth step. Omit the chilli and replace the shallots with 1 bunch chopped spring onions.

SPICY FISH

Serves **2**
Preparation time **10 minutes, plus marinating**
Cooking time **5 minutes**

1 **garlic clove**, peeled
2 **red shallots**, chopped
1 **lemon grass stalk**
½ teaspoon **ground turmeric**
½ teaspoon **ground ginger**
1 **mild red chilli**, deseeded and roughly chopped
1 tablespoon **groundnut oil**
2 teaspoon **fish sauce**
300 g (10 oz) boneless
   white fish fillets, cut into bite-sized pieces
salt and **pepper**
1 tablespoon chopped **fresh coriander**, to garnish

Put the garlic, shallots, lemon grass, turmeric, ginger, chilli and salt and pepper into a food processor or blender and process until a paste is formed, adding the oil and fish sauce to help the grinding.

Place the fish in a bowl and toss with the spice paste. Cover and refrigerate for 15 minutes.

Thread the pieces of fish on to skewers and arrange on a foil-lined tray. Cook under a preheated hot grill for 4–5 minutes, turning once so that the pieces brown evenly. Serve sprinkled with the coriander.

For Chinese greens to serve as an accompaniment, put 300 g (10 oz) raw shredded Chinese greens in a saucepan of boiling water and cook for 1–2 minutes. Drain and place on warmed serving plates. Heat 1 teaspoon groundnut oil in a small pan and cook ½ teaspoon finely chopped garlic briefly. Stir in 1 teaspoon oyster sauce, 1 tablespoon water and ½ tablespoon sesame oil, then bring to the boil. Pour over the greens and toss together.

SEAFOOD LEMON GRASS CRUMBLE

Serves **4**
Preparation time **20 minutes**
Cooking time **40 minutes**

500 g (1 lb) **swordfish steaks**
200 g (7 oz) **raw peeled prawns**
250 g (8 oz) **mascarpone cheese**
4 tablespoons **white wine**
1 **lemon grass stalk**
150 g (5 oz) **plain flour**
75 g (3 oz) **butter**, cut into pieces
4 tablespoons chopped **dill**
4 tablespoons freshly grated **Parmesan cheese**
salt and **pepper**

Cut the swordfish into large chunks, discarding any skin and bones, and scatter in a 1.5 litre (2½ pint) ovenproof dish or pie dish. Add the prawns and season with salt and pepper.

Beat the mascarpone in a bowl to soften. Stir in the wine and spoon over the fish.

Chop the lemon grass as finely as possible and process in a blender or food processor with the flour and butter until the mixture resembles fine breadcrumbs. Add the dill and pulse very briefly to mix.

Tip the mixture over the fish and sprinkle with the Parmesan. Bake in a preheated oven, 190°C (375°F), Gas Mark 5, for about 35–40 minutes until the topping is pale golden. Serve with a green salad.

For seafood puff pastry pie, omit the Parmesan cheese and replace the lemon grass crumble with 500 g (1 lb) puff pastry. Roll out the pastry on a lightly floured surface, then place on top of the fish in the dish. Brush the top with egg yolk to glaze, then sprinkle with pepper. Bake the pie in a preheated oven, 220°C (425°F), Gas Mark 7, for 15 minutes then reduce the heat to 180°C (350°F), Gas Mark 4, and bake for a further 15–20 minutes until golden.

SALT COD WITH POTATOES

Serves **4**
Preparation time **15 minutes, plus soaking**
Cooking time **35 minutes**

500 g (1 lb) **salt cod**
4 tablespoons **olive oil**
1 **onion**, finely chopped
3 **garlic cloves**, crushed
600 ml (1 pint) **fish stock**
½ teaspoon **saffron threads**
750 g (1½ lb) **floury potatoes**, cut into
  small chunks
500 g (1 lb) **cherry plum tomatoes**, roughly
  chopped
4 tablespoons chopped **parsley**
salt and **pepper**

Put the salt cod in a bowl, cover with plenty of cold water and leave to soak for 1–2 days, changing the water twice daily. Drain the cod and cut into small chunks, discarding any skin and bones.

Heat the oil in a large saucepan and gently fry the onion for 5 minutes until softened. Add the garlic and cook for 1 minute. Add the stock and crumble in the saffron. Bring to the boil, then reduce the heat to a gentle simmer.

Add the salt cod and potatoes and cover with a lid. Cook gently for about 20 minutes until the fish and potatoes are very tender.

Stir in the tomatoes and parsley and then cook for 5 minutes until the tomatoes have softened. Season to taste (you might not need any salt, depending on the saltiness of the fish). Ladle into shallow bowls and serve with warm bread.

For smoked trout with potatoes, replace the salt cod with 300 g (10 oz) smoked trout. Cut into chunks, but don't soak in the first step. Add to the saucepan once the potatoes are cooked, along with 2 tablespoons capers, rinsed and drained, and 2 teaspoons green peppercorns in brine, rinsed, drained and crushed.

MACKEREL & CIDER VICHYSSOISE

Serves **3–4 as a main course, 8 as a starter**
Preparation time **15 minutes**
Cooking time **30 minutes**

625 g (1¼ lb) **leeks**
50 g (2 oz) **butter**
625 g (1¼ lb) **new potatoes**, diced
600 ml (1 pint) **strong cider**
600 ml (1 pint) **fish stock**
2 teaspoons **Dijon mustard**
300 g (10 oz) **smoked mackerel fillets**
5 tablespoons chopped **chives**
plenty of freshly ground **nutmeg**
200 g (7 oz) **crème fraîche**
salt and **pepper**
chive sprigs, to garnish

Trim the leeks and chop, keeping the white and green parts separate. Melt the butter in a large saucepan and gently fry the white parts and half the green parts for 5 minutes. Add the potatoes, then stir in the cider, stock and mustard and bring almost to the boil. Reduce the heat and cook gently for 20 minutes until the potatoes are soft but still holding their shape.

Flake the smoked mackerel into small pieces, discarding any skin and stray bones. Add to the pan with the chopped chives, nutmeg and remaining green leeks. Simmer gently for 5 minutes.

Stir in half the crème fraîche and season to taste with salt and pepper. Spoon into bowls, top with the remaining crème fraîche and garnish with chive sprigs.

For trout and white wine vichyssoise, replace the cider with 300 ml (½ pint) dry white wine and add an extra 300 ml (½ pint) fish stock. Instead of the mackerel, use 500 g (1 lb) fresh skinned and boned trout and flake and cook as above. Replace the crème fraîche with 150 ml (¼ pint) single cream.

OVEN-STEAMED FISH WITH GREENS

Serves **2**
Preparation time **15 minutes**
Cooking time **25 minutes**

15 g (½ oz) **fresh root ginger**
¼ teaspoon **crushed dried chillies**
1 **garlic clove**, thinly sliced
2 tablespoons **rice wine vinegar**
2 chunky **cod fillets**, each 150g–200 g
 (5–7 oz), skinned
150 ml (¼ pint) hot **fish stock**
½ **cucumber**
2 tablespoons **light soy sauce**
2 tablespoons **oyster sauce**
1 tablespoon **caster sugar**
½ bunch **spring onions**, cut into 2.5 cm
 (1 inch) lengths
25 g (1 oz) **fresh coriander**, roughly chopped
200 g (7 oz) **ready-cooked rice**

Peel and slice the ginger as finely as possible. Cut across into thin shreds and mix with the crushed chillies, garlic and 1 teaspoon of the vinegar. Spoon over the pieces of cod, rubbing it in gently.

Lightly oil a wire rack and position over a small roasting pan. Pour the stock into the pan and place the cod fillets on the rack. Cover with foil and carefully transfer to a preheated oven, 180°C (350°F), Gas Mark 4, for 20 minutes or until cooked through.

Meanwhile, peel the cucumber, cut in half and scoop out the seeds. Cut the flesh into small, chip-sized pieces. Mix together the soy sauce, oyster sauce, sugar and remaining vinegar in a small bowl.

Remove the fish from the pan and keep warm. Drain off the juices from the pan and reserve. Add the cucumber, spring onions, coriander and rice to the pan and heat through, stirring, for about 5 minutes until hot, stirring in enough of the reserved juices to make the rice slightly moist.

Pile on to serving plates, top with the fish and serve with the sauce spooned over.

For oven-steamed chicken with greens, replace the fish with 4 small skinned chicken breast fillets. Use chicken stock instead of the fish stock. Make severel deep scores in the chicken fillets, then cook as per the second step but for 30–40 minutes. Replace the oyster sauce with the same quantity of hoisin sauce.

154

CHILLI & PANCETTA MARROW CUPS

Serves **4**
Preparation time **20 minutes**
Cooking time **45 minutes**

150 g (5 oz) **ciabatta**
100 g (3½ oz) **pine nuts**
1.25 kg (2½ lb) **marrow**
50 g (2 oz) **butter**
4 tablespoons **olive oil**
75 g (3 oz) **pancetta**, cubed
3 **garlic cloves**, crushed
1 **mild red chilli**, deseeded and sliced
½ teaspoon **hot smoked paprika**
2 teaspoons chopped **thyme leaves**
small handful **curly parsley**, chopped
salt

Crumble the ciabatta into small pieces and spread out on a foil-lined grill rack. Scatter with the pine nuts and grill lightly until toasted.

Peel the marrow and cut across into 4 even-sized lengths, trimming off the ends. Using a dessertspoon, scoop out the seeds, leaving a small base in each, to make cups.

Melt the butter with 2 tablespoons of the oil in a small roasting pan and gently fry the pancetta for about 5 minutes until beginning to crisp and colour. Add the garlic, chilli and paprika and cook for a further 1 minute. Drain to a large bowl, leaving a little of the spicy oil in the pan.

Off the heat, put the marrow cups in the pan, turning them in the oil. Place upright and brush the centres with more of the spicy oil in the pan. Season with salt and bake in a preheated oven, 200°C (400°F), Gas Mark 6, for 25 minutes or until tender.

Toss the pine nuts and ciabatta with the pancetta mixture and herbs and divide between the cups. Drizzle with the remaining oil and return to the oven for a further 15 minutes.

For sun-dried tomato pumpkin cups, replace the pancetta with 50 g (2 oz) finely chopped sun-dried tomatoes and fry off in the same way. Replace the marrow with small, single-portion-sized pumpkins. Slice off the tops and scoop out the seeds. Brush the spicy oil on the insides and bake for 50 minutes or until soft.

MAPLE PORK WITH ROASTED ROOTS

Serves **4**
Preparation time **20 minutes**
Cooking time 1½ **hours**

12 **baby onions** or **shallots**, peeled but left whole
500 g (1 lb) small **waxy potatoes**, cubed
300 g (10 oz) **baby carrots**
300 g (10 oz) small **parsnips**, cut into wedges
3 tablespoons **olive oil**
2 **courgettes**, cut into chunky pieces
several **rosemary sprigs**
1 tablespoon **grainy mustard**
3 tablespoons **maple syrup**
4 large **pork chops**, trimmed of fat
salt and **pepper**

Scatter the onions or shallots, potatoes, carrots and parsnips in a large, sturdy roasting pan. Drizzle with the oil and shake the pan so that the vegetables are coated in oil. Sprinkle with salt and pepper and roast in a preheated oven, 190°C (375°F), Gas Mark 5, for 30 minutes until beginning to colour.

Add the courgettes and rosemary sprigs to the pan and toss the vegetables together. Return to the oven for a further 10 minutes.

Mix together the mustard, maple syrup and a little salt. Tuck the pork chops among the vegetables and brush with about half the maple glaze. Return to the oven for 20 minutes.

Turn the pork chops over and brush with the remaining maple glaze. Return to the oven for a further 15 minutes or until the chops are cooked through.

For honey and lemon pork, replace the carrots and parsnips with 2 large courgettes and 3 red peppers, cut into chunky wedges, and roast as above. Instead of the mustard and maple syrup, mix together 3 tablespoons clear honey, 2 tablespoons lemon juice and a 2.5 cm (1 inch) piece of fresh root ginger, grated, in the third step and use in the same way as the maple glaze.

PUMPKIN & ROOT VEGETABLE STEW

Serves **8–10**
Preparation time: **20 minutes**
Cooking time: 1½–**2 hours**

1 **pumpkin**, about 1.5 kg
  (3 lb)
4 tablespoons **sunflower** or **olive oil**
1 large **onion**, finely chopped
3–4 **garlic cloves**, crushed
1 small **red chilli**, deseeded and chopped
4 **celery sticks**, cut into
  2.5 cm (1 inch) lengths
500 g (1 lb) **carrots**, cut into 2.5 cm (1 inch) pieces
250 g (8 oz) **parsnips**, cut into 2.5 cm (1 inch) pieces
2 x 400g (13 oz) cans plum **tomatoes**
3 tablespoons **tomato purée**
1–2 tablespoons **hot paprika**
250 ml (8 fl oz) **vegetable stock**
1 **bouquet garni**
2 x 400 g (13 oz) cans **red kidney beans**, drained
salt and **pepper**
3–4 tablespoons finely chopped **parsley**, to garnish

Slice the pumpkin in half across its widest part and discard the seeds and fibres. Cut the flesh into cubes, removing the skin. You should have about 1 kg (2 lb) pumpkin flesh.

Heat the oil in a large saucepan and fry the onion, garlic and chilli until soft but not coloured. Add the pumpkin and celery and fry gently for 10 minutes. Stir in the carrots, parsnips, tomatoes, tomato purée, paprika, stock and bouquet garni. Bring to the boil, then reduce the heat, cover the pan and simmer for 1–1½ hours until the vegetables are almost tender.

Add the beans and cook for 10 minutes. Season with salt and pepper and garnish with the parsley to serve. Serve with crusty bread or garlic mashed potatoes. This stew improves with reheating.

For pumpkin goulash, heat 2 tablespoons oil in a flameproof casserole and fry 1 chopped onion until soft. Stir in 1 tablespoon paprika and 1 teaspoon caraway seeds and cook for 1 minute. Add a 400 g (13 oz) can chopped tomatoes and 2 tablespoons dark muscovado sugar and bring to the boil. Add 375 g (12 oz) thickly sliced pumpkin, 250 g (8 oz) diced potatoes, a large sliced carrot and 1 chopped red pepper. Season, cover and bring to the boil, then simmer for 1–1½ hours. To serve, stir in 150 ml (¼ pint) soured cream.

CREAMY PORK & CIDER HOTPOT

Serves **4**
Preparation time **25 minutes**
Cooking time 1½ **hours**

625 g (1¼ lb) piece lean, boneless **leg of pork**
2 teaspoons **plain flour**
25 g (1 oz) **butter**
1 tablespoon **oil**
1 small **onion**, chopped
1 large **leek**, chopped
450 ml (¾ pint) **cider**
1 tablespoon chopped **sage**
2 tablespoons **grainy mustard**
100 ml (3½ fl oz) **crème fraîche**
2 **pears**, peeled, cored and thickly sliced
450 g (14½ oz) **sweet potatoes**, scrubbed and
   thinly sliced
2 tablespoons **chilli-infused oil**
salt
chopped parsley, to garnish

Cut the pork into small pieces, discarding any excess fat. Season the flour with a little salt and use to coat the meat.

Melt the butter with the oil in a shallow, flameproof casserole and gently fry the pork in batches until lightly browned, draining each batch to a plate.

Add the onion and leek to the casserole and fry gently for 5 minutes. Return the meat to the pan, along with the cider, sage and mustard. Bring just to the boil, then cover with a lid, reduce the heat and cook on the lowest setting for 30 minutes.

Stir the crème fraîche into the sauce and scatter the pear slices on top. Arrange the sweet potato slices in overlapping layers on top, putting the end pieces underneath and keeping the best slices for the top layer. Brush with the chilli oil and sprinkle with salt.

Place in a preheated oven, 160°C (325°F), Gas Mark 3, for 45 minutes or until the potatoes are tender and lightly browned. Scatter with the chopped parsley.

For creamy pork and white wine hotpot, replace the cider with the same quantity of dry white wine in the third step. Use the same quantity of ordinary potatoes as the sweet potatoes and layer on top as above in the fourth step. Increase the cooking time in the oven to about 1 hour.

PORK & TOMATO LINGUINE

Serves **4**
Preparation time **20 minutes**
Cooking time **40 minutes**

300 g (10 oz) **leg of pork**
2 teaspoons **mild paprika**
250 g (8 oz) **dried linguine**
5 tablespoons **olive oil**
50 g (2 oz) **chorizo**, diced
1 **red onion**, sliced
250 g (8 oz) **passata**
3 tablespoons **sun-dried tomato paste**
½ teaspoon **saffron threads**
750 ml (1¼ pints) **chicken stock** or **vegetable stock**
50 g (2 oz) **fresh** or **frozen peas**
3 **garlic cloves**, crushed
4 tablespoons chopped **parsley**
finely grated **rind** of 1 **lemon**
salt and **pepper**

Toss the pork in the paprika and salt and pepper. Roll up half the pasta in a tea towel. Run the tea towel firmly over the edge of a work surface so that you hear the pasta breaking into short lengths. Tip into a bowl and break the remainder in the same way.

Heat 3 tablespoons of the oil in a large frying pan and fry the pork, chorizo and onion very gently for about 10 minutes until browned.

Stir in the passata, tomato paste, saffron and stock and bring to the boil. Reduce the heat and cook very gently for 15 minutes until the meat is tender.

Sprinkle in the pasta and stir well to mix. Cook gently, stirring frequently, for 10 minutes until the pasta is tender, adding a little water to the pan if the mixture becomes dry before the pasta is cooked. Add the peas and cook for a further 3 minutes.

Stir in the garlic, parsley, lemon rind and remaining oil. Check the seasoning and serve.

For chicken and tomato linguine, omit the pork and use 4 skinned and boned chicken thighs cut into chunks. Toss the chicken in the paprika and salt and pepper as in the first step. Follow the second step to fry the chicken, replacing the chorizo with the same quantity of smoked pork sausage. Cook as above, using chicken stock.

BEAN, PANCETTA & FONTINA RISOTTO

Serves **2**
Preparation time **15 minutes**
Cooking time **30 minutes**

3 tablespoons **olive oil**
1 **onion**, finely chopped
3 **garlic cloves**, crushed
75 g (3 oz) **pancetta**, chopped
250 g (8 oz) **risotto rice**
½ teaspoon **dried mixed herbs**
900 ml (1½ pints) hot **chicken stock** or **vegetable stock**
125 g (4 oz) **broad beans**, defrosted if frozen
75 g (3 oz) **peas**
75 g (3 oz) **fontina cheese**, coarsely grated
50 g (2 oz) **butter**
2 tablespoons freshly grated **Parmesan cheese**, plus extra shavings to garnish
1 tablespoon chopped **mint leaves**
6–8 **basil leaves**, shredded, plus extra to garnish
salt and **pepper**

Heat the oil in a large saucepan and fry the onion until softened. Add the garlic and pancetta to the pan and fry until the pancetta is golden brown. Add the rice and stir the grains into the onion mixture to coat in the oil.

With the pan still over a medium heat, add the dried mixed herbs and the hot stock to the rice and bring the mixture to the boil, stirring constantly. Season with salt and pepper and reduce to a simmer. Simmer for 10 minutes, stirring frequently. Add the broad beans and peas and continue to cook for a further 10 minutes.

Remove the pan from the heat and stir the fontina through the risotto. Dot the butter on top together with the Parmesan. Cover the pan with a lid and set aside for 2–3 minutes to allow the cheese and butter to melt into the risotto.

Remove the lid and add the mint and basil and gently stir the cheese, butter and herbs through the risotto. Serve immediately, garnished with basil leaves and extra shavings of Parmesan.

For tomato and mushroom risotto, fry the onion, then 250 g (8 oz) sliced mushrooms, 2 crushed garlic cloves, 1 teaspoon dried oregano and 3 large, finely chopped tomatoes over a low heat for 5 minutes. Stir in 400 g (13 oz) risotto rice, then a ladleful from 1 litre (1¾ pints) of hot stock and cook over a low heat until absorbed. Add the remaining stock a ladleful at a time, and cook for about 25 minutes until absorbed. Stir in 25 g (1 oz) butter, 40 g (1½ oz) Parmesan and season.

BRAISED LIVER & BACON WITH PRUNES

Serves **4**
Preparation time **15 minutes**
Cooking time **1 hour**

400 g (13 oz) **lamb's liver**, sliced
2 teaspoons **plain flour**
8 **thin-cut smoked streaky bacon** rashers
16 **pitted prunes**
3 tablespoons **olive oil**
2 large **onions**, thinly sliced
750 g (1½ lb) large **potatoes**, sliced
450 ml (¾ pint) **lamb stock** or **chicken stock**
3 tablespoons roughly chopped **parsley**, to garnish
salt and **pepper**

Cut the liver into thick strips, removing any tubes. Season the flour with salt and pepper and use to coat the liver. Cut the bacon rashers in half and wrap a piece around each prune.

Heat half the oil in a flameproof casserole and fry the onions until lightly browned. Drain to a plate. Add the liver to the casserole and brown on both sides. Drain to the plate. Add the remaining oil to the pan with the bacon-wrapped prunes and fry on both sides until browned. Drain.

Arrange the potatoes in the casserole and put all the fried ingredients on top. Pour the stock over, season lightly and bring to the boil. Cover with a lid and transfer to a preheated oven, 180°C (350°F), Gas Mark 4, for 50 minutes until the potatoes are very tender. Serve sprinkled with the parsley.

For lamb's liver with cranberries and bacon, fry 2 thinly sliced onions and 150 g (5 oz) diced smoked back bacon for 10 minutes in 2 tablespoons oil. Set aside. Melt 25 g (1 oz) butter and fry 625 g (1¼ lb) sliced lamb's liver for 3 minutes over a high heat, turning once or twice, until browned on the outside and just pink in the centre. Add 75 g (3 oz) frozen cranberries and 2 tablespoons each cranberry sauce, red wine vinegar and water, season and cook for 2 minutes, stirring. Stir in the onions and bacon and heat through gently, stirring to combine.

PORK & CABBAGE BAKE

Serves **4**
Preparation time **15 minutes**
Cooking time **40 minutes**

65 g (2½ oz) **butter**
500 g (1 lb) **pork and apple sausages**, skinned
1 **onion**, chopped
2 teaspoons **caraway seeds**
625 g (1¼ lb) **Savoy cabbage**, shredded
400 g (13 oz) **floury potatoes**, diced
200 ml (7 fl oz) **chicken stock** or **vegetable stock**
1 tablespoon **cider vinegar**
salt and **pepper**

Melt half the butter in a shallow, flameproof casserole and add the sausagemeat. Fry quickly, breaking the meat up with a wooden spoon and stirring until browned.

Add the onion, caraway and a little seasoning and fry for a further 5 minutes.

Stir in the cabbage and potatoes, mixing the ingredients together thoroughly. Pour the stock and cider vinegar over them and add a little more seasoning. Dot with the remaining butter and cover with a lid.

Bake in a preheated oven, 160°C (325°F), Gas Mark 3, for 30 minutes until the cabbage and potatoes are very tender. Serve with chunks of wholegrain bread.

For chicken and cabbage bake, replace the sausages with 400 g (13 oz) skinned and boned chicken thighs, cut into chunks. Shallow-fry as above in the first step. Instead of the Savoy cabbage, use the same quantity of shredded red cabbage and replace the cider vinegar with 1 tablespoon red wine vinegar along with 2 tablespoons clear honey. Cook as above.

LAMB WITH ORANGE & CHICKPEAS

Serves **8**
Preparation time **25 minutes, plus overnight soaking**
Cooking time **2½ hours**

225 g (7½ oz) **chickpeas**, soaked in cold water overnight
4 tablespoons **olive oil**
2 teaspoons **ground cumin**
1 teaspoon each **ground cinnamon**, **ginger** and **turmeric**
½ teaspoon **saffron threads**
1.5 kg (3 lb) **shoulder of lamb**, trimmed of all fat and cut into 2.5 cm (1 inch) cubes
2 **onions**, roughly chopped
3 **garlic cloves**, finely chopped
2 **tomatoes**, skinned, deseeded and chopped
12 **pitted black olives**, sliced
grated **rind** of **1 unwaxed lemon**
grated **rind** of **1 unwaxed orange**
6 tablespoons chopped **fresh coriander**
salt and **pepper**

Drain the chickpeas and rinse under cold water. Put them in a flameproof casserole or large saucepan, cover with water and bring to the boil, then reduce the heat and simmer, covered, for about 1–1½ hours until tender.

Meanwhile, combine half the olive oil with the cumin, cinnamon, ginger, turmeric and saffron in a large bowl, plus ½ teaspoon salt and ½ teaspoon pepper. Add the cubed lamb, toss and set aside in a cool place for 20 minutes. Wipe out the pan.

Heat the remaining oil in the pan. Fry the lamb in batches until well browned, draining to a plate.

Add the onions to the pan and cook, stirring constantly until browned. Stir in the garlic and the tomatoes with 250 ml (8 fl oz) water, stirring and scraping the base of the pan. Return the lamb to the pan and add enough water to just cover. Bring to the boil over a high heat and skim off any surface foam. Reduce the heat, cover and simmer for about 1 hour or until the meat is tender.

Drain the chickpeas and reserve the cooking liquid. Add the chickpeas with about 250 ml (8 fl oz) of the cooking liquid to the lamb. Simmer for 30 minutes.

Stir in the olives and lemon and orange rind and simmer for a final 30 minutes.

Mix in half the chopped coriander then serve garnished with the remaining coriander. When cool, this dish may be frozen in a plastic container.

LAMB WITH ARTICHOKES & GREMOLATA

Serves **4**
Preparation time **20 minutes**
Cooking time **25 minutes**

500 g (1 lb) **lamb neck fillet**
2 teaspoons **plain flour**
4 tablespoons **olive oil**
1 **onion**, finely chopped
1 **celery stick**, thinly sliced
150 ml (¼ pint) **chicken stock** or **vegetable stock**
2 **garlic cloves**, finely chopped
finely grated **rind** of 1 **lemon**
4 tablespoons chopped **parsley**
150 g (5 oz) shop-bought or homemade **roasted artichokes**, thinly sliced
4 tablespoons **double cream**
salt and **pepper**

Trim any excess fat from the lamb and cut into thin slices. Season the flour with salt and pepper and use to coat the lamb. Heat half the oil in a large frying pan and fry the lamb, half at a time, until browned, draining each batch to a plate.

Gently fry the onion and celery in the remaining oil for 5 minutes until softened. Return the lamb to the pan and stir in the stock. Bring to the boil, then reduce the heat and simmer very gently for about 8 minutes until the lamb is cooked through.

Meanwhile, make the gremolata by mixing together the garlic, lemon rind and parsley.

Add the artichokes and cream to the pan and heat through for 2 minutes. Check the seasoning and serve sprinkled with the gremolata.

For home-roasted artichokes, thoroughly drain and slice a can of artichoke hearts. Drizzle with olive oil, sprinkle with dried oregano and seasoning and roast in a preheated oven, 200°C (400°F), Gas Mark 6, for 20–25 minutes.

LAMB & RED RICE PILAF

Serves **3–4**
Preparation time **20 minutes**
Cooking time **1 hour 10 minutes**

2 teaspoons **cumin seeds**
2 teaspoons **coriander seeds**
10 **cardamom pods**
3 tablespoons **olive oil**
500 g (1 lb) **shoulder of lamb**, diced
2 **red onions**, sliced
25 g (1 oz) **fresh root ginger**, grated
2 **garlic cloves**, crushed
½ teaspoon **ground turmeric**
200 g (7 oz) **red rice**
600 ml (1 pint) **lamb stock** or **chicken stock**
40 g (1½ oz) **pine nuts**
75 g (3 oz) ready-to-eat **dried apricots**,
  thinly sliced
50 g (2 oz) **rocket**
salt and **pepper**

Grind the cumin, coriander and cardamom pods using a pestle and mortar until the cardamom pods have opened to release the seeds. Discard the shells.

Heat the oil in a small, sturdy roasting pan and fry the spices for 30 seconds. Add the lamb and onions and toss with the spices. Transfer to a preheated oven, 180°C (350°F), Gas Mark 4, and cook for 40 minutes until the lamb and onions are browned.

Return to the hob and stir in the ginger, garlic, turmeric and rice. Add the stock and bring to the boil. Cover with a lid or foil and cook over the lowest setting for about 30 minutes until the rice is tender and the stock has been absorbed.

Stir in the pine nuts and apricots and season to taste. Scatter with the rocket and fold in very lightly. Pile on to serving plates and serve immediately.

For homemade lamb stock, put 750 g (1½ lb) roasted lamb bones and meat scraps in a large, heavy-based saucepan with 1 large onion, roughly chopped, 2 large carrots and 2 celery sticks, both roughly sliced, 1 teaspoon black peppercorns and several bay leaves and thyme sprigs. Just cover with cold water and bring slowly to the boil. Reduce the heat and simmer for 3 hours, skimming the surface if necessary. Strain through a sieve and leave to cool. Store for up to a week in the refrigerator or freezer.

STEAK & ALE CASSEROLE

Serves **5–6**
Preparation time **20 minutes**
Cooking time **1¾ hours**

2 tablespoons **plain flour**
1 kg (2 lb) **braising steak**, cut into chunks
25 g (1 oz) **butter**
1 tablespoon **oil**
2 **onions**, chopped
2 **celery sticks**, sliced
several **thyme sprigs**
2 **bay leaves**
400 ml (14 fl oz) **strong ale**
300 ml (½ pint) **beef stock**
2 tablespoons **black treacle**
500 g (1 lb) **parsnips**, peeled and cut
  into wedges
salt and **pepper**

Season the flour with salt and pepper and use to coat the beef. Melt the butter with the oil in a large, flameproof casserole and fry the beef in batches until deep brown. Drain with a slotted spoon while cooking the remainder.

Add the onions and celery and fry gently for 5 minutes. Return the beef to the pan and add the herbs, ale, stock and treacle. Bring just to the boil, then reduce the heat and cover with a lid. Bake in a preheated oven, 160°C (325°F), Gas Mark 3, for 1 hour.

Add the parsnips to the dish and return to the oven for a further 30 minutes or until the beef and parsnips are tender. Check the seasoning and serve.

For potato champ to serve as an accompaniment, cook 1.5 kg (3 lb) scrubbed potatoes in a large saucepan of salted boiling water for 20 minutes. Peel away the skins, then return to the pan and mash. Beat in 150 ml (¼ pint) milk, 3–4 finely chopped spring onions and 50 g (2 oz) butter. Season with salt and pepper and then serve.

BEEF & FLAT NOODLE SOUP

Serves **4–6**
Preparation time **30 minutes**
Cooking time **2 hours**

1 tablespoon **vegetable oil**
500 g (1 lb) **braising beef**
1.8 litres (3 pints) **beef stock**
4 **star anise**
1 **cinnamon stick**
1 teaspoon **black peppercorns**
4 **shallots**, thinly sliced
4 **garlic cloves**, crushed
7 cm (3 inch) piece of **fresh root ginger**, finely sliced
300 g (10 oz) **flat rice noodles**
125 g (4 oz) **bean sprouts**
6 **spring onions**, thinly sliced
handful of **fresh coriander**
250 g (8 oz) **beef fillet**, sliced
2 tablespoons **fish sauce**
salt and **pepper**
hot red chillies, to garnish

nuoc cham sauce
2 **red chillies**, chopped
1 **garlic clove**, chopped
1½ tablespoons **caster sugar**
1 tablespoon **lime juice**
1 tablespoon **rice wine vinegar**
3 tablespoons **fish sauce**

Heat the oil in a large saucepan or casserole and sear the beef on all sides until thoroughly brown.

Add the stock, star anise, cinnamon, black peppercorns, half the shallots, the garlic and ginger. Bring to the boil, removing any scum. Reduce the heat, cover the pan with a lid and simmer very gently for about 1½ hours or until the beef is tender.

To make the nuoc cham sauce, pound the chilli, garlic and sugar until smooth, using a pestle and mortar. Add the lime juice, vinegar, fish sauce and 4 tablespoons water and blend together well.

When the beef from the broth is tender, lift it out and slice it thinly. Add the noodles to the broth and cook gently for 2–3 minutes to soften. Add the bean sprouts, along with the sliced beef and heat for 1 minute. Strain the broth, noodles and bean sprouts to warmed serving bowls. Scatter with the beef fillet, spring onions, coriander and remaining onions or shallots. Garnish with the chillies. Serve with the nuoc cham sauce.

For tofu and flat noodle soup, replace the beef with 250 g (8 oz) tofu, cut into small squares and drained on kitchen paper. Sear as above. Replace the beef stock with the same quantity of vegetable stock and replace the fish sauce with the same quantity of soy sauce throughout. Reduce the cooking time to 20 minutes. Add 150 g (5 oz) frozen soya beans with the noodles.

VENISON & CHESTNUT STEW

Serves **6**
Preparation time **30 minutes**
Cooking time **2½ hours**

2 tablespoons **plain flour**
875 g (1¾ lb) lean **stewing venison**, cut into small pieces
10 **juniper berries**
3 tablespoons **oil**
150 g (5 oz) **bacon lardons**
1 **large onion**, chopped
3 **carrots**, sliced
½ teaspoon **ground cloves**
300 ml (½ pint) **red wine**
200 ml (7 fl oz) **game stock** or **chicken stock**
1 tablespoon **red wine vinegar**
2 tablespoons **redcurrant jelly**
350 g (12 oz) **cooked chestnuts**
1 kg (2 lb) large **potatoes**, thinly sliced
2 teaspoons chopped **rosemary**
40 g (1½ oz) **butter**, softened
salt and **pepper**

Season the flour with salt and pepper and use to coat the venison. Crush the juniper berries using a pestle and mortar.

Heat the oil in a large, flameproof casserole and fry the meat in batches until browned, draining each batch to a plate. Add the bacon, onion and carrots to the casserole and fry gently for 5 minutes or until browned.

Stir in the crushed juniper berries, cloves, wine, stock, vinegar and redcurrant jelly and bring to the boil. Reduce the heat and stir in the chestnuts and venison.

Cover with a lid and place in a preheated oven, 160°C (325°F), Gas Mark 3, for 1 hour. Check the seasoning, then scatter with the potatoes and return to the oven, covered, for a further 30 minutes.

Blend the rosemary with the butter and a little seasoning and dot over the potatoes. Return to the oven, uncovered, for a further 45 minutes or until the potatoes are lightly browned.

For homemade game stock, brown 500 g (1 lb) game trimmings (for example pheasant or pigeon bones) in a roasting pan in a preheated oven, 200°C (400°F), Gas Mark 6, for 15 minutes. Tip into a saucepan with 1 unpeeled, roughly chopped onion, 1 chopped carrot, 2 chopped celery sticks, 1 glass red wine, 1 teaspoon juniper berries and 3 bay leaves. Cover with water. Bring to a simmer and cook very gently for 1½ hours. Strain through a sieve and leave to cool.

STIFADO

Serves **3–4**
Preparation time **20 minutes**
Cooking time **2½ hours**

½ teaspoon **ground black pepper**
½ teaspoon **ground allspice**
2 teaspoons finely chopped **rosemary**
1 **rabbit** (about 750–875 g/1½–1¾ lb), jointed
3 tablespoons **olive oil**
3 large **onions**, sliced
2 teaspoons **caster sugar**
3 **garlic cloves**, crushed
75 ml (3 fl oz) **red wine vinegar**
300 ml (½ pint) **red wine**
50 g (2 oz) **tomato purée**
salt
flat leaf parsley, to sprinkle

Mix together the pepper, allspice and rosemary and rub over the rabbit.

Heat the oil in a large, flameproof casserole and fry the meat in batches on all sides until thoroughly browned. Drain the meat to a plate.

Add the onions to the pan with the sugar and fry, stirring frequently, for about 15 minutes until caramelized. Stir in the garlic and then cook for a further 1 minute.

Add the vinegar and wine to the pan. Bring to the boil and continue to boil until the mixture has reduced by about a third. Stir in the tomato purée and a little salt and return the meat to the pan.

Cover with a lid and place in a preheated oven, 150°C (300°F), Gas Mark 2, for about 2 hours until the meat is very tender and the juices thick and glossy. Check the seasoning and sprinkle with the parsley.

For Greek salad to serve as an accompaniment, combine 6 roughly chopped tomatoes, 1 thickly sliced cucumber, ½ small, thinly sliced red onion and 125 g (4 oz) kalamata olives together in a large bowl. Drizzle with olive oil and lemon juice to taste. Crumble 200 g (8 oz) feta cheese into pieces and scatter over the salad. Season with plenty of black pepper.

BEEF, PUMPKIN & GINGER STEW

Serves **6**
Preparation time **20 minutes**
Cooking time 1½ **hours**

2 tablespoons **plain flour**
750 g (1½ lb) **lean stewing beef**, diced
25 g (1 oz) **butter**
3 tablespoons **oil**
1 **onion**, chopped
2 **carrots**, sliced
2 **parsnips**, sliced
3 **bay leaves**
several **thyme sprigs**
2 tablespoons **tomato purée**
625 g (1¼ lb) **pumpkin**, peeled, deseeded and
  cut into small chunks
1 tablespoon **dark muscovado sugar**
50 g (2 oz) **fresh root ginger**, finely chopped
small handful of **parsley**, chopped, plus extra
  to garnish
salt and **pepper**

Season the flour with salt and pepper and use to coat the beef. Melt the butter with the oil in a large saucepan and fry the meat in 2 batches until browned, draining with a slotted spoon.

Add the onion, carrots and parsnips to the saucepan and fry gently for 5 minutes.

Return the meat to the pan and add the herbs and tomato purée. Add just enough water to cover the ingredients and bring slowly to the boil. Reduce the heat to its lowest setting, cover with a lid and simmer very gently for 45 minutes.

Add the pumpkin, sugar, ginger and parsley and cook for a further 30 minutes until the pumpkin is soft and the meat is tender. Check the seasoning and serve scattered with extra parsley.

For beef, sweet potato and horseradish stew, replace the pumpkin with 500 g (1 lb) sweet potato, cut into chunks and cooked as above. Replace the ginger with 3 tablespoons hot horseradish sauce.

DAUBE OF BEEF

Serves **5–6**
Preparation time **20 minutes**
Cooking time 1½ **hours**

1 tablespoon **plain flour**
1 kg (2 lb) **braising beef**, diced
4 tablespoons **olive oil**
100 g (3½ oz) **streaky bacon**, chopped
1 large **onion**, chopped
4 **garlic cloves**, crushed
several pared strips **orange rind**
200 g (7 oz) **carrots**, sliced
several **thyme sprigs**
300 ml (½ pint) **red wine**
300 ml (½ pint) **beef stock**
100 g (3½ oz) **pitted black olives**
4 tablespoons **sun-dried tomato paste**
salt and **pepper**

Season the flour with salt and pepper and use to coat the beef. Heat the oil in a large, flameproof casserole and fry the meat in batches until browned, draining each batch to a plate. Add the bacon and onion to the casserole and fry for 5 minutes.

Return all the meat to the casserole with the garlic, orange rind, carrots, thyme sprigs, wine and stock. Bring almost to the boil, then cover with a lid and transfer to a preheated oven, 160°C (325°F), Gas Mark 3, for 1¼ hours or until the meat is very tender.

Put the olives and sun-dried tomato paste in a blender or food processor and blend very lightly until the olives are chopped but not puréed. Stir into the casserole and return to the oven for a further 15 minutes. Check the seasoning and serve with crusty bread, beans or mashed potato.

For beef bourguignon, place the same quantity of beef overnight in a marinade of sliced onion, parsley and thyme sprigs, crumbled bay leaf, 400 ml (14 fl oz) red burgundy and 2 tablespoons each brandy and olive oil. Cook 150 g (5 oz) diced bacon in 50 g (2 oz) butter in a flameproof casserole, then 24 small pickling onions and 500 g (1 lb) button mushrooms and set aside. Remove the beef from the marinade. Brown the beef in the casserole, stir in 1 tablespoon plain flour, then the strained marinade, 300 ml (½ pint) beef stock, 1 crushed garlic clove, 1 bouquet garni and seasoning. Simmer, covered, for 2 hours. Return the bacon, pickling onions and mushrooms, cover and simmer for 30 minutes.

VEAL WITH WINE & LEMON

Serves **5–6**
Preparation time **20 minutes**
Cooking time **40 minutes**

2 tablespoons **olive oil**
1 kg (2 lb) **veal**, chopped into cubes
2 **onions**, sliced
4 **garlic cloves**, sliced
2 **baby fennel bulbs**, roughly chopped
300 ml (½ pint) **white wine**
300 ml (½ pint) **chicken stock**
rind of ½ **lemon**, cut into julienne strips (matchsticks)
4 **bay leaves**
1 tablespoon chopped **thyme**
salt and **pepper**

Heat the oil in a frying pan over a high heat, then fry off the meat in batches, draining to a plate with a slotted spoon.

Add the onions and garlic to the pan and cook over a medium heat until golden. Add the fennel and fry for a further 3–4 minutes or until softened.

Return the veal to the pan and add the wine, stock, lemon rind, bay leaves and thyme. Bring to the boil.

Reduce the heat and simmer, covered, for a further 20–25 minutes. Season to taste and serve.

For fragrant brown rice to serve as an accompaniment, wash 400 g (13 oz) brown basmati rice in a sieve until the water runs clear. Put crushed seeds from 4 cardamom pods, a large pinch of saffron threads, 1 cinnamon stick, ½ teaspoon cumin seeds and 2 bay leaves in a flameproof casserole and dry-fry over a medium heat for 2–3 minutes. Add 1 tablespoon olive oil, and when hot, stir in 1 chopped onion and cook for 10 minutes, stirring frequently. Add the rice, then stir in 600 ml (1 pint) water, 2 tablespoons lemon juice and salt and pepper. Bring to the boil, then cover and simmer for 15 minutes until all the water has been absorbed, adding a little more water if the mixture dries out before it is cooked. Leave to stand for a few minutes before serving.

VEAL WITH TOMATOES & CAPERS

Serves **4**
Preparation time **20 minutes**
Cooking time **2¼ hours**

1 tablespoon **plain flour**
4 thick slices **shin of veal**
4 tablespoons **olive oil**
2 **onions**, finely chopped
2 **garlic cloves**, crushed
75 g (3 oz) **prosciutto**, torn into small pieces
pared **rind** of 1 **lemon**
300 ml (½ pint) **white wine**
several **thyme sprigs**
4 **tomatoes**, skinned and cut into wedges
2 tablespoons **capers**, rinsed and drained
salt and **pepper**

Season the flour with salt and pepper and use to coat the meat. Heat the oil in a flameproof casserole and fry the pieces of meat on all sides until browned. Drain.

Add the onions to the pan and fry gently for 5 minutes. Add the garlic, prosciutto and strips of lemon rind and cook for 1 minute. Add the wine and thyme sprigs and bring to the boil.

Return the veal to the casserole and tuck the tomatoes around. Scatter with the capers and cover with a lid. Place in a preheated oven, 160°C (325°F), Gas Mark 3, for about 2 hours until the meat is very tender. Check the seasoning and serve.

For spicy polenta with garlic to serve as an accompaniment, bring to the boil 900 ml (1½ pints) salted water in a large saucepan. Meanwhile, melt 25 g (1 oz) butter and fry 1 crushed garlic clove with pinch of dried chilli flakes for 1 minute. Remove from heat. Gradually whisk 150 g (5 oz) polenta into the boiling water, add the garlic butter and 2 tablespoons chopped, fresh mixed herbs. Stir over a low heat for 8–10 minutes until the polenta thickens. Remove from heat, beat in 25 g (1 oz) butter and 50 g (2 oz) freshly grated Parmesan cheese and season.

CHICKEN & PICKLED WALNUT PILAF

Serves **4**
Preparation time **20 minutes**
Cooking time **35 minutes**

400 g (13 oz) skinned and boned **chicken thighs**, cut
   into small pieces
2 teaspoons **Moroccan spice blend**
4 tablespoons **olive oil**
50 g (2 oz) **pine nuts**
1 large **onion**, chopped
3 **garlic cloves**, sliced
½ teaspoon **ground turmeric**
250 g (8 oz) mixed **long-grain** and **wild rice**
300 ml (½ pint) **chicken stock**
3 pieces of **stem ginger**, finely chopped
3 tablespoons chopped **parsley**
2 tablespoons chopped **mint**
50 g (2 oz) **pickled walnuts**, sliced
salt and **pepper**

Toss the chicken pieces in the spice blend and a little salt.

Heat the oil in a large frying pan or sauté pan and fry the pine nuts until
they begin to colour. Drain with a slotted spoon.

Add the chicken to the pan and fry gently for 6–8 minutes, stirring until
lightly browned.

Stir in the onion and fry gently for 5 minutes. Add the garlic and turmeric
and fry for a further 1 minute. Add the rice and stock and bring to the
boil. Reduce the heat to its lowest setting and simmer very gently for
about 15 minutes until the rice is tender and the stock absorbed.
Add a little water if the liquid has been absorbed before the rice is
cooked through.

Stir in the ginger, parsley, mint, walnuts and pine nuts. Season to taste
and heat through gently for 2 minutes before serving.

For homemade Moroccan spice blend, mix together ½ teaspoon
each of crushed fennel, cumin, coriander and mustard seeds with
¼ teaspoon each of ground cloves and cinnamon.

AROMATIC BRAISED DUCK

Serves **4**
Preparation time **25 minutes**
Cooking time **2 hours**

4 **duck portions**
2 teaspoons **Chinese
   five-spice powder**
2 **lemon grass stalks**, bruised
5 **garlic cloves**, crushed
4 **red shallots**, chopped
125 g (4 oz) **dried shiitake mushrooms**, soaked for
   30 minutes
5 cm (2 inch) piece of **fresh root ginger**, peeled and
   cut into thick julienne strips
600 ml (1 pint) **chicken stock**
25 g (1 oz) dried **medlar berries** or **Chinese
   red dates**
15 g (½ oz) dried **black fungus**, broken into pieces
1 tablespoon **fish sauce**
2 teaspoons **cornflour**
4 **spring onions**, quartered
salt and **pepper**
handful of **fresh coriander**,
   to garnish

Season the duck portions with the five-spice powder. Place them skin-
side down in a very hot frying pan or casserole to brown the skin. Turn
the pieces over. Add the lemon grass, garlic, shallots, mushrooms and
ginger to the pan, then cover the duck with the stock. Cover the pan
with a lid and simmer very gently for 1½ hours.

Remove the duck from the pan and add the medlar berries or Chinese
red dates, black fungus and fish sauce. Season with salt and pepper to
taste. Mix the cornflour to a smooth paste with a little water and add to
the pan. Bring the sauce to the boil, stirring constantly, and cook until
thickened. Return the duck to the pan and simmer gently for 30 minutes.

Add the spring onions to the sauce and garnish the duck with
the coriander.

For stir-fried pak choi to serve as an accompaniment, heat tablespoon
olive oil in a nonstick sauté pan over a high heat. Add 500 g (1 lb) pak
choi, halved, a handful at a time, stirring occasionally. Cover the pan
and cook for 2–3 minutes until the bok choi leaves have wilted. Mix
together 1 teaspoon tamari sauce, 1 tablespoon Chinese rice wine and
3 tablespoons vegetable stock in a small bowl. Add a cornflour paste
made from ½ tablespoon cornflour mixed with 1 tablespoon water and
pour over the pak choi, stirring constantly until the sauce thickens.

CHICKEN, OKRA & RED LENTIL DHAL

Serves **4**
Preparation time **15 minutes**
Cooking time **45 minutes**

2 teaspoons **ground cumin**
1 teaspoon **ground coriander**
½ teaspoon **cayenne pepper**
¼ teaspoon **ground turmeric**
500 g (1 lb) skinned and boned **chicken thighs**, cut into large pieces
3 tablespoons **oil**
1 **onion**, sliced
2 **garlic cloves**, crushed
25 g (1 oz) **fresh root ginger**, finely chopped
750 ml (1¼ pints) **water**
300 g (10 oz) **red lentils**, rinsed
200 g (7 oz) **okra**
small handful of **fresh coriander**, chopped
salt
lime wedges, to garnish

Mix together the cumin, coriander, cayenne and turmeric and toss with the chicken pieces.

Heat the oil in a large saucepan. Fry the chicken pieces in batches until deep golden, draining each batch to a plate. Add the onion to the pan and fry for 5 minutes until browned. Stir in the garlic and ginger and cook for a further 1 minute.

Return the chicken to the pan and add the measurement water. Bring to the boil, then reduce the heat and simmer very gently, covered, for 20 minutes until the chicken is cooked through. Add the lentils and cook for 5 minutes. Stir in the okra, coriander and a little salt and cook for a further 5 minutes until the lentils are tender but not completely pulpy.

Check the seasoning and serve in shallow bowls with lime wedges, chutney and poppadums.

For chicken, courgette and chilli dhal, use 3 medium courgettes, thinly sliced, instead of the okra. For a hotter flavour, add a thinly sliced medium-strength red chilli with the garlic and ginger.

CHICKEN & MUSHROOMS WITH POLENTA

Serves **4**
Preparation time **20 minutes**
Cooking time **55 minutes**

25 g (1 oz) **butter**
1 **onion**, chopped
500 g (1 lb) lean **chicken**, diced
250 g (8 oz) **mushrooms**, sliced
2 teaspoons **plain flour**
150 ml (¼ pint) **chicken stock**
1 tablespoon **grainy mustard**
4 tablespoons chopped **parsley**
100 ml (3½ fl oz) **single cream**
200 g (7 oz) **fresh soya beans** or 400 g (13 oz) can **flageolet beans**, drained
500 g (1 lb) pack **ready-cooked polenta**
50 g (2 oz) **Gruyère cheese**, grated
salt and **pepper**

Melt the butter in a shallow, flameproof casserole. Add the onion and chicken and fry gently for 6–8 minutes, stirring frequently, until lightly browned.

Add the mushrooms and fry for a further 5 minutes. Sprinkle in the flour, then add the stock, mustard, parsley and a little seasoning. Bring to the boil, then reduce the heat and stir in the cream and beans.

Slice the polenta very thinly and arrange, overlapping the slices, on top of the chicken. Sprinkle with the cheese and a little black pepper.

Place in a preheated oven, 190°C (375°F), Gas Mark 5, for 30–40 minutes until the cheese is melted and beginning to brown. Serve with a leafy salad.

For chicken and mushrooms with cheese toasts, replace the polenta with 8 thin slices of French bread. Arrange over the chicken, then sprinkle with the same quantity of Cheddar cheese instead of the Gruyère. Cook as above, until the cheese has melted and the bread is turning golden.

TURKEY CHILLI POBLANO

Serves **6**
Preparation time **25 minutes**
Cooking time **1 hour**

125 g (4 oz) **flaked almonds**
50 g (2 oz) **peanuts**
½ tablespoon **coriander seeds**
1 teaspoon **ground cloves**
3 tablespoons **sesame seeds**
½ **cinnamon stick**
1 teaspoon **fennel seeds** or **aniseed**
4 large **dried chillies**
1 **green jalapeño chilli**, chopped
400 g (13 oz) can **chopped tomatoes**
75 g (3 oz) **raisins**
6 tablespoons **vegetable oil**
2 **onions**, finely chopped
3 **garlic cloves**, crushed
625 g (1¼ lb) **turkey fillets**, finely sliced or cubed
300 ml (½ pint) **vegetable stock**
50 g (2 oz) **bitter plain chocolate**, roughly chopped

To garnish
red and green chillies, finely chopped

Spread the almonds, peanuts, coriander seeds, cloves, sesame seeds, cinnamon, fennel or aniseed and dried chillies over a baking sheet and roast in a preheated oven, 200°C (400°F), Gas Mark 6, for 10 minutes, stirring once or twice.

Remove from the oven and put the nuts and spices in a food processor or blender and process until well combined. Add the chopped green chilli and process once more until well mixed.

Spoon the spice mixture into a bowl and mix in the tomatoes and raisins.

Heat the oil in a large saucepan and fry the onions and garlic with the turkey on all sides until browned. Remove the turkey and set aside.

Add the spice mixture to the oil remaining in the saucepan and cook, stirring frequently, for 5–6 minutes or until the spice paste has heated through and is bubbling. Add the stock and chocolate and simmer gently until the chocolate has melted.

Reduce the heat, return the turkey to the pan and mix well. Cover the pan and simmer gently for 30 minutes, adding extra water if the sauce begins to dry out. Garnish with the chopped red and green chillies.

For Mexican-style rice to serve as an accompaniment, gently heat 2 tablespoons vegetable oil in a saucepan and cook 325 g (11 oz) basmati rice for 5 minutes, stirring. Add 200 g (7 oz) chopped tomatoes, 1 crushed garlic clove, 50 g (2 oz) diced carrot and 1 chopped green chilli. Bring to boil, then simmer for 10 minutes.

SPRING BRAISED DUCK

Serves **4**
Preparation time **20 minutes**
Cooking time **1¾ hours**

4 **duck legs**
2 teaspoons **plain flour**
25 g (1 oz) **butter**
1 tablespoon **olive oil**
2 **onions**, sliced
2 **streaky bacon** rashers, finely chopped
2 **garlic cloves**, crushed
1 glass **white wine**, about 150 ml (¼ pint)
300 ml (½ pint) **chicken stock**
3 **bay leaves**
500 g (1 lb) small **new potatoes**, e.g. Jersey Royals
200 g (7 oz) **fresh peas**
150 g (5 oz) **asparagus tips**
2 tablespoons chopped **mint**
salt and **pepper**

Halve the duck legs through the joints. Mix the flour with a little seasoning and use to coat the duck pieces.

Melt the butter with the oil in a sturdy roasting pan or flameproof casserole and gently fry the duck pieces for about 10 minutes until browned. Drain to a plate and pour off all but 1 tablespoon of the fat left in the pan.

Add the onions and bacon to the pan and fry gently for 5 minutes. Add the garlic and fry for a further 1 minute. Add the wine, stock and bay leaves and bring to the boil, stirring. Return the duck pieces and cover with a lid or foil. Place in a preheated oven, 160°C (325°F), Gas Mark 3, for 45 minutes.

Add the potatoes to the pan, stirring them into the juices. Sprinkle with salt and return to the oven for 30 minutes.

Add the peas, asparagus and mint to the pan and return to the oven for a further 15 minutes or until all the vegetables are tender. Check the seasoning and serve.

For spring braised chicken, replace the duck with 4 chicken thighs and omit the bacon. Add the following spring vegetables when adding the peas, asparagus and mint: 200 g (7 oz) baby turnips, 100 g (3½ oz) baby carrots, 2 small, sliced courgettes. Cook as above.

COQ AU VIN

Serves **6–8**
Preparation time: **20 minutes**
Cooking time: 1½ **hours**

3 tablespoons **oil**
3–4 slices of **bread**, crusts removed, diced
50 g (2 oz) **butter**
2.5 kg (5 lb) **chicken**, cut into 12 serving pieces
24 **small pickling onions**, peeled
125 g (4 oz) **smoked bacon**, diced
1 tablespoon **plain flour**
1 bottle **red wine**
1 **bouquet garni**
2 **garlic cloves**, peeled
freshly grated **nutmeg**
24 **button mushrooms**, sliced
1 tablespoon **brandy**
salt and **pepper**

To garnish
chopped **parsley**
pared strips of **orange rind**

Heat 1 tablespoon of the oil in a large, flameproof casserole and fry the bread until golden. Drain. Add the remaining oil, the butter and chicken pieces. Fry gently over a low heat until golden on all sides, turning occasionally. Remove with a slotted spoon and keep warm. Pour off a little of the fat from the casserole, then add the onions and bacon. Sauté until lightly coloured, then sprinkle in the flour and stir well.

Pour in the wine and bring to the boil, stirring. Add the bouquet garni, garlic cloves, nutmeg and salt and pepper to taste. Return the chicken to the casserole. Reduce the heat, cover and simmer for 15 minutes.

Add the mushrooms and continue cooking gently for a further 45 minutes or until the chicken is cooked and tender. Remove the chicken with a slotted spoon and arrange the pieces on a warmed serving plate. Keep hot. Pour the brandy into the sauce and boil, uncovered, for 5 minutes until the sauce is thick and reduced. Remove the bouquet garni and garlic cloves.

Pour the sauce over the chicken and serve with the bread croûtes. Garnish with the chopped parsley and orange rind.

For creamy mashed potatoes to serve as an accompaniment, cook 8 large potatoes, cut into chunks, in a saucepan of salted boiling water for 20 minutes. Mash, then beat until very smooth. Add 50 g (2 oz) butter, then gradually beat in 75 ml (3 fl oz) hot milk until fluffy. Season and add a pinch of nutmeg.

CHICKEN & TARRAGON RISOTTO

Serves **6**
Preparation time **15 minutes**
Cooking time **30 minutes**

500 g (1lb) skinned **chicken breast fillets**, cut into small chunks
25 g (1 oz) **butter**
1 **onion**, finely chopped
2 **garlic cloves**, crushed
300 g (10 oz) **risotto rice**
1 glass **white wine**, about 150 ml (¼ pint)
400 ml (14 fl oz) **chicken stock** or **vegetable stock**
1 teaspoon **saffron threads**
250 g (8 oz) **mascarpone cheese**
3 tablespoons roughly chopped **tarragon**
3 tablespoons chopped **parsley**
100 g (3½ oz) **mangetout** or **sugarsnap peas**, halved
salt and **pepper**

Season the chicken with salt and pepper. Melt the butter in a flameproof casserole, then add the chicken and gently fry for 5 minutes until lightly browned. Add the onion and cook for a further 5 minutes. Add the garlic and rice and cook for a further 1 minute, stirring.

Pour in the wine and let the mixture bubble until the wine has almost evaporated. Stir in the stock and saffron and bring to the boil.

Cover with a lid and bake in a preheated oven, 180°C (350°F), Gas Mark 4, for 10 minutes until the stock is absorbed and the rice is almost tender.

Stir in the mascarpone, tarragon, parsley and mangetout or peas. Mix well until the cheese has melted, then cover and return to the oven for a further 5 minutes. Stir in a little boiling water if the mixture has dried out. Check the seasoning and serve with a leafy salad.

For creamy swordfish and tarragon risotto, replace the chicken with 4 swordfish fillets, cut into chunks, and fry off as above in the first step. Replace the mascarpone with 150 ml (¼ pint) single cream.

CHICKEN WITH CORNMEAL DUMPLINGS

Serves **4**
Preparation time **25 minutes**
Cooking time 1½ **hours**

3 tablespoons **olive oil**
8 skinned and boned **chicken thighs**, cut into small pieces
4 teaspoons **Cajun spice blend**
1 large **onion**, sliced
100 g (3½ oz) **smoked streaky bacon**, chopped
2 each **red** and **yellow peppers**, deseeded and roughly chopped
200 ml (7 fl oz) **chicken stock**
125 g (4 oz) **self-raising flour**
125 g (4 oz) **cornmeal**
½ teaspoon **dried chilli flakes**
3 tablespoons chopped **fresh coriander**
75 g (3 oz) **Cheddar cheese**, grated
50 g (2 oz) **butter**, melted
1 **egg**
100 ml (3½ fl oz) **milk**
4 small **tomatoes**, skinned and quartered
100 ml (3½ fl oz) **double cream**
salt and **pepper**

Heat the oil in a large, shallow flameproof casserole and fry the chicken pieces for about 5 minutes until lightly browned. Stir in the spice blend and cook for a further 1 minute. Drain to a plate.

Add the onion, bacon and peppers and fry for 10 minutes, stirring frequently, until beginning to colour.

Return the chicken to the casserole and stir in the stock and a little seasoning. Bring to the boil, then cover with a lid and bake in a preheated oven, 180°C (350°F), Gas Mark 4, for 45 minutes until the chicken is tender.

While the chicken is cooking, prepare the dumplings: mix together the flour, cornmeal, chilli flakes, coriander and cheese in a bowl. Beat the butter with the egg and milk and add to the bowl. Mix together to make a thick paste, that is fairly sticky but holds its shape.

Stir the tomatoes and cream into the chicken mixture and season to taste. Place spoonfuls of the dumpling mixture over the top. Return to the oven, uncovered, for a further 30 minutes or until the dumplings have slightly risen and form a firm crust.

For traditional dumplings, mix together 175 g (6 oz) self-raising flour, 50 g (2 oz) vegetable suet and 4 tablespoons chopped parsley in a bowl with a little salt and pepper. Add enough water to mix to a soft, slightly sticky dough. Spoon over the casserole and cook, covered, for 20–25 minutes until the dumplings are light and fluffy.

GUINEA FOWL & BEAN SOUP

Serves **4–6**
Preparation time **20 minutes, plus overnight soaking**
Cooking time 1½ **hours**

250 g (8 oz) **dried black-eyed beans**
1 kg (2 lb) oven-ready **guinea fowl**
1 **onion**, sliced
2 **garlic cloves**, crushed
1.5 litres (2½ pints) **chicken stock**
½ teaspoon **ground cloves**
50 g (2 oz) can **anchovies**, drained and finely chopped
100 g (3½ oz) **watercress**
150 g (5 oz) **wild mushrooms**
3 tablespoons **tomato purée**
salt and **pepper**

Put the beans in a bowl, cover with plenty of cold water and leave to soak overnight.

Drain the beans and put in a large saucepan. Cover with water and bring to the boil. Boil for 10 minutes, then drain the beans through a colander.

Put the guinea fowl in the pan and add the drained beans, onion, garlic, stock and cloves. Bring just to the boil, then reduce the heat to its lowest setting and cover with a lid. Cook very gently for 1¼ hours until the guinea fowl is very tender.

Drain the guinea fowl to a plate and leave until cool enough to handle. Flake all the meat from the bones, discarding the skin. Chop up any large pieces of meat and return all the meat to the pan.

Scoop a little of the stock into a small bowl with the anchovies and mix together so that the anchovies are blended with the stock. Discard the tough stalks from the watercress.

Add the anchovy mixture, mushrooms and tomato purée to the pan and season with salt and plenty of black pepper. Reheat gently for a few minutes and stir in the watercress just before serving.

For chicken and haricot bean soup, use the same quantity of haricot beans rather than the black-eyed. Take 4 chicken legs, cook and flake the meat from the bones as above. Finally, replace the watercress with the same quantity of rocket, chopped.

GAME & CHESTNUT CASSEROLE

Serves **6**
Preparation time **40 minutes**
Cooking time **1 hour 40 minutes**

500 g (1 lb) **pork sausagemeat**
3 **onions**, finely chopped
2 tablespoons chopped **thyme**
400 g (13 oz) **mixed game**,
350 g (12 oz) **mixed poultry**,
2 tablespoons **plain flour**
100 g (3½ oz) **butter**
2 **celery sticks**, chopped
2 **garlic cloves**, crushed
750 ml (1¼ pints) **chicken** or **game stock**
10 **juniper berries**, crushed
200 g (7 oz) **self-raising flour**
1 teaspoon **baking powder**
Approx 150 ml (½ pint) **milk**, plus a little extra
    to glaze
200 g (7 oz) whole **cooked chestnuts**
3 tablespoons **Worcestershire sauce**
salt and **pepper**

Mix the sausagemeat with one-third of the onions, half the thyme and plenty of seasoning. Shape into balls about 1.5 cm (¾ inch) in diameter.

Cut all the meat into small pieces. Season the plain flour and use to coat the meat. Melt 25 g (1 oz) of the butter in a large, flameproof casserole and brown the meat in batches, draining each batch to a plate.

Melt another 25 g (1 oz) of the butter and fry the remaining onions and the celery for 5 minutes. Add the garlic and fry for 1 minute. Stir in any remaining coating flour, then blend in the stock. Return the meat to the pan with the juniper berries. Cover and place in a preheated oven, 160°C (325°F), Gas Mark 3, for 1 hour until the meat is tender.

Meanwhile, put the self-raising flour and baking powder in a food processor with a little salt, the remaining thyme and the remaining butter, cut into pieces. Blend to breadcrumb consistency. Add most of the milk to make a dough, adding the rest if it is very dry. Turn out on to a floured surface and roll out to 1.5 cm (¾ inch) thick. Cut out rounds using a 4 cm (1¾ inch) cutter.

Stir the chestnuts and the Worcestershire sauce into the casserole and check the seasoning. Arrange the scones around the edge and glaze with milk. Raise the oven temperature to 220°C (425°F), Gas Mark 7, and cook for 20 minutes or until the scones are cooked through.

ITALIAN CHICKEN WITH TOMATO SAUCE

Serves **4**
Preparation time **20 minutes**
Cooking time 1¼ **hours**

4 **chicken legs**, halved through the joints
4 tablespoons **olive oil**
1 large **onion**, finely chopped
1 **celery stick**, finely chopped
75 g (3 oz) **pancetta**, diced
2 **garlic cloves**, crushed
3 **bay leaves**
4 tablespoons **dry vermouth** or **white wine**
2 x 400 g (13 oz) cans **chopped tomatoes**
1 teaspoon **caster sugar**
3 tablespoons **sun-dried tomato paste**
25 g (1 oz) **basil leaves**, torn into pieces
8 **black olives**
salt and **pepper**

Season the chicken pieces with salt and pepper. Heat the oil in a large saucepan or sauté pan and fry the chicken pieces on all sides to brown. Drain to a plate.

Add the onion, celery and pancetta to the pan and fry gently for 10 minutes. Add the garlic and bay leaves and fry for a further 1 minute.

Add the vermouth or wine, tomatoes, sugar, tomato paste and seasoning and bring to the boil. Return the chicken pieces to the pan and reduce the heat to its lowest setting. Cook very gently, uncovered, for about 1 hour or until the chicken is very tender.

Stir in the basil and olives and check the seasoning before serving.

For fennel, orange and olive salad to serve as an accompaniment, toss 1 large fennel bulb, thinly sliced, with 8–10 black olives, 1 tablespoon olive oil and 2 tablespoons lemon juice in a large bowl. Season with salt and pepper. Cut away the skin and pith of 2 oranges and slice thinly into rounds. Add the orange slices to the salad and toss gently to combine.

BEAN CHILLI WITH AVOCADO SALSA

Serves **4–6**
Preparation time **15 minutes**
Cooking time **30 minutes**

3 tablespoons **olive oil**
2 teaspoons **cumin seeds**, crushed
1 teaspoon **dried oregano**
1 **red onion**, chopped
1 **celery stick**, chopped
1 **medium-strength red chilli**, deseeded and sliced
2 x 400 g (13 oz) cans **chopped tomatoes**
50 g (2 oz) **sun-dried tomatoes**, thinly sliced
2 teaspoons **sugar**
300 ml (½ pint) **vegetable stock**
2 x 400 g (13 oz) cans **red kidney beans**
handful of **fresh coriander**, chopped
1 small **avocado**
2 **tomatoes**
2 tablespoons **sweet chilli sauce**
2 teaspoons **lime juice**
100 g (3½ oz) **soured cream**
salt and **pepper**

Heat the oil in a large saucepan. Add the cumin seeds, oregano, onion, celery and chilli and cook gently, stirring, for about 6–8 minutes until the vegetables start to colour.

Add the canned tomatoes, sun-dried tomatoes, sugar, stock, beans and coriander and bring to the boil. Reduce the heat and simmer for about 20 minutes until the juices are thickened and pulpy.

To make the salsa, finely dice the avocado and put it in a small bowl. Halve the tomatoes, scoop out the seeds and finely dice the flesh. Add to the bowl with the chilli sauce and lime juice. Mix well.

Season the bean mixture and spoon into bowls. Top with spoonfuls of soured cream and the avocado salsa. Serve with toasted pitta or flat breads.

For bean stew, heat 4 tablespoons olive oil in a small saucepan and gently fry 2 crushed garlic cloves, 1 tablespoon chopped rosemary and 2 teaspoons grated lemon rind for 3 minutes. Add 2 x 400 g (13 oz) cans butter beans with their liquid, 4 large skinned and chopped tomatoes and a little chilli powder. Bring to the boil, then simmer over a high heat for 8–10 minutes until the sauce is thickened. Season and serve with the avocado salsa and soured cream.

PASTA IN CREAMY VEGETABLE BROTH

Serves **3–4**
Preparation time **10 minutes**
Cooking time **15 minutes**

3 tablespoons **olive oil**
1 large **fennel bulb**, finely chopped
150 g (5 oz) **button mushrooms**, halved
2 tablespoons chopped **tarragon, parsley** or **fennel**
750 ml (1¼ pints) **vegetable stock**
200 g (7 oz) **purple sprouting broccoli**, halved
    lengthways and cut into 5 cm (2 inch) lengths
300 g (10 oz) **ready-made cheese** or **spinach**
    tortellini or **ravioli**
6 tablespoons **double cream**
plenty of **freshly grated nutmeg**
salt and **pepper**
freshly grated **Parmesan cheese**, to garnish

Heat the oil in a large saucepan. Add the fennel and cook gently, stirring frequently, for about 5 minutes until soft. Add the mushrooms and cook for a further 5 minutes.

Add the herbs and stock and bring to the boil. Tip in the broccoli and return to the boil. Add the pasta and cook for about 3 minutes until the pasta is tender.

Stir in the cream and nutmeg and season to taste. Ladle into soup bowls and serve garnished with Parmesan.

For pasta in chickpea and spinach soup, heat 2 tablespoons oil in a large saucepan and fry 2 crushed garlic cloves, 1 chopped onion and 1 tablespoon chopped rosemary for 5 minutes until soft. Add 2 x 400 g (13 oz) cans chickpeas with their liquid and 1.2 litres (2 pints) vegetable stock and bring to the boil, then cover and simmer for 30 minutes. Add 75 g (3 oz) small pasta shapes and return to the boil, then simmer for 8 minutes. Stir in 125 g (4 oz) shredded spinach and cook for 5 minutes until the pasta and spinach are tender. Season and serve topped with grated nutmeg, Parmesan and croûtons.

TOMATO & BREAD SOUP

Serves **4**
Preparation time **15 minutes**
Cooking time **30 minutes**

1 kg (2 lb) **ripe vine tomatoes,** skinned, deseeded
   and chopped
300 ml (½ pint) **vegetable stock**
6 tablespoons **extra-virgin olive oil**
2 **garlic cloves,** crushed
1 teaspoon **sugar**
2 tablespoons chopped **basil**
100 g (3½ oz) **day-old bread,** without crusts
1 tablespoon **balsamic vinegar**
salt and **pepper**

Put the tomatoes in a saucepan with the stock, 2 tablespoons of the oil, the garlic, sugar and basil and bring gradually to the boil. Cover the pan, reduce the heat and simmer gently for 30 minutes.

Crumble the bread into the soup and stir over a low heat until it has thickened. Stir in the vinegar and the remaining oil and season with salt and pepper to taste. Serve immediately or leave to cool to room temperature.

For tomato and almond soup, bring the tomatoes, oil, garlic and sugar to the boil as above, omitting the basil. Reduce the heat and simmer uncovered for 15 minutes. Meanwhile, blend 150 ml (¼ pint) extra-virgin olive oil with 15 g (½ oz) basil leaves and a pinch of salt, until really smooth. Set aside. Stir 100 g (3½ oz) toasted ground almonds into the soup and serve drizzled with the basil oil.

SPICY BEAN & YOGURT BAKE

Serves **4**
Preparation time **15 minutes**
Cooking time **1 hour**

2 teaspoons **cumin seeds**
2 teaspoons **fennel seeds**
10 **cardamom pods**
2 x 400 g (13 oz) cans **red kidney beans,** drained
4 tablespoons **olive oil**
1 **large onion,** chopped
1 **medium-strength red chilli,** deseeded and
   thinly sliced
finely grated **rind** of 1 **lemon**
2 **garlic cloves,** crushed
25 g (1 oz) **breadcrumbs**
100 g (3½ oz) **blanched almonds,** chopped
50 g (2 oz) **sultanas** or **raisins,** chopped
2 **eggs**
300 g (10 oz) **natural yogurt**
2 teaspoons **honey**
50 g (2 oz) **Cheddar cheese,** grated
3 **bay leaves**
salt and **pepper**

Crush the cumin, fennel and cardamom using a pestle and mortar. Once the cardamom pods have opened, discard the shells and lightly crush the seeds. Mix with the beans in a bowl and crush the beans lightly by mashing them against the side of the bowl with a fork.

Heat the oil in a small, 1.5 litre (2½ pint) roasting pan or flameproof casserole and gently fry the onion for 5 minutes. Add two-thirds of the chilli, reserving a few slices for a garnish, the lemon rind and the garlic and remove from the heat.

Add to the bowl with the breadcrumbs, almonds, sultanas or raisins, 1 egg and a little salt. Mix well and tip back into the pan. Spread the mixture in an even layer and pack down gently.

Beat the remaining egg in a bowl with the yogurt, honey and a little seasoning. Pour it over the bean mixture, spreading in an even layer. Scatter with the bay leaves and remaining chilli slices. Bake in a preheated oven, 160°C (325°F), Gas Mark 3, for about 50 minutes until the topping is very lightly set. Serve the bake hot.

For shredded iceberg salad to serve as an accompaniment, shred a small iceberg lettuce into a bowl and add ¼ cucumber, peeled and thinly sliced, and ½ bunch spring onions, finely chopped. Mix the grated rind and juice of 1 lime with 3 tablespoons groundnut oil and 1 tablespoon clear honey and season with salt and pepper. Toss together and serve.

BEANS WITH COCONUT & CASHEWS

Serves **4**
Preparation time **8 minutes**
Cooking time **25 minutes**

3 tablespoons **groundnut** or **vegetable oil**
2 **onions**, chopped
2 **small carrots**, thinly sliced
3 **garlic cloves**, crushed
1 **red pepper**, deseeded and chopped
2 **bay leaves**
1 tablespoon **paprika**
3 tablespoons **tomato purée**
400 ml (14 fl oz) can **coconut milk**
200 g (7 oz) can **chopped tomatoes**
150 ml (¼ pint) **vegetable stock**
400 g (13 oz) can **red kidney beans**, rinsed and
   drained
100 g (3½ oz) **unsalted cashew nuts**, toasted
small handful of **fresh coriander**, roughly chopped
salt and **pepper**

Heat the oil in a large saucepan. Add the onions and carrots and fry for 3 minutes. Add the garlic, red pepper and bay leaves and fry for 5 minutes until the vegetables are soft and well browned.

Stir in the paprika, tomato purée, coconut milk, tomatoes, stock and beans and bring to the boil. Reduce the heat and simmer, uncovered, for 15 minutes until the vegetables are tender.

Stir in the cashew nuts and coriander, season to taste with salt and pepper and heat through for 2 minutes. Serve with warmed grainy bread or boiled rice.

For red rice pilaf, to serve as an accompaniment, place 275 g (9 oz) Camargue red rice in a saucepan with 900 ml (1½ pints) hot vegetable stock and 1 crushed garlic clove. Bring to the boil, then reduce the heat and simmer gently for 20–25 minutes or until the rice is tender, adding a little water if the mixture boils dry. Stir in 2 tablespoons chopped parsley, the finely grated rind and juice of 1 lemon, 2 tablespoons olive oil and 1 teaspoon caster sugar, then season to taste with salt and pepper.

GREEN RISOTTO

Serves **4**
Preparation time **10 minutes**
Cooking time **30 minutes**

125 g (4 oz) **butter**
1 tablespoon **olive oil**
1 **garlic clove**, crushed or chopped
1 **onion**, finely diced
300 g (10 oz) **risotto rice**
1 litre (1¾ pints) hot **vegetable stock**
125 g (4 oz) **green beans**,
   cut into short lengths
125 g (4 oz) **peas**
125 g (4 oz) **broad beans**
125 g (4 oz) **asparagus**, cut into short lengths
125 g (4 oz) **baby spinach**, chopped
75 ml (3 fl oz) **dry vermouth** or **white wine**
2 tablespoons chopped **parsley**
125 g (4 oz) **Parmesan cheese**, freshly grated
salt and **pepper**

Melt half the butter with the oil in a large saucepan, add the garlic and onion and fry gently for 5 minutes.

Add the rice and stir well to coat each grain with the butter and oil. Add enough stock to just cover the rice and stir well. Simmer gently, stirring frequently.

When most of the liquid is absorbed, add more stock and stir well. Continue adding the stock a little at a time, stirring until it is absorbed and the rice is tender but retaining a little bite – this will take about 25 minutes. You may not need all the stock. Add the vegetables and vermouth or wine, mix well and cook for 2 minutes.

Remove the pan from the heat, season and add the remaining butter, the parsley and the Parmesan. Mix well and serve.

For saffron and tomato risotto, omit the peas, asparagus and spinach from the above recipe. Add 75 g (3 oz) pine nuts to the pan when melting the butter. Fry until golden, then drain before adding the garlic and onions. Crumble in 1 teaspoon saffron threads with the rice. Add 300 g (10 oz) halved cherry tomatoes at the end of the third step, cooking for 2–3 minutes until heated through, then stir in the pine nuts and a handful of shredded basil leaves.

BUDGET MEALS

JERK CHICKEN WINGS

Serves **4**
Preparation time **5 minutes**, plus marinating
Cooking time **12 minutes**

12 large **chicken wings**
2 tablespoons **olive oil**
1 tablespoon **jerk seasoning mix**
juice of ½ **lemon**
1 teaspoon **salt**
chopped **flat leaf parsley**, to garnish
lemon wedges, to serve

Put the chicken wings in a glass or ceramic dish. In a small bowl, whisk together the oil, jerk seasoning mix, lemon juice and salt, pour over the wings and stir well until evenly coated. Cover and leave to marinate in the refrigerator for at least 30 minutes or overnight.

Arrange the chicken wings on a grill rack and cook under a preheated grill, basting halfway through cooking with any remaining marinade, for 6 minutes on each side or until cooked through, tender and lightly charred at the edges. Increase or reduce the temperature setting of the grill, if necessary, to ensure that the wings cook through. Garnish with the chopped parsley and serve immediately with lemon wedges for squeezing over.

For jerk lamb kebabs, coat 750 g (1½ lb) boneless lamb, cut into bite-sized pieces in the jerk marinade as above, leaving to marinate overnight if time allows. Thread the meat on to 8 metal skewers and cook under a preheated grill or over a barbecue for 6–8 minutes on each side or until cooked to your liking.

DUCK BREASTS WITH FRUITY SALSA

Serves **4**
Preparation time **15 minutes**
Cooking time **about 15 minutes**

2 large **boneless duck breasts**, skin on, halved lengthways
2 tablespoons **dark soy sauce**
1 tablespoon **clear honey**
1 teaspoon grated **fresh root ginger**
1 teaspoon **chilli powder**

For the fruity salsa
1 large ripe **mango**, peeled, stoned and finely diced
6–8 **plums**, stoned and finely diced
grated rind and juice of 1 **lime**
1 small **red onion**, finely chopped
1 tablespoon **olive oil**
1 tablespoon roughly chopped **mint leaves**
1 tablespoon roughly chopped **coriander leaves**
salt and **pepper**

Use a sharp knife to score the skin on the duck breasts lightly, cutting down into the fat but not through to the meat.

Heat a frying pan until very hot, then add the duck breasts, skin-side down, and cook for 3 minutes or until sealed and browned. Turn over and cook for 2 minutes. Use a slotted spoon to transfer the duck breasts to a baking sheet, skin-side up.

In a small bowl, mix together the soy sauce, honey, ginger and chilli powder. Spoon over the duck. Cook in a preheated oven, 200°C (400°F), Gas Mark 6, for 6–9 minutes, until cooked to your liking. The duck may be served pink in the centre or more well cooked.

Meanwhile, in a bowl, mix together all the ingredients for the salsa and season well with salt and pepper.

Thinly slice the cooked duck and fan out the slices slightly on individual plates. Spoon some of the salsa over the duck and serve immediately, offering the remaining salsa separately.

For apricot & lime salsa as an alternative to the plum and mango salsa, in a bowl mix together 250 g (8 oz) drained and finely chopped canned apricots in natural juice, the grated rind and juice of 1 lime, 1 finely chopped shallot, 1 tablespoon finely chopped fresh root ginger, 1 tablespoon olive oil and 2 teaspoons clear honey.

COCONUT CHICKEN

Serves **4**
Preparation time **10 minutes**
Cooking time **20 minutes**

1 tablespoon **vegetable oil**
1 **onion**, diced
1 **red pepper**, cored, deseeded and diced
8 **chicken thighs**, boned, skinned and cut into
   bite-sized pieces
200 g (7 oz) **mangetout**
2 tablespoons **medium curry paste**
1 teaspoon finely chopped **lemon grass stalks**
1 teaspoon finely chopped **fresh root ginger**
2 **garlic cloves**, crushed
1 tablespoon **soy sauce**
400 ml (14 fl oz) **coconut milk**
1 handful of **basil leaves**
salt and **pepper** (optional)

Heat the oil in a saucepan, add the onion and red pepper and cook for 5 minutes until soft and just starting to brown. Add the chicken and cook for 5 minutes until browned all over.

Add the mangetout, curry paste, lemon grass, ginger, garlic and soy sauce and cook, stirring, for 2–3 minutes. Add the coconut milk and stir well. Cover and simmer gently for 5–8 minutes.

Remove from the heat, check and adjust the seasoning if necessary and stir in the basil just before serving with boiled basmati rice.

For spicy fried rice to serve as an alternative accompaniment, heat 2 tablespoons vegetable oil in a wok or large frying pan and crack 2 eggs into it, breaking the yolks and stirring them around. Add 250 g (8 oz) cold, cooked long-grain rice, 3 teaspoons caster sugar, 1½ tablespoons soy sauce, 2 teaspoons crushed dried chillies and 1 teaspoon Thai fish sauce and stir-fry over a high heat for 2 minutes. Serve immediately with the coconut chicken and garnished with coriander leaves.

RICE NOODLES WITH LEMON CHICKEN

Serves **4**
Preparation time **10 minutes**
Cooking time **10 minutes**

4 **boneless chicken breasts**, skin on
juice of 2 **lemons**
4 tablespoons **sweet chilli sauce**
250 g (8 oz) **dried rice noodles**
1 small bunch of **flat leaf parsley**, chopped
1 small bunch of **coriander**, chopped
½ **cucumber**, peeled into ribbons with a vegetable
    peeler
salt and **pepper**
finely chopped **red chilli**, to garnish

Mix the chicken with half the lemon juice and the sweet chilli sauce in a large bowl and season to taste with salt and pepper.

Lay a chicken breast between 2 sheets of clingfilm and lightly pound with a mallet to flatten. Repeat with the remaining chicken breasts.

Arrange the chicken on a grill rack in a single layer. Cook under a preheated grill for 4–5 minutes on each side or until cooked through. Finish on the skin side so that it is crisp.

Meanwhile, put the noodles in a heatproof bowl, pour over boiling water to cover and leave for 10 minutes until just tender, then drain. Add the remaining lemon juice, herbs and cucumber to the noodles and toss well to mix. Season to taste with salt and pepper.

Top the noodles with the cooked chicken and serve immediately, garnished with the chopped red chilli.

For stir-fried ginger broccoli to serve as an accompaniment, trim the stalks from 500 g (1 lb) broccoli. Divide the heads into florets, then diagonally slice the stalks. Blanch the broccoli in a saucepan of salted boiling water for 30 seconds. Drain, refresh under cold running water and drain thoroughly. Heat 2 tablespoons vegetable oil in a large frying pan, add 1 thinly sliced garlic clove and a 2.5 cm (1 inch) piece of fresh root ginger, peeled and finely chopped, and stir-fry for a few seconds. Add the broccoli and stir-fry over a high heat for 2 minutes. Sprinkle over 1 teaspoon sesame oil and stir-fry for a further 30 seconds.

PESTO TURKEY KEBABS

Serves **4**
Preparation time **15 minutes**
Cooking time **about
12 minutes**

4 **turkey breast steaks**, about 500 g (1 lb) in total
2 tablespoons **pesto**
4 slices of **Parma ham**
125 g (4 oz) **sun-dried tomatoes**, finely chopped
125 g (4 oz) **mozzarella cheese**, finely diced
1 tablespoon **olive oil**
salt and **pepper**
chopped parsley, to garnish
lemon wedges, to serve

Lay a turkey steak between 2 sheets of clingfilm and pound lightly with a mallet until about 1 cm ($^1/_2$ inch) thick. Repeat with the remaining steaks.

Spread the pesto over each beaten turkey steak and lay 1 slice of Parma ham on top of each. Sprinkle the tomatoes and mozzarella evenly over the turkey steaks, then season to taste with salt and pepper and roll up each one from the long side.

Cut the turkey rolls into 2.5 cm (1 inch) slices. Carefully thread the slices of roll evenly on to 4 metal skewers.

Brush the turkey rolls lightly with the oil and grill under a preheated grill for 6 minutes on each side or until cooked through. Increase or reduce the temperature setting of the grill, if necessary, to ensure that the rolls cook through and brown on the outside. Garnish with chopped parsley and serve hot with lemon wedges for squeezing over.

For homemade pesto, put 50 g (2 oz) pine nuts and 2 crushed garlic cloves in a food processor or blender and process to a thick paste. Alternatively, put in a mortar and pound with a pestle. Tear 50 g (2 oz) basil leaves into shreds and process or pound to a thick paste. Transfer both pastes to a bowl. Stir in 150 g (5 oz) finely grated Parmesan cheese and 2 tablespoons lemon juice. Add 150 ml ($^1/_4$ pint) olive oil a little at a time, beating well. Season to taste with salt and pepper.

CHICKEN RATATOUILLE

Serves **2**
Preparation time **15 minutes**
Cooking time **25 minutes**

2 tablespoons **olive oil**
2 **boneless, skinless chicken breasts**, cut into
    bite-sized pieces
65 g (2$^1/_2$ oz) **courgettes**, thinly sliced
75 g (3 oz) **aubergine**, cubed
150 g (5 oz) **onion**, thinly sliced
50 g (2 oz) cored, deseeded **green pepper**, thinly
    sliced
75 g (3 oz) **mushrooms**, sliced
400 g (13 oz) can **plum tomatoes**
2 **garlic cloves**, finely chopped
1 teaspoon **organic vegetable bouillon powder**
1 teaspoon **dried basil**
1 teaspoon **dried parsley**
$^1/_2$ teaspoon **ground black pepper**

Heat the oil in a large frying pan, add the chicken and cook, stirring, for 3–4 minutes until browned all over. Add the courgettes, aubergine, onion, green pepper and mushrooms and cook, stirring occasionally, for 15 minutes or until tender.

Add the tomatoes to the pan and gently stir. Stir in the garlic, bouillon powder, herbs and pepper and simmer, uncovered, for 5 minutes or until the chicken is tender. Serve immediately.

For roasted potatoes with rosemary and garlic, to serve as an accompaniment, heat 2 tablespoons olive oil in a large roasting tin in a preheated oven, 230°C (450°F), Gas Mark 8. Meanwhile, cut 750 g (1$^1/_2$ lb) scrubbed, unpeeled potatoes into quarters lengthways and pat dry with kitchen paper. Mix together 2 tablespoons olive oil and 2 tablespoons chopped rosemary in a bowl, add the potatoes and toss to coat. Add to the roasting tin, shake carefully to form an even layer, then roast at the top of the oven for 20 minutes. Meanwhile, peel and thinly slice 4 garlic cloves. Remove the tin and move the potatoes around so that they cook evenly. Scatter the garlic slices among the potatoes, then return to the oven and cook for a further 5 minutes. Season to taste with salt and pepper and serve immediately with the chicken ratatouille.

CHICKEN THIGHS WITH FRESH PESTO

Serves **4**
Preparation time **15 minutes**
Cooking time **25 minutes**

1 tablespoon **olive oil**
8 **chicken thighs**
chopped basil leaves, to garnish

For the pesto
6 tablespoons **olive oil**
50 g (2 oz) **pine nuts**, toasted
50 g (2 oz) freshly grated **Parmesan**
50 g (2 oz) **basil leaves**
15 g (½ oz) **parsley**
2 **garlic cloves**, chopped
salt and **pepper**

Heat the oil in a nonstick frying pan over a medium heat. Add the chicken thighs and cook gently, turning frequently until the chicken is cooked through (about 20 minutes).

Meanwhile, make the pesto by placing all the ingredients in a food processor or blender and whizzing until smooth and well combined.

Remove the chicken from the pan and keep hot. Reduce the heat and add the pesto to the pan. Heat through for 2–3 minutes.

Pour the warmed pesto over the chicken thighs, garnish with basil and serve with courgette ribbons and grilled tomatoes.

For tomato rice as an accompaniment, cut 400 g (13 oz) cherry tomatoes in half and place on a nonstick baking tray. Sprinkle with 2 tablespoons of finely chopped garlic and sea salt and pepper to taste. Place in a hot oven for 12–15 minutes, then transfer to a mixing bowl with 250 g (8 oz) cooked basmati or long grain rice. Toss well to mix and serve with the chicken cooked as above.

FAST CHICKEN CURRY

Serves **4**
Preparation time **5 minutes**
Cooking time **20–25 minutes**

3 tablespoons **olive oil**
1 **onion**, finely chopped
4 tablespoons **medium curry paste**
8 **chicken thighs**, boned, skinned and cut into thin strips
400 g (13 oz) can **chopped tomatoes**
250 g (8 oz) **broccoli**, broken into small florets, and stalks peeled and sliced
100 ml (3½ fl oz) **coconut milk**
salt and **pepper**

Heat the oil in a deep nonstick saucepan, add the onion and cook for 3 minutes until soft. Add the curry paste and cook, stirring, for 1 minute.

Add the chicken, tomatoes, broccoli and coconut milk to the pan. Bring to the boil, then reduce the heat, cover and cook over a low heat for 15–20 minutes.

Remove from the heat, season well with salt and pepper and serve immediately.

For seafood patties with curry sauce, follow the first stage of the recipe above, then add the tomatoes, 200 g (7 oz) young spinach leaves and the coconut milk and cook as directed. Meanwhile, put 375 g (12 oz) roughly chopped white fish fillets and 175 g (6 oz) frozen cooked peeled prawns, defrosted and roughly chopped, in a food processor and process until well combined. Alternatively, finely chop and mix together by hand. Transfer to a bowl, add 4 finely chopped spring onions, 2 tablespoons chopped coriander leaves, 50 g (2 oz) fresh white breadcrumbs, a squeeze of lemon juice, 1 beaten egg, and salt and pepper to taste. Mix well, then form into 16 patties. Roll in 25 g (1 oz) fresh white breadcrumbs to coat. Heat a shallow depth of vegetable oil in a large frying pan, add the patties, in batches, and cook for 5 minutes on each side or until crisp and golden brown. Serve hot with the curry sauce.

MINI CHICKEN & BROCCOLI FRITTATAS

Makes **12**
Preparation time **15 minutes**
Cooking time **15 minutes**

250 g (8 oz) **broccoli**, cut into small florets
oil, for greasing
125–150 g (4–5 oz) **cooked chicken**, diced
6 **eggs**
125 ml (4 fl oz) **milk**
40 g (1½ oz) **Parmesan cheese**, freshly grated
salt and **pepper**

Add the broccoli to a saucepan of boiling water and cook for 3 minutes, then drain into a colander. Brush the insides of a 12-section nonstick muffin tin with a little oil, then divide both the broccoli and the chicken between the sections.

Beat the eggs, milk and Parmesan together in a jug, season generously, then pour the mixture over the broccoli and chicken.

Bake in a preheated oven, 190°C (375°F), Gas Mark 5, for 15 minutes until well risen and golden. Loosen the edges of the frittatas, then turn out and serve with a tomato salad or baked beans.

For chicken, bacon & red onion frittata, heat 1 tablespoon olive oil in a medium frying pan, add 125 g (4 oz) diced streaky bacon and 1 sliced red onion and fry for 5 minutes until golden. Add 125–150 g (4–5 oz) diced cooked chicken and fry until piping hot. Beat the eggs and milk together, then season. Add an extra 1 tablespoon oil to the pan, then pour in the egg mixture. Fry until the underside is golden, then finish off under a hot grill until set and golden. Cut into wedges to serve.

TERIYAKI CHICKEN

Serves **4**
Preparation time **10 minutes**, plus marinating
Cooking time **8 minutes**

2 **boneless, skinless chicken breasts**, cut into thin strips
2 tablespoons **soy sauce**
1 tablespoon **olive oil**
2 **large carrots**, peeled and cut into small matchsticks
2 **red peppers**, cored, deseeded and cut into small matchsticks
200 g (7 oz) jar **teriyaki stir-fry sauce**
6 **spring onions**, chopped

Put the chicken in a glass or ceramic bowl, add the soy sauce and toss well to coat. Cover and leave to marinate in a cool place for 10 minutes.

Heat the oil in a wok or large frying pan, add the chicken and marinade and stir-fry for 2 minutes. Add the carrots and peppers and stir-fry for 4 minutes. Add the sauce and spring onions and cook briefly, stirring, to heat through. Serve immediately over egg noodles.

For pork teriyaki with crispy garlic, substitute the chicken with 625 g (1¼ lb) pork steaks. Place the steaks between sheets of clingfilm and flatten with a wooden mallet. Cut into thin strips and cook as above. To make the crispy garlic, thinly slice 4 garlic cloves. Heat a 5 cm (2 inch) depth of oil in a deep, heavy-based saucepan to 180–190°C (350–375°F) or until a cube of bread browns in 30 seconds. Add the garlic slices and cook until golden and crispy. Remove with a slotted spoon and drain on kitchen paper. Sprinkle over the finished dish.

TANDOORI CHICKEN

Serves 4
Preparation time **5 minutes**, plus marinating
Cooking time **25–30 minutes**

8 **chicken drumsticks**
8 **chicken thighs**
2 tablespoons **tikka spice mix or paste**
2 **garlic cloves**, crushed
1 tablespoon **tomato purée**
juice of 1 **lemon**
75 ml (3 fl oz) **natural yogurt**

To garnish
grated lime rind
chopped coriander

Make deep slashes all over the chicken pieces. In a large glass or ceramic bowl, mix together all the remaining ingredients, then add the chicken and turn to coat thoroughly with the marinade. Cover and leave to marinate in the refrigerator for at least 30 minutes or overnight.

Transfer the chicken to an ovenproof dish and cook in a preheated oven, 240°C (475°F), Gas Mark 9, for 25–30 minutes until cooked through, tender and lightly charred at the edges. Serve garnished with lime rind and chopped coriander.

For blackened tandoori salmon, use the marinade above to coat 4 thick, skinless salmon fillets, then cover and leave to marinate in the refrigerator for 30 minutes–1 hour. Transfer to a nonstick baking sheet and bake at 180°C (350°F), Gas Mark 4, for 20 minutes or until cooked through. Serve with plain rice or couscous.

GRIDDLED SALSA CHICKEN

Serves 4
Preparation time **10 minutes**
Cooking time **6 minutes**

4 **boneless chicken breasts**, skin on
3 tablespoons **olive oil**
salt and pepper

For the cucumber and tomato salsa
1 **red onion**, finely chopped
2 **tomatoes**, deseeded and diced
1 **cucumber**, finely diced
1 **red chilli**, finely chopped
1 small handful of **coriander leaves**, chopped
juice of 1 **lime**

Remove the skin from the chicken breasts. Using kitchen scissors, cut each breast in half lengthways but without cutting the whole way through. Open each breast out flat. Brush with the oil and season well with salt and pepper. Heat a griddle pan until very hot. Add the chicken breasts and cook for 3 minutes on each side or until cooked through and grill-marked.

Meanwhile, to make the salsa, mix together the onion, tomatoes, cucumber, red chilli, coriander and lime juice. Season well with salt and pepper.

Serve the chicken hot with the spicy salsa spooned over and around.

For griddled tuna with pineapple salsa, prepare and cook 4 thick fresh tuna steaks, about 175 g (6 oz) each, as for the butterflied chicken breasts above. Meanwhile, in a bowl, mix together 6 tablespoons drained and roughly diced canned pineapple, 1 finely chopped red onion, 1 tablespoon finely chopped fresh root ginger, 1 finely chopped red chilli, grated rind and juice of 1 lime, 2 teaspoons clear honey, and salt and pepper to taste. Serve the pineapple salsa with the griddled tuna.

PEA & LAMB KORMA

Serves **4**
Preparation time **10 minutes**
Cooking time **30 minutes**

2 tablespoons **olive oil**
1 **onion**, chopped
2 **garlic cloves**, crushed
250 g (8 oz) **potatoes**, cut into 1.5 cm (¾ inch) dice
500 g (1 lb) **minced lamb**
1 tablespoon **korma curry powder**
200 g (7 oz) **frozen peas**
200 ml (7 fl oz) **vegetable stock**
2 tablespoons **mango chutney**
salt and **pepper**
chopped **coriander leaves**, to garnish

Heat the oil in a saucepan, add the onion and garlic and cook for 5 minutes until the onion is soft and starting to brown. Add the potatoes and minced lamb and cook, stirring and breaking up the mince with a wooden spoon, for 5 minutes or until the meat has browned.

Add the curry powder and cook, stirring, for 1 minute. Add the remaining ingredients and season to taste with salt and pepper. Bring to the boil, then reduce the heat, cover tightly and simmer for 20 minutes.

Remove from the heat, garnish with chopped coriander and serve with natural yogurt and steamed rice.

For spicy Indian wraps, finely shred 200 g (7 oz) iceberg lettuce and place in a bowl with 1 coarsely grated carrot. Heat 8 large flour wraps (or tortillas) on a griddle pan for 1–2 minutes on each side and then add the lettuce mixture on to the centre of each one. Divide the korma mixture (cooked as above) between the wraps and roll each one to enclose the filling. Serve accompanied with a dollop of yogurt if liked.

MINTED LAMB SKEWERS

Serves **4**
Preparation time **10 minutes**
Cooking time **10 minutes**

500 g (1 lb) **minced lamb**
2 teaspoons **curry powder**
6 tablespoons finely chopped **mint leaves**
salt and **pepper**

Mix together the minced lamb, curry powder and mint in a bowl and season to taste with salt and pepper. Using your hands, knead to combine the mixture evenly.

Divide the mixture into small sausages and thread evenly on to metal skewers. Cook under a preheated grill for 10 minutes, turning once. Serve hot with warmed naan bread, soured cream and a lime wedge. Sprinkle with chopped mint leaves and a little curry powder.

For cucumber raita to serve as an accompaniment, cut ½ large cucumber in half lengthways, scoop out and discard the seeds, then thinly slice each half. In a bowl, mix together with 250 ml (8 fl oz) natural yogurt, 1 tablespoon chopped mint leaves and 1 tablespoon chopped coriander leaves. Season to taste with salt and pepper. Toast 2 teaspoons cumin seeds in a dry frying pan until fragrant. Sprinkle over the raita just before serving.

MEXICAN PIE

Serves **4**
Preparation time **10 minutes**
Cooking time **30 minutes**

2 tablespoons **olive oil**
1 **onion**, finely chopped
2 **garlic cloves**, crushed
2 **carrots**, diced
250 g (8 oz) **minced beef**
1 **red chilli**, finely chopped
400 g (13 oz) can **chopped tomatoes**
400 g (13 oz) can **red kidney beans**, drained
　and rinsed
50 g (2 oz) **tortilla chips**
100 g (3½ oz) **Cheddar cheese**, grated
salt and **pepper**
chopped parsley or coriander, to garnish

Heat the oil in saucepan, add the onion, garlic and carrots and cook until softened. Add the minced beef and chilli and cook, stirring and breaking up with a wooden spoon, for 5 minutes or until the meat has browned. Add the tomatoes and beans, mix well and season to taste with salt and pepper.

Transfer to an ovenproof dish, cover with the tortilla chips and sprinkle with the Cheddar. Bake in a preheated oven, 200°C (400°F), Gas Mark 6, for 20 minutes or until golden brown. Garnish with chopped parsley or coriander before serving.

For tortilla-wrapped chilli with guacamole, follow the first stage of the recipe above, but then cover and simmer on the hob for 20 minutes. Meanwhile, halve 2 large, ripe avocados lengthways and remove the stones. Scoop the flesh into a bowl, add 3 tablespoons lime juice and roughly mash. Add 125 g (4 oz) tomatoes, skinned, deseeded and chopped, 2 crushed garlic cloves, 40 g (1½ oz) chopped spring onions, 1 tablespoon finely chopped green chillies and 2 tablespoons chopped coriander leaves, mix well and season to taste with salt and pepper. Divide the chilli between 4 warmed flour tortillas and wrap up. Serve with the guacamole, and soured cream, if liked.

BEEF MEATBALLS WITH RIBBON PASTA

Serves **4**
Preparation time **20 minutes**
Cooking time **1 hour**
　20 minutes

400 g (13 oz) **dried tagliatelle** or **fettuccine**
2 slices of **stale bread**, crusts removed, broken into
　small pieces
75 ml (3 fl oz) **milk**
4 tablespoons **olive oil**
6 **spring onions** or **1 small onion**, finely chopped
1 **garlic clove**, chopped
750 g (1½ lb) **minced beef**
2 tablespoons freshly grated **Parmesan cheese**, plus
　extra to serve
freshly grated **nutmeg**, to taste
300 ml (½ pint) **dry white wine**
400 g (13 oz) can **chopped tomatoes**
2 **bay leaves**
salt and **black pepper**
basil leaves, to garnish

For the meatballs, soak the bread in the milk in a large bowl. Meanwhile, heat half the oil in a frying pan over a medium heat, add the spring onions or onion and garlic and cook, stirring frequently, for 5 minutes until soft and just beginning to brown.

Add the minced meat to the bread and mix well. Add the cooked onion and garlic, the Parmesan and nutmeg and season with salt and pepper. Work together with your hands until well combined and smooth. Shape into 28 even-sized balls. Heat the remaining oil in a large, nonstick frying pan, add the meatballs, in batches, and cook over a high heat, turning frequently, until golden brown. Transfer to a shallow ovenproof dish.

Pour the wine and tomatoes into the frying pan and bring to the boil, scraping up any sediment from the base. Add the bay leaves, season with salt and pepper and boil rapidly for 5 minutes. Pour the sauce over the meatballs, cover with foil and bake in a preheated oven, 180°C (350°F), Gas Mark 4, for 1 hour, or until tender.

When the meatballs and sauce are almost ready, cook the pasta in a large saucepan of salted boiling water according to the packet instructions until al dente. Drain thoroughly and serve with the meatballs and sauce. Garnish with basil leaves and a scattering of Parmesan cheese.

For pork meatballs with walnuts, replace the beef with 750 g (1½ lb) minced pork. Grind 100 g (3½ oz) walnuts and add to the meat mixture, omitting the Parmesan, then cook as above.

BEEF WITH BLACK BEAN SAUCE

Serves **4**

Preparation time **15 minutes**

Cooking time **15 minutes**

750 g (1½ lb) **minute steak**

2 tablespoons **groundnut oil**

1 **onion**, thinly sliced

100 g (3½ oz) **mangetout**, halved lengthways

1 **garlic clove**, finely chopped

15 g (½ oz) **fresh ginger root**, peeled and finely chopped

1 small **red chilli**, finely chopped

200 g (7 oz) jar **black bean sauce**

salt and **pepper**

Trim the steak of all fat and then cut the meat into thin slices across the grain. Heat half the oil in a wok or large frying pan, add the beef, in 2 batches, and cook, stirring, until well browned all over. Transfer to a bowl.

Heat the remaining oil in the pan, add the onion and mangetout and stir-fry for 2 minutes. Add the garlic, ginger and chilli and stir-fry for 1 minute. Add the black bean sauce and cook, stirring, for 5 minutes or until the sauce begins to thicken. Season to taste with salt and pepper and serve immediately with steamed rice or egg-fried rice.

For seafood with black bean sauce, stir-fry 500 g (1 lb) raw tiger prawns and 200 g (7 oz) squid rings in a hot wok for 2–3 minutes. Add 8 roughly sliced spring onions and 2 sliced red peppers and stir-fry for a further 2–3 minutes. Add the black bean sauce and cook for 5 minutes, stirring often. Serve hot with egg noodles.

PORK & RED PEPPER CHILLI

Serves **4**
Preparation time **10 minutes**
Cooking time **30 minutes**

2 tablespoons **olive oil**
1 large **onion**, chopped
2 **garlic cloves**, crushed
1 **red pepper**, cored, deseeded and diced
450 g (14½ oz) **minced pork**
1 **red chilli**, finely chopped
1 teaspoon **dried oregano**
500 g (1 lb) **passata (sieved tomatoes)**
400 g (13 oz) can **red kidney beans**, drained
 and rinsed
salt and **pepper**
soured cream, to serve

Heat the oil in a saucepan, add the onion, garlic and red pepper and cook for 5 minutes until soft and starting to brown. Add the minced pork and cook, stirring and breaking up with a wooden spoon, for 5 minutes or until browned.

Add all the remaining ingredients and bring to the boil. Reduce the heat and simmer gently for 20 minutes. Remove from the heat, season well with salt and pepper and serve immediately with a dollop of soured cream and boiled rice or crusty bread.

For lamb & aubergine chilli, substitute the pork mince and red pepper with 1 medium aubergine and 450 g (14¼ oz) lamb mince. Cut the aubergine into small cubes and fry as above with the lamb mince. Garnish the finished dish with 2 tablespoons of finely chopped mint leaves and serve with rice or pasta.

MOROCCAN MEATBALL TAGINE

Serves 4
Preparation time **15 minutes**
Cooking time **40 minutes**

2 small **onions**, finely chopped
2 tablespoons **raisins**
750 g (1½ lb) **minced beef**
1 tablespoon **tomato purée**
3 teaspoons **curry powder**
3 tablespoons **olive oil**
½ teaspoon **ground cinnamon**
625 g (1¼ lb) can **chopped tomatoes**
juice of ½ **lemon**
2 **celery sticks**, thickly sliced
1 large or 2 medium **courgettes**, roughly chopped
175 g (6 oz) **frozen peas**

Mix together half the onions, the raisins, minced beef, tomato purée and curry powder in a bowl. Using your hands, knead to combine the mixture evenly. Form the mixture into 24 meatballs.

Heat 1 tablespoon of the oil in a saucepan, add the meatballs, in small batches, and cook until browned all over. Tip out the excess fat and put all the meatballs in the pan. Add the cinnamon, tomatoes and lemon juice, cover and simmer gently for 25 minutes until the meatballs are cooked.

Meanwhile, heat the remaining oil in a large frying pan, add the celery and courgettes and cook until soft and starting to brown. Add the peas and cook for a further 5 minutes until the peas are tender.

Just before serving, stir the courgette mixture into the meatball mixture.

For coriander & apricot couscous, to serve as an accompaniment, put 200 g (7 oz) instant couscous in a large, heatproof bowl with 50 g (2 oz) chopped ready-to-eat dried apricots. Pour over boiling hot vegetable stock to just cover the couscous. Cover and leave to stand for 10–12 minutes until all the water has been absorbed. Meanwhile, chop 2 large, ripe tomatoes and finely chop 2 tablespoons coriander leaves. Fluff up the couscous grains with a fork and tip into a warmed serving dish. Stir in the tomatoes and coriander with 2 tablespoons olive oil and season to taste with salt and pepper. Toss well to mix and serve with the tagine.

BOBOTIE

Serves 4
Preparation time **10 minutes**, plus cooling
Cooking time **40 minutes**

2 tablespoons **olive oil**
1 **onion**, chopped
2 **garlic cloves**, chopped
2 tablespoons **medium curry paste**
500 g (1 lb) **minced beef**
2 tablespoons **tomato purée**
1 tablespoon **white wine vinegar**
50 g (2 oz) **sultanas**
1 slice of **white bread**, soaked in 3 tablespoons milk
   and mashed
4 **eggs**, beaten
100 ml (3½ fl oz) **double cream**
salt and **pepper**

Heat the oil in a saucepan, add the onion and garlic and cook until soft and starting to brown. Add the curry paste and minced beef and cook, stirring and breaking up with a wooden spoon, for 5 minutes or until browned.

Add the tomato purée, vinegar, sultanas and mashed bread. Season to taste with salt and pepper and transfer to a deep, medium-sized ovenproof dish or a 20 cm (8 inch) heavy cake tin.

Mix together the eggs and cream in a bowl, season to taste with salt and pepper and pour over the meat mixture.

Bake in a preheated oven, 180°C (350°F), Gas Mark 4, for 30 minutes or until the egg is set and golden brown. Remove from the oven and leave to cool for 10–15 minutes before serving.

For individual boboties to serve as a stylish starter for an elegant dinner, divide the meat mixture between 4 individual ramekin dishes and pour the egg mixture over each one. Bake in a preheated oven, 180°C (350°F), Gas Mark 4, for 20–25 minutes or until the tops are just set. Meanwhile, toast thin slices of bread in a preheated griddle pan or under a preheated grill. Serve with the boboties.

MUSTARD & HAM MACARONI CHEESE

Serves **4**
Preparation time **5 minutes**
Cooking time **15 minutes**

350 g (11½ oz) **dried quick-cook macaroni**
250 g (8 oz) **mascarpone cheese**
100 g (3½ oz) **Cheddar cheese**, grated
100 ml (3½ fl oz) **milk**
2 teaspoons **Dijon mustard**
400 g (13 oz) can **premium cured ham**, cut into
  small cubes
salt and **pepper**
chopped **flat leaf parsley**, to garnish

Cook the macaroni in a large saucepan of salted boiling water according to the packet instructions until al dente, then drain and put in a warmed serving bowl. Cover and keep warm.

Gently heat the mascarpone, Cheddar, milk and mustard in a saucepan until melted into a sauce. Stir in the ham and cook gently for 1–2 minutes. Season to taste with salt and pepper.

Serve the macaroni with the cheese sauce spooned over, garnished with chopped parsley.

For spinach with olive oil & lemon dressing, an ideal accompaniment to the above dish, rinse 625 g (1¼ lb) spinach leaves in cold water, then put in a large saucepan with just the water that is clinging to the leaves, sprinkling with salt to taste. Cover and cook over a medium heat for 5–7 minutes until wilted and tender, shaking the pan vigorously from time to time. Drain thoroughly in a colander, then return to the rinsed-out pan and toss over a high heat until any remaining water has evaporated. Add 2 tablespoons butter and 2 finely chopped garlic cloves, and continue tossing until combined with the spinach. Transfer to a warmed serving dish, drizzle over 4 tablespoons olive oil and 2 tablespoons lemon juice, season to taste with salt and pepper and serve immediately with the macaroni dish.

THAI GREEN PORK CURRY

Serves **4**
Preparation time **10 minutes**
Cooking time **20 minutes**

2 tablespoons **olive oil**
4 **boneless pork steaks**, cut into bite-sized pieces
2 tablespoons **Thai green curry paste**
400 ml (14 fl oz) **coconut milk**
100 g (3½ oz) **green beans**
200 g (7 oz) can **water chestnuts**, drained, rinsed and cut in half
juice of 1 **lime**, or to taste
1 handful of **coriander leaves**

Heat the oil in a large saucepan, add the pork and cook, stirring, for 3–4 minutes until browned all over. Add the curry paste and cook, stirring, for 1 minute until fragrant.

Add the coconut milk, stir and reduce the heat to a gentle simmer. Cook for 10 minutes, then add the beans and water chestnuts. Cook for a further 3 minutes.

Remove from the heat, add lime juice to taste and stir through the coriander. Serve immediately with boiled rice.

For Thai red pork curry, replace the Thai green curry paste with Thai red curry paste. To prepare your own Thai red curry paste, put 10 large red chillies, 2 teaspoons coriander seeds, 5 cm (2 inch) piece of fresh root ginger, peeled and finely chopped, 1 finely chopped lemon grass stalk, 4 halved garlic cloves, 1 roughly chopped shallot, 1 teaspoon lime juice and 2 tablespoons groundnut oil in a food processor or blender and process to a thick paste. Alternatively, pound the ingredients together using a pestle and mortar. Transfer the paste to an airtight container; it can be stored in the refrigerator for up to 3 weeks.

RISI E BISI

Serves **4**
Preparation time **5 minutes**
Cooking time **about 25 minutes**

1 tablespoon **butter**
1 tablespoon **olive oil**
1 **onion**, finely chopped
2 **garlic cloves**, crushed
250 g (8 oz) **risotto rice**
900 ml (1½ pints) **hot chicken stock**, made with
   1 chicken stock cube and boiling water, heated
   to simmering
450 g (14½ oz) **frozen peas**
25 g (1 oz) **Parmesan cheese**, grated
100 g (3½ oz) **cooked ham**, finely chopped
1 bunch of **parsley**, finely chopped
salt and **pepper**

Melt the butter with the oil in a saucepan, add the onion and garlic and cook until the onion is soft and starting to brown. Add the rice and stir until coated with the butter mixture.

Add the hot stock, a ladleful at a time, and cook, stirring constantly, until each addition has been absorbed before adding the next. Continue until all the stock has been absorbed and the rice is creamy and cooked but still retains a little bite — this will take around 15 minutes.

Add the peas and heat through for 3–5 minutes. Remove from the heat and stir in the Parmesan, ham and parsley. Season to taste with salt and pepper and serve immediately.

For tuna & tomato risotto, after cooking the onion and garlic, add 3 tablespoons white wine and cook, stirring, until it has evaporated. Then follow the recipe above, but use fish stock instead of chicken stock and add 2 chopped tomatoes in place of the peas, along with a 200 g (7 oz) can tuna, drained and flaked, and heat through for 3–5 minutes. Remove from the heat and stir in 2 tablespoons chopped basil leaves with the Parmesan cheese and salt and pepper to taste. Serve immediately.

TOMATO & BACON RICE

Serves **4**
Preparation time **10 minutes**, plus standing
Cooking time **about 20 minutes**

2 tablespoons **olive oil**
2 **large leeks**, sliced
1 **garlic clove**, crushed
200 g (7 oz) **back bacon**, chopped
400 g (13 oz) can **chopped tomatoes**
250 g (8 oz) **long-grain rice**
750 ml (1¼ pints) **chicken stock**
salt and **pepper**
chopped **flat leaf parsley**, to garnish

Heat the oil in a saucepan, add the leeks, garlic and bacon and cook over a medium heat for a few minutes until soft and starting to brown. Add the tomatoes and rice and cook, stirring, for 1 minute.

Add the stock and season to taste with salt and pepper. Reduce the heat, cover tightly and cook for 12–15 minutes or until all the stock has been absorbed and the rice is tender.

Remove from the heat and leave to stand, covered, for 10 minutes. Stir, then garnish with parsley and serve immediately.

For homemade chicken stock, chop a cooked chicken carcass into 3–4 pieces and put in a large saucepan with 1 chopped onion, 2–3 chopped carrots, 1 chopped celery stick, 1 bay leaf, 3–4 parsley stalks and 1 thyme sprig. Add 1.8 litres (3 pints) cold water and bring to the boil, skimming any scum that rises to the surface. Reduce the heat and simmer gently for 2–2½ hours. Strain through a muslin-lined sieve. If not using straight away, leave to cool before covering and refrigerating.

QUICK SAUSAGE & BEAN CASSEROLE

Serves **4**
Preparation time **5 minutes**
Cooking time **25 minutes**

2 tablespoons **olive oil**
16 **cocktail sausages**
2 **garlic cloves**, crushed
400 g (13 oz) can **chopped tomatoes**
400 g (13 oz) can **baked beans**
200 g (7 oz) can **mixed beans**, drained and rinsed
½ teaspoon **dried thyme**
salt and **pepper**
3 tablespoons chopped **flat leaf parsley**, to garnish

Heat the oil in a frying pan, add the sausages and cook until browned all over.

Transfer the sausages to a large saucepan and add all the remaining ingredients. Bring to the boil, then reduce the heat, cover tightly and simmer for 20 minutes. Season to taste with salt and pepper and serve hot, garnished with the chopped herbs.

For mustard mash to serve as an accompaniment, cook 1 kg (2 lb) chopped potatoes in a large saucepan of salted boiling water until tender. Drain well and return to the pan. Mash with 75 g (3 oz) butter, 1 tablespoon wholegrain mustard, 3 teaspoons prepared English mustard and 1 crushed garlic clove. Season to taste with salt and pepper, then beat in 2 tablespoons chopped parsley and a dash of olive oil. Serve hot with the casserole.

SPICY PORK ROLLS WITH MINTED YOGURT

Serves **4**
Preparation time **15 minutes**
Cooking time **10–12 minutes**

4 **pork escalopes**, about 125–150 g (4–5 oz) each
1 **small onion**, roughly chopped
1 **red chilli**, deseeded and roughly chopped
4 tablespoons roughly chopped **coriander leaves**
grated rind and juice of 1 **lime**
1 tablespoon **Thai fish sauce**
2 **garlic cloves**, crushed
1 teaspoon grated **fresh root ginger**
1 teaspoon **ground cumin**
½ teaspoon **ground coriander**
50 ml (2 fl oz) **coconut milk**
mint leaves (optional)

For the minted yogurt
200 ml (7 fl oz) **Greek yogurt**
4 tablespoons roughly chopped **mint leaves**
salt and **pepper**

Lay a pork escalope between 2 sheets of clingfilm and pound lightly with a mallet until about 5 mm (¼ inch) thick. Repeat with the remaining escalopes.

Process the remaining ingredients in a food processor or blender to a coarse paste. Spread a quarter of the paste over a pork escalope and roll up to enclose the filling. Secure the roll with a wooden cocktail stick. Repeat with the remaining paste and pork.

Put the rolls on a baking sheet and cook in a preheated oven, 200°C (400°F), Gas Mark 6, for 10–12 minutes or until cooked through.

Meanwhile, to make the minted yogurt, put the yogurt in a small bowl, stir in the mint and season to taste with salt and pepper. Serve the rolls hot, with a dollop of the minted yogurt on the side and garnished with mint leaves, if liked.

For satay sauce to serve with the pork rolls instead of the minted yogurt, heat 1 tablespoon groundnut oil in a small frying pan, add 1 crushed garlic clove and cook, stirring, over a low heat for 2–3 minutes until softened. Stir in 4 tablespoons crunchy peanut butter, ¼ teaspoon dried chilli flakes, 1 tablespoon dark soy sauce, 1 tablespoon lime juice, 1 teaspoon clear honey and 2 tablespoons coconut cream and heat gently, stirring, until boiling. Serve warm with the pork rolls.

PASTA PIE

Serves **4**
Preparation time **10 minutes**
Cooking time **30 minutes**

1 tablespoon **olive oil**
450 g (14½ oz) **leeks**, sliced
2 **garlic cloves**, crushed
4 **eggs**, beaten
150 ml (¼ pint) **single cream**
125 g (4 oz) **Gruyère cheese**, grated
125 g (4 oz) **cooked fusilli**
salt and **pepper**

Heat the oil in a frying pan, add the leeks and garlic and cook until soft.

Mix the leek mixture with all the remaining ingredients, season to taste with salt and pepper and transfer to a greased ovenproof dish or medium-sized cake tin.

Bake in a preheated oven, 180°C (350°F), Gas Mark 4, for 25 minutes or until the eggs have set and the pie is golden brown. Serve with a crisp green salad.

For chicken & mozzarella macaroni pie, follow the first stage of the recipe, then add 200 g (7 oz) cooked chicken, cut into small bite-sized pieces, and 2 tablespoons finely chopped tarragon with the eggs and cream, together with 125 g (4 oz) grated mozzarella cheese and 125 g (4 oz) cooked macaroni. Bake in the oven as above.

SUMMER PRAWN & FISH FILO PIE

Serves **4**
Preparation time **10 minutes**
Cooking time **20–25 minutes**

750 g (1½ lb) **skinless white fish fillets**
100 g (3½ oz) **frozen cooked peeled prawns**, defrosted
100 g (3½ oz) **frozen peas**, defrosted
grated rind and juice of 1 **lemon**
600 ml (1 pint) **bottled white sauce**
1 bunch of **dill**, chopped
8 sheets of **filo pastry**
melted butter, for brushing
salt and **pepper**

Cut the fish into large, bite-sized pieces and put in a bowl with the prawns and peas. Add the lemon rind and juice, stir in the white sauce and dill and season well with salt and pepper.

Tip the fish mixture into 4 individual gratin or pie dishes. Cover the surface of each pie with 2 sheets of filo pastry, scrunching up each sheet into a loosely crumpled ball. Brush the pastry with melted butter.

Bake in a preheated oven, 200°C (400°F), Gas Mark 6, for 20–25 minutes until the pastry is golden brown and the fish is cooked through.

For seafood & potato pie, prepare the fish mixture as above, but use 2 tablespoons chopped parsley in place of the dill. Put into a medium-sized ovenproof dish. Cook 800 g (1 lb 10 oz) chopped potatoes in a large saucepan of salted boiling water until tender. Meanwhile, put 2 large eggs in a separate saucepan and bring to the boil. Cook for 10 minutes, then plunge into cold water to cool. Shell the eggs and cut in half lengthways. Drain the potatoes and mash with 2 tablespoons butter. Season well with salt and pepper. Gently press the egg halves, at evenly spaced intervals, into the fish mixture, then spoon or pipe the mash over the fish mixture. Bake in a preheated oven, 200°C (400°F), Gas Mark 6, for 20–25 minutes or until the top is lightly golden.

MACKEREL WITH AVOCADO SALSA

Serves **4**
Preparation time **10 minutes**
Cooking time **6–8 minutes**

8 **mackerel fillets**
2 **lemons**, plus extra wedges to serve
salt and pepper

For the avocado salsa
2 **avocados**, peeled, stoned and finely diced
juice and rind of 1 **lime**
1 **red onion**, finely chopped
½ **cucumber**, finely diced
1 handful of **coriander leaves**, finely chopped

Make 3 diagonal slashes across each mackerel fillet on the skin side and season well with salt and pepper. Cut the lemons in half, then squeeze the juice over the fish.

Lay on a grill rack, skin-side up, and cook under a preheated grill for 6–8 minutes or until the skin is lightly charred and the flesh is just cooked through.

Meanwhile, to make the salsa, mix together the avocados and lime juice and rind, then add the onion, cucumber and coriander. Toss well to mix and season to taste with salt and pepper.

Serve the mackerel hot with the avocado salsa and lemon wedges for squeezing over.

For grilled sardines with tomato relish, replace the mackerel fillets with 12 whole, cleaned and gutted sardines and grill for 4–5 minutes on each side. Meanwhile, put the chopped white parts of 4 spring onions, 2 tablespoons lime juice, 250 g (8 oz) ripe tomatoes, skinned, deseeded and chopped, ½ chopped sun-dried tomato, 1 deseeded and chopped red chilli and 3 tablespoons chopped coriander leaves in a food processor or blender and process until well combined. Serve the sardines hot with the relish.

FISH KEBABS & SPRING ONION MASH

Serves **4**
Preparation time **15 minutes**, plus marinating
Cooking time **18–20 minutes**

600 g (1 lb 3 oz) **skinless haddock, cod or coley fillets**, cut into 2.5 cm (1 inch) cubes
125 ml (4 fl oz) **natural yogurt**
1 teaspoon crushed **garlic**
1 teaspoon grated **fresh root ginger**
1 teaspoon **hot chilli powder**
1 tablespoon **ground coriander**
1 tablespoon **ground cumin**

For the spring onion mash
6 large **Desirée or King Edward potatoes**, diced
150 ml (¼ pint) **crème fraîche**
4 tablespoons finely chopped **coriander leaves**
1 **red chilli**, deseeded and thinly sliced
4 **spring onions**, thinly sliced
salt and **pepper**

Lay the fish cubes in a large, shallow glass or ceramic dish. In a small bowl, mix together the yogurt, garlic, ginger, chilli powder, ground coriander and cumin. Season the mixture to taste and pour over the fish. Cover and leave to marinate in a cool place while you make the mash.

Cook the potatoes in a large saucepan of salted boiling water for 10 minutes or until tender. Drain in a colander and return to the pan. Mash the potatoes and add the crème fraîche. Continue mashing until smooth, then stir in the chopped coriander, chilli and spring onions. Season to taste with salt and pepper, cover and set aside.

Heat the grill on the hottest setting. Thread the cubes of fish evenly on to 4 metal skewers and cook under the grill for 8–10 minutes, turning once. Serve immediately, with the mash and a green salad.

For spinach mash, to serve as an alternative accompaniment, while the potatoes are cooking, heat 2 tablespoons oil in a saucepan, add 1 finely chopped onion and 1 finely chopped garlic clove and cook for 5 minutes. Add 500 g (1 lb) chopped spinach leaves and cook, stirring, for 2 minutes or until the spinach just starts to wilt. Stir in 1 teaspoon ground ginger. Mash the potatoes with the spinach mixture and 4 tablespoons milk. Season to taste with salt and pepper.

MOROCCAN GRILLED SARDINES

Serves **4**
Preparation time **10 minutes**
Cooking time **6–8 minutes**

12 **sardines**, cleaned
  and gutted
2 tablespoons **harissa**
2 tablespoons **olive oil**
juice of 1 **lemon**
salt flakes and **pepper**
chopped coriander, to garnish
lemon wedges, to serve

Heat the grill on the hottest setting. Rinse the sardines and pat dry with kitchen paper. Make 3 deep slashes on both sides of each fish with a sharp knife.

Mix the harissa with the oil and lemon juice to make a thin paste. Rub into the sardines on both sides. Put the sardines on a lightly oiled baking sheet. Cook under the grill for 3–4 minutes on each side, depending on their size, or until cooked through. Season to taste with salt flakes and pepper and serve immediately garnished with coriander and with lemon wedges for squeezing over.

For baked sardines with pesto, line a medium ovenproof dish with 2 sliced tomatoes and 2 sliced onions. Prepare the sardines as above, then rub 4 tablespoons pesto over the fish and arrange in a single layer on top of the tomatoes and onions. Cover with foil and bake in a preheated oven, 200°C (400°F), Gas Mark 6, for 20–25 minutes or until the fish is cooked through.

RED SALMON & ROASTED VEGETABLES

Serves **4**
Preparation time **10 minutes**
Cooking time **25 minutes**

1 **aubergine**, cut into bite-sized pieces
2 **red peppers**, cored, deseeded and cut into bite-sized pieces
2 **red onions**, quartered
1 **garlic clove**, crushed
4 tablespoons **olive oil**
pinch of **dried oregano**
200 g (7 oz) can **red salmon**, drained and flaked
100 g (3½ oz) **pitted black olives**
salt and **pepper**
basil leaves, to garnish

Mix together the aubergine, red peppers, onions and garlic in a bowl with the oil and oregano and season well with salt and pepper.

Spread the vegetables out in a single layer in a nonstick roasting tin and roast in a preheated oven, 220°C (425°F), Gas Mark 7, for 25 minutes or until the vegetables are just cooked.

Transfer the vegetables to a warmed serving dish and gently toss in the salmon and olives. Serve warm or at room temperature, garnished with basil leaves.

For rocket & cucumber couscous to serve with the salmon and vegetables, put 200 g (7 oz) instant couscous in a large, heatproof bowl. Season well with salt and pepper and pour over boiling hot water to just cover the couscous. Cover and leave to stand for 10–12 minutes until all the water has been absorbed. Meanwhile, finely chop 4 spring onions, halve, deseed and chop ½ cucumber and chop 75 g (3 oz) rocket leaves. Fluff up the couscous grains with a fork and tip into a warmed serving dish. Stir in the prepared ingredients with 2 tablespoons olive oil and 1 tablespoon lemon juice. Toss well to mix and serve with the salmon and vegetables.

CREAMY PRAWN CURRY

Serves **4**
Preparation time **10 minutes**
Cooking time **about**
10 minutes

2 tablespoons **vegetable oil**
1 **onion**, halved and finely sliced
2 **garlic cloves**, finely sliced
2.5 cm (1 inch) piece of **fresh root ginger**, peeled and
   finely chopped
1 tablespoon **ground coriander**
1 tablespoon **ground cumin**
½ teaspoon **turmeric**
200 ml (7 fl oz) **coconut milk**
125 ml (4 fl oz) **vegetable stock**
600 g (1 lb 3 oz) **frozen large cooked peeled**
   prawns, defrosted
grated rind and juice of **1 lime**
4 tablespoons finely chopped **coriander leaves**
salt and **pepper**

Heat the oil in a large saucepan, add the onion, garlic and ginger and cook for 4–5 minutes. Add the ground coriander, cumin and turmeric and cook, stirring, for 1 minute.

Pour in the coconut milk and stock and bring to the boil. Reduce the heat and simmer for 2–3 minutes. Stir in the prawns and lime rind and juice, then simmer for 2 minutes or until the prawns are heated through.

Stir in the chopped coriander and season well with salt and pepper. Serve immediately with boiled basmati or jasmine rice.

For spiced coconut rice to serve with the curry, rinse 375 g (12 oz) basmati rice in cold water until the water runs clear. Drain and put in a large, heavy-based saucepan. Dissolve 125 g (4 oz) chopped creamed coconut in 750 ml (1¼ pints) boiling water and add to the rice with a 7 cm (3 inch) piece of lemon grass stalk, halved lengthways, 2 x 2.5 cm (1 inch) pieces of cinnamon stick, 1 teaspoon salt, and pepper to taste. Bring the rice to the boil, then cover and cook for 10 minutes until almost all the liquid has been absorbed. Turn off the heat and leave to stand for 10 minutes until the rice is tender. Fluff up with a fork before serving with the curry.

THAI-STYLE COCONUT MUSSELS

Serves **4**
Preparation time **20 minutes**
Cooking time **about**
10 minutes

2 kg (4 lb) **fresh, live mussels**
600 ml (1 pint) **vegetable stock**
400 ml (14 fl oz) **coconut milk**
grated rind and juice of **2 limes**
2 **lemon grass stalks**, lightly bruised, plus extra stalks
   to garnish (optional)
1 tablespoon **Thai green curry paste**
3 **red chillies**, deseeded and finely sliced
4 tablespoons chopped **coriander leaves**, plus extra
   to garnish (optional)
2 **spring onions**, shredded
salt and **pepper**
1 **red chilli**, deseeded and chopped (optional)

Scrub the mussels in cold water, scrape off any barnacles and pull away the hairy beards that protrude from the shells. Discard any with broken shells or any open mussels that do not close when tapped sharply.

Pour the stock and coconut milk into a large saucepan and bring to the boil. Stir in the lime rind and juice, lemon grass, curry paste, chillies, coriander and spring onions. Season to taste with salt and pepper.

Add the mussels, cover and return to the boil. Cook for 3–4 minutes or until all the mussels have opened. Discard any shells that remain closed. Use a slotted spoon to divide the mussels between 4 serving bowls and keep warm until ready to serve.

Bring the liquid to a vigorous boil and boil rapidly for 5 minutes or until reduced. Strain through a fine sieve, then ladle over the mussels. Garnish with chopped red chilli, chopped coriander leaves and lemon grass stalks.

For homemade Thai green curry paste, put 15 small green chillies, 4 halved garlic cloves, 2 finely chopped lemon grass stalks, 2 torn lime leaves, 2 chopped shallots, 50 g (2 oz) coriander leaves, stalks and roots, 2.5 cm (1 inch) piece of fresh root ginger, peeled and finely chopped, 2 teaspoons black peppercorns, 1 teaspoon pared lime rind, ½ teaspoon salt and 1 tablespoon groundnut oil into a food processor or blender and process to a thick paste. Alternatively, use a pestle and mortar to crush the ingredients, working in the oil at the end. Transfer the paste to an airtight container; it can be stored in a refrigerator for up to 3 weeks.

TROUT WITH CUCUMBER RELISH

Serves **4**
Preparation time **10 minutes**
Cooking time **10–12 minutes**

4 **rainbow trout**, cleaned and gutted
1 tablespoon **sesame oil**
crushed **Szechuan pepper**, to taste
salt

For the cucumber relish
1 **cucumber**, about 20 cm (8 inches) long
2 teaspoons **salt**
4 tablespoons **rice vinegar**
3 tablespoons **caster sugar**
1 **red chilli**, deseeded and sliced
3 cm (1¼ inch) piece **fresh root ginger**, peeled
 and grated
4 tablespoons **cold water**

To garnish
chopped chives
lemon wedges

Cut the cucumber in half lengthways, scoop out and discard the seeds and cut the flesh into 1 cm (½ inch) slices. Put in a glass or ceramic bowl. In a small bowl, put the salt, vinegar, sugar, chilli and ginger, add the water and mix well. Pour over the cucumber, cover and leave to marinate at room temperature while you cook the trout.

Brush the trout with the oil and season to taste with crushed Szechuan pepper and salt. Place the trout in a single layer on a grill rack and grill for 5–6 minutes on each side or until cooked through. Leave to rest for a few moments, then garnish with chopped chives and serve with the cucumber relish and lemon wedges.

For trout with ground almond dressing, brush the trout with 1 tablespoon olive oil and season to taste with salt and black pepper. While the trout is cooking as above, put 125 g (4 oz) ground almonds in a small saucepan over a medium heat and cook, stirring constantly, until lightly browned. Remove from the heat, add 6 tablespoons olive oil, 4 tablespoons lemon juice and 2 tablespoons chopped parsley, and season to taste with salt and pepper. Stir well, then return to the heat for 2 minutes. Pour the dressing over the cooked trout, garnish with parsley sprigs and serve immediately.

TUNA NIÇOISE SPAGHETTI

Serves **4**
Preparation time **10 minutes**
Cooking time **10 minutes**

4 **eggs**
350 g (11½ oz) **dried spaghetti**
3 x 200 g (7 oz) cans **tuna in brine**, drained
100 g (3½ oz) **green beans**, trimmed and blanched
50 g (2 oz) **kalamata olives**, pitted
100 g (3½ oz) **semi-dried tomatoes**
1 teaspoon grated **lemon rind**
2 tablespoons **lemon juice**
3 tablespoons **capers**
salt and **pepper**

Put the eggs in a saucepan of cold water and bring to the boil. Cook for 10 minutes, then plunge into cold water to cool. Shell the eggs, then roughly chop and set aside.

Meanwhile, cook the pasta in a large saucepan of salted boiling water according to the packet instructions until al dente.

Mix together the tuna, beans, olives, semi-dried tomatoes, lemon rind and juice and capers in a bowl. Season to taste with pepper.

Drain the pasta and return to the pan. Add the tuna mixture and gently toss to combine. Serve immediately garnished with the eggs.

For tuna, pea & sweetcorn rice cook 200 g (7 oz) easy-cook basmati rice in a large saucepan of lightly salted boiling water for 12–15 minutes or until tender. Drain, refresh under cold running water and drain again. Meanwhile, cook the eggs as above, then shell and cut into quarters. In a separate saucepan, cook 100 g (3½ oz) frozen sweetcorn and 100 g (3½ oz) frozen peas in salted boiling water for 5 minutes or until tender. Drain, refresh under cold running water and drain again. In a large bowl, mix together the rice, sweetcorn and peas, together with the tuna and olives, as above, and 2 tablespoons chopped basil. Whisk together 2 tablespoons lemon juice, 1 tablespoon olive oil and 1 crushed garlic clove, add to the rice and toss well to coat. Serve garnished with the egg quarters.

TUNA & SWEETCORN PILAFF

Serves **4**
Preparation time **10 minutes**
Cooking time **15–20 minutes**

2 tablespoons **olive oil**
1 **onion**, chopped
1 **red pepper**, cored, deseeded and diced
1 **garlic clove**, crushed
250 g (8 oz) **easy-cook long-grain rice**
750 ml (1¼ pints) **chicken stock**
325 g (11 oz) can **sweetcorn**, drained
200 g (7 oz) can **tuna in spring water**, drained
salt and **pepper**
6 chopped **spring onions**, to garnish

Heat the oil in a saucepan, add the onion, red pepper and garlic and cook until soft. Stir in the rice, then add the stock and season to taste with salt and pepper.

Bring to the boil, then reduce the heat and simmer, stirring occasionally, for 10–15 minutes until all the stock has been absorbed and the rice is tender.

Stir in the sweetcorn and tuna and cook briefly over a low heat to heat through. Serve immediately garnished with the spring onions.

For picnic pilaff cake, put the cooked rice mixture in a 23 cm (9 inch) square nonstick cake tin. In a bowl, beat 4 eggs with 4 tablespoons finely chopped parsley, season well with salt and pepper and pour over the rice mixture. Bake in a preheated oven, 180°C (350°F), Gas Mark 4, for 25–30 minutes or until set. Leave to cool, then remove from the tin and serve cut into thick wedges.

LEMON & CHILLI PRAWN LINGUINE

Serves **4**
Preparation time **15 minutes**
Cooking time **about**
  10 minutes

375 g (12 oz) **dried linguine or spaghetti**
15 g (½ oz) **butter**
1 tablespoon **olive oil**
1 **garlic clove**, finely chopped
2 **spring onions**, thinly sliced
2 **red chillies**, deseeded and thinly sliced
450 g (14½ oz) **frozen large peeled prawns**, defrosted
2 tablespoons **lemon juice**
2 tablespoons finely chopped **coriander leaves**
salt and **pepper**

Cook the pasta in a large saucepan of salted boiling water according to the packet instructions until al dente. When the pasta is about half cooked, melt the butter with the oil in a large nonstick frying pan. Add the garlic, spring onions and chillies and cook, stirring, for 2–3 minutes.

Add the prawns and cook briefly until heated through. Pour in the lemon juice and stir in the coriander until well mixed, then remove from the heat and set aside.

Drain the pasta and toss it with the prawn mixture, either in the frying pan (if large enough) or in a large, warmed serving bowl. Season well with salt and pepper and serve immediately.

For lime & chilli squid noodles, slit the bodies of 450 g (14½ oz) small squid down one side and lay flat on a board, insides up. Using a sharp knife, score the flesh with a criss-cross pattern. Cut any tentacles into small pieces. Cook 375 g (12 oz) dried medium egg noodles in a saucepan of boiling water according to the packet instructions until just tender. Meanwhile, heat 2 tablespoons groundnut oil in a large nonstick frying pan or wok, add 2 thinly sliced garlic cloves and a 2.5 cm (1 inch) piece of fresh root ginger, peeled and chopped, together with the spring onions and chillies as above, and stir-fry over a high heat for 2 minutes. Add the squid and stir-fry for 2–3 minutes. Add the juice of 1 lime, 2 tablespoons dark soy sauce, 1 tablespoon Thai fish sauce and 2 tablespoons finely chopped coriander leaves, stir briefly, then remove from the heat. Drain the noodles, toss with the squid mixture and serve immediately.

SPICED CALAMARI WITH PARSLEY SALAD

Serves **4**
Preparation time **15 minutes**, plus standing
Cooking time **about 5 minutes**

150 g (5 oz) **besan** (chickpea or gram flour)
1½ teaspoons **paprika**
1½ teaspoons **ground cumin**
½ teaspoon **baking powder**
¼ teaspoon **pepper**
250 ml (8 fl oz) **soda water**
vegetable oil, for deep-frying
6 **whole squid**, cleaned and cut into 1 cm (½ inch)
   thick rings
salt

For the parsley salad
4 tablespoons **lemon juice**
4 tablespoons **olive oil**
2 **garlic cloves**, finely chopped
20 g (¾ oz) **flat leaf parsley**
1 **red onion**, halved and thinly sliced
2 **tomatoes**, roughly chopped

Sift the besan, paprika, cumin and baking powder into a bowl, add the pepper and mix together. Make a well in the centre. Gradually add the soda water and whisk until it is a smooth batter. Season to taste with salt. Cover and leave to stand for 30 minutes.

Meanwhile, for the salad dressing, in a bowl, whisk together the lemon juice, olive oil and garlic.

Fill a deep, heavy-based saucepan one-third full with vegetable oil and heat until a cube of bread browns in 15 seconds. Dip the squid rings in the batter, add to the oil, in batches, and cook for 30–60 seconds until golden brown. Remove with a slotted spoon and drain on kitchen paper.

Add the parsley, red onion and tomatoes to the dressing and toss well to mix. Top with the battered squid and serve immediately.

For pan-fried squid with chilli, slit the bodies of the squid down one side and lay flat, inside up. Using a sharp knife, score the flesh with a criss-cross pattern. Cut any tentacles into small pieces. In a bowl, mix together 2 tablespoons olive oil, 3 crushed garlic cloves, 1 finely chopped red chilli and 4 tablespoons lemon juice. Add the squid, cover and leave to marinate in a cool place for 15 minutes. Remove the squid from the marinade. Heat 2 tablespoons olive oil in a frying pan until just smoking, add the squid and season to taste with salt and pepper. Cook, stirring, over a high heat for 2–3 minutes until browned. Strain the marinade and stir into the pan with 2 tablespoons finely chopped flat leaf parsley.

EGG POTS WITH SMOKED SALMON

Serves **4**
Preparation time **5 minutes**
Cooking time **10–15 minutes**

200 g (7 oz) **smoked salmon trimmings**
2 tablespoons chopped **chives**
4 **eggs**
4 tablespoons **double cream**
toasted bread, to serve
pepper

Divide the smoked salmon and chives between 4 buttered ramekins. Make a small indent in the salmon with the back of a spoon and break an egg into the hollow, sprinkle with a little pepper and spoon the cream over the top.

Put the ramekins in a roasting tin and half-fill the tin with boiling water. Bake in a preheated oven, 180°C (350°F), Gas Mark 4, for 10–15 minutes or until the eggs have just set.

Remove from the oven and leave to cool for a few minutes, then serve with the toasted bread.

For homemade Melba toast, to serve with the baked egg pots, toast 4 slices of bread lightly on both sides. While hot, trim off the crusts, then split the toast in half widthways. Lay the toast, cut-side up, on a baking sheet and bake in the bottom of the oven with the egg pots until dry.

SESAME PRAWNS WITH PAK CHOI

Serves **4**
Preparation time **10 minutes**, plus marinating
Cooking time **about 3 minutes**

600 g (1 lb 3 oz) **large frozen peeled prawns**,
  defrosted
1 teaspoon **sesame oil**
2 tablespoons **light soy sauce**
1 tablespoon **clear honey**
1 teaspoon grated **fresh root ginger**
1 teaspoon crushed **garlic**
1 tablespoon **lemon juice**
500 g (1 lb) **pak choi**
2 tablespoons **vegetable oil**
salt and **pepper**

Put the prawns in a glass or ceramic bowl. Add the sesame oil, soy sauce, honey, ginger, garlic and lemon juice. Season to taste with salt and pepper and mix well, then cover and leave to marinate in a cool place for 5–10 minutes.

Cut the heads of pak choi in half lengthways, then blanch in a large saucepan of boiling water for 40–50 seconds. Drain well, cover and keep warm.

Heat the vegetable oil in a wok or large frying pan. Add the prawns and marinade and stir-fry over a high heat for 2 minutes until thoroughly hot.

Divide the pak choi between 4 serving plates, then top with the prawns and any juices from the pan. Serve immediately.

For sesame chicken with broccoli & red pepper, use 600 g (1 lb 3 oz) boneless, skinless chicken breast, cut into thin strips, in place of the prawns. Coat with the marinade as above, then cover and leave to marinate in the refrigerator for 1–2 hours. Meanwhile, trim the stalks from 400 g (13 oz) broccoli. Divide the heads into small florets, then peel and diagonally slice the stalks. Blanch the florets and stalks in a large saucepan of salted boiling water for 30 seconds. Drain well, refresh under cold running water and drain again thoroughly. Core, deseed and thinly slice 1 large red pepper. Heat the oil in the wok or large frying pan as above, add the chicken and marinade and stir-fry over a high heat for 2 minutes. Add the broccoli and red pepper and stir-fry for a further 2 minutes. Serve immediately.

216

PRAWN & CRAB CAKES WITH CHILLI JAM

Serves **4**
Preparation time **15 minutes**, plus cooling and chilling
Cooking time **15 minutes**

2 x 175 g (6 oz) cans **white crab meat**
grated rind and juice of 1 **lime**
4 **spring onions**, chopped
1 **red chilli**, deseeded and finely chopped
1 teaspoon grated **fresh root ginger**
1 teaspoon crushed **garlic**
3 tablespoons chopped **coriander leaves**, plus extra
  leaves to garnish
3 tablespoons **mayonnaise**
125 g (4 oz) **fresh white breadcrumbs**
200 g (7 oz) **frozen cooked peeled prawns**, defrosted
salt and **pepper**
vegetable oil, for shallow-frying

For the chilli jam
2 **red chillies**, deseeded and finely diced
6 tablespoons **caster sugar**
2 tablespoons **water**

Put the crab meat, lime rind and juice, spring onions, chilli, ginger, garlic, coriander, mayonnaise and breadcrumbs in a food processor and process until well combined. Transfer the mixture to a bowl. Chop the prawns and fold into the mixture with salt and pepper to taste. Alternatively, the ingredients can be mixed together by hand. Cover and chill while making and cooling the chilli jam.

Put all the chilli jam ingredients in a small saucepan and heat gently until simmering. Cook for 4–5 minutes until the sugar has dissolved and the mixture has thickened slightly. Leave to cool.

Form the prawn mixture into 12 cakes.

Heat the oil in a large nonstick frying pan, add the cakes and cook for 3–4 minutes on each side or until golden. Drain on kitchen paper and serve immediately garnished with coriander leaves. Serve the chilli jam spooned over the cakes or separately. A crisp rocket salad or green salad is a good accompaniment.

For coconut coriander sauce to serve as an alternative to the chilli jam, put 250 ml (8 fl oz) coconut milk, 2 tablespoons smooth peanut butter, 2 finely chopped spring onions, white parts only, 1 crushed garlic clove, 1 finely chopped green chilli, 2 tablespoons chopped coriander leaves, 1 tablespoon lime juice and 1 teaspoon sugar in a food processor or blender and process until smooth.

SALMON WITH LIME COURGETTES

Serves **4**
Preparation time **10 minutes**
Cooking time **10–15 minutes**

4 **salmon fillet** portions, about 200 g (7 oz) each
1 tablespoon prepared **English mustard**
1 teaspoon grated **fresh root ginger**
1 teaspoon crushed **garlic**
2 teaspoons **clear honey**
1 tablespoon **light soy sauce** or **tamari**
salt and **pepper**

For the lime courgettes
2 tablespoons **olive oil**
500 g (1 lb) **courgettes**, thinly sliced lengthways
grated rind and juice of 1 **lime**
2 tablespoons chopped **mint**

Lay the salmon fillet portions, skin-side down, in a shallow flameproof dish, to fit snugly in a single layer. In a small bowl, mix together the mustard, ginger, garlic, honey and soy sauce or tamari, then spoon evenly over the fillets. Season to taste with salt and pepper.

Heat the grill on the hottest setting. Cook the salmon fillets under the grill for 10–15 minutes, until lightly charred on top and cooked through.

Meanwhile, to prepare the lime courgettes, heat the oil in a large nonstick frying pan, add the courgettes and cook, stirring frequently, for 5–6 minutes or until lightly browned and tender. Stir in the lime rind and juice and mint and season to taste with salt and pepper.

Serve the salmon hot with the courgettes.

For stir-fried green beans to serve in place of the lime courgettes, cut 500 g (1 lb) green beans into 5 cm (2 inch) lengths. Heat 2 tablespoons vegetable oil in a wok or large frying pan, add 2 crushed garlic cloves, 1 teaspoon grated fresh root ginger and 2 thinly sliced shallots and stir-fry over a medium heat for 1 minute. Add the beans and $1/2$ teaspoon salt and stir-fry over a high heat for 1 minute. Add 1 tablespoon light soy sauce and 150 ml ($1/4$ pint) chicken or vegetable stock and bring to the boil. Reduce the heat and cook, stirring frequently, for a further 4 minutes, or until the beans are tender and the liquid has thickened. Season with pepper and serve immediately with the salmon.

CREAMY GARLIC MUSSELS

Serves **4**
Preparation time **15 minutes**
Cooking time **about 8 minutes**

1.5 kg (3 lb) **fresh, live mussels**
1 tablespoon **butter**
1 **onion**, finely chopped
6 **garlic cloves**, finely chopped
100 ml ($3^{1}/_{2}$ fl oz) **white wine**
150 ml ($1/4$ pint) **single cream**
1 large handful of **flat leaf parsley**, roughly chopped
salt and **pepper**

Scrub the mussels in cold water, scrape off any barnacles and pull away the dark hairy beards that protrude from the shells. Discard any with broken shells or any open mussels that do not close when tapped sharply.

Melt the butter in a large saucepan, add the onion and garlic and cook for 2–3 minutes until transparent and softened.

Increase the heat and tip in the mussels with the wine, then cover and cook for 3 minutes or until all the shells have opened. Discard any that remain closed.

Pour in the cream and heat through briefly, stirring well. Add the parsley, season well with salt and pepper and serve immediately in large bowls, with crusty bread to mop up the juices.

For mussels in spicy tomato sauce, cook the onion and garlic in 1 tablespoon olive oil instead of the butter, together with 1 deseeded and finely chopped red chilli. Add 1 teaspoon paprika and cook, stirring, for 1 minute, then add 400 g (13 oz) can chopped tomatoes. Season to taste with salt and pepper, cover and simmer gently for 15 minutes. Meanwhile, clean the mussels, as in the first stage above. Stir the mussels into the tomato sauce and increase the heat. Cover and cook for 3 minutes or until all the shells have opened. Discard any that remain closed. Add the parsley and serve as above.

CARROT, PEA & BROAD BEAN RISOTTO

Serves **4**
Preparation time **15 minutes**
Cooking time **about**
   25 minutes

4 tablespoons **butter**
2 tablespoons **olive oil**
1 **large onion**, finely chopped
2 **carrots**, finely chopped
2 **garlic cloves**, finely chopped
350 g (11½ oz) **risotto rice**
200 ml (7 fl oz) **white wine**
1.5 litres (2½ pints) **vegetable stock**, heated to
   simmering
200 g (7 oz) **frozen peas**, defrosted
100 g (3½ oz) **frozen broad beans**, defrosted and
   peeled
50 g (2 oz) **Parmesan cheese**, finely grated
1 handful of **flat leaf parsley**, roughly chopped
salt and **pepper**

Melt the butter with the oil in a saucepan, add the onion, carrots and garlic and cook for about 3 minutes until soft. Add the rice and stir until coated with the butter mixture. Add the wine and cook rapidly, stirring, until it has evaporated.

Add the hot stock, a ladleful at a time, and cook, stirring constantly, until each addition has been absorbed before adding the next. Continue until all the stock has been absorbed and the rice is creamy and cooked but still retains a little bite – this will take around 15 minutes.

Add the peas and broad beans and heat through for 3–5 minutes. Remove from the heat and stir in the Parmesan and parsley. Season to taste with salt and pepper and serve immediately.

For Italian-style risotto balls, leave the risotto to cool, then chill overnight in the refrigerator. Form the chilled mixture into walnut-sized balls. Beat 2 eggs together in a shallow bowl. Roll the rice balls through the egg, then in 100 g (3½ oz) dried breadcrumbs to coat. Fill a deep, heavy-based saucepan one-third full with vegetable oil and heat to 180–190°C (350–375°F) or until a cube of bread browns in 30 seconds. Add the rice balls, in batches, and cook for 2–3 minutes until golden. Remove with a slotted spoon, drain on kitchen paper and serve.

PASTA WITH TOMATO & BASIL SAUCE

Serves **4**
Preparation time **10 minutes**
Cooking time **10 minutes**

400 g (13 oz) **dried spaghetti**
5 tablespoons **olive oil**
5 **garlic cloves**, finely chopped
6 **vine-ripened tomatoes**, deseeded and chopped
25 g (1 oz) **basil leaves**
salt and **pepper**

Cook the pasta in a large saucepan of salted boiling water according to the packet instructions.

Meanwhile, heat the oil in a frying pan, add the garlic and cook over a low heat for 1 minute. As soon as the garlic begins to change colour, remove the pan from the heat and add the remaining oil.

Drain the pasta and return to the pan. Add the garlic oil with the chopped tomatoes and basil leaves. Season to taste with salt and pepper and toss well to mix. Serve immediately.

For quick tomato & basil pizza, prepare the garlic oil as above, but use 4 tablespoons oil and 4 garlic cloves. Meanwhile, skin the tomatoes and deseed and chop them as above. Pour off half the oil and reserve, add the tomatoes and half the basil to the pan, season well and leave to simmer while you make the dough. Sift 250 g (8 oz) self-raising flour and 1 teaspoon salt into a large bowl, then gradually add 150 ml (1/4 pint) warm water, mixing well to form a soft dough. Work the dough into a ball with your hands. Knead on a lightly floured surface until smooth and soft. Roll out the dough to a 30 cm (12 inch) round, making the edge slightly thicker than the centre, and lay on a warmed baking sheet. Spread the tomato mixture over the dough base, top with 125 g (4 oz) sliced mozzarella cheese and drizzle with the remaining garlic oil. Bake in a preheated oven, 240°C (475°F), Gas Mark 9, for 15 minutes or until the base is golden. Scatter with the remaining basil leaves and serve immediately.

SUMMER VEGETABLE FETTUCCINE

Serves **4**
Preparation time **10 minutes**
Cooking time **15 minutes**

250 g (8 oz) **asparagus**, trimmed and cut into 5 cm
   (2 inch) lengths
125 g (4 oz) **sugarsnap peas**
400 g (13 oz) **dried fettuccine or pappardelle**
200 g (7 oz) **baby courgettes**
150 g (5 oz) **button mushrooms**
1 tablespoon **olive oil**
1 **small onion**, finely chopped
1 **garlic clove**, finely chopped
4 tablespoons **lemon juice**
2 teaspoons chopped **tarragon**
2 teaspoons chopped **parsley**
100 g (3½ oz) **smoked mozzarella cheese**, diced
salt and **pepper**

Cook the asparagus and sugarsnap peas in a saucepan of boiling water for 3–4 minutes, then drain and refresh under cold running water. Drain well and set aside.

Cook the pasta in a large saucepan of salted boiling water according to the packet instructions until al dente.

Meanwhile, halve the courgettes lengthways and cut the mushrooms in half. Heat the oil in a large frying pan, add the onion and garlic and cook for 2–3 minutes. Add the courgettes and mushrooms and cook, stirring, for 3–4 minutes. Stir in the asparagus and sugarsnap peas and cook for 1–2 minutes before adding the lemon juice and herbs.

Drain the pasta and return to the pan. Add the vegetable mixture and mozzarella and season to taste with salt and pepper. Toss gently to mix and serve.

For cheesy garlic bread to serve with the pasta, cut a baguette into 2.5 cm (1 inch) thick slices, cutting almost through to the bottom crust but keeping the slices together at the base. In a bowl, beat 125 g (4 oz) softened butter with 1 crushed garlic clove, 1½ tablespoons finely chopped parsley and 125 g (4 oz) finely grated Parmesan cheese. Spread the butter on either side of the bread slices and over the top of the loaf. Wrap tightly in foil, place on a baking sheet and bake in a preheated oven, 190°C (375°F), Gas Mark 5, for 15 minutes. Carefully open up the foil and fold back, then bake for a further 5 minutes. Cut into slices and serve hot.

RED PEPPER & CHEESE TORTELLINI

Serves **4**
Preparation time **10 minutes**, plus cooling
Cooking time **15 minutes**

2 **red peppers**
2 **garlic cloves**, chopped
8 **spring onions**, finely sliced
500 g (1 lb) **fresh cheese-stuffed tortellini or any
   other fresh stuffed tortellini**
175 ml (6 fl oz) **olive oil**
25 g (1 oz) **Parmesan cheese**, finely grated
salt and **pepper**

Cut the peppers into large pieces, removing the cores and seeds. Lay skin-side up under a preheated grill and cook until the skin blackens and blisters. Transfer to a plastic bag, tie the top to enclose and leave to cool, then peel away the skin.

Place the peppers and garlic in a food processor and blend until fairly smooth. Stir in the spring onions and set aside.

Cook the tortellini in a large saucepan of boiling water according to the packet instructions until al dente. Drain and return to the pan.

Toss the pepper mixture into the pasta and add the oil and Parmesan. Season to taste with salt and pepper and serve immediately.

For warm ham & red pepper tortellini salad, grill and peel the red peppers as above, then thinly slice. While the tortellini is cooking, thinly slice 1 red onion. Drain the pasta and toss with 125 g (4 oz) chopped cooked ham, 200 g (7 oz) rocket leaves and the onion and red peppers. Serve immediately.

COURGETTE & HERB RISOTTO

Serves **4**
Preparation time **10 minutes**
Cooking time **about**
20 minutes

4 tablespoons **butter**
2 tablespoons **olive oil**
1 **large onion**, finely chopped
2 **garlic cloves**, finely chopped
350 g (11½ oz) **risotto rice**
200 ml (7 fl oz) **white wine**
1.5 litres (2½ pints) **vegetable stock**, heated to
  simmering
200 g (7 oz) **baby leaf spinach**, chopped
100 g (3½ oz) **courgettes**, finely diced
50 g (2 oz) **Parmesan cheese**, finely grated
1 small handful of **dill, mint and chives**, roughly
  chopped
salt and **pepper**

Melt the butter with the oil in a saucepan, add the onion and garlic and cook for about 3 minutes until soft. Add the rice and stir until coated with the butter mixture. Add the wine and cook rapidly, stirring, until it has evaporated.

Add the hot stock, a ladleful at a time, and cook, stirring constantly, until each addition has been absorbed before adding the next. Continue until all the stock has been absorbed and the rice is creamy and cooked but still retains a little bite – this will take around 15 minutes.

Stir in the spinach and courgettes and heat through for 3–5 minutes. Remove from the heat and stir in the Parmesan and herbs. Season to taste with salt and pepper and serve immediately.

For courgette & carrot risotto, cook the onion and garlic in the butter and oil as above, but add 2 finely chopped celery sticks and 3 small diced carrots. Continue with the recipe above until the end of the second stage. Meanwhile, cut 3 courgettes into 1 cm (½ inch) cubes. Add the courgettes to the risotto and heat through for 3–5 minutes. Remove from the heat and stir in 1 tablespoon chopped basil with the Parmesan. Season to taste with salt and pepper and serve immediately.

MIXED BEAN KEDGEREE

Serves **4**
Preparation time **10 minutes**
Cooking time **15–20 minutes**

2 tablespoons **olive oil**
1 **onion**, chopped
2 tablespoons **mild curry powder**
250 g (8 oz) **long-grain rice**
750 ml (1¼ pints) **vegetable stock**
4 **eggs**
2 x 400 g (13 oz) cans **mixed beans**, drained
  and rinsed
150 ml (¼ pint) **soured cream**
salt and **pepper**
2 **tomatoes**, finely chopped, to garnish
flat leaf parsley, to garnish

Heat the oil in a saucepan, add the onion and cook until soft. Stir in the curry powder and rice. Add the stock and season to taste with salt and pepper. Bring to the boil, then reduce the heat, cover and simmer, stirring occasionally, for 10–15 minutes until all the stock has been absorbed and the rice is tender.

Meanwhile, put the eggs in a saucepan of cold water and bring to the boil. Cook for 10 minutes, then plunge into cold water to cool. Shell the eggs, then cut them into wedges.

Stir through the beans and soured cream and cook briefly over a low heat to heat through. Serve garnished with the eggs, tomatoes and parsley.

For chicken & pineapple pilaff, follow the first stage of the recipe above, but stir in 2 teaspoons turmeric with the curry powder and use chicken stock in place of the vegetable stock. Stir 400 g (13 oz) chopped cooked chicken breast and a 250 g (8 oz) can pineapple pieces in natural juice, drained, into the rice with the soured cream and cook briefly over a low heat to heat through. Serve garnished with 3 tablespoons chopped coriander leaves.

PAPPARDELLE PUTTANESCA

Serves **4**
Preparation time **10 minutes**
Cooking time **15 minutes**

2 tablespoons **olive oil**
1 **onion**, chopped
2 **red chillies**, deseeded and finely chopped
2 **garlic cloves**, crushed
1 tablespoon **capers**
2 x 400 g (13 oz) cans **chopped tomatoes**
100 g (3½ oz) **pitted black olives**
50 g (2 oz) can **anchovy fillets in oil**, drained
400 g (13 oz) **dried pappardelle or fettuccine**
25 g (1 oz) **Parmesan cheese**, finely grated
salt and **pepper**

Heat the oil in a saucepan, add the onion, chillies and garlic and cook until soft. Add the capers, tomatoes, olives and anchovies, cover tightly and simmer for 10 minutes. Season to taste with salt and pepper.

Meanwhile, cook the pasta in a large saucepan of salted boiling water according to the packet instructions until al dente.

Drain the pasta. Serve immediately topped with the sauce and the Parmesan.

For tuna & olive pasta sauce, cook the onion and garlic as above but with ½ teaspoon dried red chilli flakes instead of the chillies. Then, in place of the anchovies, add a 200 g (7 oz) can tuna in oil, drained and flaked, to the pan with the capers, tomatoes and olives. Simmer for 10 minutes, then stir in 200 ml (7 fl oz) half-fat crème fraîche and season to taste with salt and pepper just before serving on top of the drained pasta. Scatter with the Parmesan and 1 tablespoon finely chopped parsley.

CREAMY BLUE CHEESE PASTA

Serves **4**
Preparation time **10 minutes**
Cooking time **10 minutes**

375 g (12 oz) **dried pasta shells**
2 tablespoons **olive oil**
6 **spring onions**, thinly sliced
150 g (5 oz) **dolcelatte cheese**, diced
200 g (7 oz) **cream cheese**
salt and **pepper**
3 tablespoons chopped **chives**, to garnish

Cook the pasta shells in a large saucepan of salted boiling water according to the packet instructions until al dente.

Meanwhile, heat the oil in a large frying pan, add the spring onions and cook over a medium heat for 2–3 minutes. Add the cheeses and stir while they blend into a smooth sauce.

Drain the pasta shells and transfer to a warmed serving bowl. Stir in the sauce and season to taste with salt and pepper. Sprinkle with the chives and serve immediately.

For cheese & leek filo parcels, fry 3 leeks, thinly sliced, until soft and starting to brown, then leave to cool. Mix with the cheeses as above and 3 tablespoons chives. Melt 75 g (3 oz) butter in a saucepan. Put 8 sheets of filo pastry on a plate and cover with a damp tea towel. Working with 1 pastry sheet at a time, cut into 3 equal strips and brush well with melted butter. Put a teaspoon of the cheese mixture at one end of each strip. Fold one corner diagonally over to enclose and continue folding to the end of the strip to make a triangular parcel. Brush with melted butter and lay on a baking sheet. Repeat with the remaining cheese mixture and pastry to make about 24 small parcels. Bake in a preheated oven, 220°C (425°F), Gas Mark 7, for 8–10 minutes until golden brown. Serve hot.

PASTA WITH AUBERGINES & PINE NUTS

Serves **4**
Preparation time **10 minutes**
Cooking time **15 minutes**

8 tablespoons **olive oil**
2 **aubergines**, diced
2 **red onions**, sliced
75 g (3 oz) **pine nuts**
3 **garlic cloves**, crushed
5 tablespoons **sun-dried tomato paste**
150 ml (¼ pint) **vegetable stock**
300 g (10 oz) **cracked pepper-, tomato- or
   mushroom-flavoured fresh ribbon pasta**
100 g (3½ oz) **pitted black olives**
salt and **pepper**
3 tablespoons roughly chopped **flat leaf parsley**,
   to garnish

Heat the oil in a large frying pan, add the aubergines and onions and cook for 8–10 minutes until tender and golden. Add the pine nuts and garlic and cook, stirring, for 2 minutes. Stir in the sun-dried tomato paste and stock and simmer for 2 minutes.

Meanwhile, cook the pasta in a large saucepan of salted boiling water for 2 minutes or until al dente.

Drain the pasta and return to the pan. Add the vegetable mixture and olives, season to taste with salt and pepper and toss together over a medium heat for 1 minute until combined. Serve scattered with the chopped parsley.

For potato-topped aubergine & tomato casserole, cook 4 potatoes in a large saucepan of salted boiling water until just tender. Meanwhile, follow the first stage of the recipe above, but omit the pine nuts, and add just 2 tablespoons sun-dried tomato paste together with 3 large skinned and chopped tomatoes and the stock. Simmer for 5 minutes, then slice the olives and stir into the mixture. Transfer to a shallow ovenproof dish. Drain the potatoes, cut into slices and arrange, overlapping, on top of the vegetable mixture. Sprinkle with 4 tablespoons finely grated Parmesan cheese and bake in a preheated oven, 200°C (400°F), Gas Mark 6, for 35–40 minutes until golden brown on top.

LEBANESE LENTIL & BULGAR SALAD

Serves **4**
Preparation time **10 minutes**
Cooking time **30 minutes**

100 g (3½ oz) **Puy lentils**
1 tablespoon **tomato purée**
750 ml (1½ pints) **vegetable stock**
100 g (3½ oz) **bulgar wheat**
juice of 1 **lemon**
1 tablespoon **olive oil**
2 **onions**, sliced
1 teaspoon **granulated sugar**
1 bunch of **mint**, chopped
salt and **pepper**
3 **tomatoes**, finely chopped

Put the lentils, tomato purée and stock in a saucepan and bring to the boil. Reduce the heat, cover tightly and simmer for 20 minutes. Add the bulgar wheat and lemon juice and season to taste with salt and pepper. Cook for 10 minutes until all the stock has been absorbed.

Meanwhile, heat the oil in a frying pan, add the onions and sugar and cook over a low heat until deep brown and caramelized.

Stir the mint into the lentil and bulgar wheat mixture, then serve warm, topped with the fried onions and chopped tomato.

For Lebanese-style chicken salad, season 3 chicken breasts with salt and pepper. Brush each one with a little olive oil and place on a very hot griddle pan. Cook for 4–5 minutes on each side or until cooked through and lightly charred on the edges. Cut the breasts into thin slices and stir into the lentil salad above with 1 finely chopped cucumber and 10–12 sliced radishes.

GOLDEN MUSHROOM & LEEK PIES

Serves **4**
Preparation time **15 minutes**
Cooking time **25–30 minutes**

25 g (1 oz) **butter**
2 **leeks**, thinly sliced
300 g (10 oz) **chestnut mushrooms**, quartered
300 g (10 oz) **button mushrooms**, quartered
1 tablespoon **plain flour**
250 ml (8 fl oz) **milk**
150 ml (¼ pint) **double cream**
100 g (3½ oz) **strong Cheddar cheese**, grated
4 tablespoons finely chopped **parsley**
2 sheets of **ready-rolled puff pastry**, defrosted
    if frozen
1 **egg**, beaten

Melt the butter in a large saucepan, add the leeks and cook for 1–2 minutes. Add the mushrooms and cook for 2 minutes. Stir in the flour and cook, stirring, for 1 minute, then gradually add the milk and cream and cook, stirring constantly, until the mixture thickens. Add the Cheddar and the parsley and cook, stirring, for 1–2 minutes. Remove from the heat.

Cut 4 rounds from the pastry sheets to cover 4 individual pie dishes. Divide the mushroom mixture between the pie dishes. Brush the rims with the beaten egg, then place the pastry rounds on top. Press down around the rims and crimp the edges with a fork. Cut a couple of slits in the top of each pie to let the steam out. Brush the pastry with the remaining egg.

Bake in a preheated oven, 220°C (425°F), Gas Mark 7, for 15–20 minutes until the pastry is golden brown. Serve immediately.

For curried ham & mushroom pies, follow the first stage above, but after cooking the mushrooms add 1 teaspoon medium curry powder and ½ teaspoon turmeric to the pan and cook, stirring, for 1 minute, before adding the flour and continuing with the recipe. Once the sauce has thickened, stir in 200 g (7 oz) cooked ham, cut into small bite-sized pieces, in place of the Cheddar and 4 tablespoons chopped coriander leaves instead of the parsley. Make and bake the pies as above.

GRILLED CHICORY WITH SALSA VERDE

Serves **4**
Preparation time **15 minutes**
Cooking time **10 minutes**

4 **heads of chicory**, about 150 g (5 oz) each, trimmed
    and halved lengthways
2 tablespoons **olive oil**
125 g (4 oz) **Parmesan cheese**, coarsely grated
chopped **parsley**, to garnish

For the salsa verde
200 g (7 oz) **flat leaf parsley**
50 g (2 oz) **pine nuts**, toasted
2 **pickled gherkins**
8 **pitted green olives**
1 **garlic clove**, chopped
1 tablespoon **lemon juice**
150 ml (¼ pint) **olive oil**
salt and **pepper**

Coarsely purée all the ingredients for the salsa verde, except the oil, in a food processor or blender. With the motor still running, gradually trickle in the oil to make a creamy paste. Transfer to a serving dish, cover and set aside. (The salsa will keep for up to 1 week in the refrigerator.)

Heat the grill on the hottest setting. Arrange the chicory halves on the grill rack, cut-sides down, brush with some of the oil and cook under the grill for 5 minutes. Turn the chicory halves over, brush with the remaining oil and sprinkle the Parmesan over the top. Cook for a further 4 minutes or until the cheese has melted and the edges of the chicory begin to char.

Transfer the chicory to plates and garnish with chopped parsley. Add a little salsa verde to each plate and serve immediately, offering the remaining salsa verde separately. Toasted ciabatta bread is a good accompaniment.

For grilled sardines with salsa verde, arrange 750 g (1½ lb) whole, cleaned and gutted sardines in a large, shallow, glass or ceramic dish. Whisk together 3 tablespoons olive oil, 2 garlic cloves, the grated rind and juice of 1 lemon and 2 teaspoons dried oregano. Pour over the fish and turn them in the marinade to coat, then cover and leave to marinate in the refrigerator for about 1 hour. Meanwhile, prepare the salsa verde as above. Cook the sardines under a preheated grill or over a barbecue for 4–5 minutes on each side, basting with the marinade. Serve with the salsa verde.

VEGETARIAN

GOATS' CHEESE & CHIVE SOUFFLÉS

Serves **4**
Preparation time **10 minutes**
Cooking time **20–25 minutes**

25 g (1 oz) **unsalted butter**
2 tablespoons **plain flour**
250 ml (8 fl oz) **milk**
100 g (3½ oz) **soft goats' cheese**
3 **eggs**, separated
2 tablespoons chopped **chives**
salt and **pepper**

Melt the butter in a saucepan, add the flour and cook over a low heat, stirring, for 30 seconds. Remove the pan from the heat and gradually stir in the milk until smooth. Return to the heat and cook, stirring constantly, until the mixture thickens. Cook for 1 minute.

Leave to cool slightly, then beat in the goats' cheese, egg yolks, chives, and salt and pepper to taste.

Whisk the egg whites in a large, perfectly clean bowl, until soft peaks form. Fold the egg whites into the cheese mixture. Spoon the mixture into 4 greased, individual soufflé ramekins and set on a baking sheet. Bake in a preheated oven, 200°C (400°F), Gas Mark 6, for 15–18 minutes until risen and golden. Serve immediately.

For Cheddar & chilli soufflés, use 100 g (3½ oz) grated Cheddar cheese instead of soft goats' cheese and 2 tablespoons finely chopped coriander leaves in place of the chives, and also beat 2 finely chopped red chillies, deseeded according to taste, into the egg yolk mixture.

TOMATO & MOZZARELLA TARTLETS

Serves **6**
Preparation time **20 minutes**
Cooking time **20 minutes**

250 g (8 oz) **puff pastry**, defrosted if frozen
6 tablespoons **sun-dried tomato paste**
3 **plum tomatoes**, deseeded and roughly chopped
125 g (4 oz) **mozzarella cheese**, roughly diced
8 **pitted black olives**, roughly chopped
1 **garlic clove**, finely chopped
2 tablespoons roughly chopped **oregano**
1 tablespoon **pine nuts**
olive oil, for drizzling
salt and **pepper**

Line a large baking sheet with nonstick baking paper. Roll out the pastry on a lightly floured work surface to 2.5 mm (⅛ inch) thick. Use a 12 cm (5 inch) round cutter to stamp out 6 rounds and lay on the prepared baking sheet.

Spread 1 tablespoon sun-dried tomato paste over each pastry round. In a small bowl, mix together the tomatoes, mozzarella, olives, garlic, oregano and pine nuts and season well with salt and pepper. Divide the mixture between the pastry rounds.

Drizzle a little olive oil over the tartlets and bake in a preheated oven, 200°C (400°F), Gas Mark 6, for 20 minutes or until the pastry is golden. Serve immediately with mixed salad leaves.

For tomato & anchovy tartlets, follow the first stage of the recipe, then spread 1 tablespoon pesto over each pastry round instead of the sun-dried tomato paste. In a bowl, mix the tomatoes, olives and garlic, as above, with a 50 g (2 oz) can anchovy fillets in oil, drained and snipped into small pieces, 50 g (2 oz) drained and chopped bottled roasted red peppers in oil and 2 tablespoons chopped basil and season well with salt and pepper. Divide between the pastry rounds, drizzle with olive oil and bake as above.

MUSHROOM STROGANOFF

Serves **4**
Preparation time **10 minutes**
Cooking time **10 minutes**

1 tablespoon **butter**
2 tablespoons **olive oil**
1 **onion**, thinly sliced
4 **garlic cloves**, finely chopped
500 g (1 lb) **chestnut mushrooms**, sliced
2 tablespoons **wholegrain mustard**
250 ml (8 fl oz) **crème fraîche**
salt and **pepper**
3 tablespoons chopped **parsley**, to garnish

Melt the butter with the oil in a large frying pan, add the onion and garlic and cook until soft and starting to brown.

Add the mushrooms to the pan and cook until soft and starting to brown. Stir in the mustard and crème fraîche and just heat through. Season to taste with salt and pepper, then serve immediately, garnished with the chopped parsley.

For mushroom soup with garlic croûtons, while the mushrooms are cooking, remove the crusts from 2 thick slices of day-old white bread and rub with 2 halved garlic cloves. Cut the bread into cubes. Fry the cubes of bread in a shallow depth of vegetable oil in a frying pan, turning constantly, for 5 minutes or until browned all over and crisp. Drain on kitchen paper. After adding the mustard and crème fraîche to the mushroom mixture as above, add 400 ml (14 fl oz) boiling hot vegetable stock, then purée the mixture in a food processor or blender until smooth. Serve in warmed bowls, topped with the croûtons and garnished with the chopped parsley.

MUSHROOMS À LA GRECQUE

Serves **4**
Preparation time **10 minutes**, plus standing
Cooking time **10 minutes**

8 tablespoons **olive oil**
2 **large onions**, sliced
3 **garlic cloves**, finely chopped
600 g (1 lb 3½ oz) **button mushrooms**, halved
8 **plum tomatoes**, roughly chopped or 400 g (13 oz) can **chopped tomatoes**
100 g (3½ oz) **pitted black olives**
2 tablespoons **white wine vinegar**
salt and **pepper**
chopped **parsley**, to garnish

Heat 2 tablespoons of the oil in a large frying pan, add the onions and garlic and cook until soft and starting to brown. Add the mushrooms and tomatoes and cook, stirring gently, for 4–5 minutes. Remove from the heat.

Transfer the mushroom mixture to a serving dish and garnish with the olives.

Whisk the remaining oil with the vinegar in a small bowl, season to taste with salt and pepper and drizzle over the salad. Garnish with the chopped parsley, cover and leave to stand at room temperature for 30 minutes to allow the flavours to mingle before serving.

For mushroom pasta salad, prepare the mushroom mixture as above. Cook 200 g (7 oz) dried pennette or farfalle in a large saucepan of salted boiling water according to the packet instructions until al dente. Meanwhile, cook 125 g (4 oz) green beans in a saucepan of salted boiling water until just tender. Drain the beans, refresh under cold running water, and drain again. Drain the pasta thoroughly and toss into the mushroom mixture with the beans and 2 tablespoons torn basil leaves. Serve at room temperature.

SPINACH & POTATO GRATIN

Serves **4**
Preparation time **10 minutes**
Cooking time **35 minutes**

625 g (1¼ lb) **potatoes**, thinly sliced
500 g (1 lb) **spinach leaves**
200 g (7 oz) **mozzarella cheese**, grated
4 **tomatoes**, sliced
3 **eggs**, beaten
300 ml (½ pint) **whipping cream**
salt and **pepper**

Cook the potato slices in a large saucepan of salted boiling water for 5 minutes, then drain well.

Meanwhile, cook the spinach in a separate saucepan of boiling water for 1–2 minutes. Drain and squeeze out the excess water.

Grease a large ovenproof dish and line the bottom with half the potato slices. Cover with the spinach and half the mozzarella, seasoning each layer well with salt and pepper. Cover with the remaining potato slices and arrange the tomato slices on top. Sprinkle with the remaining mozzarella.

Whisk the eggs and cream together in a bowl and season well with salt and pepper. Pour over the ingredients in the dish.

Bake in a preheated oven, 180°C (350°F), Gas Mark 4, for about 30 minutes. Serve immediately with a salad and crusty bread.

For tomato, lime & basil salad to serve as an accompaniment, slice or quarter 1 kg (2 lb) tomatoes while the gratin is baking, and arrange in a large serving bowl. Scatter over ½ red onion, thinly sliced, and 1 handful of basil leaves. Whisk together 4 tablespoons olive oil, 2 tablespoons chopped basil, 1 tablespoon lime juice, 1 teaspoon grated lime rind, ½ teaspoon clear honey, 1 crushed garlic clove, a pinch of cayenne pepper, and salt and pepper to taste. Pour over the salad. Cover and leave to stand at room temperature for about 30 minutes to allow the flavours to mingle, then serve with the gratin.

SWEETCORN & PEPPER FRITTATA

Serves **4**
Preparation time **10 minutes**
Cooking time **about 10 minutes**

2 tablespoons **olive oil**
4 **spring onions**, thinly sliced
200 g (7 oz) can **sweetcorn**, drained
150 g (5 oz) bottled **roasted red peppers** in oil, drained and cut into strips
4 **eggs**, lightly beaten
125 g (4 oz) **strong Cheddar cheese**, grated
1 small handful of **chives**, finely chopped
salt and **pepper**

Heat the oil in a frying pan, add the spring onions, sweetcorn and red peppers and cook for 30 seconds.

Add the eggs, Cheddar, chives, and salt and pepper to taste and cook over a medium heat for 4–5 minutes until the base is set. Remove from the hob, place under a preheated grill and cook for 3–4 minutes or until golden and set. Cut into wedges and serve immediately with a green salad and crusty bread.

For courgette, pepper & Gruyère frittata, use 200 g (7 oz) finely chopped courgettes instead of the sweetcorn, 125 g (4 oz) grated Gruyère cheese in place of the Cheddar and substitute 4 tablespoons chopped mint leaves for the chives.

STUFFED MUSHROOMS WITH TOFU

Serves **1**
Preparation time **15 minutes**
Cooking time **20 minutes**

300 ml (½ pint) **boiling water**
1 teaspoon **organic vegetable bouillon powder**
2 large **portobello mushrooms**, stalks removed
1 tablespoon **olive oil**
40 g (1½ oz) **red onion**, finely chopped
125 g (4 oz) **firm tofu**, diced
1 tablespoon **pine nuts**, toasted
¼ teaspoon **cayenne pepper**
1 tablespoon **chopped basil**
25 g (1 oz) **Parmesan cheese**, finely grated
75 g (3 oz) **baby spinach leaves**
salt and **pepper**

Pour the boiling water into a wide pan, then stir in the bouillon powder. Add the mushrooms and poach for 2–3 minutes, then remove with a slotted spoon and drain on kitchen paper.

Heat a little of the oil in a pan, add the onion and cook until soft. Remove from the heat and leave to cool.

Mix together the onion, tofu, pine nuts, cayenne pepper, basil and the remaining oil. Season well with salt and pepper.

Sprinkle some Parmesan over each mushroom, then stuff the mushrooms with the onion mixture. Arrange in a flameproof dish and cook about 15 cm (6 inches) below a preheated medium grill for 10 minutes or until heated through and the cheese has melted.

To serve, scatter the spinach leaves on a plate and arrange the hot mushrooms on top.

For baba ghanoush, a Middle Eastern aubergine dip that makes a great accompaniment to this dish, prick 1 aubergine all over with a fork, cut lengthways in half, then lay, cut-side down, on a greased baking sheet. Bake in a preheated oven, 190°C (375°F), Gas Mark 5, for 30–40 minutes until softened. When cool enough to handle, peel, then purée in a food processor or blender with ½ crushed garlic clove and 1 teaspoon lemon juice. With the motor still running, gradually trickle in 1 tablespoon olive oil to make a creamy paste. Stir in 1 tablespoon chopped parsley and season to taste with salt and pepper. Add a generous dollop on the side of the mushrooms.

233

GREEK VEGETABLE CASSEROLE

Serves **4**
Preparation time **10 minutes**
Cooking time **25 minutes**

4 tablespoons **olive oil**
1 **onion**, thinly sliced
3 **peppers** of mixed colours, cored, deseeded and sliced into rings
4 **garlic cloves**, crushed
4 **tomatoes**, chopped
200 g (7 oz) **feta cheese**, cubed
1 teaspoon **dried oregano**
salt and pepper
chopped **flat leaf parsley**, to garnish

Heat 3 tablespoons of the oil in a flameproof casserole, add the onion, peppers and garlic and cook until soft and starting to brown. Add the tomatoes and cook for a few minutes until softened. Mix in the feta and oregano, season to taste with salt and pepper and drizzle with the remaining oil.

Cover and cook in a preheated oven, 200°C (400°F), Gas Mark 6, for 15 minutes. Garnish with the parsley and serve with warmed crusty bread.

For Middle Eastern vegetable casserole, heat 1 tablespoon olive oil in a flameproof casserole, add 1 red onion, cut into wedges, 3 sliced celery sticks and 3 thinly sliced carrots and cook until soft and starting to brown. Add 2 teaspoons harissa and cook, stirring, for 1 minute. Add about 625 g (1¼ lb) aubergines, trimmed and chopped, 2 large chopped tomatoes and 250 ml (8 fl oz) water. Bring to the boil, then cover and cook in a preheated oven, 180°C (350°F), Gas Mark 4, for about 25 minutes. Stir in 2 large potatoes, peeled and thickly sliced, and cook for a further 15 minutes or until tender but still firm. Serve hot garnished with chopped coriander.

MUSHROOM & BROCCOLI PIE

Serves **4**

Preparation time **8 minutes**

Cooking time **30 minutes**

350 g (11½ oz) **broccoli florets**

3 tablespoons **olive oil**

350 g (11½ oz) **mushrooms**, trimmed and thickly sliced

150 g (5 oz) **Gorgonzola cheese**

3 tablespoons **mascarpone cheese**

4 tablespoons **crème fraîche**

2 tablespoons chopped **chives**

1 large sheet ready-rolled **puff pastry** (thawed if frozen)

1 **egg**, lightly beaten

salt and **pepper**

Cook the broccoli in lightly salted boiling water for about 2 minutes or until the florets are just beginning to soften.

Meanwhile, heat the oil in a large frying pan and cook the mushrooms over a medium heat, stirring occasionally, for about 5 minutes. Stir in the Gorgonzola, mascarpone and crème fraîche. Add the drained broccoli florets and the chives, season and tip into 4 individual ovenproof dishes or 1 large rectangular ovenproof dish.

Lay the pastry over the filling, pressing it to the sides of the dish to seal. Brush the top with beaten egg and cut two slits. Cook in a preheated oven, 220°C (425°F), Gas Mark 7, for about 25 minutes until the pastry is crisp and golden. Serve immediately.

For puff-crust cauliflower cheese pie, use 450 g (14½ oz) cauliflower florets instead of the broccoli and 200 g (7 oz) grated strong Cheddar cheese instead of the Gorgonzola. Omit the mushrooms.

CUMIN LENTILS WITH YOGURT DRESSING

Serves **4**

Preparation time **10 minutes**

Cooking time **13 minutes**

4 tablespoons **olive oil**

2 **red onions**, thinly sliced

2 **garlic cloves**, chopped

2 teaspoon **cumin seeds**

500 g (1 lb) cooked **Puy lentils**

125 g (4 oz) **peppery leaves**, such as beetroot or rocket

1 large raw **beetroot**, peeled and coarsely grated

1 **Granny Smith apple**, peeled and coarsely grated (optional)

lemon juice, to serve

salt and **pepper**

Yogurt dressing

300 ml (½ pint) **Greek yogurt**

2 tablespoons **lemon juice**

½ teaspoon **ground cumin**

15 g (½ oz) **mint leaves**, chopped

Heat the oil in a frying pan and fry the red onions over a medium heat for about 8 minutes until soft and golden. Add the garlic and cumin seeds and cook for a further 5 minutes.

Mix the onion mixture into the lentils, season well and leave to cool.

Make the dressing by mixing together the ingredients in a small bowl.

Serve the cooled lentils on a bed of leaves, with the grated beetroot and apple (if used), a couple of spoonfuls of minty yogurt and a generous squeeze of lemon juice.

For cumin chickpeas with apricots, use 2 x 425 g (14 oz) cans chickpeas instead of the lentils. Chop and add 100 g (3½ oz) ready-to-eat dried apricots to replace the beetroot and apple.

CURRIED DHAL WITH SPINACH

Serves **4**
Preparation time **5 minutes**
Cooking time **15 minutes**

500 g (1 lb) **red lentils**
100 g (3½ oz) **butter**
1 **onion**, sliced
1 **garlic clove**, crushed
2 tablespoons **cider vinegar**
1 tablespoons **ground coriander**
1 teaspoon **turmeric**
1 teaspoon **ground cumin**
2 tablespoons medium **curry powder**
½ teaspoon **chilli powder**
200 g (7 oz) chopped **spinach**
1 teaspoon **garam masala**
salt and **pepper**

To serve
8 **chapattis**
mango chutney

Cook the lentils in plenty of unsalted boiling water for about 12 minutes or until they are soft but holding their shape.

Meanwhile, melt the butter in a saucepan and gently cook the onion for about 8 minutes until it is softened but not coloured. Add the garlic and cook for 1 minute, then stir in the vinegar and all the spices except the garam masala and fry gently for 2 minutes.

Drain the lentils and stir them into the spice mix with the chopped spinach. Heat until the spinach has wilted and the lentils are hot. Season to taste, stir in the garam masala and serve immediately with plenty of chapattis and mango chutney.

For potato & spinach curry, dice 500 g (1 lb) potatoes and cook them for 10 minutes, until just tender and substitute for the lentils. Increase the quantity of spinach to 500 g (1 lb). Serve sprinkled with toasted, chopped cashew nuts.

236

HERBY CHICKPEA FATOUSH

Serves **4**
Preparation time **15 minutes**
Cooking time **4 minutes**

3 **pitta breads**
1 **garlic clove**, peeled and halved
1 **green pepper**, cored, deseeded and thinly sliced
10–12 **radishes**, thinly sliced
400 g (13 oz) can **chickpeas**, rinsed and drained
15 g (½ oz) **parsley**, chopped
15 g (½ oz) **mint**, chopped
2 ripe **tomatoes**, deseeded and sliced
½ **red onion**, finely chopped, or 4 **spring onions**, finely sliced
½ **cucumber**, deseeded and diced
75 ml (3 fl oz) **olive oil**
3 tablespoons **lemon juice**
1 tablespoon **tahini** (optional)
1 teaspoon **sumac** (optional)
8 cos (romaine) **lettuce leaves**, to serve

Heat a griddle pan and toast the pitta breads for 2 minutes on each side until crisp and slightly charred. Remove from the pan and rub immediately with the cut garlic. Cut the bread into squares.

Combine the pitta cubes with the green pepper, radishes, chickpeas, parsley, mint, tomatoes, onion and cucumber. Pour over the oil and lemon juice and stir in the tahini (if used). Mix until the salad is well coated. Tip into a serving dish and scatter over the sumac (if used).

Put 2 lettuce leaves on each serving plate and let people help themselves to the fatoush.

For cannellini & French bread salad, replace the pitta bread with French bread cubes, baked in a preheated oven, 180°C (350°F), Gas Mark 4, for about 15 minutes until crisp and browning. Use cannellini beans instead of chickpeas and replace the tahini with 2 tablespoons pesto. Omit the sumac and garlic.

BALSAMIC BRAISED LEEKS & PEPPERS

Serves **4**
Preparation time **5 minutes**
Cooking time **20 minutes**

2 tablespoons **olive oil**
2 **leeks**, cut into 1 cm (½ inch) pieces
1 **orange pepper**, deseeded and cut into 1 cm
    (½ inch) chunks
1 **red pepper**, deseeded and cut into 1 cm
    (½ inch) chunks
3 tablespoons **balsamic vinegar**
handful of **flat leaf parsley**, chopped
salt and **pepper**

Heat the oil in a saucepan, add the leeks and orange and red peppers and stir well. Cover the pan and cook very gently for 10 minutes.

Add the balsamic vinegar and cook for a further 10 minutes without a lid. The vegetables should be brown from the vinegar and all the liquid should have evaporated.

Season well, then stir in the chopped parsley just before serving.

For balsamic braised onions, place 500 g (1 lb) peeled baby onions in a saucepan with 3 tablespoons balsamic vinegar, 3 tablespoons oilve oil, 40 g (1½ oz) light muscovado sugar, 2 tablespoons sun-dried tomato paste, several thyme spigs, a handful of sultanas and 300 ml (½ pint) water. Bring to the boil, then reduce the heat and simmer gently for about 40 minutes until the onions are tender and the sauce syrupy. Serve warm or cold.

ASPARAGUS & MANGETOUT STIR-FRY

Serves **4**
Preparation time **10 minutes**
Cooking time **7–9 minutes**

2 tablespoons **vegetable oil**
100 g (3½ oz) **fresh root ginger**, peeled and thinly
    shredded
2 large **garlic cloves**, thinly sliced
4 **spring onions**, diagonally sliced
250 g (8 oz) thin **asparagus spears**, cut into 3 cm
    (1¼ inch) lengths
150 g (5 oz) **mangetout**, cut in half diagonally
150 g (5 oz) **bean sprouts**
3 tablespoons **light soy sauce**

To serve
steamed rice
extra **soy sauce** (optional)

Heat a large wok until it is smoking then add the oil. Stir-fry the ginger and garlic for 30 seconds, add the spring onions and cook for a further 30 seconds. Add the asparagus and cook, stirring frequently, for another 3–4 minutes.

Add the mangetout and cook for 2–3 minutes until the vegetables are still crunchy but beginning to soften. Finally, add the bean sprouts and toss in the hot oil for 1–2 minutes before pouring in the soy sauce and removing from the heat.

Serve immediately with steamed rice and extra soy sauce, if liked.

For stir-fried vegetable omelettes, for each omelette, beat together 3 eggs with 2 tablespoons water and seasoning. Cook in a frying pan until lightly set. Top with a quarter of the cooked vegetables and fold in half. Set aside to keep warm and make three more.

RÖSTI WITH TOMATO & THREE CHEESES

Serves **2**
Preparation time **20 minutes**
Cooking time **25 minutes**

400 g (13 oz) **waxy potatoes**
½ small **onion**, grated
1 teaspoon **dried oregano**
25 g (1 oz) **butter**
1 tablespoon **olive oil**
3 small **tomatoes**, sliced
50 g (2 oz) **Gruyère cheese**, grated
75 g (3 oz) **mozzarella cheese**, sliced
2 tablespoons freshly grated **Parmesan cheese**
handful of **pitted black olives**
salt and **pepper**
small **basil leaves**, to garnish

Coarsely grate the potatoes and pat dry between sheets of kitchen paper. Mix in a bowl with the onion, oregano and plenty of seasoning.

Melt the butter with the oil in a medium-sized, heavy-based frying pan. Tip in the rösti mixture and spread it out in an even layer, pressing down gently to compact it. Cook over a very gentle heat for about 10 minutes or until the underside has turned golden. Test by lifting at the edge. To turn the rösti, invert it on to a plate and then slide it back into the pan to cook the base for a further 5–10 minutes until crisp and golden.

Arrange the tomato slices on top, seasoning with a little pepper. Sprinkle the Gruyère over the tomatoes and arrange the mozzarella slices on top. Sprinkle with the Parmesan and scatter with the olives. Cook under a preheated moderate grill for about 5 minutes until the cheese bubbles and begins to colour. Garnish with basil leaves and serve with a green salad.

For rösti with mushroom and soured cream, grate 375 g (12 oz) waxy potatoes and pat dry. Combine with 1 sliced onion, 1 tablespoon chopped dill, ½ teaspoon salt and 15 g (½ oz) plain flour, then add 1 beaten egg. Heat a little oil in a nonstick pan, divide the rösti mixture into 8 and fry for 3–4 minutes on each side. Keep warm. For the sauce, melt 25 g (1 oz) butter and fry 2 chopped shallots and 1 crushed garlic clove for 5 minutes, then stir-fry 375 g (12 oz) button mushrooms for 5–6 minutes. Stir in 2 tablespoons chopped dill, 6 tablespoons soured cream and 2 teaspoons horseradish sauce, season and serve with the rösti.

BAKED AUBERGINES & MOZZARELLA

Serves **4**
Preparation time **10 minutes**
Cooking time **about**
   25 minutes

2 **aubergines**, sliced in
   half lengthways
3 tablespoons **olive oil**
1 **onion**, chopped
1 **garlic clove**, crushed
250 g (8 oz) can **chopped tomatoes**
1 tablespoon **tomato purée**
300 g (10 oz) **mozzarella cheese**, cut into thin slices
salt and **pepper**
basil, to garnish

Brush the aubergines with 2 tablespoons of the oil and arrange, cut-side up, on a baking sheet. Roast in a preheated oven, 200°C (400°F), Gas Mark 6, for 20 minutes.

Meanwhile, heat the remaining oil in a frying pan, add the onion and garlic and cook until the onion is soft and starting to brown. Add the tomatoes and tomato purée and simmer for 5 minutes or until the sauce has thickened.

Remove the aubergines from the oven and cover each half with some sauce and 2 of the mozzarella slices. Season to taste with salt and pepper and return to the oven for 4–5 minutes to melt the cheese. Serve immediately scattered with basil leaves.

For roasted garlic bread to serve as an accompaniment, separate 2 garlic bulbs into separate cloves. Put on a square of foil and drizzle generously with olive oil. Bring up the sides of the foil and twist together at the top. Bake in the oven alongside the aubergines, then unwrap and allow to cool slightly before squeezing the flesh from the skins and spreading on to slices of hot French bread. Serve with the baked aubergines.

BEETROOT RISOTTO

Serves **4**
Preparation time **5–10 minutes**
Cooking time **30 minutes**

1 tablespoon **olive oil**
15 g (½ oz) **butter**
1 teaspoon **crushed** or **coarsely ground coriander seeds**
4 **spring onions**, thinly sliced
400 g (13 oz) **freshly cooked beetroot**, cut into 1 cm (½ inch) dice
500 g (1 lb) **risotto rice**
1.5 litres (2½ pints) **hot vegetable stock**
200 g (7 oz) **cream cheese**
4 tablespoons **finely chopped dill**
salt and **pepper**

To garnish
dill sprigs (optional)
crème fraîche (optional)

Heat the oil and butter in a large saucepan. Add the crushed or ground coriander seeds and spring onions and stir-fry briskly for 1 minute.

Add the beetroot and the rice. Cook, stirring, for 2–3 minutes to coat all the grains with oil and butter. Gradually pour in the hot stock a ladleful at a time, stirring frequently until each ladleful is absorbed before adding the next. This should take about 25 minutes, by which time the rice should be tender, but retaining a little bite.

Stir in the cream cheese and dill and season to taste. Serve immediately, garnished with dill sprigs and a little crème fraîche, if using.

For spinach and lemon risotto, heat the oil and butter and cook 2 finely chopped shallots and 2 crushed garlic cloves for 3 minutes. Stir in 300 g (10 oz) risotto rice and gradually add 1 litre (1¾ pints) vegetable stock as above. Before you add the last of the stock, stir in 500 g (1 lb) chopped spinach, the grated rind and juice of 1 lemon and season. Increase the heat and stir, then add the remaining stock and 50 g (2 oz) butter and cook for a few minutes. Stir in 50 g (2 oz) grated Parmesan. Garnish with more Parmesan, and grated lemon rind, if you like, before serving.

VEGGIE SAUSAGE HOTPOT

Serves **4**
Preparation time **10 minutes**
Cooking time **40 minutes**

40 g (1½ oz) **butter**, softened
1 tablespoon **olive oil**
8 **vegetarian sausages**
100 g (3½ oz) **chestnut mushrooms**, sliced
1 **red onion**, sliced
200 g (7 oz) **Puy lentils**, rinsed
400 ml (13 fl oz) **vegetable stock**
2 tablespoons chopped **oregano**
2 tablespoons **sun-dried tomato paste**
300 g (10 oz) **cherry tomatoes**, halved
1 **garlic clove**, crushed
2 tablespoons chopped **parsley**
8 small or 4 large slices **ciabatta**
salt and **pepper**

Melt half the butter with the oil in a sauté pan or flameproof casserole and fry the sausages with the mushrooms and onion until lightly browned.

Add the lentils, stock, oregano and tomato paste and mix the ingredients together. Bring to the boil and cover with a lid, then reduce the heat and cook very gently for about 20 minutes until the lentils are tender and the stock is nearly absorbed.

Stir in the tomatoes and check the seasoning. Cook for a further 5 minutes.

Meanwhile, mix the garlic and parsley with the remaining butter and spread thinly over the ciabatta slices. Arrange over the hotpot and cook under a preheated moderate grill for about 5 minutes until the bread is lightly toasted.

For spicy veggie burgers, heat 1 tablespoon oil and fry ½ red onion, 1 garlic clove and 1 teaspoon each grated ginger, ground cumin and coriander and chilli powder for 10 minutes. Cool slightly, then blend with a 400 g (13 oz) can red kidney beans, 75 g (3 oz) fresh breadcrumbs, 2 tablespoons each fresh coriander and soy sauce and salt and pepper. With wet hands, form the mixture into 8 small burgers and fry for 2–3 minutes on each side. Use the veggie burgers instead of the vegetarian sausages in the hotpot or serve them with a fresh tomato sauce.

CURRIED CAULIFLOWER WITH CHICKPEAS

Serves **4**
Preparation time **10 minutes**
Cooking time **20 minutes**

2 tablespoons **olive oil**
1 **onion**, chopped
2 **garlic cloves**, crushed
4 tablespoons **medium curry paste**
1 **small cauliflower**, divided into florets
375 ml (13 fl oz) **vegetable stock**, made with
   1 vegetable stock cube and boiling water
4 **tomatoes**, roughly chopped
400 g (13 oz) canned **chickpeas**, drained and rinsed
2 tablespoons **mango chutney**
salt and **pepper**
4 tablespoons chopped **coriander**, to garnish
whisked **natural yogurt**, to serve (optional)

Heat the oil in a saucepan, add the onion and garlic and cook until the onion is soft and starting to brown. Stir in the curry paste, add the cauliflower and stock and bring to the boil. Reduce the heat, cover tightly and simmer for 10 minutes.

Add the tomatoes, chickpeas and chutney and continue to cook, uncovered, for 10 minutes. Season to taste with salt and pepper. Serve garnished with coriander and drizzled with a little whisked yogurt, if liked.

For homemade mango chutney, put the peeled, stoned and sliced flesh of 6 ripe mangoes in a large saucepan with 300 ml (½ pint) white wine vinegar and cook over a low heat for 10 minutes. Add 250 g (8 oz) soft dark brown sugar, 50 g (2 oz) fresh root ginger, peeled and finely chopped, 2 crushed garlic cloves, 2 teaspoons chilli powder and 1 teaspoon salt and bring to the boil, stirring constantly. Reduce the heat and simmer for 30 minutes, stirring occasionally. Ladle into a sterilized screw-top jar and replace the lid. Store in the refrigerator and use within 1 month.

CALDO VERDE

Serves **4**
Preparation time **15 minutes**
Cooking time **35 minutes**

125 g (4 oz) **dark green cabbage, e.g. Cavolo Nero**
4 tablespoons **olive oil**
1 large **onion**, chopped
625 g (1½ lb) **floury potatoes**, cut into small chunks
2 **garlic cloves**, chopped
1 litre (1¾ pints) **vegetable stock**
400 g (13 oz) can **cannellini beans**, drained
15 g (½ oz) **fresh coriander**, roughly chopped
salt and **pepper**

Discard any tough stalk ends from the cabbage and roll the leaves up tightly. Using a large knife, shred the cabbage as finely as possible.

Heat the oil in a large saucepan and gently fry the onion for 5 minutes. Add the potatoes and cook, stirring occasionally, for 10 minutes. Stir in the garlic and cook for a further 1 minute.

Add the stock and bring to the boil. Reduce the heat and simmer gently, covered, for about 10 minutes until the potatoes are tender. Use a potato masher to lightly mash the potatoes into the soup so that they are broken up but not completely puréed.

Stir in the beans, shredded cabbage and coriander and cook gently for a further 10 minutes. Season to taste with salt and pepper.

For colcannon, boil 500 g (l lb) unpeeled potatoes until tender. Drain and add 150 ml (¼ pint) milk. Meanwhile, boil 500 g (1 lb) finely shredded green cabbage for 10 minutes or until the cabbage is tender. Drain and add 6 finely chopped spring onions. When cool enough to handle, peel and mash the potatoes in a bowl, then beat in the cabbage and spring onions. Season and beat in 50 g (2 oz) butter.

GOATS' CHEESE & BROAD BEAN TORTILLA

Serves **4**
Preparation time **15 minutes**
Cooking time **40 minutes**

75 ml (3 fl oz) **olive oil**
1 **onion**, chopped
625 g (1¼ lb) medium-sized **waxy potatoes**, sliced
6 **eggs**
2 teaspoons **green peppercorns in brine**, rinsed, drained and lightly crushed
200 g (7 oz) **goats' cheese**, e.g. **chèvre blanc**, roughly crumbled
125 g (4 oz) **frozen baby broad beans**
salt

Heat the oil in a 24–25 cm (9½–10 inch) sturdy frying pan. Add the onion and potatoes and sprinkle with salt. Gently fry on the lowest setting for about 15–20 minutes, turning frequently, until softened. If a lot of oil is left in the pan once the potatoes are softened, drain it off, but leave a little to finish cooking.

Beat the eggs in a bowl with the green peppercorns and a little extra salt.

Toss the cheese and beans with the potato mixture until evenly combined. Spread the mixture in a thin layer and pour the eggs over the top. Reduce the heat to its lowest setting and cook gently for 10–15 minutes until almost set. Finish by cooking under a preheated moderate grill for 5 minutes until lightly browned. Serve warm or cold with a mixed salad.

For a French bean and pepper tortilla, omit the peppercorns, goats' cheese and beans and add 2 sliced red peppers, or 1 red and 1 green, and some sliced green beans with the onion and potatoes. Pour over the eggs and cook as above.

242

GRILLED POLENTA & CHEESE BAKE

Serves **4**
Preparation time **8 minutes**
Cooking time **25–30 minutes**

200 g (7 oz) **roasted red peppers in olive oil**
1 kg (2 lb) ready-made, firm **polenta**, cut into 5 mm (¼ inch) slices
150 g (5 oz) **fontina cheese**, grated
150 g (5 oz) **pecorino cheese**, grated
1 **garlic clove**, chopped
350 ml (12 fl oz) **passata**
1 teaspoon finely grated **lemon rind**
pinch of **caster sugar**
small bunch of **basil**, shredded, plus extra whole leaves to garnish
salt and **pepper**

Drain and slice the red peppers, reserving 3 tablespoons of the oil.

Arrange half the polenta slices in a lightly buttered ovenproof dish and scatter over half the sliced peppers and cheeses.

Repeat the layers and cook in a preheated oven, 240°C (475°F), Gas Mark 9, for 15 minutes.

Meanwhile, heat the oil from the peppers in a pan and fry the garlic over a medium heat until soft and beginning to turn golden. Stir in the remaining ingredients, season to taste and bring to the boil, then reduce the heat and leave to bubble gently for 15–20 minutes.

Put the polenta bake under a preheated hot grill for 5 minutes to brown the top. Garnish with basil leaves and serve immediately with the tomato sauce.

For semolina gnocchi, add 250 g (8 oz) semolina to 900 ml (1½ pints) boiling milk, reduce the heat and simmer for 5 minutes, stirring the mixture constantly with a whisk until thick. Add a little butter then pour into a 1 kg (2 lb) loaf tin. Cook in a preheated oven, 180°C (350°F), Gas Mark 4, until firm, and slice. Layer and grill as above.

VEGETABLE & CHEESE WRAP

Serves **4**
Preparation time **10 minutes**
Cooking time **6–8 minutes**

200 g (7 oz) **soft, mild goats' cheese**
8 medium-sized **soft tortilla wraps**
16 **basil leaves**
150 g (5 oz) **grilled artichokes in oil**, drained
150 g (5 oz) **grilled aubergines in oil**, drained
150 g (5 oz) **grilled peppers in oil**, drained
8 **sun-dried tomatoes**
50 g (2 oz) **pine nuts**, lightly toasted
75 g (3 oz) **wild rocket**
4 tablespoons **Parmesan cheese** shavings (optional)

Spread the cheese over the tortillas and arrange the basil leaves lengthways in the centre of each wrap. Top with the vegetables and finish with the pine nuts, rocket and Parmesan shavings, if used.

Roll up each tortilla by bringing in the sides and then rolling the wrap so that the sides are closed and the filling is concealed.

Heat a large, dry, griddle pan or frying pan over a medium heat. Cook the wraps for about 6–8 minutes, turning frequently. Remove from the heat, cut each one diagonally and serve immediately.

For cheese & tomato wraps with peppers, replace the goats' cheese with a soft cheese with herbs and garlic. Omit the artichokes and aubergines and replace the sun-dried tomatoes with 400 g (13 oz) fresh cherry tomatoes, which you should halve.

VEGETARIAN

STUFFED SWEET POTATO MELT

Serves **4**
Preparation time **10 minutes**
Cooking time **50 minutes**

4 **sweet potatoes**
350 g (11½ oz) **taleggio cheese**, sliced
½ teaspoon **dried thyme**
sprigs of **parsley**, to garnish

Caramelized onions
75 ml (3 fl oz) **vegetable oil**
6 large **onions**, sliced
4 tablespoons **white wine**
3 tablespoons **white wine vinegar**
1 tablespoon **soft brown sugar**
1 teaspoon **dried thyme**
salt and **pepper**

Prick the sweet potatoes with a sharp knife and put them in a preheated oven, 220°C (425°F), Gas Mark 7, for about 45 minutes or until the flesh is soft when tested with a knife.

Meanwhile, make the caramelized onions. Heat the oil in a large frying pan over a low heat and add all the remaining ingredients. Cook slowly, stirring occasionally, for about 30 minutes until the onions are nut brown and soft.

Remove the potatoes from the oven and put them on a baking sheet. Carefully slice the potatoes in half and pile over the caramelized onions. Top with the sliced taleggio and a sprinkling of thyme and cook under a preheated hot grill for 4–5 minutes until bubbling and beginning to brown.

Garnish with sprigs of parsley and serve immediately with a crisp green salad and a dollop of soured cream, if liked.

For polenta with caramelized onions & goats' cheese rounds, cut 2 x 500 g (1 lb) packets of ready-made polenta into 8 slices and cut 2 x 100 g (3½ oz) goats' cheeses into 4 slices each. Grill the polenta slices on one side. Turn them over and top each one with some caramelized onions, prepared as above, and 1 slice of goats' cheese. Return to the grill for about 5 minutes, until the cheese is brown on top and soft.

POTATO GRATIN WITH CHICORY

Serves **4**
Preparation time **10 minutes**
Cooking time **43–45 minutes**

1.5 kg (3 lb) **floury potatoes,** peeled and cut into
 3–4 mm (about ¼ inch) sliced
50 g (2 oz) **butter**
1 tablespoon **olive oil**
1 **onion**, sliced
3 **garlic cloves**, chopped
200 g (7 oz) **Cheddar cheese**, grated
400 ml (14 fl oz) **double cream** or full-fat **crème**
 fraîche
375 g (12 oz) **Reblochon** or **Brie cheese**, sliced
salt and **pepper**

To serve
3–4 heads **chicory**, separated
ready-made **French dressing**

Cook the potatoes in lightly salted boiling water for 10 minutes,
then drain.

Melt the butter with the oil in a medium saucepan and cook the onion for
about 5 minutes, or until soft and golden. Add the garlic and cook for a
further 2 minutes.

Add the grated cheese and cream or crème fraîche. Stir until the mixture
is hot and the cheese has melted. Season to taste.

Arrange half the potatoes in a lightly buttered, shallow, ovenproof dish.
Place half the cheese slices over the potatoes and pour over half the
cheese sauce. Cover with the remaining potato slices, the rest of
the cheese sauce and top with the remaining cheese slices.

Cook in a preheated oven, 220°C (425°F), Gas Mark 7, for
30–35 minutes until bubbling and golden brown. Serve immediately
with the chicory and dressing.

For Italian-style gratin, use 150 g (5 oz) grated pecorino and
400 g (13 oz) fontina for the hard and soft cheeses. Sprinkle over a
teaspoon of dried Italian herbs and add 1 teaspoon finely chopped
rosemary before baking.

PEA & LEEK OMELETTE

Serves **4**
Preparation time **5–6 minutes**
Cooking time **19–22 minutes**

250 g (8 oz) baby **new potatoes**
75 g (3 oz) **butter**
1 tablespoon **olive oil**
500 g (1 lb) **leeks**, trimmed, cleaned and cut into 1 cm
 (½ inch) slices
200 g (7 oz) frozen or fresh **peas**
6 **eggs**
150 ml (5 fl oz) **milk**
2 tablespoons chopped **chives**
125 g (4 oz) **soft garlic and chive cheese**
salt and **pepper**

To serve
125 g (4 oz) **salad leaves**
4 tablespoons ready-made **salad dressing**

Cook the potatoes in boiling water for about 10 minutes or until cooked
but still firm.

Meanwhile, melt the butter with the oil in a large frying pan, add the
leeks, cover and cook, stirring frequently, for 8–10 minutes or until soft.
Stir in the peas.

Drain the potatoes, cut them into quarters and add to the frying pan.
Continue cooking for 2–3 minutes.

Whisk the eggs with the milk and chives, season well and pour into the
frying pan. Move around with a spatula so that the vegetables are well
coated and the egg begins to cook. Crumble the cheese on top and
leave over a medium heat for 2–3 minutes until the egg becomes firm.

Place under a preheated hot grill for 3–4 minutes until the omelette is
completely set and the top is golden brown. Serve in thick slices with a
prepared salad and ready-made dressing.

For quick herb salad dressing, whisk together 6 tablespoons olive oil,
2 tablespoons wine vinegar, 3 tablespoons chopped parsley, ½ grated
small onion, ½ teaspoon mustard, ¼ teaspoon caster sugar and a little
ground coriander. Season to taste.

PUMPKIN, LEEK & POTATO BAKE

Serves **4**
Preparation time **30 minutes**
Cooking time **2 hours**

4 tablespoons **hot horseradish sauce**
1 tablespoon chopped **thyme**
300 ml (½ pint) **double cream**
1 large **leek**, finely shredded
100 g (3½ oz) **walnuts**, roughly chopped
500 g (1 lb) **pumpkin**
750 g (1½ lb) **baking potatoes**, thinly sliced
150 ml (¼ pint) **vegetable stock**
50 g (2 oz) **breadcrumbs**
40 g (1½ oz) **butter**, melted
2 tablespoons **pumpkin seeds**
salt

Mix the horseradish sauce in a large bowl with the thyme and half the cream. Add the leek and all but 2 tablespoons of the walnuts and mix well.

Cut the pumpkin into chunks, discarding the skin and seeds. Thinly slice the chunks.

Scatter half the potatoes in a 2 litre (3½ pint) shallow, ovenproof dish, seasoning lightly with salt, and cover with half the pumpkin chunks. Spoon the leek mixture on top, spreading in an even layer. Arrange the remaining pumpkin slices on top and then the remaining potato slices. Sprinkle with salt.

Mix the remaining cream with the stock and pour over the potatoes. Mix the breadcrumbs with the butter and sprinkle over the top. Scatter with the pumpkin seeds and remaining nuts. Cover with foil and bake in a preheated oven, 180°C (350°F), Gas Mark 4, for 1 hour. Remove the foil and bake for a further 45–60 minutes until golden and the vegetables feel tender when pierced with a knife.

For spicy pumpkin and potato bake, use a finely chopped chilli or 50 g (2 oz) grated fresh root ginger instead of the horseradish. Replace the leek with 1 large bunch spring onions, finely chopped. Bake as above until the vegetables are tender.

GNOCCHI WITH SPINACH & GORGONZOLA

Serves **3–4**
Preparation time **5 minutes**
Cooking time **10 minutes**

250 g (8 oz) **baby spinach**
300 ml (½ pint) **vegetable stock**
500 g (1 lb) **potato gnocchi**
150 g (5 oz) **Gorgonzola cheese**, cut into small pieces
3 tablespoons **double cream**
plenty of freshly grated **nutmeg**
pepper

Wash the spinach leaves thoroughly, if necessary. Pat them dry on kitchen paper.

Bring the stock to the boil in a large saucepan. Tip in the gnocchi and return to the boil. Cook for 2–3 minutes or until plumped up and tender.

Stir in the cheese, cream and nutmeg and heat until the cheese melts to make a creamy sauce.

Add the spinach to the pan and cook gently for 1–2 minutes, turning the spinach with the gnocchi and sauce until wilted. Pile on to serving plates and season with plenty of black pepper.

For homemade vegetable stock, heat 2 tablespoons olive oil in a large saucepan. Add 1 large chopped onion, 2 chopped carrots, 125 g (4 oz) chopped turnip or parsnip, 3 sliced celery sticks and 125 g (4 oz) sliced mushrooms and fry gently for 5 minutes. Add 2 bay leaves, several thyme and parsley sprigs, 2 chopped tomatoes, 2 teaspoons black peppercorns and the onion skin and cover with 1.8 litres (3 pints) water. Bring to the boil, then partially cover and simmer gently for 1 hour. Cool, then strain. Refrigerate for up to 2 days or freeze.

SPINACH & SWEET POTATO CAKES

Serves **4**

Preparation time **35 minutes**, plus infusing

Cooking time **about 40 minutes**

500 g (1 lb) **sweet potatoes**, peeled and cut
　into chunks

125 g (4 oz) **spinach leaves**

4–5 **spring onions**, finely sliced

olive oil, for deep-frying

3 tablespoons **sesame seeds**

4 tablespoons **plain flour**

salt and **pepper**

Red chilli & coconut dip

200 ml (7 fl oz) **coconut cream**

2 **red chillies**, deseeded and finely chopped

1 **lemon grass stalk**, thinly sliced

3 **kaffir lime leaves**, shredded

small bunch of fresh **coriander**, chopped

2 tablespoons **sesame oil**

To garnish

lime wedges

spring onions, shredded

Cook the sweet potatoes in lightly salted boiling water for about
20 minutes or until tender. Drain, then return them to the pan and place
over a low heat for 1 minute, stirring constantly, so the excess moisture
evaporates. Lightly mash the potatoes with a fork.

Meanwhile, put the spinach in a colander and pour over a kettle of
boiling water. Refresh the spinach in cold water and squeeze dry. Stir the
spinach into the potatoes. Add the spring onions, season and set aside.

Make the dip. Gently warm the coconut cream in a pan with the chillies,
lemon grass and lime leaves for about 10 minutes. Don't let it boil. Set
aside to infuse.

Heat the oil in a large pan or deep-fat fryer to 180°C (350°F) or until a
cube of bread browns in 20 seconds. Use your hands to form the potato
mixture into 12 cakes. Mix together the sesame seeds and flour and
sprinkle over the cakes, then carefully lower them into the oil and fry
in batches for about 3 minutes until they are golden and crispy. Drain
on kitchen paper and keep warm while you cook the rest.

Stir the coriander and sesame oil into the dip and pour it into 4 individual
dishes. Serve immediately with the potato cakes.

For sage-seasoned spinach & sweet potato cakes, shred 6 large fresh
sage leaves and add to the potato cakes. Cook 400 g (13 oz) cooking
apples and beat to a purée with 3–4 tablespoons sugar. Add 25 g melted
butter and the rind of 1 lemon. Serve the hot cakes with the apple sauce.

248

ASPARAGUS WITH TARRAGON DRESSING

Serves **4**
Preparation time **20 minutes**
Cooking time **about 5 minutes**

3 tablespoons **olive oil** (optional)
500 g (1 lb) **asparagus**
750 g (1½ lb) **rocket** or other **salad leaves**
2 **green onions**, finely sliced
4 **radishes**, thinly sliced
salt and **pepper**

Tarragon & lemon dressing
finely grated rind of 2 **lemons**
4 tablespoons **tarragon vinegar**
2 tablespoons chopped **tarragon**
½ teaspoon **Dijon mustard**
pinch of **caster sugar**
150 ml (¼ pint) **olive oil**

To garnish
roughly chopped **herbs**, such as tarragon, parsley,
  chervil or dill
thin strips of **lemon rind**

Make the dressing. Combine the lemon rind, vinegar, tarragon, mustard and sugar in a small bowl and season to taste. Stir to mix, then gradually whisk in the oil. Alternatively, place all the ingredients in a screw-top jar and shake well to combine. Set aside.

Heat the oil (if used) in a large frying pan. Add the asparagus in a single layer and cook for about 5 minutes, turning occasionally. (The asparagus should be tender when pierced with the tip of a sharp knife and lightly patched with brown.)

Transfer the asparagus to a shallow dish and sprinkle with salt and pepper. Cover with the dressing, toss gently and leave to stand for 5 minutes.

Arrange the salad leaves in a serving dish, sprinkle over the onions and radishes and pile the asparagus in the centre of the leaves. Garnish with chopped herbs and thin strips of lemon rind. Serve on its own with bread or as an accompaniment to a main dish.

For garlic & mustard dressing as an alternative to tarragon and lemon, place in a screw-top jar 1 finely chopped small garlic clove, 1 finely chopped small shallot, 2 tablespoons wholegrain mustard, a pinch each of salt, pepper and sugar, 125 ml (4 fl oz) olive oil and 2–3 tablespoons shallot or red wine vinegar. Place the lid on the jar and shake until the ingredients are well combined. Serve drizzled over the asparagus.

QUICK & EASY MISO SOUP

Serves **4**

Preparation time **10 minutes**
Cooking time **10 minutes**

1 quantity **vegetable stock**
2 tablespoons **miso paste**
125 g (4 oz) **shiitake mushrooms**, sliced
200 g (7 oz) **firm tofu**, cubed

Put the stock in a saucepan and heat until simmering.

Add the miso paste, shiitake mushrooms and tofu to the stock and simmer gently for 5 minutes. Serve immediately with rice.

For sticky rice, to serve as an accompaniment, wash 300 g (10 oz) glutinous rice in several changes of water and drain. Put in a large mixing bowl, cover with cold water and leave to soak for about 1 hour. Drain the rice and wash it again. Put in a saucepan with 300 ml (½ pint) water and bring to a simmer. Cover and cook very gently for 20 minutes or until the water is absorbed and the rice is tender. Add a little more water if the pan dries out before the rice is cooked.

BUTTER BEAN & TOMATO SOUP

Serves **4**

Preparation time **10 minutes**
Cooking time **20 minutes**

3 tablespoons **olive oil**
1 **onion**, finely chopped
2 **celery sticks**, thinly sliced
2 **garlic cloves**, thinly sliced
2 x 400 g (13 oz) cans **butter beans**, rinsed
   and drained
4 tablespoons **sun-dried tomato paste**
900 ml (1½ pints) **vegetable stock**
1 tablespoon chopped **rosemary** or **thyme**
salt and **pepper**
Parmesan cheese shavings, to serve

Heat the oil in a saucepan. Add the onion and fry for 3 minutes until softened. Add the celery and garlic and fry for 2 minutes.

Add the butter beans, sun-dried tomato paste, stock, rosemary or thyme and a little salt and pepper. Bring to the boil, then reduce the heat, cover and simmer gently for 15 minutes. Serve sprinkled with the Parmesan shavings. This soup makes a light main course served with bread and plenty of Parmesan.

For spiced carrot and lentil soup, in a saucepan, heat 2 tablespoons oil and fry 1 chopped onion, 2 crushed garlic cloves and 375 g (12 oz) chopped carrots for 10 minutes. Add a 400 g (13 oz) can lentils, drained, 2 teaspoons ground coriander, 1 teaspoon ground cumin and 1 tablespoon chopped thyme and fry for 1 minute. Stir in 1 litre (1¾ pints) vegetable stock, a 400 g (13 oz) can chopped tomatoes and 2 teaspoons lemon juice and bring to the boil. Cover and simmer gently for 20 minutes. Blend until smooth then warm through.

FENNEL & LEMON SOUP

Serves **4**
Preparation time **20 minutes**, plus chilling
Cooking time **25 minutes**

50 ml (2 fl oz) **olive oil**
3 fat **spring onions**, chopped
250 g (8 oz) **fennel bulb**, trimmed, cored and thinly
    sliced
1 **potato**, diced
finely grated rind and juice of 1 **lemon**
about 1.8 litres (3 pints) hot **vegetable stock**
pepper

Gremolata

1 small **garlic clove**, finely chopped
finely grated rind of 1 **lemon**
4 tablespoons chopped **parsley**
16 **black olives**, pitted and chopped

Heat the oil in a large saucepan, add the spring onions and cook for 5 minutes or until beginning to soften. Add the fennel, potato and lemon rind and cook for 5 minutes until the fennel begins to soften. Pour in the stock and bring to the boil. Reduce the heat, cover and simmer for about 15 minutes or until the ingredients are tender.

Meanwhile, make the gremolata. Mix together the garlic, lemon rind and parsley, then stir the chopped olives into the mixture. Cover and chill.

Liquidize the soup in a food processor or blender and pass it through a sieve. The soup should not be too thick, so add more stock if necessary. Return it to the rinsed pan and warm through. Taste and season with pepper and plenty of lemon juice. Pour into warm bowls and sprinkle each serving with gremolata, to be stirred in before eating. Serve with slices of toasted crusty bread, if liked.

For butter bean & fennel soup, heat 900 ml (1 ½ pints) vegetable stock with 2 trimmed, cored and sliced fennel bulbs, 1 sliced onion, 1 sliced carrot, 1 sliced courgette and 2 crushed garlic cloves. Boil gently for 20 minutes, then add 2 x 400 g (13½ oz) cans butter beans and a 400 g (13½ oz) can chopped tomatoes. Heat, stir in 2 tablespoons chopped sage, process to blend and serve.

SPICED PUMPKIN & SPINACH SOUP

Serves **4**
Preparation time **10 minutes**
Cooking time **30–32 minutes**

50 g (2 oz) **butter**
2 tablespoons **olive oil**
1 **onion**, roughly chopped
2 **garlic cloves**, peeled
1.5 kg (3 lb) **pumpkin**, peeled and roughly chopped
1 teaspoon **ground coriander**
½ teaspoon **cayenne pepper**
½ teaspoon **ground cinnamon**
¼ teaspoon **ground allspice**
750 ml (1¼ pints) hot **vegetable stock**
150 g (5 oz) **frozen spinach**
salt and **pepper**

To serve

2 tablespoons **pumpkin seeds**, lightly toasted
4 teaspoons **pumpkin seed oil**

Heat the butter and oil in a large, heatproof casserole and add the onion and garlic. Cook over a medium heat for 5–6 minutes until soft and golden.

Add the pumpkin and continue cooking for a further 8 minutes, stirring frequently, until beginning to soften and turn golden. Add the spices and cook for 2–3 minutes, making sure that the pumpkin is well coated.

Pour in the hot stock and bring to the boil, then reduce the heat, cover and leave to bubble gently for about 15 minutes until the pumpkin is soft.

Use a hand-held blender to liquidize the pumpkin until smooth, then stir in the spinach. Reheat for about 5 minutes until the spinach has melted and the soup is hot. Season to taste.

Spoon the soup into bowls, scatter over the lightly toasted pumpkin seeds and a drizzle of pumpkin oil and serve immediately.

For butternut, spinach & coconut soup, use 500 g (1 lb) butternut squash, peeled, deseeded and cubed, instead of the pumpkin and cook as above. Stir in 200 ml (7 fl oz) coconut milk before serving.

GREEN BEAN, MISO & NOODLE SOUP

Serves **2**
Preparation time **10 minutes**
Cooking time **10 minutes**

3 tablespoons **brown miso paste**
1 litre (1¾ pints) **vegetable stock**
25 g (1 oz) **fresh root ginger**, grated
2 **garlic cloves**, thinly sliced
1 small **hot red chilli**, deseeded and thinly sliced
100 g (3½ oz) **soba, wholemeal** or **plain noodles**
1 bunch **spring onions**, finely shredded
100 g (3½ oz) **fresh** or **frozen peas**
250 g (8 oz) **runner beans**, trimmed and shredded
3 tablespoons **mirin**
1 tablespoon **sugar**
1 tablespoon **rice wine vinegar**

Blend the miso paste with a dash of the stock in a saucepan to make a thick, smooth paste. Add a little more stock to thin the paste and then pour in the remainder. Add the ginger, garlic and chilli and bring almost to the boil.

Reduce the heat to a gentle simmer and stir in the noodles, stirring until they have softened into the stock – about 5 minutes.

Add the spring onions, peas, runner beans, mirin, sugar and vinegar and stir well.

Cook gently for 1–2 minutes until the vegetables have softened slightly. Ladle into bowls and serve immediately.

For miso soup with tofu, make dashi stock by boiling 15 g (½ oz) kombu seaweed in 1.8 litres (3 pints) water, skimming any scum. Add 1½ tablespoons dried bonito flakes and simmer, uncovered, for 20 minutes. Off the heat, stir in ½ tablespoon dried bonito flakes and set aside for 5 minutes. Strain and return to the pan. Mix 2 tablespoons red or white miso with a little dashi stock, then add 1 tablespoon at a time to the stock, stirring until dissolved. Cut 1 small leek into fine julienne strips and 125 g (4 oz) firm tofu into small squares and add to the warm soup with 1 tablespoon wakame seaweed. Garnish with chopped chives.

RED PEPPER SOUP

Serves **4**
Preparation time **15 minutes**
Cooking time **35 minutes**

2 **onions**, finely chopped
2 tablespoons **olive oil**
1 **garlic clove**, crushed
3 **red peppers**, deseeded and roughly chopped
2 **courgettes**, finely chopped
900 ml (1½ pints) **vegetable stock**
   or **water**
salt and **pepper**

To garnish
natural yogurt or **double cream**
chopped **chives**

Put the onions in a large saucepan with the oil and gently fry for 5 minutes or until softened and golden brown. Add the garlic and cook gently for 1 minute.

Add the red peppers and half the courgettes and fry for 5–8 minutes or until softened and brown.

Add the stock or water to the pan with salt and pepper and bring to the boil. Reduce the heat, cover the pan and simmer gently for 20 minutes.

When the vegetables are tender, blend the mixture in batches, to a smooth soup and return to the pan. Season to taste, reheat and serve topped with the remaining chopped courgette and garnished with yogurt or a swirl of cream and chopped chives. This vibrant and warming soup is ideal for any meal and tastes just as good warm or cold.

For Provençal peppers, heat 1 tablespoon oil and fry 2 sliced onions until soft. Add 4 sliced red peppers and 1 crushed garlic clove and cook for 5 minutes. Stir in a 400 g (13 oz) can of tomatoes, 2 tablespoons chopped fresh herbs and season. Bring to the boil, then reduce the heat and simmer, uncovered, for 15 minutes. Serve hot or cold.

TABBOULEH WITH FRUIT & NUTS

Serves **4**
Preparation time **10 minutes**, plus soaking

150 g (5 oz) **bulgar wheat**
75 g (3 oz) **unsalted, shelled pistachio nuts**
1 small **red onion**, finely chopped
3 **garlic cloves**, crushed
25 g (1 oz) **flat leaf parsley**, chopped
15 g (½ oz) **mint**, chopped
finely grated rind and juice of 1 **lemon** or **lime**
150 g (5 oz) **ready-to-eat prunes**, sliced
4 tablespoons **olive oil**
salt and **pepper**

Put the bulgar wheat in a bowl, cover with plenty of boiling water and leave to soak for 15 minutes.

Meanwhile, put the nuts in a separate bowl and cover with boiling water. Leave to stand for 1 minute, then drain. Rub the nuts between several thicknesses of kitchen paper to remove most of the skins, then peel away any remaining skins with your fingers.

Mix the nuts with the onion, garlic, parsley, mint, lemon or lime rind and juice and prunes in a large bowl.

Drain the bulgar wheat thoroughly in a sieve, pressing out as much moisture as possible with the back of a spoon. Add to the other ingredients with the oil and toss together. Season to taste with salt and pepper and chill until ready to serve.

For classic tabbouleh, omit the nuts and prunes and add 6 chopped tomatoes and 50 g (2 oz) chopped black olives. Use only 2 garlic cloves and be sure to use a lemon not a lime.

ZESTY QUINOA SALAD

Serves **4**
Preparation time **15 minutes**
Cooking time **15–20 minutes**

150 g (5 oz) **quinoa**, rinsed
1 small **yellow pepper**, cored, deseeded and diced
1 small **red pepper**, cored, deseeded and diced
4 **spring onions**, sliced
⅓ **cucumber**, deseeded and diced
½ **fennel bulb**, finely diced
2 tablespoons finely chopped **curly parsley**
2 tablespoons finely chopped **mint**
2 tablespoons finely chopped **coriander**
2 tablespoons **sunflower seeds**
juice and finely grated rind of **2 limes**
8 **physalis**, quartered

Dressing
4 teaspoons **harissa paste**
juice and finely grated rind of **2 limes**
8 tablespoons **sunflower oil**
salt and **pepper**

Put the quinoa in a pan of cold water, bring to the boil and cook for 15–20 minutes or until the quinoa is translucent and just cooked. Drain and rinse thoroughly in cold water.

Meanwhile, make the dressing by mixing together the harissa paste, lime juice and rind and oil. Season to taste and set aside.

Mix the cooked quinoa with the prepared vegetables and herbs, 1 tablespoon of the sunflower seeds and the lime juice and rind.

Scatter over the physalis and the remaining sunflower seeds and serve with the dressing.

For baked potatoes with quinoa salad, coat 4 large potatoes, about 400 g each, with olive oil and salt, prick all over with a fork and bake in a preheated oven, 220°C (425°F), Gas Mark 7, for about an hour, until the skins are crisp and a skewer slides in easily. Make the salad as above, omitting the sunflower seeds, limes and physalis. Mix 200 ml (7 fl oz) soured cream with 2 tablespoons chopped chives and a little nutmeg. Fill the potatoes with the salad and top with the soured cream instead of the dressing.

SPICY FRIED RICE WITH SPINACH SALAD

Serves **3–4**
Preparation time **10 minutes**
Cooking time **10 minutes**

4 **eggs**
2 tablespoons **sherry**
2 tablespoons **light soy sauce**
1 bunch **spring onions**
4 tablespoons **stir-fry or wok oil**
75 g (3 oz) **unsalted cashew nuts**
1 **green pepper**, deseeded and finely chopped
½ teaspoon **Chinese five-spice powder**
250 g (8 oz) **ready-cooked long-grain rice**
150 g (5 oz) **baby spinach**
100 g (3½ oz) **sprouted mung beans** or 50 g (2 oz) **pea shoots**
salt and **pepper**
sweet chilli sauce, to serve

Beat the eggs with the sherry and 1 tablespoon of the soy sauce in a small bowl. Cut 2 of the spring onions into 7 cm (3 inch) lengths, then cut lengthways into fine shreds. Leave in a bowl of very cold water to curl up slightly. Finely chop the remaining spring onions, keeping the white and green parts separate.

Heat half the oil in a large frying pan or wok and fry the cashew nuts and green parts of the spring onions, turning in the oil, until the cashew nuts are lightly browned. Drain with a slotted spoon.

Add the white parts of the spring onions to the pan and stir-fry for 1 minute. Add the beaten eggs and cook, stirring constantly, until the egg starts to scramble into small pieces, rather than one omelette.

Stir in the green pepper and five-spice powder with the remaining oil and cook for 1 minute, then tip in the cooked rice and spinach with the remaining soy sauce, mixing the ingredients together well until thoroughly combined and the spinach has wilted.

Return the cashew nuts and spring onions to the pan with the mung beans or pea shoots and season to taste. Pile on to serving plates, scatter with the drained spring onion curls and serve with sweet chilli sauce.

For spicy fried rice with baby corn, replace the spinach with ½ small Chinese cabbage, shredded, and 200 g (7 oz) baby corn, sliced, and add to the pan in the fourth step with the green pepper.

BROAD BEAN SALAD

Serves **4**
Preparation time **10 minutes**
Cooking time **20 minutes**

2 **aubergines**, thinly sliced into rounds
2 **yellow courgettes**, thinly sliced lengthways
4–6 tablespoons **olive oil**
300 g (10 oz) **frozen baby broad beans**
1 tablespoon chopped **dill**
1 tablespoon chopped **mint**
1 small **fennel bulb**, thinly sliced
200 g (7 oz) **feta cheese**, crumbled
salt and **pepper**
mint leaves, to garnish
1 **lemon**, cut into wedges, to serve

Brush the aubergines and courgettes with oil and cook in a griddle pan for 2–3 minutes on each side until soft and golden. You will have to do this in several batches.

Cook the broad beans in boiling water until tender. Drain and toss with 1 tablespoon of the oil, the herbs and plenty of seasoning.

Leave the broad beans, aubergines and courgettes to cool before assembling or serve them as a warm salad. Arrange the aubergine and courgette slices on serving plates, scatter over the broad beans and sliced fennel and then the feta. Sprinkle over a few mint leaves and serve with lemon wedges.

For broad bean & celeriac salad, replace the courgettes with 2 thinly sliced red peppers and the fennel with 250 g (8 oz) coarsely grated celeriac.

WILD RICE & GOATS' CHEESE SALAD

Serves **4**
Preparation time **10 minutes**
Cooking time **about**
  15 minutes

250 g (8 oz) mixed **long grain** and **wild rice**
100 g (3½ oz) **fine green beans**
4 tablespoons **olive oil**
3 **red onions**, thinly sliced
150 ml (5 fl oz) **balsamic vinegar**
1 teaspoon chopped **thyme**
125 g (4 oz) **goats' cheese**, sliced
8 **baby plum tomatoes**, halved
small bunch of **basil**
salt and **pepper**

Cook the rice in lightly salted boiling water for about 15 minutes until tender or according to the instructions on the packet. Add the green beans for the final 2 minutes of cooking. Drain and set aside.

Meanwhile, heat the oil in a large frying pan and cook the onions gently for about 12 minutes or until soft and golden. Add the balsamic vinegar and thyme, season with salt and pepper and allow to bubble gently for 2–3 minutes until the mixture thickens slightly.

Stir the onions into the rice and beans and leave to cool. Once cool, scatter over the cheese, tomatoes and basil leaves and serve.

For pearl barley salad with smoked cheese, replace the rice with the same quantity of pearl barley and cook in boiling water for 25–35 minutes until tender, then drain. Substitute the goats' cheese for diced smoked cheese.

256

BEETROOT & SQUASH SPAGHETTI

Serves **4**

Preparation time **8 minutes**

Cooking time **10 minutes**

300 g (10 oz) dried **spaghetti** or **fusilli**

150 g (5 oz) **fine green beans**

500 g (1 lb) **butternut squash**, peeled, deseeded and cut into 1 cm (½ inch) dice

4 tablespoons **olive oil**

500 g (1 lb) raw **beetroot**, cut into 1 cm (½ inch) dice

50 g (2 oz) **walnuts**, crushed

150 g (5 oz) **goats' cheese**, diced

2 tablespoons **lemon juice**

freshly grated **Parmesan cheese** (optional)

Cook the pasta in lightly salted boiling water for 10 minutes or until just cooked. Add the beans and squash for the final 2 minutes of cooking time.

Meanwhile, heat the oil in a large frying pan, add the beetroot and cook, stirring occasionally, for 10 minutes until cooked but still firm.

Toss the drained pasta mixture with the beetroot, walnuts and goats' cheese. Squeeze over the lemon juice and serve immediately with a bowl of Parmesan, if liked.

For baby carrot & squash spaghetti, replace the beetroot with the same quantity of baby carrots, cooked in boiling water for about 5 minutes, until tender. Roast the butternut squash with 4 garlic cloves and the oil in a preheated oven, 240°C (475°F), Gas Mark 9, for about 40 minutes or until softened. Replace the goats' cheese with havarti or dolcelatte.

RICOTTA-BAKED LARGE PASTA SHELLS

Serves **4**
Preparation time **20 minutes**
Cooking time **30 minutes**

250 g (8 oz) **dried conchiglie rigate**
400 g (13 oz) **ricotta cheese**
1 small **garlic clove**, crushed
125 g (4 oz) **Parmesan cheese**, freshly grated
20 g (¾ oz) **basil**, finely chopped
125 g (4 oz) **baby spinach**, roughly chopped
1 quantity **Quickest-ever Tomato Pasta Sauce** 150 g
   (5 oz) **mozzarella cheese**, cut into cubes
salt and **black pepper**

Cook the pasta in a large saucepan of salted boiling water according to the packet instructions until al dente. Drain, refresh in cold water, then drain again thoroughly.

Meanwhile, make the filling. Put the ricotta in a large bowl and break up with a fork. Stir in the garlic, half the Parmesan, the basil and spinach. Season generously with salt and pepper and use this mixture to stuff the pasta shells.

Spoon one quarter of the tomato sauce over the base of an ovenproof dish and arrange the pasta shells, open-side uppermost, on top. Pour the remaining sauce evenly over, then scatter with the mozzarella and the remaining Parmesan.

Bake in a preheated oven, 220°C (425°F), Gas Mark 7, for 20 minutes until golden brown.

For watercress & chickpea shells with béchamel, use 1 quantity béchamel sauce from the Spring Cannelloni recipe instead of the tomato sauce. Finely chop 150 g (5 oz) watercress and combine with 2 chopped spring onions and a 400 g (13 oz) can chickpeas, drained and chopped. Mix with the ricotta, parmesan and basil as above, omitting the garlic and spinach. Layer the béchamel and filled pasta shells, then top with cheese as above.

SPRING CANNELLONI

Serves **4**
Preparation time **30 minutes**
Cooking time **30–40 minutes**

500 ml (17 fl oz) **milk**
1 **bay leaf**
1 small **onion**, quartered
125 g (4 oz) shelled **broad beans**, fresh or frozen
125 g (4 oz) shelled **peas**, fresh or frozen
20 g (¾ oz) **mint**, chopped
20 g (¾ oz) **basil**, chopped
1 **garlic clove**, crushed
300 g (10 oz) **ricotta cheese**
75 g (3 oz) **Parmesan cheese**, plus extra for sprinkling
40 g (1½ oz) **butter**
30 g (1¼ oz) **plain flour**
75 ml (3 fl oz) **dry white wine**
150 g (5 oz) **dried lasagne sheets**
salt and **black pepper**

Bring the milk with the bay leaf and onion to a simmer in a saucepan. Infuse off the heat for 20 minutes. Strain.

Meanwhile, cook the beans and peas in boiling water until tender: 6–8 minutes for fresh or 2 minutes for frozen. Drain and refresh in cold water. Process half in a food processor with the herbs and garlic to a rough purée. Combine with the ricotta, Parmesan and remaining vegetables. Season with salt and pepper.

Melt the butter in a saucepan over a very low heat. Add the flour and cook, stirring, for 2 minutes until a light biscuity colour. Remove from the heat and slowly add the infused milk, stirring away any lumps as you go. Return to the heat, bring to a simmer, stirring, and pour in the wine. Simmer for 5–6 minutes until thick. Season with salt and pepper.

Cook the pasta in a large saucepan of salted boiling water according to the packet instructions until just al dente. Drain, refresh in cold water, then cut into 16 pieces 8 x 9 cm (3¼ x 3½ inches).

Spread 1½ tablespoons of filling on to each pasta piece and roll up. Spread half the sauce in an ovenproof dish and top with the rolls in a single layer. Spoon over the remaining sauce. Sprinkle with Parmesan. Bake in a preheated oven, 200°C (400°F), Gas Mark 6, for 15 minutes until golden brown.

For spinach cannelloni, chop and wilt 250 g (8 oz) spinach in a little butter in a covered pan and use instead of the beans and peas. Cook as above, replacing the mint and basil with grated nutmeg.

DOLCELATTE & SPINACH GNOCCHI

Serves **4**
Preparation time **5 minutes**
Cooking time **20 minutes**

500 g (1 lb) **bought gnocchi** or **1 quantity Classic
    Potato Gnocchi**
15 g (½ oz) **unsalted butter**
125 g (4 oz) **baby spinach**
large pinch of freshly grated **nutmeg**
175 g (6 oz) **dolcelatte cheese**, cut into cubes
125 ml (4 fl oz) **double cream**
3 tablespoons freshly grated **Parmesan cheese**
salt and **black pepper**

Cook the gnocchi in a large saucepan of salted boiling water until they rise to the surface: according to the packet instructions for bought gnocchi or for 3–4 minutes if using homemade. Drain thoroughly.

Meanwhile, melt the butter in a saucepan over a high heat, and when it starts to sizzle, add the spinach and cook, stirring, for 1 minute, or until just wilted. Remove from the heat and season with nutmeg, salt and pepper, then stir in the dolcelatte, cream and gnocchi.

Transfer to an ovenproof dish and scatter with the Parmesan. Bake in a preheated oven, 220°C (425°F), Gas Mark 7, for 12–15 minutes until the sauce is bubbling and golden.

For dolcelatte, kale & leek gnocchi, replace the spinach with 250 g (8 oz) finely shredded kale and 1 finely sliced leek, cooked in butter for 3–4 minutes. Omit the nutmeg. Season with salt and pepper and combine with the dolcelatte, cream and gnocchi. Bake as above.

260

VEGETARIAN

AUBERGINE & RIGATONI BAKE

Serves **4–6**
Preparation time **30 minutes**, plus standing
Cooking time **40 minutes**

olive oil, for frying
3 large **aubergines**, cut into
    5 mm (¼ inch) slices
1½ tablespoons **dried oregano**
375 g (12 oz) **dried penne** or **rigatoni**
1 quantity **Tomato Pasta Sauce**
2 x 150 g (5 oz) **mozzarella balls**, roughly chopped
75 g (3 oz) **Parmesan cheese**, freshly grated
2 tablespoons **fresh white breadcrumbs**
salt and **black pepper**

Heat 1 cm (½ inch) oil in a large frying pan over a high heat until the surface of the oil seems to shimmer slightly. Add the aubergines, in batches, and fry until golden on both sides. Remove with a slotted spoon and drain on a dish lined with kitchen paper. Scatter with the oregano and season lightly with salt.

Cook the pasta in a large saucepan of salted boiling water according to the packet instructions until almost al dente. Drain, then stir in a bowl with the tomato sauce, mozzarella and Parmesan. Season with salt and pepper.

Meanwhile, line the base and sides of an 18 cm (7 inch) springform cake tin with the aubergine slices. Overlap the slices slightly, to ensure that there are no gaps, then fill the tin with the pasta mixture. Press down so that the pasta is tightly packed, then cover with the remaining aubergine slices.

Scatter the breadcrumbs over the top of the pasta cake and bake on a baking sheet in a preheated oven, 200°C (400°F), Gas Mark 6, for 15 minutes until golden brown. Leave the cake to stand for 15 minutes before unclipping and removing the ring to serve. Don't attempt to remove the cake from its base, as it will most probably break in the process.

For courgette & rigatoni bake, use 6–7 large courgettes instead of the aubergines and cut them into long slices before frying.

TOMATO, PINE NUT & ROCKET PESTO

Serves **4–6**
Preparation time **10 minutes**
Cooking time **10–12 minutes**

400–600 g (13–1 lb 2 oz) **dried pasta twists**, such as fusilli
3 **ripe tomatoes**
4 **garlic cloves**, peeled
50 g (2 oz) **rocket leaves**, plus extra to garnish
100 g (3½ oz) **pine nuts**
150 ml (¼ pint) **olive oil**
salt and **black pepper**

Cook the pasta in a large saucepan of salted boiling water according to the packet instructions until al dente.

Meanwhile, finely chop the tomatoes, garlic cloves, rocket and pine nuts by hand, then stir in the oil. Season with salt and pepper. Transfer to a bowl.

Drain the pasta, add to the bowl with the pesto and toss to combine. Serve immediately, garnished with a few basil leaves.

For tomato, parsley & almond pesto, put 4 ripe tomatoes, 2 cloves garlic, 50 g (2 oz) parsley, 100 g (3½ oz) almonds and 150 ml (½ pint) olive oil in a food processor and process until smooth.

CLASSIC BASIL PESTO

Serves **4**
Preparation time **2 minutes**
Cooking time **10–12 minutes**

400 g (13 oz) **dried trofie**
75 g (3 oz) **basil leaves**
50 g (2 oz) **pine nuts**
2 **garlic cloves**
50 g (2 oz) **Parmesan cheese**, freshly grated, plus extra to serve
100 ml (3½ fl oz) **olive oil**
salt and **black pepper**
basil leaves, to garnish

Cook the pasta in a large saucepan of salted boiling water according to the packet instructions until al dente.

Meanwhile, put the basil, pine nuts and garlic in a food processor and process until well blended. Transfer to a bowl and stir in the Parmesan and oil. Season with salt and pepper.

Drain the pasta, reserving a ladleful of the cooking water, and return to the pan. Stir in the pesto, adding enough of the reserved pasta cooking water to loosen the mixture. Serve immediately with a scattering of grated Parmesan and garnished with basil leaves.

For potato & bean pesto pasta, the classic Genovese way of serving pesto, start by cooking 250 g (8 oz) peeled and sliced potatoes in a large saucepan of salted boiling water for 5 minutes, then add the pasta and cook according to the packet instructions until al dente. When there are 5 minutes of the cooking time remaining, add 150 g (5 oz) trimmed French beans to the pan. After draining the pasta, stir in the pesto as above. A long pasta shape such as linguine suits this variation better.

ROASTED TOMATO & RICOTTA PASTA

Serves **4**
Preparation time **10 minutes**
Cooking time **15–20 minutes**

500 g (1 lb) **cherry tomatoes**, halved
4 tablespoons **extra virgin olive oil**
2 teaspoons chopped **thyme leaves**
4 **garlic cloves**, sliced
pinch of **crushed dried chillies**
400 g (13 oz) **dried pasta**
1 bunch of **basil leaves**, torn
125 g (4 oz) **ricotta cheese**, crumbled
salt and **black pepper**

Put the tomatoes in a roasting tin with the oil, thyme, garlic and chillies, and season with salt and pepper. Roast in a preheated oven, 200°C (400°F), Gas Mark 6, for 15–20 minutes until the tomatoes have softened and released their juices.

Meanwhile, cook the pasta in a large saucepan of salted boiling water according to the packet instructions until al dente. Drain and return to the pan.

Stir the tomatoes with all their pan juices and most of the basil leaves into the pasta and toss gently until combined. Season with salt and pepper and spoon into serving bowls.

Chop the remaining basil, mix into the ricotta and season with salt and pepper. Spoon into a small dish for guests to spoon on to the pasta.

For roasted tomato & goats' cheese sauce, replace the ricotta with 125 g (4 oz) crumbly goats' cheese. This piquant, herb-scented dish goes well with pasta verde, spinach-flavoured pasta shapes.

VEGGIE CARBONARA

Serves **4**
Preparation time **5 minutes**
Cooling time **15 minutes**

2 tablespoons **olive oil**
2 **garlic cloves**, finely chopped
3 **courgettes**, thinly sliced
6 **spring onions**, cut into
   1 cm (½ inch) lengths
400 g (13 oz) **dried penne**
4 **egg yolks**
100 ml (3½ fl oz) **crème fraîche**
75 g (3 oz) freshly grated **Parmesan cheese**, plus
   extra to serve
salt and **black pepper**

Heat the oil in a heavy-based frying pan over a medium-high heat. Add the garlic, courgettes and spring onions and cook, stirring, for 4–5 minutes until the courgettes are tender. Set aside.

Cook the pasta in a large saucepan of salted boiling water according to the packet instructions until al dente.

Meanwhile, crack the egg yolks into a bowl and season with salt and a generous grinding of pepper. Mix together with a fork.

Just before the pasta is ready, return the pan with the courgette mixture to the heat. Stir in the crème fraîche and bring to the boil.

Drain the pasta thoroughly, return it to the pan and immediately stir in the egg mixture, Parmesan and the creamy courgette mixture. Stir vigorously and serve immediately with a scattering of grated Parmesan.

For asparagus carbonara, replace the courgettes with 250 g (8 oz) asparagus spears. Cut the spears into 2.5 cm (1 inch) lengths and cook in exactly the same way as the courgettes.

WILD MUSHROOM PAPPARDELLE

Serves **4**
Preparation time **15 minutes**
Cooking time **12–25 minutes**

375 g (12 oz) **mixed wild mushrooms**, cleaned
6 tablespoons **olive oil**
1 **garlic clove**, thinly sliced
1 **fresh red chilli**, deseeded and finely chopped
juice of ½ **lemon**
3 tablespoons roughly chopped **flat leaf parsley**
50 g (2 oz) **unsalted butter**, cut into cubes
400 g (13 oz) **dried pappardelle** or **homemade pappardelle**
salt and **black pepper**
fresh **Parmesan cheese shavings**, to serve

Trim the mushrooms, slicing porcini mushrooms (if you can find some fresh) and tearing large delicate mushrooms, such as chantarelles or oyster mushrooms.

Heat the oil in a large, heavy-based frying pan over a low heat. Add the garlic and chilli and leave the flavours to infuse for 5 minutes. If the garlic begins to colour, simply remove the pan from the hob and leave to infuse in the heat of the pan.

Increase the heat to high, add the mushrooms and cook, stirring, for 3–4 minutes until they are tender and golden. Remove from the heat and stir in the lemon juice, parsley and butter. Season with salt and pepper.

Cook the pasta in a large saucepan of salted boiling water until it is al dente: according to the packet instructions for dried pasta or for 2–3 minutes for fresh pasta. Drain thoroughly, reserving a ladleful of the cooking water.

Return the pan with the mushroom mixture to a medium heat and stir in the pasta. Toss until well combined, then pour in the reserved pasta cooking water and continue stirring until the pasta is well coated. Serve immediately with Parmesan shavings.

For creamy mushroom pappardelle, omit the chilli, halve the quantity of oil and stir 200 g (7 oz) crème fraîche into the mushrooms with the butter. Bring to the boil before removing from the heat, then continue with the recipe as above. Drizzle with 2 teaspoons truffle oil before serving.

264

VEGETARIAN

CHILLI POLENTA WITH CHERRY TOMATOES

Serves **4**

Preparation time **10 minutes**

Cooking time **30 minutes**

3 tablespoons **chilli-infused olive oil**

1 **garlic clove**, crushed

25 g (1 oz) **Parmesan cheese**, freshly grated

100 g (3½ oz) **sun-dried tomato pesto**

500 g (1 lb) **ready-made polenta**

250 g (8 oz) **cherry tomatoes**, halved

½ small **red onion**, thinly sliced

15 g (½ oz) chopped **parsley**

15 g (½ oz) chopped **chives**

50 g (2 oz) **black olives**, sliced

50 g (2 oz) **pine nuts**

2 tablespoons **balsamic glaze**

salt

Mix 1 tablespoon of the oil with the garlic, Parmesan and pesto. Slice the polenta horizontally into 2 thin slabs, then cut each in half to make 4 chunky slices. Cut each of the slices in half horizontally and use to sandwich the filling, making 4 sandwiches.

Arrange, slightly apart, in a shallow, ovenproof dish and bake in a preheated oven, 190°C (375°F), Gas Mark 5, for 15 minutes.

Meanwhile, mix the tomatoes in a bowl with the red onion, parsley, chives, olives, pine nuts and a little salt. Pile on top of the polenta and return to the oven for a further 15 minutes.

Beat the remaining oil with the balsamic glaze. Transfer the polenta stacks to serving plates and drizzle with the dressing. Serve with a rocket salad.

For homemade sun-dried tomato pesto, drain 125 g (4 oz) sun-dried tomatoes in oil and chop finely. Grind or process with 50 g (2 oz) pine nuts, 2 garlic cloves and 65 g (2 ½ oz) grated Parmesan. Blend to a thick paste with 125 g (4 oz) olive oil, then season. This sauce can be kept, covered and chilled, for up to 5 days.

GOATS' CHEESE & PEPPER LASAGNE

Serves **4**
Preparation time **20 minutes, plus standing**
Cooking time **50 minutes–1 hour**

325 g (11 oz) can or jar of **pimientos**
6 **tomatoes**, skinned and roughly chopped
1 **yellow pepper**, deseeded and finely chopped
2 **courgettes**, thinly sliced
75 g (3 oz) **sun-dried tomatoes**, thinly sliced
100 g (3½ oz) **sun-dried tomato pesto**
25 g (1 oz) **basil**
4 tablespoons **olive oil**
150 g (5 oz) **soft fresh goats' cheese**
600 ml (1 pint) **bought** or **homemade cheese sauce**
150 g (5 oz) **dried egg lasagne**
6 tablespoons **grated Parmesan cheese**
salt and **pepper**

Drain the pimientos and roughly chop. Mix in a bowl with the tomatoes, yellow pepper, courgettes, sun-dried tomatoes and pesto. Tear the basil leaves and add to the bowl with the oil and a little salt and pepper. Mix the ingredients together thoroughly.

Spoon a quarter of the ingredients into a 1.8 litre (3 pint) shallow, ovenproof dish and dot with a quarter of the goats' cheese and 4 tablespoons of the cheese sauce. Cover with a third of the lasagne sheets in a layer, breaking them to fit where necessary. Repeat the layering, finishing with a layer of the tomato mixture and goats' cheese.

Spoon the remaining cheese sauce on top and sprinkle with the Parmesan. Bake in a preheated oven, 190°C (375°F), Gas Mark 5, for 50–60 minutes until deep golden. Leave to stand for 10 minutes before serving with a leafy salad.

For homemade cheese sauce, put 500 ml (17 fl oz) milk in a saucepan with 1 small onion and 1 bay leaf. Heat until just boiling, then remove from the heat and leave to infuse for 20 minutes. Strain the milk into a jug. Melt 50 g (2 oz) butter, tip in 50 g (2 oz) plain flour and stir in quickly. Cook, stirring, for 1–2 minutes, then, off the heat, gradually whisk in the milk until blended. Bring gently to the boil, stirring, and cook for 2 minutes. Off the heat, stir in 125 g (4 oz) grated Cheddar or Gruyère.

ORECCHIETTE WITH WALNUT SAUCE

Serves **4**
Preparation time **5 minutes**
Cooking time **10–12 minutes**

375 g (12 oz) **dried orecchiette**
50 g (2 oz) **butter**
15 **sage leaves**, roughly chopped
2 **garlic cloves**, finely chopped
125 g (5 oz) **walnuts**, finely chopped
150 ml (¼ pint) **single cream**
65 g (2½ oz) **Parmesan cheese**, freshly grated
salt and **black pepper**

Cook the pasta in a large saucepan of salted boiling water according to the packet instructions until al dente.

Meanwhile, melt the butter in a frying pan over a medium heat. When it begins to foam and sizzle, stir in the sage and garlic and cook, stirring, for 1–2 minutes until golden. Remove from the heat and stir in the walnuts, cream and Parmesan.

Drain the pasta and stir it thoroughly into the sauce. Season with salt and pepper and serve immediately.

For spinach, spring onion & avocado salad, to serve with the pasta, use 150 g (5 oz) baby spinach leaves, 4 finely sliced spring onions and 2 peeled, stoned and sliced avocados. Toss together and spoon into separate side dishes.

FUN RECIPES
FOR KIDS

HERBY BEANS & BACON

Serves **4**
Preparation time **10 minutes**
Cooking time **15 minutes**

1 tablespoon **olive oil**
6 rindless **streaky bacon** rashers, thickly chopped
1 small **carrot**, finely grated
400 g (13 oz) can **chopped tomatoes**
3 tablespoons **tomato purée**
2 tablespoons **clear honey**
400 g (13 oz) can **borlotti beans**, drained and rinsed
3 tablespoons chopped **flat leaf parsley** (optional)
4 thick slices **wholemeal** or **granary bread**
25 g (1 oz) freshly grated **Parmesan cheese** (optional)

Heat the oil in a large, heavy-based frying pan, then cook the bacon over a moderate heat for 2–3 minutes until beginning to turn pale golden. Add the carrot and cook for 1 minute more.

Add the tomatoes, tomato purée and honey and heat until the tomato juice is bubbling. Add the beans, then reduce the heat and simmer for 4 minutes, uncovered, until the tomato juice has reduced and thickened slightly. Stir in the parsley, if liked, and set aside.

Lightly toast the bread under a grill until golden and just crisp. Place on warmed serving plates and pile the herby beans and bacon on top. Sprinkle with the Parmesan, if liked.

For sausage & beans, cook 4 good-quality sausages in the oil for 5–6 minutes, turning until golden. Remove from the pan and slice, then return to the pan with 100 g (3½ oz) thinly sliced chorizo sausage and cook for 2 minutes, stirring occasionally until the sausages are golden. Continue as above and serve scattered with Parmesan, if liked.

BREAKFAST CRUMBLE

Serves **8**
Preparation time **30 minutes**
Cooking time **45–50 minutes**

500 g (1 lb) **eating apples**, peeled, cored and roughly chopped
250 g (8 oz) **pears**, peeled, cored and roughly chopped
finely grated rind and juice of 1 **orange**
4 tablespoons **clear honey**
½ teaspoon **ground ginger**
175 g (6 oz) **strawberries**, hulled and quartered

Crumble

50 g (2 oz) **plain flour**
3 tablespoons **cold-milled flaxseed (ground linseed)**
50 g (2 oz) **butter**, cubed
50 g (2 oz) **porridge oats**
50 g (2 oz) **mixed seeds** (such as pumpkin, sunflower, sesame and hemp)
75 g (3 oz) **demerara sugar**

Place the apples and pears in a medium, heavy-based saucepan with the orange rind and juice, honey and ginger. Bring to a gentle simmer, stirring occasionally, then cover and simmer for 10 minutes until soft and slightly pulpy. Add the strawberries and cook for a further 2–3 minutes until soft, yet still retaining their shape. Remove the pan from the heat and transfer the mixture to an ovenproof gratin dish. Set aside while making the crumble.

Put the flour in a bowl and stir in the flaxseed. Add the butter and rub into the mixture until it resembles chunky breadcrumbs. Add the oats and again rub the fat into the mixture using your fingertips to distribute well. Stir in the seeds and sugar then sprinkle over the fruit.

Bake the crumble in a preheated oven, 200°C (400°F), Gas Mark 6, for 30–35 minutes until the topping is golden. Serve the crumble warm.

For amber crumble, omit the apples, pears and strawberries, roughly chop 4 ripe peaches and 6 ripe apricots and segment 4 oranges, then toss with 4 tablespoons clear honey and 1 teaspoon ground cinnamon. Place the uncooked fruit in the gratin dish, sprinkle with the crumble and bake as above.

TOFFEE-APPLE PORRIDGE

Serves **4**
Preparation time **10 minutes**
Cooking time **15 minutes**

500 g (1 lb) **eating apples**, peeled, cored and roughly
  chopped
½ teaspoon **ground mixed spice**
½ teaspoon **ground ginger**
5 tablespoons **soft brown sugar**
8 tablespoons **water**
600 ml (1 pint) **milk**
150 g (5 oz) **porridge oats**

Place the apples in a medium, heavy-based saucepan with the spices, 3 tablespoons of the sugar and the measured water. Bring to the boil, then reduce the heat to a simmer. Cover and simmer over a very gentle heat for 4–5 minutes, stirring occasionally, until the apples are soft yet still retaining some of their shape. Set aside with a lid to keep warm while making the porridge.

Bring the milk and remaining sugar to the boil, stirring occasionally. Remove from the heat and add the porridge oats. Stir well, then return to a low heat, stirring continuously for 4–5 minutes until the porridge has thickened.

Stir half the apple mixture through the porridge until well mixed, then ladle into 4 warmed serving bowls. Spoon over the remaining apple mixture and drizzle with the toffee apple syrup to serve, if liked.

For hot-pink, swirled porridge, mash 250 g (8 oz) fresh raspberries with 1 teaspoon golden caster sugar. Make up the porridge following the method above, then remove from the heat and spoon in the mashed raspberries. Using 1–2 stirs only, swirl the raspberries into the porridge, then ladle the swirled porridge into warmed bowls and serve with spoonfuls of Greek yogurt on top, if liked.

HUMMUS PITTA POCKETS

Serves **6**
Preparation time **15 minutes**
Cooking time **3 minutes**

400 g (13 oz) can **chickpeas**, drained and rinsed
3 tablespoons **tahini paste**
finely grated rind and juice of ½ **lemon**
1 tablespoon **olive oil**
3 tablespoons chopped **chives** (optional)
4 tablespoons **water**
2 medium **carrots**, grated
½ **cucumber**, chopped
handful of freshly cut **cress**
4 wholemeal or white **pitta breads**

Place the chickpeas in a food processor with the tahini paste and whiz until thick. Add the lemon rind and juice, olive oil, chives and measured water. Whiz again until smooth and creamy.

Toss the carrots, cucumber and cress in a bowl.

Lightly toast the pitta breads for 1 minute in a toaster until warm and slightly 'puffed'. Halve each pitta and fill, while warm, with the hummus and salad. Serve immediately.

For pockets with beetroot hummus, place 175 g (6 oz) cooked, drained beetroot (not in vinegar) into a food processor with 2 tablespoons tahini paste, the juice of ½ lemon and 1 teaspoon horseradish sauce. Whiz until smooth and creamy. Use to fill the pitta pockets as above, with the salad.

TUNA MELTS

Serves **2**
Preparation time **10 minutes**
Cooking time **11–13 minutes**

200 g (7 oz) can **tuna**, in oil or brine, drained
75 g (3 oz) frozen **sweetcorn**
3 tablespoons **mayonnaise**
2 **panini**, cut in half horizontally
75 g (3 oz) **Gruyère** or **Emmenthal cheese**, thinly sliced

Flake the tuna into a bowl. Put the sweetcorn in a small saucepan and pour boiling water over to just cover it. Cook for 3 minutes and drain through a sieve. Rinse the sweetcorn under cold water and add it to the tuna. Stir in the mayonnaise until well mixed.

Spread the tuna mixture over the two bread bases. Arrange the cheese on top of the tuna. Press the bread tops down firmly on the filling.

Heat a heavy-based frying pan or ridged grill pan for 2 minutes. Add the breads and cook on a gentle heat for 3–4 minutes on each side, turning them carefully with a fish slice or tongs. Wrap the tuna melts in nonstick baking paper and chill in the refridgerator until ready to serve.

For warm haloumi & vegetable melts, heat 1 tablespoon olive oil in a frying pan and cook 1 small, thinly sliced courgette and 1 thinly sliced red pepper for 3–4 minutes until softened. Fill the paninis with the vegetables and top with 125 g (4 oz) thinly sliced haloumi cheese. Cook as above, then transfer to serving plates and serve.

BEAN, COCONUT & SPINACH SOUP

Serves **4**
Preparation time **5 minutes**
Cooking time about **20 minutes**

1 tablespoon **olive oil**
1 **onion**, chopped
2 large **garlic cloves**, crushed
1 teaspoon **ground coriander**
2 x 400 g (13 oz) cans **mixed beans**, drained
400 g (13 oz) can **coconut milk**
150 ml (¼ pint) **vegetable stock**
250 g (8 oz) fresh **spinach**

Heat the oil in a large, heavy-based saucepan and cook the onion and garlic over a moderate heat for 3–4 minutes until softened. Add the coriander and beans and cook for 1 minute, then add the coconut milk and stock. Bring to the boil, then reduce the heat, cover and simmer for 10 minutes.

Add the spinach to the pan. Stir well and cook for a further 5 minutes.

Whiz the soup in a food processor in 2 batches until smooth, then ladle into warmed serving bowls and serve immediately.

For red lentil & bacon soup, heat 1 tablespoon olive oil and cook 1 chopped onion, 100 g (3½ oz) roughly chopped streaky bacon, 2 large carrots (cut into large chunks) and 1 crushed garlic clove for 3–4 minutes. Add 250 g (8 oz) red lentils, ½ teaspoon ground nutmeg and 900 ml (1½ pints) chicken stock and bring to the boil. Reduce the heat, cover and simmer for 40 minutes until the lentils are soft and cooked. Whiz the soup in a food processor in 2 batches until smooth.

TRAFFIC-LIGHT SCRAMBLED EGGS

Serves **4**
Preparation time **10 minutes**
Cooking time **10 minutes**

3 tablespoons **olive oil**
1 small **onion**, finely chopped
½ **green pepper**, cored, deseeded and roughly chopped
½ **red pepper**, cored, deseeded and roughly chopped
½ **yellow pepper**, cored, deseeded and roughly chopped
1 **garlic** clove, crushed
3 tablespoons **water**
6 **eggs**, beaten
100 ml (3½ fl oz) **single cream**
4 thick slices **wholemeal bread**, to serve

Heat the oil in a large, nonstick frying pan and cook the onion and peppers over a moderate heat for about 4–5 minutes until softened. Add the garlic and cook for a further 1 minute, then add the measured water. Cover the pan and simmer for 2 minutes.

Beat together the eggs and cream in a jug. Remove the lid from the pan, pour in the eggs and stir over a low heat with a wooden spoon until the eggs are creamy and cooked.

Meanwhile, lightly toast the bread slices. Serve the eggs spooned over the warm toast.

For cheesy eggs & cress, beat together the eggs, cream and 50 g (2 oz) grated Cheddar cheese in a jug. Heat 15 g (½ oz) butter in a large nonstick frying pan and add the egg mixture. Stir over a low heat with a wooden spoon until creamy and cooked. Serve on warm wholemeal toast with freshly cut cress sprinkled over.

JEWELLED COUSCOUS

Serves **2–3**
Preparation time **20 minutes**
Cooking time **2 minutes**

150 g (5 oz) **couscous**
200 ml (7 fl oz) hot **vegetable stock**
50 g (2 oz) **green beans**, trimmed and cut into 1 cm (½ inch) lengths
1 small **orange**
2 tablespoons **olive oil**
1 tablespoon **clear honey**
1 **pomegranate**
½ small **pineapple**, chopped into small pieces
1 small **red pepper**, cored, deseeded and finely diced

Put the couscous in a heatproof bowl and add the stock. Cover and leave to stand for 20 minutes.

Meanwhile, bring a small pan of water to the boil and add the beans. Cook for 2 minutes. Drain the beans through a colander and rinse in cold water.

Finely grate half the rind of the orange and mix it in a small bowl with 3 tablespoons of orange juice, the oil and the honey. Whisk lightly with a fork.

Cut the pomegranate in half. Pull the fruit apart with your hands and ease out the clusters of seeds. Separate the seeds, discarding any white parts of the fruit, which are bitter. Add the pomegranate seeds, beans, pineapple and red pepper to the couscous along with the orange and honey dressing. Mix well and chill in the refrigerator until ready to serve.

For chicken, pea & mint couscous, make the couscous as above and leave to stand. Replace all the above vegetables with 175 g (6 oz) cooked chicken, 125 g (4 oz) cooked peas and 3 tablespoons fresh chopped mint. Mix the rind and juice of half a lemon into a 200 ml (7 fl oz) pot of crème fraîche and serve spooned over the couscous.

PEKING WRAPS

Serves **2**
Preparation time **10 minutes**
Cooking time **about 10 minutes**

1 **duck breast**, weighing about 175 g (6 oz), with skin,
cut across into very thin slices
½ teaspoon **Chinese 5-spice powder**
1 tablespoon **vegetable oil**
2 large **soft flour tortillas**
2 tablespoons **hoisin sauce**
2 **iceberg lettuce leaves**, thinly shredded
5 cm (2 inch) piece **cucumber**, sliced into matchstick-
sized pieces
2 **spring onions**, thinly sliced diagonally

Put the slices of duck on a plate and sprinkle with the 5-spice powder. Turn the slices in the spice until coated all over. Heat the oil in a small frying pan for 1 minute. Add the duck and fry gently for 5 minutes, turning the pieces with a fish slice. Using the fish slice, transfer the duck to a plate and leave to cool while you prepare the filling.

Heat the tortillas one at a time in the microwave on full power for 8 seconds. Alternatively, warm them under a hot grill or in a frying pan for approximately 10 seconds.

Spread the hoisin sauce over one side of each tortilla. Scatter a line of lettuce, then the cucumber, spring onions and duck down the centre of each tortilla, keeping the ingredients away from the ends.

Fold 2 sides of each tortilla over the ends of the filling, then roll them up tightly from an unfolded side so that the filling is completely enclosed. Cut the wraps in half, wrap in nonstick baking paper and chill in the refrigerator until ready to go.

For crispy lamb & lettuce Peking wraps, toss 175 g (6 oz) lamb fillet strips in the 5-spice powder and cook as above. Use shredded lettuce, spring onion and cucumber as before, as well as strips of finely sliced carrot.

CHINESE-STYLE TURKEY WRAPS

Serves **2**
Preparation time **10 minutes**
Cooking time **1–2 minutes**

½ teaspoon **vegetable oil**
100 g (3½ oz) **turkey breast**, thinly sliced
1 tablespoon **clear honey**
2 tablespoons **soy sauce**
1 tablespoon **sesame oil**
2 **soft flour tortillas**
50 g (2 oz) **bean sprouts**
¼ **red pepper**, cored, deseeded and thinly sliced
¼ **onion**, thinly sliced
25 g (1 oz) **mangetouts**, sliced
2 **baby sweetcorn**, thinly sliced

Heat the oil in a frying pan over a moderate heat and add the turkey to the pan. Stir for 1–2 minutes until cooked through. Reduce the heat and stir in the honey, soy sauce and sesame oil, making sure that the turkey is well coated. Set aside to cool.

Assemble a wrap by placing half the turkey mixture down the centre of a tortilla. Add half the bean sprouts and pepper, onion, mangetouts and baby sweetcorn. Repeat with the other tortilla. (Alternatively, retain the remaining tortilla and mixture for use another day; the mixture will keep for up to 24 hours in the refrigerator.)

Roll up the tortilla securely and wrap in nonstick baking paper (clingfilm can make the wrap rather soggy).

For Chinese-style pork & pak choi wraps, replace the turkey with 125 g (4 oz) tenderloin pork strips tossed with ½ teaspoon Chinese five spice and cook as above for 3–4 minutes. Add 1 small head pak choi, shredded with the honey, soy sauce and sesame oil and cook for a further 2 minutes. Assemble as above with 125 g (4 oz) beansprouts, omitting the mangetouts, onion and sweetcorn.

SPICY CHORIZO WRAP

Serves **2**
Preparation time **15 minutes**
Cooking time **5–7 minutes**

4 **eggs**
½ teaspoon **mild chilli powder**
50 g (2 oz) sliced **chorizo sausage**, cut into
   thin shreds
2 tablespoons **olive oil**
1 punnet **mustard and cress**
2 large **soft flour tortillas**
2 tablespoons **red pesto**

Break the eggs into a bowl and add the chilli powder. Whisk well until the eggs are completely broken up. Stir in the chorizo. Heat the oil in a small frying pan for 1 minute. Tip the egg mixture into the pan. When the eggs start to set around the edges, use a fork to push the cooked parts into the centre of the pan so the uncooked egg flows into the space. Keep doing this until the eggs are no longer runny, then let the omelette cook until just set (3–5 minutes). Slide the omelette on to a plate and leave to cool.

Cut the mustard and cress from the punnet and put it in a sieve. Rinse under cold water and leave to drain.

Prepare the tortillas by heating in the microwave on full power for 10 seconds. Alternatively, warm them under a hot grill or heat in the frying pan for approximately 10 seconds (wipe out the pan with kitchen paper first, taking care as it might still be hot).

Spread one side of each of the tortillas with the pesto and lay the omelette on top. Sprinkle with the mustard and cress. Roll up tightly so the filling is completely enclosed. Cut the wraps in half, wrap in nonstick baking paper and chill in the refrigerator until ready to serve.

For pesto chicken wraps, replace the chorizo with 75 g (3 oz) cooked and torn chicken pieces and 50g (2 oz) black olives, sliced. Spread the tortilla with 1 tablespoon green pesto and top with the omelette. Omit the mustard and cress, roll up and serve warm.

278

SWEETCORN FRITTERS & TOMATO DIP

Makes **20**
Preparation time **15 minutes**
Cooking time **20–30 minutes**

75 g (3 oz) **plain flour**
½ teaspoon **paprika**
150 ml (¼ pint) **milk**
1 **egg**, beaten
275 g (9 oz) can **sweetcorn**, drained
3 tablespoons chopped **parsley**
2 **spring onions**, finely chopped
½ **red pepper**, finely chopped

Tomato dip
1 tablespoon **olive oil**
6 ripe **tomatoes**, roughly chopped
1 tablespoon **soft brown sugar**
½ teaspoon **paprika**
1 tablespoon **red wine vinegar**
4 tablespoons **vegetable oil**

Sift the flour and paprika into a bowl, then add the milk and egg and whisk together to form a thick batter. Add the sweetcorn, parsley, spring onions and red pepper and mix well. If the mixture is too thick, add 1 tablespoon water to loosen. Set aside while making the tomato dip.

Heat the oil in a medium heavy-based pan, add the tomatoes and cook over a moderate heat for 5 minutes, stirring occasionally. Add the sugar, paprika and vinegar, reduce the heat, cover and simmer over a very gentle heat for 10–15 minutes, stirring occasionally until the tomatoes are thick and pulpy. Remove from the heat and transfer to a bowl to cool.

Heat the vegetable oil in a large, nonstick frying pan and spoon tablespoons of the sweetcorn mixture into the pan, well spaced apart, and cook for 1–2 minutes on each side, in batches, until golden and firm. Remove the fritters from the pan using a fish slice and drain on kitchen paper.

Serve the sweetcorn fritters with a pot of the sauce, to dip or wrap in foil to keep warm for transport.

For minted courgette fritters, replace the sweetcorn with 1 finely chopped large courgette. Heat 1 teaspoon of oil in a large frying pan and cook the courgette over a moderate heat for 3–4 minutes, stirring occasionally until pale golden. Add to the batter with 2 tablespoons of chopped mint.

CHICKPEA & HERB SALAD

Serves **4**
Preparation time **10 minutes**
Cooking time **5 minutes** (optional)

100 g (3½ oz) **bulgar wheat**
4 tablespoons **olive oil**
1 tablespoon **lemon juice**
2 tablespoons chopped **flat leaf parsley**
1 tablespoon chopped **mint**
400 g (13 oz) can **chickpeas**, drained and rinsed
125 g (4 oz) **cherry tomatoes**, halved
1 tablespoon chopped mild **onion**
100 g (3½ oz) **cucumber**, diced
150 g (5 oz) **feta cheese**, diced

Put the bulgar wheat in a heatproof bowl and pour over sufficient boiling water just to cover. Set aside until the water has been absorbed. (If you want to give a fluffier finish to the bulgar wheat, transfer it to a steamer and steam for 5 minutes. Spread out on a plate to cool.)

Mix together the oil, lemon juice, parsley and mint in a large bowl. Add the chickpeas, tomatoes, onion, cucumber and bulgar wheat. Mix well and add the feta, stirring lightly to avoid breaking up the cheese.

Serve immediately, or pack into an airtight container to transport.

For tuna, bean & black olive salad, replace the chickpeas, tomatoes, onion and cucumber for 1 x 200 g (7 oz) can tuna, drained and flaked, 1 x 400 g (13 oz) can mixed beans, drained and rinsed, 100 g (4 oz) black olives and 4 tablespoons lemon juice. Toss well before serving.

CHICKEN FAJITAS & NO-CHILLI SALSA

Serves **4**
Preparation time **20 minutes**
Cooking time **about 5 minutes**

½ teaspoon **ground coriander**
½ teaspoon **ground cumin**
½ teaspoon **ground paprika**
1 **garlic clove**, crushed
3 tablespoons chopped **fresh coriander**
375 g (12 oz) boneless, skinless **chicken breasts**, cut into bite-sized strips
1 tablespoon **olive oil**
4 **soft flour tortillas**
soured cream (optional)

Salsa
3 large, ripe **tomatoes**, finely chopped
3 tablespoons chopped **fresh coriander**
⅛ **cucumber**, finely chopped
1 tablespoon **olive oil**

Guacamole
1 large **avocado**, roughly chopped
grated rind and juice of ½ **lime**
2 teaspoons **sweet chilli sauce** (optional)

Place all the ground spices, garlic and coriander in a mixing bowl. Toss the chicken in the oil, then add to the spices and toss to coat lightly in the spice mixture.

Make the salsa, mix the tomatoes, coriander and cucumber in a bowl and drizzle over the oil. Transfer to a serving bowl.

Make the guacamole, mash the avocado with the lime rind and juice and sweet chilli sauce, if using, until soft and rough-textured. Transfer to a serving bowl.

Heat a griddle pan or heavy-based frying pan and cook the chicken for 3–4 minutes, turning occasionally, until golden and cooked through. Fill the tortillas with the hot chicken slices, guacamole and salsa, and fold into quarters. Spoon over a little soured cream, if liked.

For beef fajitas, replace the chicken with rump or sirloin steak, cut into bite-sized strips. For a slightly 'warmer' version, replace the paprika with mild chilli powder.

VEGETABLE BURGERS

Serves **8**
Preparation time **20 minutes**, plus chilling
Cooking time **12–15 minutes**

250 g (8 oz) **spinach**, washed and patted dry
1 tablespoon **olive oil**
1 small **red pepper**, cored, deseeded and very finely chopped
4 **spring onions**, finely sliced
400 g (13 oz) can **chickpeas**, drained and rinsed
125 g (4 oz) **ricotta cheese**
1 **egg yolk**
½ teaspoon **ground coriander**
50 g (2 oz) **plain flour**
1 **egg**, beaten
175 g (6 oz) **wholemeal breadcrumbs**
4 tablespoons **vegetable oil**

To serve
8 mini **burger buns**
tomato ketchup
cherry tomatoes (optional)

Put the moist spinach in a pan over a moderate heat for 2–3 minutes, stirring continuously, until wilted. Remove from the heat, drain well, and set aside.

Heat the olive oil in a frying pan and cook the pepper and spring onions over a moderate heat for 4–5 minutes until soft. Set aside.

Place the chickpeas in a food processor with the ricotta and blend until smooth. Add the spinach, egg yolk and coriander and blend again to mix well. Transfer to a mixing bowl and fold in the pepper and spring onion mixture. Shape the mixture into 8 patties, toss them lightly in the flour, then roll first in the beaten egg and then in the breadcrumbs, to coat. Chill for 30 minutes.

Heat the vegetable oil in a large, heavy-based frying pan and cook the burgers over a moderate heat for 6–7 minutes, turning once, until golden and crisp. Serve in the buns with tomato ketchup and cherry tomatoes, if liked.

For sausage & pepper burgers, cook the spinach, peppers and onions as above. Chop the spinach roughly. Place 375 g (12 oz) good-quality sausagemeat in a bowl and add 1 tablespoon tomato chutney and 1 teaspoon Dijon mustard. Mix well, then stir in the spinach, peppers and onions and mix well. Do not coat, but simply heat the oil and cook for 2–3 minutes on each side until golden. Serve as above.

MINI SCONE PIZZAS

Serves **4**
Preparation time **25 minutes**
Cooking time **15–20 minutes**

250 g (8 oz) **self-raising wholemeal flour**
50 g (2 oz) **butter**, cubed
150 ml (¼ pint) **milk**
150 ml (¼ pint) **tomato passata**
3 tablespoons **tomato purée**
2 tablespoons chopped **basil**
4 thick slices good-quality **ham**, shredded
125 g (4 oz) **pitted black olives**, halved
150 g (5 oz) **mozzarella cheese**, grated

Sift the flour into a bowl and rub in the butter until the mixture resembles fine breadcrumbs. Make a well in the centre and stir in enough of the milk to give a fairly soft dough. Turn it out on to a lightly floured surface and knead gently. Cut into 4 pieces, then knead again to shape each into a rough round. Roll out 4 rough circles each to about 15 cm (6 inch) and place on a baking sheet.

Mix together the passata, tomato purée and basil. Divide between the scone bases and spread to within 1 cm (½ inch) of the edges. Pile each with the ham and olives, then sprinkle with the mozzarella.

Drizzle with a little oil and bake in a preheated oven, 200°C (400°F), Gas Mark 6, for 15–20 minutes until the bases are risen and the cheese is golden. Wrap in foil and serve warm or cold.

For egg & bacon scone pizzas, form each pizza base into a slight bowl shape with a ridge around the edge. Spread with the tomato sauce. Heat 1 tablespoon olive oil and cook 6 roughly chopped back bacon rashers for 2 minutes until golden. Drain on kitchen paper. Sprinkle the pizzas with the bacon pieces, then crack an egg over the top of each. Bake in the oven as above without the cheese. Remove from the oven and, while still warm, sprinkle each with 1 tablespoon grated mozzarella and some chopped parsley.

SPAGHETTI BOLOGNAISE

Serves **6**
Preparation time **30 minutes**
Cooking time **35 minutes**

2 tablespoons **olive oil**
1 **onion**, finely chopped
2 **carrots**, grated
1 **courgette**, grated
500 g (1 lb) **lean beef mince**
2 tablespoons **plain flour**
2 tablespoons **tomato purée**
600 ml (1 pint) **rich beef stock**
200 g (7 oz) can **chopped tomatoes**
250 g (8 oz) **spaghetti** or **linguine**
freshly grated **Parmesan cheese**, to serve

Heat 1 tablespoon of the oil in a large, heavy-based saucepan and cook the onion, carrots and courgette over a moderate heat for 5–6 minutes, stirring occasionally until soft. Remove the vegetables from the pan and set aside.

Add the mince to the pan and cook over a high heat for 4–5 minutes, stirring frequently until browned all over. Return the vegetables to the pan, add the flour and stir well to coat lightly. Add the tomato purée to the beef stock and stir well, then add the stock to the meat along with the chopped tomatoes. Bring to the boil, then reduce the heat, cover with a lid and simmer for 20 minutes.

Meanwhile, cook the pasta for 8–10 minutes or according to packet instructions until tender. Drain and toss with the remaining oil. Arrange the pasta in warmed serving bowls and pile the bolognaise sauce on top. Sprinkle with the Parmesan.

For bolognaise pasta bake, cook 250 g (8 oz) macaroni until just tender. Drain and toss with 1 tablespoon olive oil. Make up the bolognaise sauce as above and mix with the macaroni. Transfer to a large gratin dish. Mix 200 ml (7 fl oz) crème fraîche with 3 tablespoons freshly grated Parmesan cheese and 2 tablespoons chopped parsley, and spoon over the top of the macaroni. Bake in a preheated oven, 200°C (400°F), Gas Mark 6, for 20–25 minutes until the topping is golden and bubbling.

CHICKEN RICE SALAD

Serves **4**
Preparation time **10 minutes**, plus cooling
Cooking time **about 15 minutes**

4 **chicken thighs**, skinned
  and boned
175 g (6 oz) **long-grain rice**
2 teaspoons **lemon juice**
2 tablespoons **peanut butter** (optional)
2 tablespoons **olive oil**
2 **pineapple rings**, chopped
1 **red pepper**, cored, deseeded and chopped
75 g (3 oz) **sugar snap peas**, sliced
4 tablespoons **peanuts** (optional)

Place the chicken thighs in a steamer set over boiling water for 10–12 minutes until cooked through. Alternatively, simmer them in shallow water in a frying pan for 10 minutes. Remove from the steamer or pan and set aside to cool.

Meanwhile, cook the rice according to the packet instructions. Drain and rinse under cold water to cool the rice completely, then tip it into a large bowl.

Make the dressing: mix together the lemon juice and peanut butter, if using, until well combined, then whisk in the oil.

Dice the chicken thighs into bite-sized pieces and stir into the rice. Add the pineapple, red pepper, sugar snap peas and peanuts, if using. Pour the dressing over the chicken rice salad and serve.

For prawn rice salad, make up the peanut dressing as above. Replace the chicken with 150 g (5 oz) prawns tossed with 2 tablespoons toasted sesame seeds. Cut ¼ cucumber into thin sticks and toss with the rice, peanut sauce, prawns and seeds.

BAKED SWEET POTATOES & PRAWNS

Serves **4**
Preparation time **10 minutes**
Cooking time **25–30 minutes**

1 tablespoon **olive oil**
4 large **sweet potatoes**, skin on, scrubbed, patted dry
250 g (8 oz) medium **prawns**, defrosted if frozen
1 ripe **avocado**, cut into small chunks
2 tablespoons **mayonnaise**
2 tablespoons **milk** or **water**
3 tablespoons **crème fraîche**
1 tablespoon **tomato purée**

To serve
ground paprika
1 small pot **sprouting alfalfa** (or other sprouting seeds)

Drizzle a little of the oil over each sweet potato, then rub it all over the skin. Put the potatoes on a baking sheet. Bake in a preheated oven, 200°C (400°F), Gas Mark 6, for 25–30 minutes until tender and cooked through.

Meanwhile, place the prawns and avocado in a bowl and toss together. Mix the mayonnaise with the milk or water until smooth, then add the crème fraîche and tomato purée and mix until well blended. Add the prawns and avocado and toss well to coat lightly.

Remove the sweet potatoes from the oven. Split the hot potatoes and fill them with the prawn mixture. Serve garnished with a pinch of paprika and some freshly cut sprouting seeds.

For baked sweet potatoes & creamy mushrooms, bake the sweet potatoes as above. Heat 1 tablespoon olive oil in a heavy-based frying pan and cook 250 g (8 oz) quartered chestnut mushrooms over a high heat for 3–4 minutes until golden and softened. Remove from the heat, add 200 ml (7 fl oz) crème fraîche and 1 teaspoon Dijon mustard and stir well for a few seconds until piping hot. Spoon into the sweet potatoes as above.

SWEET POTATO-TOPPED FISH PIE

Serves **4**
Preparation time **45 minutes**
Cooking time **45 minutes**

375 g (12 oz) **cod fillet**
300 ml (½ pint) **water**
250 g (8 oz) **prawns**, thawed if frozen, drained
1 large **carrot**, roughly chopped
250 g (8 oz) **broccoli**, cut into small florets
25 g (1 oz) **butter**
25 g (1 oz) **plain flour**
300 ml (½ pint) **milk**
50 g (2 oz) **Cheddar cheese**, grated

Potato topping
625 g (1¼ lb) **sweet potatoes**, peeled and chopped
50 g (2 oz) **butter**
3 tablespoons chopped **parsley**
25 g (1 oz) **Cheddar cheese**, finely grated

Place the cod fillet in a heavy-based frying pan and pour over the measured water. Bring to the boil, reduce the heat, cover and simmer for 3 minutes until the fish is opaque and cooked through. Drain and reserve the fish stock. Flake the fish into chunks and gently toss with the prawns.

Cook the carrot and broccoli in boiling water for 5 minutes, drain and set aside. Melt the butter in a pan, remove from the heat and add the flour. Stir over a gentle heat for 30 seconds. Remove from the heat and gradually add the milk a little at a time, stirring well after each addition, then add the reserved fish stock and stir well.

Return the pan to the heat and bring to the boil, stirring continuously until thickened. Remove from the heat and add the Cheddar. Pour over the fish, add the vegetables and very gently fold together. Transfer to a large gratin dish and set aside.

Meanwhile, cook the sweet potatoes for 8–10 minutes until tender. Drain, add the butter and mash well. Stir in the parsley, spoon over the top of the fish and sauce and sprinkle with the Cheddar. Bake in a preheated oven, 200°C (400°F), Gas Mark 6, for 30 minutes until a golden crust forms.

For cheesy tuna & prawn pie, replace the cod with 2 x 200 g (7 oz) cans tuna in brine, drained and flaked. Cook 750 g (1½ lb) white potatoes and mash with the butter, an extra 50 g (2 oz) Cheddar and 6 tablespoons milk. Fold in the parsley, spoon over the pie, sprinkle with the remaining cheese and bake as above.

POTATO & CHEESE RÖSTIS

Makes **4**
Preparation time **10 minutes**
Cooking time **25 minutes**

500 g (1 lb) **red** or **waxy potatoes**, unpeeled
50 g (2 oz) **mild Cheddar cheese**, grated
1 **red onion**, finely chopped
3 tablespoons **vegetable oil**
Tomato ketchup (see page 12), to serve

Put the potatoes in a large pan of water and bring to the boil. Boil for about 20 minutes until the potatoes are just cooked but firm. Drain and cool.

Peel the potatoes and grate them into a bowl. Stir in the grated Cheddar and onion. With wet hands, shape into 4 rounds, then press down with 2 fingers to form into röstis. Neaten up the edges.

Brush lightly with oil on both sides and grill on a foil-lined grill rack at a medium heat for 2–3 minutes on each side until golden brown.

Serve the röstis warm with the ketchup. (Any that are not needed straight away may be stored in an airtight container in the refrigerator for up to 3 days.)

For potato, bacon & tomato röstis, make the potato mixture as above, omitting the onion. Add 1 finely chopped large tomato and 2 rashers finely chopped cooked streaky bacon to the mixture along with 2 tablespoons tomato ketchup. Shape into 4 patties and cook as above. Use to fill warm toasted wholemeal pitta breads with watercress and extra ketchup.

GREEN CHEESE PASTA

Serves **4**
Preparation time **10 minutes**
Cooking time **10 minutes**

250 g (8 oz) **pasta shapes**
300 g (10 oz) fresh **spinach**
1 teaspoon **ground nutmeg**
50 g (2 oz) **butter**
50 g (2 oz) **plain flour**
600 ml (1 pint) **milk**
100 g (4 oz) **Cheddar cheese**, grated

Cook the pasta shapes for 8–10 minutes or according to packet instructions until just tender. Drain and set aside.

Meanwhile, place the spinach in a pan of boiling water and cook, stirring continuously, over a moderate heat for 2 minutes until wilted. Remove from the heat and drain well, then return to the pan and toss with the nutmeg. Set aside.

Melt the butter in a medium, heavy-based saucepan. Remove from the heat, add the flour and stir to form a thick paste. Return to the heat and cook gently for a few seconds, stirring continuously. Remove from the heat and gradually add the milk, stirring well after each addition. Return to the heat and bring to the boil, stirring continuously until the sauce has boiled and thickened.

Remove from the heat and add the spinach and cheese. Stir, then transfer to a food processor and whiz until smooth. Return to the pan and add the pasta. Stir well to coat, then divide between 4 warmed serving bowls.

For courgette & garlic pasta, replace the spinach with 3 large courgettes, trimmed and grated. Heat 1 tablespoon olive oil in a nonstick frying pan and cook the courgettes and 1 crushed garlic clove over a moderate heat for 4–5 minutes until soft and tender. Add 3 tablespoons of chopped chives, then add to the sauce in place of the spinach and whiz until smooth before tossing with the pasta.

SALMON PASTA BAKE

Serves **6**
Preparation time **20 minutes**
Cooking time **30 minutes**

250 g (8 oz) **pasta shapes**
25 g (1 oz) **butter**
25 g (1 oz) **plain flour**
300 ml (½ pint) **milk**
200 ml (7 fl oz) **crème fraîche**
100 g (4 oz) freshly grated **Parmesan cheese**
3 tablespoons chopped **herbs** (such as chives or dill)
2 x 200 g (7 oz) cans **red salmon**, drained and flaked
100 g (4 oz) frozen **peas**

Cook the pasta for 8–10 minutes or according to packet instructions until tender. Drain and set aside.

Heat the butter in a nonstick pan until melted. Remove from the heat, add the flour and stir well to form a thick paste. Return the pan to the heat and cook, stirring continuously, for 1 minute. Remove from the heat and gradually add the milk, a little at a time, stirring well until all the milk is used.

Return the pan to the heat and bring to the boil, stirring continuously until boiled and thickened. Add the crème fraîche and half the Parmesan and stir well. Add the drained pasta, herbs, flaked salmon and peas and toss gently to mix, taking care not to break up the fish. Transfer to 6 individual gratin dishes and sprinkle over the remaining Parmesan.

Bake in a preheated oven, 180°C (350°F), Gas Mark 4, for 20 minutes until golden and bubbling. Serve with warm bread and a simple salad.

For tuna pasta bake with sweetcorn, replace the salmon with 2 x 200 g (7 oz) cans of tuna in brine, drained and flaked, and replace the peas with 100 g (4 oz) sweetcorn. Add 1 tablespoon wholegrain mustard and mix well. Cut a garlic baguette into slices and place on top of the pasta. Sprinkle with the remaining Parmesan and bake as above until the bread is crisp and golden and the sauce is bubbling.

ASIAN NOODLES WITH PRAWNS

Serves **2**
Preparation time **20 minutes**
Cooking time **10 minutes**

3 tablespoons **plum sauce**
2 tablespoons **seasoned rice vinegar**
2 tablespoons **soy sauce**
100 g (3½ oz) fine or medium **egg noodles**
1 tablespoon **vegetable oil**
2 **spring onions**, sliced diagonally into chunky pieces
½ mild **red chilli**, cored, deseeded and finely chopped
150 g (5 oz) **pak choi** or **cabbage**, thinly sliced
100 g (3½ oz) **baby sweetcorn**, cut in half diagonally
200 g (7 oz) peeled **prawns**, thawed if frozen, drained

Mix the plum sauce with the rice vinegar and soy sauce in a small bowl and set aside.

Pour plenty of freshly boiled water into a medium saucepan and bring back to the boil. Add the noodles and cook for 3 minutes. Drain through a colander.

Heat the oil in a large frying pan or wok for 1 minute. Add the spring onions and chilli and fry for 1 minute, stirring with a wooden spoon. Add the pak choi or cabbage and the sweetcorn and fry for a further 2–3 minutes until the vegetables are softened.

Tip the noodles, prawns and sauce into the pan and cook, stirring gently, over a low heat until the ingredients are mixed together and hot. Serve immediately.

For Asian noodles with beef & coconut, replace the red chilli and pak choi with 175 g (6 oz) blanched broccoli florets. Add to the wok with the spring onions and cook for 1 minute. Add 175 g (6 oz) rump steak, cut into thin strips and cook in the pan for a further 2–3 minutes until golden. Add a 400 ml (14 fl oz) can coconut milk with 2 tablespoons soy sauce to replace the plum sauce and toss with the noodles. Heat for 1 minute until hot.

KORMA-STYLE CURRIED PRAWNS

Serves **4**
Preparation time **5 minutes**
Cooking time **about 25 minutes**

1 tablespoon **vegetable oil**
1 **onion**, roughly chopped
1 cm (½ inch) piece **root ginger**, peeled and finely grated
1 teaspoon **ground coriander**
½ teaspoon **ground cumin**
½ teaspoon **curry powder**
400 g (13 oz) can **chopped tomatoes**
1 tablespoon **soft brown sugar**
400 ml (13 fl oz) can **coconut milk**
250 g (8 oz) **prawns**, thawed if frozen
125 g (4 oz) frozen **peas**
3 tablespoons chopped **coriander**
rice or **naan**, to serve

Heat the oil in a large nonstick frying pan and cook the onion and ginger over a gentle heat for 3–4 minutes, stirring regularly until soft, but not golden. Add the spices and cook for a further 1 minute. Add the chopped tomatoes and sugar and increase the heat slightly, continuing to cook for a further 5 minutes, stirring occasionally, until the tomatoes have reduced slightly and thickened.

Pour in the coconut milk and bring to the boil. Reduce the heat and simmer, uncovered, for 10 minutes until the sauce has reduced and thickened. Drain the prawns well, then add to the sauce with the peas and coriander and cook for a further 2–3 minutes until piping hot.

Serve the mild curry in warmed serving bowls, with either rice or naan breads to mop up the juices.

For mild chicken & squash curry, omit the ginger and replace the prawns with 250 g (8 oz) roughly chopped chicken breast and the peas with 250 g (8 oz) butternut squash, peeled and cubed. Cook both the chicken and the squash with the onion as above, then add the spices and continue to follow the remaining recipe as above.

NO-MESS CHEESY PEPPERONI CALZONES

Serves **8**
Preparation time **30–40 minutes**
Cooking time **25–30 minutes**

300 g (10 oz) **pizza dough mix**
flour, for dusting
1 tablespoon **olive oil**
1 small **red pepper**, cored, deseeded and roughly chopped
1 small **yellow pepper**, cored, deseeded and roughly chopped
175 g (6 oz) **chorizo sausage**, sliced
1 large **tomato**, roughly chopped
½ teaspoon mixed **dried herbs**
150 g (5 oz) packet **mozzarella cheese**, drained and cubed

Make up the pizza dough according to packet instructions and turn out on to a lightly floured surface. Divide the dough into 8 pieces. Knead each lightly to produce smooth rounds, then roll into a 20 cm (8 inch) circle. Loosely cover with clingfilm.

Heat the oil in a large, nonstick frying pan and cook the peppers over a moderate heat for 5 minutes, stirring occasionally. Add the chorizo slices and cook for 2 minutes before adding the tomato. Cook for a further 3–4 minutes, stirring occasionally, until the tomato has softened. Remove from the heat and stir in the herbs and mozzarella.

Allow to cool slightly before dividing the filling between the 8 dough circles. Lightly brush the edges with a little water, then fold the circles in half to enclose the filling and press to seal. Place on a baking sheet and bake in a preheated oven, 220°C (425°F), Gas Mark 7, for 15–20 minutes. Serve warm.

For butternut squash & feta cheese calzones, heat 1 tablespoon olive oil in a pan and cook 250 g (8 oz) cubed butternut squash over a moderate heat for 5–6 minutes until beginning to soften. Add 5 tablespoons water, cover and cook over a gentle heat for 3 minutes. Remove from the heat and allow to cool. Add 2 tablespoons chopped parsley and 100 g (4 oz) crumbled feta. Use the filling as above.

BAKED CABBAGE WITH NUTS & CHEESE

Serves **4**

Preparation time **15 minutes**

Cooking time **30 minutes**

375 g (12 oz) **white cabbage**, shredded

125 g (4 oz) **green** or **savoy cabbage**, shredded

1 teaspoon **ground nutmeg**

125 g (4 oz) roasted unsalted **peanuts**, toasted

25 g (1 oz) **butter**

25 g (1 oz) **plain flour**

450 ml (¾ pint) **milk**

125 g (4 oz) strong **Cheddar cheese**, grated

1 teaspoon **Dijon mustard**

2 tablespoons chopped **parsley**

25 g (1 oz) **wholemeal breadcrumbs**

Cook the two types of cabbage in boiling water for 5 minutes until just tender. Drain and place in a large mixing bowl and toss with the nutmeg and peanuts.

Heat the butter in a nonstick saucepan until melted. Remove from the heat, add the flour and mix to a paste. Return to the heat and cook for a few seconds. Remove from the heat and add the milk a little at a time, stirring well between each addition. Return to the heat and bring to the boil, stirring continuously until boiled and thickened.

Remove the pan from the heat and add 75 g (3 oz) of the grated Cheddar and the mustard. Mix well, then pour over the cabbage and mix it in.

Transfer the mixture to a gratin dish, or 4 individual gratin dishes. Toss the remaining cheese with the parsley and breadcrumbs, then sprinkle over the top and bake in a preheated oven, 200°C (400°F), Gas Mark 6, for 20 minutes until golden and bubbling.

For root vegetable bake with nuts & cheese, replace the cabbage with 375 g (12 oz) sliced butternut squash and 250 g (8 oz) sliced parsnips. Cook in boiling water for 5 minutes and drain. Mix with the nuts and cheese sauce, sprinkle with the cheesy breadcrumbs and bake as above.

SPANISH TORTILLA

Serves **8**
Preparation time **10 minutes**
Cooking time **20–25 minutes**

2 tablespoons **olive oil**
2 **onions**, sliced
1 **garlic clove**, crushed
500 g (1 lb) cooked **waxy potatoes**, sliced
6 **eggs**
50 ml (2 fl oz) **milk**

Heat 1 tablespoon of the olive oil in a medium frying pan, with a metal handle, over a low heat and add the onions and garlic. Cook for 5 minutes until golden, then add the cooked potatoes and heat through.

Meanwhile, in a large bowl, beat together the eggs and milk. Add the potatoes, onion and garlic to the egg mixture and stir well.

Return the pan to the heat, and heat the remaining oil. Tip the potato and egg mixture into the pan and cook over a low heat for 7–8 minutes, until beginning to set. Preheat the grill to a medium heat and cook the tortilla in its pan under the grill for 3–5 minutes until the top is golden and set.

Turn out the tortilla on to a plate and allow to cool. Cut into slices and serve warm or cold. (You can wrap any unused tortilla securely and refrigerate it – eat within 3 days.)

For meaty chorizo Spanish tortilla, layer the potatoes with a 75 g (3 oz) packet sliced chorizo and 2 tablespoons chopped parsley and cook as above. Serve either warm or cold with cherry tomatoes.

CRUMB-TOPPED MACARONI CHEESE

Serves **4**
Preparation time **15 minutes**
Cooking time **about 25 minutes**

200 g (7 oz) **macaroni**
100 g (3½ oz) fresh or frozen **peas**
65 g (2½ oz) **butter**
40 g (1½ oz) **plain flour**
500 ml (17 fl oz) **milk**
1 teaspoon **Dijon mustard**
150 g (5 oz) **Cheddar cheese**, coarsely grated
100 g (3½ oz) **ham**, chopped into small pieces
65 g (2½ oz) **breadcrumbs**

Cook the macaroni for about 10 minutes or according to packet instructions until just tender. Add the peas to the pan and cook for a further 2 minutes. Drain and put on one side.

Melt 40 g (1½ oz) of the butter in the rinsed and dried saucepan. Add the flour and stir it in with a wooden spoon. Cook over a gentle heat, stirring, for 1 minute. Remove the pan from the heat and gradually pour in the milk, whisking well. Return the pan to the heat and cook over a gentle heat, stirring continuously until the sauce is thickened and smooth.

Add the mustard, Cheddar and ham and stir until the cheese has melted. Tip in the macaroni and peas and stir until coated in the sauce, then pour into a shallow heatproof dish.

Melt the remaining butter in a small saucepan and stir in the breadcrumbs until they are coated. Sprinkle the breadcrumbs over the macaroni and cook under a moderate grill for about 5 minutes or until golden, watching closely as the breadcrumbs will brown quickly. Use oven gloves to remove the dish from under the grill, and serve.

For crumb-topped aubergine & macaroni cheese, omit the peas and ham and replace with half a roughly chopped aubergine cooked in 2 tablespoons olive oil until soft, and 3 roughly chopped tomatoes. Top with the crumbs and bake as above.

SALMON RÖSTI CAKES

Serves **6**
Preparation time **30 minutes**
Cooking time **25–30 minutes**

500 g (1 lb) **white potatoes**, peeled but left whole
25 g (1 oz) **butter**
250 g (8 oz) **salmon fillets**
2 tablespoons **sunflower oil**
200 ml (7 fl oz) **crème fraîche**
3 **spring onions**, finely sliced
2 tablespoons chopped **chives**
lemon wedges, to serve

Bring a large pan of lightly salted water to the boil. Cook the potatoes for 10 minutes until beginning to soften. Drain and set aside to cool.

Heat the butter in a small frying pan and add the salmon. Cover with a tight-fitting lid and reduce the heat to very low. Cook for 8–10 minutes until the salmon is just cooked. Remove from the heat and set aside until the salmon is cool enough to handle. Flake the salmon and place in a bowl with the pan juices.

Grate the cooled potatoes, add to the bowl with the salmon and toss together to mix. Divide the mixture into 6 and form into flattened patty shapes. Heat the oil in a large nonstick frying pan and cook the rösti over a moderate heat for 2–3 minutes on each side until golden and cooked through, turning with a fish slice.

Meanwhile, place the crème fraîche in a bowl with the spring onions and chives and mix well. Drain the rösti on kitchen paper, then spoon over the crème fraîche and serve with lemon wedges.

For rösti with bacon & eggs, follow the recipe above, omitting the salmon and adding 1 tablespoon chopped parsley before shaping. Serve the crisp rösti each with 2 lightly fried bacon rashers and a poached egg on top, and homemade ketchup.

BUTTERNUT SQUASH RISOTTO

Serves **4**
Preparation time **15 minutes**
Cooking time **about
  25 minutes**

2 tablespoons **olive oil**
1 **onion**, finely chopped
500 g (1 lb) **butternut squash**, peeled, deseeded and
  roughly chopped
250 g (8 oz) **arborio rice**
900 ml (1½ pints) **rich chicken stock**
75 g (3 oz) freshly grated **Parmesan cheese**, plus
  extra to serve
4 tablespoons **pine nuts**, toasted
250 g (8 oz) fresh **spinach leaves**

Heat the oil in a large heavy-based frying pan and cook the onion and squash over a low to moderate heat for 10 minutes until softened. Add the rice and cook for 1 minute, then add half the stock. Bring to the boil, then reduce the heat and simmer gently for 5 minutes until almost all the stock has been absorbed, stirring occasionally.

Continue to add the stock 150 ml (¼ pint) at a time and cook over a gentle heat until the almost all the stock has been absorbed before adding more. Once the rice is tender, remove the pan from the heat, add the Parmesan, pine nuts and spinach and stir well to combine and wilt the spinach, returning to the heat for 1 minute if necessary.

Serve in warmed serving bowls with extra freshly grated Parmesan.

For chicken & pea risotto, replace the butternut squash with 3 x 150 g (5 oz) chicken breasts, chopped and cooked with the onion. Cook in the same way as above, adding an additional 125 g (4 oz) frozen peas and adding the spinach if liked. Serve with extra Parmesan sprinkled over.

MINI QUICHES

Makes **18**
Preparation time **45 minutes**
Cooking time **20 minutes**

vegetable oil, for greasing
plain flour, for dusting
375 g (12 oz) ready-rolled **shortcrust pastry**, thawed if
  frozen and taken out of the refrigerator 15 minutes
  before use
2 **eggs**
200 ml (7 fl oz) **milk**
4 slices **ham**, diced
2 **spring onions**, chopped
5 **cherry tomatoes**, chopped
50 g (2 oz) **Cheddar cheese**, grated

Smear some oil all around the cups of 2 bun tins. Sprinkle some flour on to a work surface and unroll the pastry. Flatten it with the balls of your hands. Stamp circles out of the pastry with a cutter and place each circle in a cup of the tin, gently pressing it down with your fingertips.

Place the eggs and milk in a measuring jug and beat with a fork.

Put the ham, spring onions and cherry tomatoes in a bowl and mix together. Put a dessertspoonful of the mixture into each pastry cup.

Pour some of the egg and milk mixture into each cup. Sprinkle some Cheddar over the top. Bake the quiches in a preheated oven, 220°C (425°F), Gas Mark 7, for 20 minutes or until set and golden. Serve the quiches hot or cold.

For red pepper, garlic & Parmesan quiches, replace the ham, spring onions and cherry tomatoes with the following – heat 1 tablespoon olive oil in a small pan and cook 1 roughly chopped red pepper and 1 crushed garlic clove for 2–3 minutes until soft. Place in the pastry cases with 50 g (2 oz) freshly grated Parmesan cheese and pour over the egg and milk as above. Omit the Cheddar and bake as above.

CHICKEN SATAY SKEWERS

Serves **4**
Preparation time **20 minutes**, plus marinating
Cooking time **8–10 minutes**

6 tablespoons **dark soy sauce**
2 tablespoons **sesame oil**
1 teaspoon **Chinese 5-spice powder**
375 g (12 oz) boneless, skinless **chicken breasts**, cut into long, thin strips

Sauce
4 tablespoons **peanut butter**
1 tablespoon **dark soy sauce**
½ teaspoon **ground coriander**
½ teaspoon **ground cumin**
pinch of **paprika** or **chilli powder**
8 tablespoons **water**
cucumber, cut into strips, to serve

Place the soy sauce, sesame oil and 5-spice powder into a bowl and mix. Add the chicken and toss together to coat in the marinade. Cover and set aside for 1 hour, stirring occasionally.

Thread the chicken, zigzag fashion, on to 10 soaked bamboo skewers (soaking them in warm water for 30 minutes will prevent the sticks burning while cooking), and place the chicken under a hot grill for 8–10 minutes, turning once, until golden and cooked through.

Meanwhile, put all the sauce ingredients in a small pan and heat, stirring, until warm and well mixed. Transfer to a small serving bowl.

Place the bowl of sauce on a serving plate with the cucumber on one side and the hot chicken skewers around it.

For pork satay skewers, replace the chicken with 375 g (12 oz) pork fillet, cut into long strips along its length. Complete and cook as above. For children who can handle a hotter sauce, fry ½ small red chilli, finely chopped, in 1 teaspoon cooking oil and add to the peanut sauce.

CHICKEN & BACON WRAPS

Serves **2**
Preparation time **15 minutes**
Cooking time **5 minutes**

1 tablespoon **olive oil**
2 x 150 g (5 oz) boneless, skinless **chicken breasts**
2 **unsmoked back bacon** rashers
2 **soft flour tortillas**
4 tablespoons **mayonnaise**
2 handfuls **spinach**

Lightly oil 2 sheets of clingfilm with the oil. Place the 2 chicken breasts, well spaced apart, between the 2 clingfilm sheets and bash with a rolling pin until the chicken is 5 mm (¼ inch) thick.

Heat a griddle or heavy-based frying pan and cook the chicken for 5 minutes, turning once, until golden and cooked through, adding the bacon to the pan for the final 2 minutes.

Spread the tortillas each with 2 tablespoons mayonnaise. Place the chicken breast over the top, then lay 2 bacon rashers on top of the chicken. Sprinkle with the spinach, then roll up tightly, securing with cocktail sticks. Cut in half and serve immediately, or wrap tightly in greaseproof paper and secure with string to transport.

For tuna & coleslaw wraps, drain a 200 g (7 oz) can of tuna in brine, and mix with 2 roughly chopped tomatoes and 1 tablespoon chopped chives. Mix ⅛ cabbage, finely shredded, with 1 large grated carrot and 1 teaspoon poppy seeds and set aside. Mix 4 tablespoons mayonnaise with 2 tablespoons water until well blended, then pour over the cabbage and carrot and toss to mix. Spread the tuna mixture over 4 flour tortillas, then spoon over the coleslaw. Roll tightly and secure with cocktail sticks as above.

ROASTED VEGETABLE COUSCOUS

Serves **6**
Preparation time **15 minutes**, plus soaking
Cooking time **30–35 minutes**

175 g (6 oz) **couscous**
1 **chicken stock cube**
450 ml (¾ pint) **hot water**
2 **courgettes**, cut into chunks
1 **red pepper**, cored, deseeded and cut into chunks
1 **yellow pepper**, cored, deseeded and cut into chunks
375 g (12 oz) **butternut squash**, peeled, deseeded and cut into chunks
1 **red onion**, chopped
5 tablespoons **olive oil**
3 tablespoons chopped **parsley** or **basil**
5 tablespoons **pine nuts**, toasted

Place the couscous in a bowl, crumble in the stock cube and stir well. Add the measured water, stir, then cover and set aside, while preparing and cooking the vegetables, to soak and swell.

Put all the prepared vegetables into a large roasting tin and drizzle over 3 tablespoons of the oil and toss to coat lightly. Roast in a preheated oven, 200°C (400°F), Gas Mark 6, for 30–35 minutes until the vegetables are soft and lightly charred.

Lightly fork the soaked couscous to fluff it up, then drizzle over the remaining oil and toss well. Add the warm vegetables, parsley or basil and pine nuts and toss well before serving.

For roasted vegetable quinoa with toasted cashews, replace the couscous with quinoa. Wash 175 g (6 oz) quinoa in a sieve, then drain. Place in a large, heavy-based nonstick frying pan and lightly toast over a moderate heat for 2–3 minutes until the grain turns a shade darker. Add 450 ml (¾ pint) water and 1 chicken stock cube and cook over a moderate heat for 8–10 minutes until the grain is tender and cooked. Drain and set aside. Add the roasted vegetables and parsley as above and replace the pine nuts with 100 g (4 oz) roughly chopped toasted cashews.

SUNSET WEDGES & SOURED CREAM

Serves **6**
Preparation time **20 minutes**
Cooking time **30–35 minutes**

3 **sweet potatoes**, skins on
2 large **baking potatoes**, skins on
3 tablespoons **olive oil**
1 teaspoon **Cajun spice**
2 tablespoons chopped **parsley**

Dip
150 ml (¼ pint) **Greek yogurt**
4 tablespoons **soured cream**
4 tablespoons chopped **chives**
2 tablespoons freshly grated **Parmesan cheese**

Cut the sweet potatoes in half, then cut each half into 4 wedges and place in a large mixing bowl. Cut the baking potatoes in half, then cut each half into 6 thick wedges and place in the bowl. Drizzle over the olive oil, then toss well to coat all the potato wedges.

Transfer the potatoes to a large baking sheet or oven tray in a single layer. Sprinkle over the Cajun spice. Roast in a preheated oven, 200°C (400°F), Gas Mark 6, for 30–35 minutes until golden and cooked through. Turn on to a serving platter and sprinkle with the parsley.

Mix the yogurt, soured cream, chives and Parmesan in a small mixing bowl. Serve the dip with the warm potato wedges.

For creamy cucumber & garlic dip to serve as an alternative accompaniment, replace the chives and Parmesan with ¼ grated cucumber and 1 crushed garlic clove. Stir in 2 tablespoons freshly chopped mint and mix well. Serve the dip with the warm potato wedges.

TOMATO-GARLIC BREAD WITH HAM

Serves 2
Preparation time **10 minutes**

1 **garlic clove**, halved
4 slices **soft white bread**
2 **tomatoes**, 1 halved and 1 thinly sliced
150 g (5 oz) finely sliced **ham**
75 g (3 oz) **Manchego cheese**, sliced

Rub the cut faces of the garlic all over the bread, concentrating particularly on the crusts. Repeat with the tomato halves.

Sandwich the bread with the ham, cheese and sliced tomato. Halve and wrap securely. The sandwiches can be kept in the refrigerator for 1 day.

For tomato-garlic bread with salami & mozzarella, flavour the bread with the garlic and tomato as above and fill with 150 g (5 oz) finely sliced salami and 75 g (3 oz) mozzarella. Add 1 sliced tomato. Warm on a baking sheet in a preheated oven, 200°C (400°F), Gas Mark 6, for 10 minutes before serving warm, cut into triangles.

SUPPER IN A HURRY

Serves 4
Preparation time **25 minutes**
Cooking time **20 minutes**

1 **ciabatta bread loaf**
small handful **chives**
125 g (4 oz) **garlic butter**, softened
5 tablespoons **olive oil**
4 boneless, skinless **chicken breasts**, cut in half
  horizontally
4 **tomatoes**, sliced
150 g (5 oz) **mozzarella cheese**, drained and sliced
1 tablespoon **white wine vinegar**
1 tablespoon **wholegrain mustard**
1 teaspoon **caster sugar**

Cut the bread at 1.5 cm (¾ inch) intervals, leaving the slices only just attached at the base.

Snip the chives with scissors and mix half in a bowl with the garlic butter. Roughly spread a dot of butter into each cut of the bread. Lay the loaf on a piece of foil and bring the edges up over the top, scrunching them together. Bake in a preheated oven, 220°C (425°F), Gas Mark 7, for 10 minutes.

Meanwhile, heat 1 tablespoon of the oil in a large frying pan. Add the chicken and fry gently for 5 minutes until golden on the underside (check by lifting a piece with a fish slice). Turn the pieces over and fry for a further 5 minutes.

Using oven gloves, carefully open out the foil on the garlic bread and bake for a further 10 minutes.

Scatter the tomato and mozzarella slices in a shallow dish.

Make a dressing by whisking together the remaining oil with the vinegar, mustard and sugar in a bowl. Scatter the remaining chives over the salad and drizzle with the dressing. Using oven gloves, remove the garlic bread from the oven and serve with the salad and chicken.

For speedy breaded pork escalopes, toss 4 pork escalopes in a little flour, dip in 4 beaten eggs, then coat in 200 g (7 oz) breadcrumbs tossed with 2 pinches smoked paprika. Heat tablespoons oil in a nonstick frying pan and cook the escalopes for 2–3 minutes on each side until golden. Serve with the tomato and mozzarella salad as above.

ASPARAGUS IN BLANKETS

Serves **4**
Preparation time **10 minutes**
Cooking time **15 minutes**

2 bunches thick **asparagus spears**, trimmed to about
   15 cm (6 inches) long
1 tablespoon **olive oil**
25 g (1 oz) **butter**, softened
16 slices **Parma, prosciutto** or **serrano ham**
4 tablespoons freshly grated **Parmesan cheese**

Bring a large pan of water to the boil. Cook the asparagus for 5 minutes in the boiling water, then remove with a slotted spoon and place in a bowl. Toss with the olive oil.

Grease a gratin dish with the butter. Wrap each of the asparagus spears in a piece of ham and place them in the greased dish side by side. Sprinkle with the Parmesan and bake in a preheated oven, 200°C (400°F), Gas Mark 6, for 10 minutes until the cheese is golden and melted.

Serve the asparagus in blankets with chunks of warm fresh bread and homemade tomato ketchup (see page 12).

For cheesy pizza-style asparagus, replace the Parma, prosciutto or serrano ham with thin slices of honey-roast ham and place the wrapped asparagus in the gratin dish. Sprinkle with 50 g (2 oz) chopped black olives and 100 g (4 oz) grated mozzarella instead of the Parmesan, and bake as above. Serve the pizza-style asparagus with garlic bread.

BEANFEAST

Serves **4**
Preparation time **10 minutes**
Cooking time **about 15 minutes**

200 g (7 oz) **tomatoes**
1 tablespoon **vegetable oil**
½ small **onion**, chopped into small pieces
1 **celery stick**, chopped into small pieces
2 x 300 g (10 oz) cans **haricot** or **cannellini beans**,
   drained and rinsed
2 teaspoons **wholegrain mustard**
2 tablespoons **black treacle**
3 tablespoons **tomato ketchup**
1 tablespoon **Worcestershire sauce**
4 slices **toast** or 4 **jacket potatoes**, to serve

Put the tomatoes into a heatproof bowl and just cover with freshly boiled water. Leave to stand for 1–2 minutes until the skins start to split. Carefully pour off the hot water and peel away the skins. Roughly chop the tomatoes on a chopping board.

Heat the oil in a medium, heavy-based saucepan for 1 minute. Add the onion and celery and fry gently for 5 minutes, stirring until just beginning to colour.

Tip in the beans, tomatoes, mustard, treacle, ketchup and Worcestershire sauce and stir the ingredients together. Heat until the liquid starts to bubble around the edges. Reduce the heat to its lowest setting and cover the pan with a lid. Cook gently for about 10 minutes until the tomatoes have softened to make a sauce.

Serve with toast or on jacket potatoes.

For lentil & paneer feast, replace the cans of beans with a 400 g (13 oz) can puy lentils, drained and rinsed and add to the pan with the tomatoes. Cook for 10 minutes, adding 250 g (8 oz) cubed paneer cheese for the final 2–3 minutes.

HAM & FRESH PINEAPPLE PIZZA

Serves 4
Preparation time **25 minutes**, plus rising
Cooking time **about 20 minutes**

250 g (8 oz) **wholemeal plain flour**
½ teaspoon **salt**
1 teaspoon fast-action **dried yeast**
150 ml (¼ pint) warm **water**
1 tablespoon **olive oil**, plus extra for oiling

Topping
2 tablespoons **olive oil**
1 small **onion**, finely chopped
150 ml (¼ pint) **passata**
3 tablespoons **tomato purée**
3 slices good-quality, thick **ham**, cut into strips
2 thick rings of fresh **pineapple**, cut into chunks
150 g (5 oz) **mozzarella cheese**, thinly sliced
thyme leaves (optional)

Sift the flour and salt into a bowl, add the yeast and mix well. Make a well in the centre and add the measured water and oil. Stir until it forms a wet dough, then beat for 2 minutes. Turn the dough out on to a well floured surface and knead for about 2 minutes until it becomes smooth and elastic. Roll out to a 30 cm (12 inch) circle, and place on a lightly oiled baking sheet. Cover with lightly oiled clingfilm and leave in a warm place while making the topping.

Heat 1 tablespoon of the oil in a small frying pan and cook the onion over a moderate heat for 2–3 minutes. Remove from the heat and add the passata and tomato purée. Spread over the pizza base to within 2.5 cm (1 inch) of the edges, and scatter over the ham.

Toss the pineapple with the remaining oil. Scatter it over the ham, then top with the mozzarella. Bake in a preheated oven, 220°C (425°F), Gas Mark 7, for 15–18 minutes until golden. Scatter with thyme leaves, if liked.

For chicken & chorizo pizza, replace the ham and pineapple with 2 x 150 g (5 oz) boneless, skinless chicken breasts and 100 g (4 oz) chorizo sausage, both thinly sliced. Heat 1 tablespoon olive oil in a frying pan and cook the chicken over a moderate heat for 3–4 minutes until golden. Add the chorizo and fry for a further 1 minute. Toss with 3 tablespoons fresh basil and pile on to the pizza base, then top with the mozzarella. Omit the thyme.

MINI STEAK BURGERS

Makes **8**
Preparation time **10 minutes**, plus chilling
Cooking time **12–15 minutes**

375 g (12 oz) **fine steak mince**
2 tablespoons **tomato ketchup**
1 tablespoon **wholegrain mustard**
3 tablespoons chopped **chives**
1 tablespoon **olive oil**
100 g (4 oz) **chestnut mushrooms**, sliced
8 thin slices **Gruyère cheese**

To serve
4 **mini burger buns**, cut in half
ketchup or **sauces**

Place the mince in a bowl with the ketchup, mustard and chives. Mix really well together, working the mixture with a fork to grind and blend the ingredients. Shape into 8 patties and place on a plate. Cover with clingfilm and chill for 30 minutes to firm.

Heat the oil in a large frying or griddle pan and cook the mushrooms over a high heat for 3–4 minutes until golden and soft. Remove from the pan using a slotted spoon. Add the burgers and cook over a moderate heat for 4–5 minutes on each side until golden and cooked through. Sit a Gruyère slice on top of each of the burgers and cover with a baking sheet for 1 minute to allow the cheese to soften.

Top the base of each bun with a burger, then spoon over the mushrooms and spread the top half of each bun with ketchup or a sauce of the child's choice. Place the lids on, and serve.

For pork & apple burgers, replace the steak mince with 375 g (12 oz) good-quality pork mince. Core 1 eating apple and grate with the skin on. Add to the mince with the mustard and chives and blend well together using a fork. Form into 8 patties, and cook as above.

NO-SUGAR BROWNIES WITH BERRIES

Serves **12**
Preparation time **20 minutes**
Cooking time **30 minutes**

250 g (8 oz) **plain dark chocolate** (70% cocoa solids)
125 g (4 oz) **unsalted butter**
4 **eggs**
150 g (5 oz) **plain flour**
50 g (2 oz) **ground almonds**
75 g (3 oz) **plain dark chocolate chips**
50 g (2 oz) **pecan nuts**, roughly chopped (optional)

To serve
fresh **blueberries**, **raspberries** and **strawberries**
ice cream or **crème fraîche**

Lightly grease a 28 x 18 cm (11 x 7 inch) baking tin and line the base with nonstick baking paper.

Melt the chocolate together with the butter. Remove from the heat and allow to cool for 2 minutes. Whisk the eggs in a separate bowl until frothy (about 3 minutes), then stir in the cooled chocolate mixture.

Fold in the flour, ground almonds, chocolate chips and pecans, if using. Transfer to the prepared baking tin and bake in a preheated oven, 180°C (350°F), Gas Mark 4, for 25–30 minutes until just firm to the touch.

Leave the brownies to cool in the tin for 20 minutes before cutting into 12 squares and serving with the fresh berries and ice cream or crème fraîche.

For white chocolate & strawberry brownies (containing sugar in the chocolate), replace the plain dark chocolate with white chocolate, and the chocolate chips and pecans with 125 g (4 oz) finely chopped strawberries. This brownie will be soft and will only keep in the refrigerator for 3 days.

STICKY FIG & BANANA TRAYBAKE

Serves **6**
Preparation time **10 minutes**
Cooking time **20 minutes**

125 g (4 oz) **margarine** or **butter**, softened
125 g (4 oz) **soft brown sugar**
1 teaspoon **ground ginger**
2 **eggs**
125 g (4 oz) **plain flour**
3 **figs**, quartered
1 large **banana**, cut into chunks
2 tablespoons **maple syrup**
ice cream or **vanilla custard**, to serve

Beat the margarine or butter and sugar until smooth and creamy. Add the ginger, eggs and flour and beat again until a smooth mixture is formed. Lightly grease a 23 cm (9 inch) square tin or ovenproof dish, then spoon in the mixture and level with the back of a spoon.

Toss the figs and banana with the maple syrup and arrange over the top of the cake, pressing the fruit into the cake in places. Bake in a preheated oven, 180°C (350°F), Gas Mark 4, for 20 minutes until the cake is well risen and golden and the fruit is soft.

Serve the cake in squares with either scoops of ice cream or vanilla custard (see below).

For vanilla custard to serve as an accompaniment, heat 300 ml (½ pint) milk, with the seeds of ½ vanilla pod scraped into it, in a nonstick pan until boiling. Meanwhile, blend 2 egg yolks with 1 teaspoon cornflour and 2 tablespoons caster sugar. Pour the milk over the egg mixture once boiled and whisk well to blend. Return to the heat, stirring continuously until just beginning to boil and thicken. It will coat the back of a spoon.

CHOCOLATE SCRIBBLE CAKE

Makes **9 squares**
Preparation time **15 minutes**
Cooking time **20 minutes**

50 g (2 oz) **plain dark chocolate**, broken into small
  pieces
50 g (2 oz) **butter** or **margarine**
2 **eggs**
150 g (5 oz) **light soft brown sugar**
50 g (2 oz) **self-raising flour**
icing pens (optional)

Melt the chocolate together with the butter.

Break the eggs into a mixing bowl, then add the sugar and sift in the flour. Stir them together vigorously.

Stir the melted chocolate and butter and carefully pour them into the mixing bowl. Stir the mixture until it is smooth, then pour into a shallow cake tin, 20 cm (8 inches) square, lined with nonstick baking paper, using the spatula to scrape every last bit from the bowl. Place on the top shelf of a preheated oven, 180°C (350°F), Gas Mark 4, for 20 minutes or until just firm when you touch it very gently in the middle.

Allow the cake to cool in the tin, then cut it into 9 pieces in the tin. Using the icing pens, decorate the squares with icing scribbles, if liked.

For pink coconut cake, make an all-in-one cake mix of 125 g (4 oz) self-raising flour, 125 g (4 oz) soft margarine, 125 g (4 oz) caster sugar and 2 eggs; beat together until smooth and creamy and then transfer to a 20 cm (8 inch) greased and base-lined square tin. Bake in the preheated oven as above for 20 minutes until golden and a skewer inserted comes out clean. Transfer to a wire rack to cool. Mix 75 g (3 oz) sifted icing sugar with 1–2 teaspoons beetroot juice until smooth and blended. Spread thinly over the cake and scatter with 1 tablespoon desiccated coconut. Cut into squares to serve.

BREAD MONSTERS

Makes **8**
Preparation time **30 minutes**, plus rising
Cooking time **15–20 minutes**

350 g (11½ oz) **strong white flour**, plus extra for
  dusting
1 teaspoon **salt**
3 g (⅛ oz) fast-action **dried yeast**
1 tablespoon **vegetable oil**
200 ml (7 fl oz) **warm water**
12 **currants**, cut in half, for the eyes and mouths
1 **egg**, beaten

Sift the flour and salt together in a mixing bowl and add the yeast, oil and water. Mix everything together with a wooden spoon, then use your hands to draw the mixture together into a firm dough. If the mixture is too dry to come together, add a little more water. If the mixture sticks to your hands, add some more flour.

Turn the dough out on to a well-floured surface and knead thoroughly for at least 5 minutes, then divide it into 8 equal pieces and knead into balls. Make a pointy snout at one end of each ball and place on a baking sheet lined with nonstick baking paper. Leave plenty of space between the rolls as they will double in size. Make prickles on the monsters by snipping into the dough with the tips of scissors. Press the currant halves into the dough to make the eyes and mouths.

Cover the rolls with a clean tea towel, then leave in a warm place for 1 hour or until they have doubled in size.

Brush the rolls with the beaten egg and bake in a preheated oven, 230°C (450°F), Gas Mark 8, for 15–20 minutes. If the rolls are cooked, they will sound hollow when tapped on the bottom (remember to pick them up with oven gloves as they will be hot). Transfer to a wire rack to cool.

For sweet bread roll snacks, add 250 g (8 oz) mixed dried fruit to the dry ingredients with 2 teaspoons ground cinnamon and 3 tablespoons caster sugar. Continue as above, shaping into 8 round balls and baking as above. Cool and serve either warm or cold, split and spread thinly with a little unsalted butter.

STRAWBERRY & VANILLA MILKSHAKE

Serves **2**
Preparation time **5–6 minutes**, plus cooling
Cooking time **5–6 minutes**

300 ml (½ pint) **milk**
300 ml (½ pint) **single cream**
½ **vanilla pod**
250 g (8 oz) **strawberries**, hulled

Put the milk and cream in a pan. Remove the vanilla seeds from the pod using the back of a teaspoon and place the pod and seeds in the pan with the milk and cream. Bring to the boil, stirring. Once boiling point has been reached, remove from the heat and allow to cool completely.

Place the strawberries in a food processor and whiz until smooth. Add the cooled vanilla milk and whiz again until pink. Pour into chilled glasses and serve with straws.

For strawberry & vanilla ice cream milkshake, put the milk and strawberries in a food processor with 5 scoops of good-quality vanilla ice cream (the variety with vanilla seeds within the ice cream) and whiz until smooth and blended. Add some ice and whiz again. Pour into chilled glasses and serve.

MANGO, MELON & ORANGE JUICE

Makes **about 400 ml (14 fl oz)**
Preparation time **5–6 minutes**

1 ripe **mango**, roughly chopped
½ **Galia melon**, deseeded and roughly chopped
200 ml (7 fl oz) **orange juice**
2 **ice cubes**

Place the mango and melon in a blender and whiz until smooth.

Add the orange juice and ice cubes, then purée until smooth. Serve immediately.

For coconut & pineapple juice, place 1 x 400 g (13 oz) can coconut milk in a food processor with ½ small pineapple, peeled, cored and roughly chopped. Whiz until smooth, then serve poured over ice and decorated with fresh cherries or strawberries for colour.

WATERMELON & RASPBERRY JUICE

Makes **about 200 ml (7 fl oz)**
Preparation time **5–6 minutes**

300 g (10 oz) **watermelon**
  (¼ an average fruit), deseeded and chopped
125 g (4 oz) **raspberries**
ice cubes, crushed (optional)

Put the watermelon and raspberries in a blender and whiz until smooth. Press the juice through a sieve to remove any raspberry pips.

Pour the juice into glasses over some crushed ice cubes, if liked.

For melon & apple juice, place half a small, deseeded and chopped, green melon into a food processor with 1 green apple, cored and cut into wedges (keep the skin on). Add 1 tablespoon lemon juice and whiz until smooth. Pour over crushed ice if liked.

FRESH LEMONADE

Makes **1.8 litres (3 pints)**
Preparation time **4–5 minutes**, plus cooling
Cooking time **4–5 minutes**

75 g (3 oz) **caster sugar**
1.8 litres (3 pints) **water**
4 **lemons**, sliced, plus extra slices to serve
ice cubes

Place the sugar in a pan with 600 ml (1 pint) of the measured water and all the sliced lemons. Bring to the boil, stirring well until all the sugar has dissolved.

Remove from the heat and add all the remaining water. Stir, then set aside to cool completely.

Once cold, roughly crush the lemons, to release all the juice. Strain through a sieve, add the ice cubes, and serve in glasses decorated with slices of lemon.

For fresh limeade, simply use 6 limes instead of 4 lemons, or use a mixture of the two. Try chopping the mint and adding while the limeade cools for a more intense mint flavour. Strain as above.

FAIRY CRUMBLE

Serves **6**
Preparation time **20 minutes**
Cooking time **30 minutes**

500 g (1 lb) **strawberries**, hulled and halved
250 g (8 oz) **raspberries**
1 **orange**, peeled and segmented
4 tablespoons **caster sugar**
½ teaspoon **ground cinnamon**

Topping
250 g (8 oz) **plain flour**
125 g (4 oz) **butter**, chilled and cubed
75 g (3 oz) **soft brown sugar**
50 g (2 oz) toasted **hazelnuts**, roughly chopped, or
   flaked almonds (optional)

Custard
2 **egg yolks**
2 tablespoons **cornflour**
3 tablespoons **caster sugar**
350 ml (12 fl oz) **milk**
2 tablespoons **beetroot juice** (from a bought cooked-
   beetroot packet) or a drop of cochineal

Place the strawberries, raspberries, orange segments (plus any juice), sugar and cinnamon in a bowl and toss together gently to coat the fruit lightly in the sugar, taking care not to break up the raspberries. Transfer the fruit to a gratin dish and set aside while making the crumble topping.

Place the flour into a bowl and using your fingertips rub the butter into it until the mixture resembles fine breadcrumbs. Stir in the sugar and nuts, if using, then spoon the crumble over the top of the fruit. Bake in a preheated oven, 200°C (400°F), Gas Mark 6, for 25–30 minutes until the topping is golden and crisp in places.

Make the pink custard: place the egg yolks, cornflour and sugar in a bowl and blend together well. Put the milk in a heavy-based nonstick saucepan and bring to the boil. Pour the milk over the egg mixture, add the beetroot juice and whisk together well. Return to the heat and cook gently, stirring continuously until thickened.

Serve the crumble in bowls with the pink custard to spoon over.

For Caribbean-style crumble, replace the red berries with 1 large mango, cut into chunks, and 6 thick slices fresh pineapple, cut into chunks. Toss with the orange and 75 g (3 oz) raisins. Replace the nuts with 4 tablespoons desiccated coconut in the crumble. Serve with ice cream rather than custard.

UPSIDE-DOWN TARTS

Serves **4**
Preparation time **10 minutes**
Cooking time **15–18 minutes**

25 g (1 oz) **unsalted butter**
25 g (1 oz) **light muscovado sugar**
50 g (2 oz) **redcurrants**
2 ripe **pears**, peeled, cored and cut into chunky pieces
½ x 375 g (12 oz) pack **ready-rolled puff pastry**,
  thawed if frozen and removed from the refrigerator

Thinly slice the butter and divide it among 4 small heatproof ramekin dishes. Sprinkle with the sugar. If the redcurrants are still attached to their stalks, reserve 4 clusters for decoration and remove the rest from the stalks (the easiest way to do this is to run the currants between the prongs of a fork). Scatter several redcurrants into each dish, then add the pears.

Unroll the pastry and cut out rounds using a 10 cm (4 inch) biscuit cutter. Lay the pastry rounds over the pears, tucking the edges down inside the dishes.

Place the dishes on a baking sheet and bake in a preheated oven, 220°C (425°F), Gas Mark 7, for 15–18 minutes or until the pastry is well risen and pale golden. Using oven gloves, remove the baking sheet from the oven and put it on a heatproof surface. Leave to cool slightly.

Loosen the edges of the pastry with a knife. Hold a ramekin dish with oven gloves and invert a small serving plate on top. Carefully flip over the dish and plate so that the plate is the right way up. Lift off the dish to reveal the tart with its fruity topping. Repeat with the remaining tarts. Serve decorated with the remaining redcurrants.

For banana & maple syrup upside-down tarts, replace the redcurrants and pears with 2 thinly sliced bananas, placing them in the bases of each of the buttered ramekins and drizzling each with 1 tablespoon maple syrup. Top with the pastry and bake as above.

NECTARINE & RASPBERRY YOGURT ICE

Serves **2**
Preparation time **5 minutes**

3 ripe **nectarines**, halved and stoned
175 g (6 oz) **raspberries**
150 ml (¼ pint) **natural yogurt**
handful of **ice cubes**

Put the nectarines and raspberries in a food processor and whiz until really smooth. Add the yogurt and whiz again, then add the ice and whiz until very crushed and the shake thickens.

Pour into chilled glasses. Decorate with cocktail umbrellas and anything else to make the drink look fun!

For banana & mango coconut ice, replace the nectarines and raspberries with 1 large ripe banana and 1 mango, cut into chunks, and whiz until smooth. Add 150 ml (¼ pint) coconut milk and whiz again. Add the ice and whiz until the shake thickens. Pour into chilled glasses to serve.

TRAFFIC-LIGHT SMOOTHIE

Makes **400 ml (14 fl oz)**
Preparation time **9–10 minutes**

3 **kiwifruits**, roughly chopped
150 ml (¼ pint)
  tangy-flavoured yogurt (such as lemon or orange)
1 small **mango**, roughly chopped
2 tablespoons **orange** or **apple juice**
150 g (5 oz) **raspberries**
1–2 teaspoons **clear honey**

Whiz the kiwifruits in a blender until smooth and spoon the mixture into 2 tall glasses. Top each with a spoonful of yogurt, spreading the yogurt to the sides of the glasses.

Blend the mango to a purée with the orange or apple juice and spoon into the glasses. Top with another layer of yogurt.

Whiz the raspberries and push through a sieve over a bowl to extract the seeds. Check their sweetness (you might need to stir in a little honey if they are very sharp). Spoon the raspberry purée into glasses to serve.

For zebra layered blackberry smoothie, place 175 g (6 oz) blackberries into a food processor with 2 tablespoons clear honey and whiz until smooth. Layer alternatively with the yogurt to replace the kiwi, mango and orange juice.

PEACH, APPLE & STRAWBERRY LOLLIES

Makes **4**
Preparation time **7–8 minutes**, plus freezing

2 **peaches**, peeled, stoned and cut into chunks
300 ml (½ pint) **water**
1 **red apple**, peeled
125 g (4 oz) **strawberries**, hulled

Place the peaches in a blender and whiz until smooth. Add one-third of the measured water and divide evenly between 4 lolly moulds. Freeze until just set.

Chop the apples into even-sized chunks and juice them. Add one-third of the water and pour on top of the frozen peach mixture, then freeze until just set.

Hull the strawberries and juice them. Add the remainder of the water and pour on top of the frozen apple mixture, then freeze until set.

For chocolate & orange lollies, place 1 x 300 g (10 oz) can mandarin segments in a food processor and whiz until smooth. Place into a pan with 125 g (4 oz) organic plain 70 per cent cocoa solids chocolate and gently heat until the chocolate has melted. Stir well with the orange pureé and pour into 4 lolly moulds. Freeze for 2 hours until firm.

PUMPKIN SEED & FRUIT BARS

Makes **8**
Preparation time **15 minutes**, plus chilling
Cooking time **5 minutes**

50 g (2 oz) **pumpkin seeds**
75 g (3 oz) **dried soya beans**
75 g (3 oz) **raisins**
75 g (3 oz) ready-to-eat **dried apricots**, roughly chopped
50 g (2 oz) **dried cranberries**
300 g (10 oz) **plain dark chocolate**, broken into pieces

Lightly grease a 28 x 18 cm (11 x 7 inch) Swiss roll tin and line the base with nonstick baking paper. Put the seeds, soya beans and all the fruit into a bowl.

Melt the chocolate. Remove from the heat, pour over the seed and fruit mixture and stir well to coat completely.

Transfer the mixture to the prepared tin and level with the back of a spoon to fill the tin evenly. Chill in the refrigerator for 1 hour until set and firm. Cut into 8 bars and keep refrigerated in an airtight container until ready to use.

For yogurt-coated bars, replace the plain dark chocolate with 200 g (7 oz) white chocolate melted over simmering water. When melted, remove from the heat and add 2 tablespoons natural yogurt and ½ teaspoon vanilla essence. Stir well, then add to the dry ingredients and stir to coat. Transfer into the tin and chill as above.

BAKED

DATE CHOCOLATE TORTE

Serves **4**
Preparation time **10 minutes,** plus cooling
Cooking time **30 minutes**

100 g (3½ oz) **flaked almonds**
125 g (4 oz) **plain dark chocolate**, roughly chopped
125 g (4 oz) **dried ready-to-eat dates**, pitted
3 **egg whites**
125 g (4 oz) **caster sugar**, plus 2 tablespoons
  for the topping
125 ml (4 fl oz) **whipping cream**
cocoa powder, to sprinkle

Grease a 23 cm (9 inch) springform tin and line with nonstick baking paper. Put the almonds and chocolate in a food processor and pulse until finely chopped. Finely chop the dates with a knife.

Whisk the egg whites in a large, perfectly clean bowl until soft peaks form. Slowly add the 125 g (4 oz) sugar and continue whisking until it has dissolved. Fold in the almond and chocolate mixture, then the dates. Spoon the mixture into the prepared tin and level the surface.

Bake in a preheated oven, 180°C (350°F), Gas Mark 4, for 30 minutes or until set and starting to come away from the side. Leave to cool in the tin before carefully turning out on to a serving plate.

Whip the cream and the remaining 2 tablespoons sugar in a small bowl until soft peaks form. Using a spatula, spread the cream evenly over the top of the torte. Serve cut into thin slices and dusted with cocoa.

For iced date chocolate muffins, spoon the chocolate mixture into 12 large, deep muffin tins lined with paper cases and bake in a preheated oven, 180°C (350°F), Gas Mark 4, for 20–25 minutes or until set. Transfer to a wire rack to cool. Melt 75 g (3 oz) chopped plain dark chocolate with 40 g (1½ oz) butter in a heatproof bowl set over a saucepan of gently simmering water. Meanwhile, toast 4 tablespoons flaked almonds in a dry frying pan, stirring constantly, until golden brown. Stir the chocolate mixture, then spoon over the muffins and sprinkle with the toasted almonds. Leave until set.

TIPSY BERRY WAFFLES

Serves **4**
Preparation time **5 minutes**
Cooking time **1–2 minutes**

15 g (½ oz) **butter**
250 g (8 oz) **mixed berries**, such as blueberries,
  blackberries and raspberries
1 tablespoon **caster sugar**
2 tablespoons **kirsch**
4 **waffles**
4 tablespoons **crème fraîche**

Melt the butter in a nonstick frying pan, add the berries, sugar and kirsch and cook over a high heat, stirring gently, for 1–2 minutes.

Meanwhile, toast or reheat the waffles according to the packet instructions. Put a waffle on each serving plate, spoon the berries over the waffles and top each portion with 1 tablespoon crème fraîche. Serve immediately.

For homemade waffles, sift 125 g (4 oz) plain flour, 1 teaspoon baking powder and a pinch of salt into a bowl. Make a well in the centre and gradually beat in 2 eggs and 150 ml (¼ pint) milk until the batter is thick and smooth. Just before cooking, beat in 3 tablespoons cooled melted butter. Heat a waffle iron and oil if necessary. Spoon in enough batter to give a good coating, close and cook for about 1 minute on each side. Lift the lid and remove the waffle. Repeat with the remaining batter.

HOT BERRY SOUFFLÉS

Serves **4**
Preparation time **10 minutes**
Cooking time **15 minutes**

15 g (½ oz) **butter**
100 g (3½ oz) **caster sugar**
50 g (2 oz) **blackberries**
200 g (7 oz) **raspberries**
4 **large egg whites**
icing sugar (optional)

Use the butter to grease 4 x 200 ml (7 fl oz) ramekins and then coat evenly with a little of the caster sugar, tipping out the excess sugar. Set the ramekins on a baking sheet.

Purée the blackberries and raspberries in a food processor or blender, reserving a few of the berries to decorate, then pour the purée into a bowl. Alternatively, the berries can be rubbed through a fine sieve to make a smooth purée.

Whisk the egg whites until stiff but not dry in a large, perfectly clean bowl. Gradually sprinkle in the remaining caster sugar, whisking continuously, and continue whisking until the whites are stiff and shiny.

Gently fold the egg whites into the berry purée, then spoon the mixture into the prepared ramekins. Bake immediately in a preheated oven, 190°C (375°F), Gas Mark 5, for 15 minutes or until risen and golden.

Dust the soufflés with icing sugar and decorate with the reserved berries. Serve immediately, with custard or ice cream, if liked.

For homemade custard to serve as an accompaniment, gently heat 300 ml (½ pint) milk in a saucepan without boiling. Meanwhile, beat 2 egg yolks in a bowl with 1 tablespoon sugar and a few drops of vanilla extract, then pour the milk into the bowl, stirring constantly. Return the mixture to the pan and heat over a low heat, stirring constantly, until the custard thickens enough to coat the back of the spoon. Serve immediately with the soufflés.

WALNUT & WHITE CHOCOLATE COOKIES

Makes **about 25**
Preparation time **15 minutes,** plus cooling
Cooking time **12–15 minutes**

1 **egg**
150 g (5 oz) **soft light brown sugar**
2 tablespoons **caster sugar**
1 teaspoon **vanilla extract**
125 ml (4 fl oz) **vegetable oil**
65 g (2½ oz) **plain flour**
3 tablespoons **self-raising flour**
¼ teaspoon **ground cinnamon**
25 g (1 oz) **shredded coconut**
175 g (6 oz) **walnuts**, toasted and chopped
125 g (4 oz) **white chocolate chips**

Grease 2 baking sheets and line with nonstick baking paper. In a bowl, beat the egg and sugars together until light and creamy. Stir in the vanilla extract and oil. Sift in the flours and cinnamon, then add the coconut, walnuts and chocolate and mix well with a wooden spoon.

Form rounded tablespoonfuls of the mixture into balls and place on the prepared baking sheets, pressing the mixture together with your fingertips if it is crumbly. Bake in a preheated oven, 180°C (350°F), Gas Mark 4, for 12–15 minutes or until golden. Leave to cool slightly on the sheets, then transfer to a wire rack to cool completely.

For hazelnut & chocolate chip cookies, follow the recipe above but use ½ teaspoon ground ginger in place of the cinnamon, toasted and chopped hazelnuts instead of the walnuts and plain dark chocolate chips in place of the white.

RHUBARB SLUMPS

Serves **4**
Preparation time **10 minutes**
Cooking time **20–25 minutes**

400 g (13 oz) **rhubarb**, cut into chunks
6 tablespoons **golden caster sugar**
grated rind and juice of 1 **orange**
100 g (3½ oz) **oats**
6 tablespoons **double cream**
2 tablespoons **dark muscovado sugar**

Mix together the rhubarb, golden caster sugar and orange rind and half the juice in a bowl. Spoon the mixture into 4 individual ramekins.

Put the oats, cream, dark muscovado sugar and remaining orange juice in the bowl and mix together. Drop spoonfuls of the oat mixture all over the surface of the rhubarb mixture.

Set the ramekins on a baking sheet and bake in a preheated oven, 180°C (350°F), Gas Mark 4, for 20–25 minutes until the topping is browned. Serve hot.

For apple and blackberry crumbles, peel, core and chop 2 dessert apples, then mix with 100 g (3½ oz) blackberries, 6 tablespoons golden caster sugar and 1 tablespoon apple juice. Spoon into the ramekins as above. Sift 125 g (4 oz) plain flour into a bowl, add 50 g (2 oz) diced butter and rub in with the fingertips until the mixture resembles coarse breadcrumbs. Stir in 50 g (2 oz) dark muscovado sugar, 25 g (1 oz) bran flakes and 50 g (2 oz) chopped mixed nuts. Spoon the mixture over the fruit and flatten slightly with the back of a spoon. Bake as above until the topping is lightly golden.

APRICOT TARTLETS

Serves **4**
Preparation time **15 minutes**
Cooking time **20–25 minutes**

375 g (12 oz) **ready-rolled puff pastry**, defrosted if frozen
100 g (3½ oz) **marzipan**
12 canned **apricot halves**, drained
light muscovado sugar, for sprinkling
apricot jam, for glazing

Using a saucer as a template, cut 4 rounds from the pastry, each approximately 8 cm (3½ inches) in diameter. Score a line about 1 cm (½ inch) from the edge of each round with a sharp knife.

Roll out the marzipan to 2.5 mm (⅛ inch) thick and cut out 4 rounds to fit inside the scored circles. Lay the pastry rounds on a baking sheet, place a circle of marzipan in the centre of each and arrange 3 apricot halves, cut-side up, on top. Sprinkle a little sugar into each apricot.

Put the baking sheet on top of a second preheated baking sheet (this helps to crisp the pastry bases) and bake in a preheated oven, 200°C (400°F), Gas Mark 6, for 20–25 minutes until the pastry is puffed and browned and the apricots are slightly caramelized around the edges. While still hot, brush the tops with apricot jam to glaze. Serve immediately.

For banana tartlets with rum mascarpone, follow the recipe above, but use 2 thickly sliced bananas in place of the apricots. While the tartlets are baking, in a bowl, mix together 4 tablespoons mascarpone cheese, 2 tablespoons rum and 2 tablespoons light muscovado sugar. Spoon on top of the hot tartlets and serve immediately.

CHOCOLATE SOUFFLÉS

Serves **4**

Preparation time **12 minutes**

Cooking time **about 15 minutes**

200 g (7 oz) **plain dark chocolate**, chopped

150 g (5 oz) **butter**, diced and softened

6 **eggs**

175 g (6 oz) **caster sugar**

125 g (4 oz) **plain flour**

icing sugar, to dust

Butter 4 x 200 ml (7 fl oz) ramekins. Melt the chocolate with the butter in a heatproof bowl set over a saucepan of gently simmering water.

Beat the eggs and sugar together in a bowl until very light and creamy. Sift the flour, then fold into the egg mixture. Fold in the chocolate mixture.

Divide the soufflé mixture between the prepared ramekins. Bake in a preheated oven, 180°C (350°F), Gas Mark 4, for 8–12 minutes. The soufflés should rise and form a firm crust, but you want them still to be slightly runny in the centre. Serve immediately dusted with icing sugar, with ice cream or cream.

For homemade vanilla ice cream to serve with the soufflés, in a heatproof bowl, mix together 1 whole egg, 1 egg yolk and 40 g (1 1/2 oz) caster sugar. Bring 250 ml (8 fl oz) single cream gently to boiling point in a saucepan and pour on to the egg mixture, stirring vigorously. Strain, then stir in 1–2 drops vanilla extract. Leave to cool, then fold in 150 ml (1/4 pint) whipped double cream. Pour into a rigid freezerproof container. Cover, seal and freeze for 1 hour. Remove and stir well, then re-freeze until firm. Transfer to the refrigerator 20 minutes before serving to soften.

BANANA & CHOC WHOLEMEAL MUFFINS

Makes **12**

Preparation time **15 minutes**

Cooking time **20–25 minutes**

150 g (5 oz) **self-raising wholemeal flour**

150 g (5 oz) **plain flour**

1 teaspoon **baking powder**

1 teaspoon **bicarbonate of soda**

1/2 teaspoon **salt**

125 g (4 oz) **golden caster sugar**

3 large ripe **bananas**, mashed

1 **egg**, beaten

75 ml (3 fl oz) **water**

75 ml (3 fl oz) **vegetable oil**

75 g (3 oz) **carob** or **plain dark chocolate**, roughly chopped

Sift the flours, baking powder, bicarbonate of soda and salt into a large bowl, then add the wheatgerm left in the sieve. Stir in the caster sugar. Mix together the bananas, egg, measured water and oil in a jug, then pour into the dry ingredients and gently mix until just combined. Fold in the carob or chocolate.

Line a 12-hole muffin tin with 12 paper muffin cases and three-quarters fill each with the mixture.

Bake in a preheated oven, 180°C (350°F), Gas Mark 4, for 20–25 minutes until they are well risen and spring back when you press them. Place on a wire rack to cool.

For fresh cherry & vanilla muffins, omit the bananas, mix 2 teaspoons vanilla extract into the egg, water and oil mixture, and fold in 250 g (8 oz) fresh pitted cherries instead of the chocolate. Bake as above.

LEMON COOKIES

Makes **18–20**
Preparation time **15 minutes**, plus cooling
Cooking time **15–20 minutes**

125 g (4 oz) **unsalted butter**, diced and softened
125 g (4 oz) **caster sugar**
2 **egg yolks**
2 teaspoons grated **lemon rind**
150 g (5 oz) **plain flour**
100 g (3½ oz) **coarse cornmeal**
saffron (optional)
icing sugar, for dusting

Line a baking sheet with nonstick baking paper. In a bowl, beat the butter and sugar together until light and fluffy. Mix in the egg yolks, lemon rind, flour and cornmeal until a soft dough forms.

Roll out the dough on a lightly floured surface to 1 cm (½ inch) thick. Using a 6 cm (2½ inch) round cutter, cut out rounds from the dough, re-rolling the trimmings. Transfer to the prepared baking sheet, then sprinkle with saffron, if liked, and bake in a preheated oven, 160°C (325°F), Gas Mark 3, for 15–20 minutes or until lightly golden. Transfer to a wire rack to cool, then dust with icing sugar.

For no-cook lemon cheesecakes, roughly crush 10 of the above biscuits and place them in the base of 4 dessert bowls or glasses. Whisk together 300 g (10 oz) cream cheese with the finely grated zest and juice of 1 lemon, 150 g (5 oz) caster sugar and 150 ml (¼ pint) double cream. Spoon this mixture into the prepared glasses and chill for 1–2 hours before serving.

DEVONSHIRE SPLITS

Makes **12 splits**

Time **1½–2½ hours**, depending on machine, plus shaping, proving and baking

Dough

300 ml (½ pint) **cold water**

2 tablespoons **butter**, at room temperature

½ teaspoon **salt**

2 tablespoons **milk powder**

500 g (1 lb) **strong white bread flour**

2 teaspoons **caster sugar**

1¼ teaspoons **fast-action dried yeast**

To finish

beaten **egg**, to glaze

250 g (8 oz) **strawberry jam**

250 g (8 oz) **clotted cream**

icing sugar, for dusting

Lift the bread pan out of the machine and fit the blade. Put the dough ingredients in the pan, following the order specified in the manual.

Fit the pan into the machine and close the lid. Set to the dough programme.

At the end of the programme turn the dough out on to a floured surface and cut it into 12 pieces. Shape each piece into a ball. Put them on large, greased baking sheets, leaving a little space around each one. Cover loosely with oiled clingfilm and leave to rise in a warm place for 20–30 minutes.

Brush the rolls with beaten egg. Bake in a preheated oven, 200°C (400°F), Gas Mark 6, for 10 minutes until golden and the bases sound hollow when tapped with the fingertips. Transfer to a wire rack to cool.

When ready to serve, cut a diagonal slice down through the rolls almost but not quite through to the base. Spoon the jam into the slit, then add spoonfuls of clotted cream. Transfer to serving plates and dust with icing sugar.

For lemon splits, make and bake the dough as above, adding the finely grated rind of 2 lemons to the dough. To finish, slice the rolls as above and fill with lightly whipped cream and lemon curd.

PEACH & RASPBERRY TARTLETS

Serves **4**
Preparation time **15 minutes**
Cooking time **8–10 minutes,** plus cooling

15 g (½ oz) **butter,** melted
4 sheets of **filo pastry,** each about 25 cm (10 inches) square
125 ml (4 fl oz) **double cream**
1 tablespoon **soft light brown sugar**
2 **peaches,** peeled, halved, stoned and diced
50 g (2 oz) **raspberries**
icing sugar, for dusting

Brush 4 deep muffin tins with the melted butter. Cut a sheet of filo pastry in half, then across into 4 equal-sized squares. Use these filo squares to line 1 muffin tin, arranging at slightly different angles, pressing down well and tucking the pastry into the tin neatly. Repeat with the remaining pastry to line the other muffin tins.

Bake the filo pastry tartlets in a preheated oven, 190°C (375°F), Gas Mark 5, for 8–10 minutes or until golden. Carefully remove the tartlet cases from the tins and leave to cool on a wire rack.

Whip the cream and brown sugar lightly in a bowl, until it holds its shape. Spoon into the tartlet cases and top with the peaches and raspberries. Dust with icing sugar. Serve immediately.

For strawberry and blueberry tartlets, grease 4 deep muffin tins as above. From ready-rolled shortcrust pastry (defrosted if frozen), cut out 4 rounds large enough to line the muffin tins. Prick the bases all over with a fork. Bake in a preheated oven, 190°C (375°F), Gas Mark 5, for 15 minutes or until golden brown. Carefully remove from the tins and leave to cool on a wire rack. Lightly whip the cream with 1 tablespoon icing sugar, then spoon into the tartlet cases. Top with 50 g (2 oz) sliced strawberries and 50 g (2 oz) blueberries. Dust with icing sugar and serve immediately.

MADELEINES

Makes **14**
Preparation time **15 minutes,** plus cooling
Cooking time **12 minutes**

3 **eggs**
100 g (3½ oz) **caster sugar**
150 g (5 oz) **plain flour**
100 g (3½ oz) **unsalted butter,** melted
grated rind of 1 **lemon**
grated rind of 1 **orange**

Brush a tray of madeleine moulds with melted butter and coat with plain flour, then tap the tray to remove the excess flour.

Whisk the eggs and sugar in a bowl until thick and pale and the whisk leaves a trail when lifted. Sift the flour, then gently fold into the egg mixture. Fold in the melted butter and lemon and orange rinds. Spoon into the moulds, leaving a little room for rising.

Bake in a preheated oven, 200°C (400°F), Gas Mark 6, for 12 minutes or until golden and springy to the touch. Remove the madeleines from the tray and leave to cool on a wire rack.

For quick sherry trifle, line the base of a dessert or trifle bowl with the madeleines and sprinkle over 2–3 tablespoons sweet sherry. Top with 300 g (10 oz) defrosted frozen mixed berries and top that with 200 ml (7 fl oz) custard. Whip 200 g (7 oz) double cream until soft peaks form and pipe or spoon over the top. Cover and chill in the refrigerator for 2–3 hours before serving.

STICKY CHELSEA BUNS

Makes **12 buns**
Time **1½–2½ hours**, depending on machine, plus
shaping, proving and baking

Dough
1 **egg**, beaten
225 ml (7½ fl oz) **milk**
50 g (2 oz) **unsalted butter**, softened
½ teaspoon **salt**
finely grated rind of 1 **lemon**
500 g (1 lb) **strong white bread flour**
75 g (3 oz) **caster sugar**
1½ teaspoon **fast-action dried yeast**

To finish
50 g (2 oz) **unsalted butter**, softened
50 g (2 oz) **light muscovado sugar**
1 teaspoon **ground mixed spice**
200 g (7 oz) luxury **mixed dried fruit**
25 g (1 oz) **fresh root ginger**, grated
50 g (2 oz) **caster sugar**

Lift the bread pan out of the machine and fit the blade. Put the dough ingredients in the pan, following the order specified in the manual. Fit the pan into the machine and close the lid. Set to the dough programme.

Mix together the butter and muscovado sugar to make a paste. Toss the spice with the fruit and ginger in a bowl.

At the end of the programme turn the dough out on to a floured surface and roll it out to a rectangle, about 45 x 25 cm (18 x 10 inches). Spread to the edges with the butter and sugar paste and scatter over the fruit mixture. Roll up the dough starting from a long side. Use a sharp knife to cut the log into 12 equal slices.

Grease a shallow 28 x 18 cm (11 x 7 inch) baking tin. Arrange the slices in the tin, and with the cut sides up. Cover loosely with oiled clingfilm and leave to rise in a warm place for about 45 minutes or until doubled in size.

Bake the buns in a preheated oven, 200°C (400°F), Gas Mark 6, for 25–35 minutes until risen and golden.

Meanwhile, put the caster sugar in a pan with 100 ml (3½ fl oz) water and heat gently until the sugar dissolves. Bring to the boil and boil for 1 minute. Transfer the buns to a wire rack and brush them with syrup. Leave to cool.

For chocolate, fruit & nut buns, substitute lemon rind for orange. Replace the butter paste and fruit mixture with 200 g (7 oz) chopped chocolate, 1 teaspoon ground ginger, 125 g (4 oz) raisins and 75 g (3 oz) chopped hazelnuts. Drizzle with melted chocolate.

A VERY HAPPY BIRTHDAY CAKE

Serves **12**
Preparation time **25 minutes**
Cooking time **35–40 minutes**

175 g (6 oz) **soft margarine**, plus extra for greasing
175 g (6 oz) **caster sugar**
2 teaspoons **vanilla essence**
300 g (10 oz) **self-raising flour**
2 teaspoons **baking powder**
3 **eggs**
50 g (2 oz) **ground rice**
150 ml (¼ pint) **low-fat**
  natural yogurt
175 g (6 oz) **strawberries**, finely chopped
300 ml (½ pint) **double cream**
3 tablespoons **reduced-sugar strawberry jam**

Grease 2 x 20 cm (8 inch) loose-bottomed, round cake tins lightly with margarine, and line the bases of the tins with nonstick baking paper. Cream the margarine and sugar in a food processor with the vanilla essence until smooth.

Sift the flour and baking powder over the creamed mixture, add the eggs, ground rice and yogurt and whiz together until creamy. Fold strawberries into the mixture.

Divide the mixture between the prepared tins and bake in a preheated oven, 180°C (350°F), Gas Mark 4, for 35–40 minutes until risen, golden and springy to the touch. Allow to cool in the tins for 10 minutes before removing to a wire rack to cool completely. Remove the baking paper.

Whisk the cream until soft peaks form. Cut the top off one of the cakes to level it, then spread with the jam and then half of the cream to the edges. Scatter with two-thirds of the strawberries. Place the other cake on top and spread with the remaining cream. Scatter with the remaining strawberries or form them into your child's initials. Add candles.

For chocolate birthday cake, replace 25 g (1 oz) of the flour with cocoa powder and bake as above. Omit the jam and simply fill with the cream. Replace the strawberries with 200 g (7 oz) chocolate-coated honeycomb balls, lightly crushed and used to fill and decorate the cake.

CHERRY, BRAN & RAISIN MUFFINS

Makes **12**
Preparation time **15 minutes**
Cooking time **20–25 minutes**

125 g (4 oz) **oatbran**
250 g (8 oz) **self-raising flour**
1 teaspoon **baking powder**
1 teaspoon **bicarbonate of soda**
1 teaspoon **ground cinnamon**
½ teaspoon **ground ginger**
125 g (4 oz) **soft brown sugar**
1 **egg**
75 ml (3 fl oz) **vegetable oil**
100 ml (3½ fl oz) **milk**
250 g (8 oz) **cherries**, stoned and halved
125 g (4 oz) **raisins**

Topping
250 g (8 oz) **mascarpone cheese**
2 tablespoons **icing sugar**

To decorate
12 **cherries**
pinch of **ground cinnamon** (optional)

Place the oatbran in a bowl. Sift the flour, baking powder, bicarbonate of soda, cinnamon and ginger over the top and mix together. Add the sugar and stir well.

Mix together in a jug the egg, oil and milk, then pour into the dry ingredients with the cherries and raisins and stir until just mixed. Line a 12-hole muffin tray with 12 paper muffin cases and divide the mixture between them. Bake in a preheated oven, 180°C (350°F), Gas Mark 4, for 20–25 minutes until well risen and golden. Remove the muffins from the tin and place on a wire rack to cool.

Beat the mascarpone and icing sugar in a bowl, then spoon and swirl on top of each cooled muffin. Decorate each with a cherry and a sprinkling of cinnamon, if liked.

For carrot-cake muffins, omit the oatbran and increase the flour to 275 g (9 oz). Add 1 teaspoon mixed spice. Replace the cherries with 2 grated carrots and add 75 g (3 oz) roughly chopped walnuts or pecans. Bake as above, then decorate with the same topping and a walnut half instead of a cherry.

CHOCOLATE & PECAN SPIRAL

Makes **1 extra-large loaf**
Time **1½–2½ hours**, depending on machine, plus shaping, proving and baking

Dough
2 **eggs**, beaten
175 ml (6 fl oz) **milk**
45 g (1¾ oz) **unsalted butter**, softened
½ teaspoon **salt**
500 g (1 lb) **strong white bread flour**
50 g (2 oz) **caster sugar**
1½ teaspoons **fast-action dried yeast**

To finish
125 g (4 oz) **plain dark chocolate**, finely chopped
125 g (4 oz) **pecan nuts**, roughly chopped
2 tablespoons **caster sugar**
1 **egg yolk**, to glaze

Lift the bread pan out of the machine and fit the blade. Put the dough ingredients in the pan, following the order specified in the manual.

Fit the pan into the machine and close the lid. Set to the dough programme.

At the end of the programme turn the dough out on to a floured surface and roll it to a 28 cm (11 inch) square. Sprinkle over three-quarters of the chocolate and the nuts and all of the sugar. Roll up the dough, then put it into a greased 1.8 litre (3 pint) loaf tin. Cover loosely with oiled clingfilm and leave in a warm place for 30 minutes or until the dough reaches just above the top of the tin.

Mix the egg yolk with 1 tablespoon of water and brush it over the dough. Sprinkle over the remaining chocolate and pecan nuts and bake in a preheated oven, 200°C (400°F), Gas Mark 6, for 35–40 minutes until the bread is well risen and deep brown and sounds hollow when tapped with the fingertips. Cover with foil after 10 minutes to prevent the nuts from over-browning.

For brandied prune & chocolate slice, roughly chop 200 g (7 oz) soft pitted prunes and put them in a bowl with 2 tablespoons brandy and steep for 2 hours. Make the dough as above. Turn the dough out on to a floured surface and work in the prunes and 100 g (3½ oz) each of plain and white chocolate. Shape into a log and drop into a greased 1.8 litre (3 pint) loaf tin. Cover loosely with oiled clingfilm and leave in a warm place until almost doubled in size. Bake as above. After baking, dust with a mixture of cocoa powder and icing sugar.

RUDOLPH'S SANTA SNACKS

Makes **about 14**
Preparation time **15 minutes**
Cooking time **15 minutes**

50 g (2 oz) **cornflakes**
100 g (3½ oz) **butter** or **margarine**, softened
75 g (3 oz) **caster sugar**
1 **egg yolk**
few drops **vanilla essence**
125 g (4 oz) **self-raising flour**
25 g (1 oz) **cornflour**
7 **glacé cherries**, sliced in half, to decorate

Place the cornflakes in a plastic bag. Crush them with your hands or bash them with a rolling pin, then tip on to a plate and set aside.

Put the butter and sugar into a mixing bowl and cream them together with a wooden spoon until pale and fluffy. Add the egg yolk and vanilla essence and stir in. Sift in the flour and cornflour and stir them into the mix.

Take walnut-sized amounts of the mixture and make them into about 14 balls. Roll the balls in the crushed cornflakes until covered, then place them on a baking sheet lined with nonstick baking paper, leaving plenty of space between them, and decorate the top of each one with half a glacé cherry.

Bake the biscuits in a preheated oven, 190°C (375°F), Gas Mark 5, for 15 minutes, or until a light golden brown, then remove from the oven and allow to cool a little before transferring to a wire cooling rack.

For Santa's chocolate snowy snacks, add 50 g (2 oz) plain chocolate drops to the mixture with the flour and cornflour, then add 1 tablespoon cocoa powder. Stir and then cook as above. Once cooked, dust with a little icing sugar to resemble snow.

BAKED

GRANOLA SQUARES

Makes **12**
Preparation time **15 minutes**, plus chilling
Cooking time **20 minutes**

175 g (6 oz) **butter**, plus extra for greasing
150 ml (¼ pint) **clear honey**
2 tablespoons **maple syrup**
1 teaspoon **ground cinnamon**
125 g (4 oz) ready-to-eat **dried apricots**, roughly chopped
100 g (4 oz) ready-to-eat **dried papaya** or **mango**, roughly chopped
125 g (4 oz) **raisins**
4 tablespoons **pumpkin seeds**
2 tablespoons **sesame seeds**
3 tablespoons **sunflower seeds**
75 g (3 oz) **pecan nuts**, roughly chopped
275 g (9 oz) **porridge oats**

Grease a 28 x 18 cm (11 x 7 inch) deep Swiss roll tin with butter and line the base with nonstick baking paper.

Place the butter, honey and maple syrup in a medium saucepan and heat, stirring continually, until the butter has melted. Add the cinnamon, dried fruit, seeds and nuts, stir the mixture and heat for 1 minute. Remove from the heat and add the porridge oats, stirring until they are well coated in the syrup.

Transfer the mixture to the prepared tin and smooth down with the back of a spoon to compact into the tin and level. Bake in a preheated oven, 180°C (350°F), Gas Mark 4, for 15 minutes until the top is just beginning to brown. Remove from the oven and allow to cool in the tin, then chill in the refrigerator for 30–60 minutes.

Turn out the chilled granola, upside down, on a chopping board, then carefully flip it back over to its correct side. Using a long, sharp knife (preferably longer than the granola itself), cut into 12 squares.

For fruity chocolate granola squares, leave out the pecans and seeds and replace with 75 g (3 oz) roughly chopped ready-to-eat dried apples. Once cooled, drizzle 50 g (2 oz) melted white chocolate over the top. Allow to set in the refrigerator for 10 minutes before cutting into squares.

BLUEBERRY & SOFT CHEESE TRAYBAKE

Serves **12**
Preparation time **20 minutes**
Cooking time **20 minutes**

175 g (6 oz) **butter**, softened
75 g (3 oz) **soft brown sugar**
375 g (12 oz) **soft cheese**
2 teaspoons **vanilla essence**
3 **eggs**
175 g (6 oz) **plain flour**
175 g (6 oz) **wholemeal flour**
175 g (6 oz) **blueberries**
75 g (3 oz) **icing sugar**, sifted
½ teaspoon **ground cinnamon** (optional)

Grease a 28 x 18 cm (11 x 7 inch) deep Swiss roll tin lightly with butter and line the base with nonstick baking paper.

Place 150 g (5 oz) of the butter into a bowl and beat well until smooth with a wooden spoon. Add the sugar, 150 g (5 oz) of the soft cheese and the vanilla essence and beat again. Add the eggs and sift in the flours. Mix together to combine well.

Fold the blueberries into the cake mixture, then transfer to the prepared tin and level. Bake in a preheated oven, 180°C (350°F), Gas Mark 4, for 20 minutes until golden and firm to the touch. Allow to cool for 10 minutes in the tin before turning the cake out on to a wire rack to cool completely.

Beat together the remaining soft cheese and remaining butter with the icing sugar and half of the cinnamon, if using, and spread over the surface of the cake. Cut into 12 squares, then sprinkle with the remaining cinnamon, if liked.

For raspberry & orange traybake, add the grated rind of ¹/₂ orange to the creamed butter, sugar and soft cheese mixture, then replace the blueberries with 125 g (4 oz) raspberries, folding in very carefully so as not to break up the fruit. Bake as above, then make up the same topping, replacing the cinnamon with the remaining orange rind, and spread over the top.

CHOC-PEANUT CAKE

Makes a **1 kg (2 lb) loaf cake**
Preparation time **15 minutes**
Cooking time **about 1 hour**

125 g (4 oz) **plain flour**
50 g (2 oz) **wholemeal flour**
1 teaspoon **baking powder**
3 tablespoons **golden caster sugar**
100 g (3½ oz) **smooth peanut butter**
125 g (4 oz) **butter**, softened
3 **eggs**, lightly beaten
1 teaspoon **vanilla extract**
50 ml (2 fl oz) **apple juice**
100 g (3½ oz) **plain chocolate chips** or **plain dark chocolate**, chopped
1 large **dessert apple**, peeled, cored and chopped

Line a 1 kg (2 lb) loaf tin with nonstick baking paper. Sift the flours and baking powder into a large bowl. Mix in the sugar, peanut butter, butter, eggs, vanilla extract and apple juice. Stir through the chocolate chips and apple.

Spoon the mixture into the prepared tin and bake in a preheated oven, 180°C (350°F), Gas Mark 4, for 1 hour. To see if it is cooked, insert a skewer in the centre of the loaf – if it comes out clean it is done, but if cake mix is attached to the skewer it will need another 10 minutes.

Remove the cake from the oven and turn out on to a wire rack. Peel off the baking paper and leave to cool. Serve cut into slices.

For honey cake, replace the peanut butter with 125 g (4 oz) thick honey and omit the chocolate chips. Drizzle with 2 tablespoons clear honey before serving.

BANANA & CHOCOLATE LOAF CAKE

Serves **8–10**
Preparation time **15 minutes**
Cooking time **55–60 minutes**

250 g (8 oz) **butter**, softened, plus extra for greasing
125 g (4 oz) **caster sugar**
1 teaspoon **vanilla extract**
3 **eggs**, beaten
300 g (10 oz) **self-raising flour**
1 teaspoon **baking powder**
3 ripe **bananas**, mashed
2 tablespoons **milk**
175 g (6 oz) **plain dark chocolate**, roughly chopped,
   or **chocolate chips**

Grease a 1 kg (2 lb) loaf tin lightly with butter and line the base with nonstick baking paper. Beat the butter, sugar and vanilla extract together in a bowl until smooth and creamy. Add the eggs and sift over the flour and baking powder. Beat together until smooth and creamy.

Add the bananas, milk and chopped chocolate and fold together until well mixed. Transfer the mixture to the prepared tin and bake in a preheated oven, 180°C (350°F), Gas Mark 4, for 55–60 minutes until the cake is well risen and golden.

Cool the cake in the tin for 10 minutes before turning out on to a wire rack to cool completely. Serve cut into slices.

For double-chocolate no-wheat banana loaf, replace the flour with 300 g (10 oz) rice flour and add 4 tablespoons of cocoa powder when sifting into the bowl.

VANILLA FLOWERS

Makes **30**
Preparation time **30 minutes**
Cooking time **10–15 minutes**

200 g (7 oz) **butter**, softened
few drops **vanilla essence**
50 g (2 oz) **icing sugar**
175 g (6 oz) **plain flour**
50 g (2 oz) **cornflour**
cake decorations, to decorate

Place the butter and vanilla essence in a mixing bowl and sift in the icing sugar. Cream the ingredients together with a wooden spoon. Sift in the flour and the cornflour a little at a time and fold in with a metal spoon.

Spoon the mixture into a piping bag, and pipe the mixture on to a baking sheet lined with nonstick baking paper, making little flower shapes. To finish a flower, push the nozzle down into the piped flower as you stop squeezing. Press a decoration into the centre of each one.

Bake the cookies in a preheated oven, 190°C (375°F), Gas Mark 5, for 10–15 minutes or until they are a pale golden colour. Remove from the oven and allow to cool for a few minutes on the baking sheet before transferring to a cooling rack.

For ginger flowers, mix 1 teaspoon ground allspice or mixed spice in with the cornflour. Decorate the centre of each with $1/4$ piece stem ginger before baking as above.

END-OF-SUMMER CUSTARD PIE

Serves **6–8**
Preparation time **20 minutes**, plus chilling
Cooking time **25 minutes**

150 g (5 oz) **plain flour**, plus extra for dusting
3 tablespoons **custard powder**
2 tablespoons **icing sugar**
75 g (3 oz) **butter**, chilled and cut into cubes
2–3 tablespoons **cold water**
500 g (1 lb) **blackberries**
2 **apples**, peeled, cored and roughly chopped
4 tablespoons **caster sugar**
1 tablespoon **clear honey**
beaten **egg**
vanilla ice cream or **crème fraîche** (optional)

Sift the flour, custard powder and icing sugar into a bowl. Rub the butter using your fingertips into the flour until the mixture resembles fine breadcrumbs. Sprinkle over the measured water, then using a round-bladed knife begin to work the mixture into a smooth, firm dough. Wrap and chill for 15 minutes.

Toss the blackberries and apples with the sugar and honey and place in a 20 cm (8 inch) round pie dish or ovenproof dish.

Roll out the pastry, on a well-floured surface, to a round slightly larger than the pie dish. Place the dish on the pastry and cut around it using a sharp knife to produce a circle the correct size for the top. Using the pastry trimmings, make a border strip about 1 cm (½ inch) wide. Dampen the edges of the pie dish and fit the strips of pastry around the edge, pressing firmly. Dampen this pastry too before placing the circle on top and pressing again firmly to hold in place. Using any remaining trimmings, decorate the pie with leaves, flowers, birds or other shapes.

Brush with beaten egg to glaze and bake in a preheated oven, 200°C (400°F), Gas Mark 6, for 20–25 minutes until golden and crisp. Serve with vanilla ice cream or crème fraîche, if liked.

For cinnamon & peach custard pie, drain 2 x 400 g (13 oz) cans of peaches in natural juice and toss with the apples, 1 tablespoon soft brown sugar and 1 teaspoon ground cinnamon. Use instead of the blackberries with the custard pastry as above.

BAKED

CHOCOLATE ORANGE BROWNIES

Makes **16**
Preparation time **15–20 minutes**
Cooking time **30–35 minutes**

250 g (8 oz) **orange-flavoured chocolate** or **plain dark chocolate** with 1 teaspoon **orange essence**
250 g (8 oz) **unsalted butter**
150 g (5 oz) **caster sugar**
4 **eggs**
finely grated rind of 1 **orange**
175 g (6 oz) **plain flour**
pinch of **salt**
1 teaspoon **baking powder**
150 g (5 oz) **milk chocolate**, roughly chopped
75 g (3 oz) **macadamia nuts**, roughly chopped

Put the chocolate and butter in a heavy-based saucepan over a very low heat and stir until both ingredients are just melted. Remove from the heat, stir in the sugar and set aside to cool a little.

Pour the chocolate mixture into a large bowl and beat in the eggs, orange rind and orange essence (if used).

Sift the flour, salt and baking powder into the bowl and fold in, together with the chocolate chunks and macadamia nuts.

Pour the mixture into a greased and lined cake tin, about 20 x 30 x 5 cm (8 x 12 x 2 inches).

Cook in a preheated oven, 180°C (350°F), Gas Mark 4, for 25–30 minutes or until set but not too firm. Leave the brownie to cool in the tin, then cut it into squares and serve.

For ginger chocolate brownies, use plain dark chocolate (not orange-flavoured chocolate) and omit the orange rind. Instead, add 1 tablespoon ground ginger to the flour and 50 g (2 oz) chopped glacé ginger to the chocolate.

BANANA & RAISIN FLAPJACKS

Serves **4**
Preparation time **10 minutes**
Cooking time **13–18 minutes**

100 g (3½ oz) **plain dark chocolate**
3 **eggs**, separated
50 g (2 oz) **self-raising flour**, sifted
40 g (1½ oz) **caster sugar**
150 g (5 oz) **raspberries**, plus extra to serve (optional)
icing sugar sifted, to decorate

Place the butter in a medium pan with the maple syrup and melt over a gentle heat. Stir in the raisins. Remove from the heat and add the bananas, stirring well. Add the oats and stir well until all the oats have been coated.

Spoon the mixture into a 28 x 18 cm (11 x 7 inch) nonstick Swiss roll tin and level the surface using a potato masher for ease. Bake in a preheated oven, 190°C (375°F), Gas Mark 5, for 10 minutes until the top is just beginning to turn a pale golden. The mixture will still seem somewhat soft.

Allow to cool for 10 minutes in the tin before cutting into 12 squares. Remove from the tin and allow to cool completely.

For ginger flapjacks, add 1 teaspoon ground ginger to the melted butter and maple syrup and replace the bananas with 75 g (3 oz) finely chopped stem ginger. Stir through with the raisins and spoon into the prepared tin and level. Bake and cut into squares as above.

RHUBARB & RASPBERRY CRUMBLE

Serves **4**
Preparation time **10 minutes**
Cooking time **25 minutes**

200 g (7 oz) **plain flour**
pinch of **salt**
150 g (5 oz) **unsalted butter**
200 g (7 oz) **soft brown sugar**
500 g (1 lb) fresh or frozen **rhubarb** (thawed if frozen), sliced
125 g (4 oz) fresh or frozen **raspberries**
3 tablespoons **orange juice**
raspberry ripple ice cream (optional)

Put the flour and salt in a bowl, add the butter and rub in with the fingertips until the mixture resembles breadcrumbs. Stir in 150 g (5 oz) of the sugar.

Mix together the fruits, the remaining sugar and orange juice and tip into a buttered dish. Sprinkle over the topping and cook in a preheated oven, 200°C (400°F), Gas Mark 6, for about 25 minutes or until golden brown and bubbling.

Remove and serve hot with raspberry ripple ice cream, if liked.

For apple & blackberry crumble, substitute the rhubarb and raspberries for 450 g (14¹/₂ oz) apples, peeled and chopped, and 450 g (14¹/₂ oz) blackberries. You could also use 450 g (14½ oz) plums, stoned and quartered, and 4 peeled and thinly sliced ripe pears.

333

MINT CHOC CHIP CHEESECAKE

Serves **4–6**
Preparation time **12 minutes**, plus setting

200 g (7 oz) **chocolate biscuits**
100 g (3½ oz) **mint-flavoured dark chocolate**,
  chopped
50 g (2 oz) **butter**, melted
200 g (7 oz) **cream cheese**
200 g (7 oz) **mascarpone cheese**
50 g (2 oz) **caster sugar**
1 tablespoon **crème de menthe** or **peppermint
  extract**
2 drops **green food colouring**
50 g (2 oz) **plain dark chocolate chips**

Put the biscuits and chocolate in a food processor or blender and process to make fine crumbs. Mix with the melted butter and press the mixture gently over the base of a 20 cm (8 inch), round, springform cake tin.
Place in the freezer to set while making the cream cheese mixture.

Beat together the cream cheese, mascarpone, sugar, mint liqueur or extract and food colouring in a large bowl. Stir in 40 g (1½ oz) of the chocolate chips and spoon the mixture over the biscuit base, smoothing with the back of a spoon.

Place in the refrigerator to chill for about 1 hour.

Loosen the edge with a knife, then remove the cheesecake from the tin carefully. Scatter over the remaining chocolate chips, roughly chopped.

For individual ginger cake cheesecakes, use 4 x 7.5 cm (3 inch) fluted tartlet tins. Make a base for each cheesecake by pressing a slice of ginger cake inside each tin. Replace the mint liqueur with ginger wine.

UPSIDE-DOWN GRAPEFRUIT CAKES

Serves **6**
Preparation time **15 minutes**
Cooking time **about
  40 minutes**

1 **grapefruit**, peeled and cut into 6 thin slices
6 tablespoons **golden syrup**
175 g (6 oz) **unsalted butter**, at room temperature
275 g (9 oz) **soft brown sugar**
2 **eggs**
175 g (6 oz) **self-raising flour**
pinch of **salt**
finely grated rind of 1 **lime**
2 tablespoons **grapefruit juice**
2–3 tablespoons **milk**

Push a slice of grapefruit to the base of each of 6 buttered pudding moulds or ramekins and drizzle with a tablespoon of golden syrup. Set aside.

Cream together the butter and sugar until light and fluffy. Add the eggs, one at a time, beating well until incorporated. Gently fold in the flour, salt and lime rind, then fold in the grapefruit juice and milk so that the mixture has a good dropping consistency.

Spoon the mixture into the moulds or ramekins and smooth down.

Put the moulds in a large roasting tin half-filled with boiling water and cook in a preheated oven, 180°C (350°F), Gas Mark 4, for about 40 minutes or until risen and golden.

Remove the cakes from the oven, lift them out of the hot water and leave to cool for 5 minutes. Loosen the sides of the cakes by running a knife around the inside of the moulds and then turn them out into serving bowls. Serve immediately with cream.

For crème anglaise to serve as an accompaniment for a special occasion, heat 475 ml (16 fl oz) milk with a split vanilla pod to boiling point. Remove from the heat. Beat together 6 egg yolks and 125 g (4 oz) caster sugar, then slowly beat in the hot milk. Return to the heat and stir continuously until the custard thickens. Remove the vanilla pod and serve.

CHRISTMAS GARLANDS

Makes **6**
Preparation time **30 minutes**
Cooking time **about**
   15 minutes

50 g (2 oz) **butter**
150 g (5 oz) **plain flour**
50 g (2 oz) **caster sugar**, plus a little for sprinkling
finely grated rind of 1 small **lemon**
1 **egg**, beaten
pieces of **angelica and glacé cherries**, to decorate

Put the butter in a bowl, sift in the flour and rub together until the mixture resembles fine breadcrumbs. Add the sugar and lemon rind and stir everything together with a wooden spoon. Add most of the egg and stir again until the mixture comes together, then use your hands to draw the dough together into a ball.

Pick off small pieces of dough and roll them into balls, each about the size of a cherry. Press 8 balls of the cookie dough together into a circle, then repeat to make a further 5 garlands. Place small pieces of glacé cherry or angelica between the balls.

Place the garlands on a baking sheet lined with nonstick baking paper and bake in a preheated oven, 190°C (375°F), Gas Mark 5, for about 15 minutes or until pale golden. Just before the end of the cooking time, brush with the remainder of the egg and sprinkle with caster sugar, then return to the oven to finish cooking.

Remove from the oven and allow to cool a little before transferring to a cooling rack. Thread on to ribbons and use as decorations.

For Christmas trees, using 10 small balls of dough per tree, create Christmas tree shapes by starting with 1 as a top row, followed by 2, 3 and 4 on the bottom row. This will create a classic triangular Christmas tree shape. Decorate the trees with angelica and glacé cherries and bake as above.

LEMON DRIZZLE CAKE

Serves **8**
Preparation time **20 minutes**
Cooking time **22–28 minutes**

5 **eggs**
100 g (3½ oz) **caster sugar**
pinch of **salt**
125 g (4 oz) **plain flour**
1 teaspoon **baking powder**
finely grated rind of 1 **lemon**
1 tablespoon **lemon juice**
100 g (3½ oz) **butter**, melted and cooled
crème fraîche or **soured cream**, to serve

Syrup
250 g (8 oz) **icing sugar**
125 ml (4 fl oz) **lemon juice**
finely grated rind of 1 **lemon**
seeds scraped from 1 **vanilla pod**

Put the eggs, sugar and salt in a large heatproof bowl set over a pan of barely simmering water. Beat the mixture with a hand-held electric whisk for 2–3 minutes or until it triples in volume and thickens to the consistency of lightly whipped cream. Remove from the heat.

Sift in the flour and baking powder, add the lemon rind and juice and drizzle the butter down the sides of the bowl. Fold in gently, pour into a greased and lined 22 cm (8½ inch) square cake tin and cook in a preheated oven, 180°C (350°F), Gas Mark 4, for 20–25 minutes or until risen, golden and coming away from the sides of the tin.

Meanwhile, put all the ingredients for the syrup in a small pan and heat gently until the sugar has dissolved. Increase the heat and boil rapidly for 4–5 minutes. Set aside to cool a little.

Remove the cake from the oven, leave it to rest for 5 minutes, then make holes over the surface with a skewer. Drizzle over two-thirds of the warm syrup. Leave the cake to cool and absorb the syrup.

Remove the cake from the tin and peel away the lining paper. Place the cake on a dish and serve in squares or slices with a heaped spoonful of crème fraîche or soured cream and an extra drizzle of syrup.

For citrus drizzle cake with sorbet, use orange rind and juice instead of lemon and serve topped with lemon sorbet.

LARDY CAKE

Makes **10 thick slices**

Time **1½–2½ hours**, depending on machine, plus shaping, proving and baking

Dough

300 ml (½ pint) **water**

25 g (1 oz) **lard**, softened

¼ teaspoon **salt**

2 tablespoons **milk powder**

1 teaspoon **ground mixed spice**

425 g (14 oz) **strong white bread flour**

2 tablespoons **golden caster sugar**

1¼ teaspoons **fast-action dried yeast**

To finish

100 g (3½ oz) **lard**, softened

25 g (1 oz) **unsalted butter**, softened

250 g (8 oz) **mixed dried fruit**

50 g (2 oz) chopped **candied peel**

100 g (3½ oz) **golden caster sugar**, plus extra for sprinkling

milk, to brush

Lift the bread pan out of the machine and fit the blade. Put the dough ingredients into the pan, following the order specified in the manual.

Fit the pan into the machine and close the lid. Set to the dough programme.

At the end of the programme turn the dough out on to a floured surface and roll it out to a rectangle, about 40 x 23 cm (16 x 9 inches), with a short end facing you. Using a knife, dot the lard over the dough, then dot over smaller pieces of butter.

Mix together the dried fruit, peel and sugar and scatter over the dough. Press down gently with your hand. Fold the bottom third of the dough over and press down gently, then fold the top third of the dough over to form a rectangle of 3 layers. Turn the dough through 45 degrees and re-roll to a similar-sized rectangle. Fold the ends in as before and re-roll to a rectangle slightly smaller than the size of a shallow, greased 28 x 18 cm (11 x 7 inch) baking tin. Lift the dough into the tin, cover loosely with oiled clingfilm and leave to rise in a warm place until risen by about half again.

Brush with a little milk and sprinkle with extra sugar. Bake in a preheated oven, 200°C (400°F), Gas Mark 6, for about 45 minutes until risen and golden. Leave in the tin for 10 minutes, then transfer to a wire rack to cool. Serve warm cut into chunky slices.

For lardy cake with ginger, grate 75 g (3 oz) fresh root ginger and add to the pan with the water when making the dough. Chop 50 g (2 oz) stem ginger and mix with the dried fruit and sugar. Finish as above.

GOOEY CHOCOLATE NUT BREAD

Makes **8–10 slices**

Time **1½–2½ hours**, depending on machine, plus shaping, proving and baking

Dough

1 large **egg**, beaten

150 ml (¼ pint) **milk**

2 teaspoons **vanilla bean paste**

75 g (3 oz) **unsalted butter**, softened

¼ teaspoon **salt**

375 g (12 oz) **strong white bread flour**

50 g (2 oz) **ground hazelnuts**

50 g (2 oz) **caster sugar**

1¼ teaspoons **fast-action dried yeast**

To finish

200 g (7 oz) **chocolate hazelnut spread**

100 g (3½ oz) **hazelnuts**, roughly chopped, plus 25 g (1 oz) to decorate

beaten **egg**, to glaze

50 g (2 oz) **plain dark chocolate**, chopped

cocoa powder and **icing sugar**, for dusting

Lift the bread pan out of the machine and fit the blade. Put the dough ingredients in the pan, following the order specified in the manual. Add the ground hazelnuts with the flour. Fit the pan into the machine and close the lid. Set to the dough programme. Grease a 20 cm (8 inch) loose-bottomed, round cake tin.

At the end of the programme turn the dough out on to a floured surface. Roll one-third of the dough to a 26 cm (10½ inch) round. Place it in the tin so it comes about 3 cm (1¼ inches) up the sides to make a case.

Dot one-third of the chocolate spread over the base and scatter with one-third of the nuts. Divide the remaining dough into 3 pieces and roll each to a 20 cm (8 inch) round. Place one layer in the tin and dot with another third of the chocolate spread and nuts. Continue layering finishing with a layer of dough.

Brush the dough with beaten egg. Press the chopped chocolate and reserved nuts into the dough. Cover loosely with oiled clingfilm and leave to rise in a warm place for 45–60 minutes or until about half the size again.

Bake in a preheated oven, 200°C (400°F), Gas Mark 6, for 50 minutes. Cover it with foil if the top starts to over-brown. Transfer to a wire rack to cool. Serve dusted with cocoa powder and icing sugar.

For white chocolate & pecan bread, instead of the chocolate spread, melt together 200 g (7 oz) white chocolate, 25 g (1 oz) unsalted butter, 1 tablespoon golden syrup and 2 tablespoons milk. Substitute pecan nuts for the hazelnuts and white chocolate for the chopped plain chocolate.

CARAMELIZED BANANA PUFF TART

Serves **4**
Preparation time **10 minutes**
Cooking time **15–20 minutes**

3 **bananas**, sliced
375 g (12 oz) **ready-made puff pastry**, defrosted
   if frozen
1 **egg**, beaten
3 tablespoons **unrefined demerara sugar**
300 ml (½ pint) **whipping cream** (optional)

Slice the bananas in half horizontally. Roll the pastry into a 20 cm (8 inch) square and cut the pastry into equal quarters. Place on a baking sheet and score a 1 cm (½ inch) border around the edge of each pastry square. Arrange the bananas, cut-side up, on the pastry inside the border, then brush the border with the beaten egg. Sprinkle the top of the bananas with the sugar.

Bake in a preheated oven, 200°C (400°F), Gas Mark 6, for 15–20 minutes or until the pastry is puffed and golden and the bananas are caramelized. Serve the tart hot with cream, if liked.

For cinnamon coffee liqueur cream as an alternative accompaniment to the tart, in a bowl whip 200 ml (7 fl oz) double cream until soft peaks form, then stir in 2 teaspoons ground cinnamon and 2 tablespoons Bailey's Irish Cream or any other creamy coffee liqueur.

BAKED

STOLLEN

Makes **1 small loaf** (about 10 thick slices)
Time **1½–2½ hours**, depending on machine, plus shaping, proving and baking

Dough
200 ml (7 fl oz) **milk**
finely grated rind of 1 **lemon**
50 g (2 oz) **unsalted butter**, softened
½ teaspoon **salt**
½ teaspoon **ground mixed spice**
350 g (11½ oz) **strong white bread flour**
50 g (2 oz) **golden caster sugar**
1¼ teaspoons **fast-action dried yeast**
75 g (3 oz) **sultanas**
50 g (2 oz) **blanched hazelnuts**, chopped
50 g (2 oz) **candied peel**, chopped

To finish
250 g (8 oz) **hazelnut marzipan** (see right)
  or **almond marzipan**
icing sugar, for dusting

Lift the bread pan out of the machine and fit the blade. Put the dough ingredients, except the sultanas, nuts and peel, in the pan, following the order specified in the manual.

Fit the pan into the machine and close the lid. Set to the dough programme, adding the sultanas, hazelnuts and peel when the machine beeps.

Roll the marzipan into a thick log about 25 cm (10 inches) long.

At the end of the programme turn the dough out on to a floured surface and roll it out to an oval, about 30 x 18 cm (12 x 7 inches). Lay the log of marzipan over the dough slightly to one side of the centre. Brush a long edge with a little water and fold the wider piece of dough over the filling, pressing it down gently.

Transfer the stollen to a large, greased baking sheet and cover loosely with oiled clingfilm. Leave to rise in a warm place until almost doubled in size. Bake in a preheated oven, 200°C (400°F), Gas Mark 6, for about 25 minutes until risen and golden. Transfer to a wire rack to cool. Dust generously with icing sugar before serving.

For homemade hazelnut marzipan, grind 150 g (5 oz) whole blanched hazelnuts in a food processor. Add 50 g (2 oz) caster sugar and 50 g (2 oz) icing sugar to the processor and blend briefly to mix. Add 1 small egg white and blend until the mixture comes together to make a paste. Gather into a ball, wrap in clingfilm and keep in a cool place until ready to use.

339

BLUEBERRY & VANILLA PLAIT

Makes **1 large plait** (about
   10 thick slices)
Time 1½–2½ hours, depending on machine, plus
   shaping, proving and baking

Dough
150 ml (¼ pint) **water**
2 teaspoons **vanilla bean paste**
1 large **egg**, beaten
75 g (3 oz) **unsalted butter**, softened
¼ teaspoon **salt**
350 g (11½ oz) **strong white bread flour**
50 g (2 oz) **ground almonds**
50 g (2 oz) **caster sugar**
1¼ teaspoons **fast-action dried yeast**

To finish
125 g (4 oz) **ricotta cheese**
250 g (8 oz) **blueberries**
3 tablespoons **caster sugar**
beaten **egg**, to glaze
vanilla sugar, for sprinkling

Lift the bread pan out of the machine and fit the blade. Put the dough ingredients in the pan, following the order specified in the manual. The vanilla bean paste should be added with the liquids and the almonds with the flour. Fit the pan into the machine and close the lid. Set to the dough programme.

At the end of the programme turn the dough out on to a floured surface and divide it into 3 equal pieces. Roll each piece to a strip about 35 x 12 cm (14 x 5 inches). Spread ricotta over each strip to about 2 cm (³/₄ inch) of the edges. Scatter with 200 g (7 oz) of the blueberries and sprinkle 1 tablespoon sugar over each strip. Bring up the edges over the filling, pinching them together firmly to make 3 thick ropes. Roll them over so the joins are underneath. Plait the strips together, tucking the ends underneath, and carefully lift on to a large, greased baking sheet. Cover loosely with oiled clingfilm and leave to rise in a warm place for 40 minutes or until nearly doubled in size.

Brush with beaten egg. Scatter with the remaining blueberries and sprinkle with vanilla sugar. Bake in a preheated oven, 200°C (400°F), Gas Mark 6, for 30 minutes or until risen and golden. Cool on a wire rack.

For red fruit & vanilla loaf, make and shape the dough as above. Use cream cheese instead of the ricotta and 200 g (7 oz) mixed dried red fruit (such as cranberries, sour cherries and strawberries) instead of the blueberries. Before cooking scatter with an extra 50 g (2 oz) chopped red fruits and sprinkle with vanilla sugar.

SPICY APPLE PARKIN

Makes **8 slices**
Time about **1 hour**, depending on machine, plus
   cooking

4 tart **dessert apples**, such as Granny Smith
5 tablespoons **apple juice**
¼ teaspoon **ground cloves**
175 g (6 oz) **black treacle**
150 g (5 oz) **golden syrup**
75 g (3 oz) **unsalted butter**, softened
100 g (3½ oz) **self-raising wholemeal flour**
100 g (3½ oz) **self-raising white flour**
1 teaspoon **bicarbonate of soda**
2 teaspoons **ground ginger**
175 g (6 oz) medium **oatmeal**

Peel, core and slice the apples and put the slices in a small saucepan with the apple juice and ground cloves. Bring to the boil, reduce the heat and cook gently, uncovered, for about 5 minutes or until the apples have softened slightly. Drain and leave to cool.

Lift the bread pan out of the machine and fit the blade. Add the treacle, syrup, butter, flour, bicarbonate of soda, ginger and oatmeal to the pan.

Fit the pan into the machine and close the lid. Set to the cake programme. After about 5 minutes use a plastic spatula to scrape the mixture down from the sides and from the corners of the pan. Stir in the apples.

Test the cake after 1 hour by inserting a skewer into the centre. If it comes out clean the cake is ready. If not, cook a little longer or complete the programme. Transfer the cake to a wire rack to cool.

For brandied prune parkin, roughly chop 200 g (7 oz) prunes. Make the cake mixture as above, omitting the first step and adding the prunes, 2 tablespoons brandy and the grated rind of 1 orange with the rest of the ingredients.

CHOCOLATE FUDGE SLICE

Makes **10 slices**

Time about **1 hour**, depending on machine

Cake

75 g (3 oz) **cocoa powder**

75 g (3 oz) **plain dark chocolate**, chopped

150 g (5 oz) **unsalted butter**, softened

250 g (8 oz) **light muscovado sugar**

2 large **eggs**, beaten

200 g (7 oz) **self-raising flour**

1/2 teaspoon **baking powder**

Icing

200 g (7 oz) **plain dark chocolate**

175 g (6 oz) **golden icing sugar**

150 g (5 oz) **unsalted butter**, softened

Whisk the cocoa powder in a bowl with 225 ml (7 1/2 fl oz) boiling water until smooth. Stir in the chopped chocolate and leave to cool, stirring occasionally, until the chocolate has melted.

Lift the bread pan out of the machine and fit the blade. Put the cake ingredients in the pan.

Fit the pan into the machine and close the lid. Set to the cake programme. After about 5 minutes use a plastic spatula to scrape the mixture down from the sides and from the corners of the pan.

Test the cake after 1 hour by inserting a skewer into the centre. If it comes out clean the cake is ready. If not, cook a little longer or complete the programme. Transfer the cake to a wire rack to cool.

Make the icing. Melt the chocolate in a small bowl and leave to cool slightly. Beat together the icing sugar and butter, then beat in the chocolate. Split the cake in half and sandwich with one quarter of the icing. Transfer to a serving plate and use a palette knife to spread the remaining icing over the top and sides.

For double chocolate fudge slice, make the cake as above, then measure 250 ml (8 fl oz) double cream and pour half into a small saucepan. Heat gently until it bubbles around the edges, then remove from the heat and tip in 250 g (8 oz) chopped white chocolate. Leave to stand for a few minutes until the chocolate has melted, then stir lightly and turn into a bowl. Leave until cool. Add the remaining cream and whisk with a hand-held electric whisk until the mixture just starts to hold its shape. Use to cover the cake.

CHERRY & ALMOND MADEIRA CAKE

Makes **8 slices**

Time about **1 1/4 hours**, depending on machine, plus cooking

75 g (3 oz) **dried black cherries**

75 ml (3 fl oz) **apple juice**

175 g (6 oz) **unsalted butter**, softened

175 g (6 oz) **caster sugar**, plus extra for dusting

3 large **eggs**, beaten

225 g (7 1/2 oz) **self-raising flour**

1/2 teaspoon **baking powder**

100 g (3 1/2 oz) **ground almonds**

1 teaspoon **almond extract**

Put the cherries and apple juice in a small saucepan and heat gently, uncovered, for about 5 minutes until the cherries have plumped up slightly and the juice has been absorbed. Leave to cool.

Lift the bread pan out of the machine and fit the blade. Put the ingredients, except the cherries, in the pan, following the order specified in the manual.

Fit the pan into the machine and close the lid. Set to the cake programme. After about 5 minutes use a plastic spatula to scrape the mixture down from the sides and from the corners of the pan. Scatter the cherries into the pan once the cake is evenly mixed.

Test the cake after 1 1/4 hours by inserting a skewer into the centre. If it comes out clean the cake is ready. If not, cook a little longer or complete the programme.

Transfer the cake to a wire rack to cool. Serve dusted with extra sugar.

For coffee & walnut madeira cake, omit the cherries, juice and almond extract. Dissolve 1 tablespoon espresso coffee powder in 2 tablespoons boiling water and add to the pan with the remaining ingredients. Make as above, adding 100 g (3 1/2 oz) roughly chopped walnuts to the pan once the cake is evenly mixed. Finish as above.

SUMMER FRUIT CHEESECAKE SLICE

Makes **8 slices**

Time **1½–2½ hours**, depending on machine, plus shaping, proving and baking

Dough

1 **egg**, beaten

150 ml (¼ pint) **milk**

1 tablespoon **vanilla bean paste** or **vanilla extract**

25 g (1 oz) **unsalted butter**, softened

1 tablespoon **milk powder**

300 g (10 oz) **strong white bread flour**, plus
1 tablespoon

50 g (2 oz) **caster sugar**

¾ teaspoon **fast-action dried yeast**

To finish

200 g (7 oz) **cream cheese**

50 g (2 oz) **caster sugar**, plus 1 tablespoon for sprinkling

1 teaspoon **vanilla bean paste** or **vanilla extract**

1 **egg**

150 g (5 oz) **raspberries**

150 g (5 oz) **strawberries**, hulled and halved

icing sugar, for dusting

Lift the bread pan out of the machine and fit the blade. Put the dough ingredients in the pan, following the order specified in the manual. Fit the pan into the machine and close the lid. Set to the dough programme.

Beat the cream cheese to soften, then beat in the sugar, vanilla paste or extract and egg until smooth.

At the end of the programme turn the dough out on to a floured surface and cut off one quarter. Roll out the remainder to a round about 28 cm (11 inches) in diameter. Grease a 23 cm (9 inch) springform cake tin. Press the dough into the tin so that it comes about 3 cm (1¼ inches) up the sides, making a case.

Divide the remaining dough into 10 equal pieces and scatter them into the case. Dot the cream cheese mixture between the dough pieces, then scatter with half the berries. Cover loosely with oiled clingfilm and leave to rise in a warm place until slightly risen.

Bake in a preheated oven, 200°C (400°F), Gas Mark 6, for about 45 minutes until the bread is risen and golden. Make sure the centre of the dough is cooked by piercing it with a skewer. Transfer to a wire rack to cool. Scatter with the remaining fruits and dust with icing sugar.

For spiced peach & redcurrant slice, add 1 teaspoon ground cinnamon instead of the vanilla paste or extract. Chop 4 ripe peaches into small chunks and use instead of the berries. After baking, drizzle the cake with melted redcurrant jelly and scatter with clusters of redcurrants.

WHITE CHOCOLATE & BANANA LOAF

Makes **1 large loaf**
Time **1–2 hours**, depending on machine

225 g (7½ oz) mashed **banana** (about 2 large
  bananas)
150 ml (¼ pint) warm **milk**
50 g (2 oz) **unsalted butter**, softened
½ teaspoon **salt**
425 g (14 oz) **strong white bread flour**
50 g (2 oz) **caster sugar**
2½ teaspoons **fast-action dried yeast**
200 g (7 oz) **white chocolate**, chopped
100 g (3½ oz) **pecan nuts**, roughly chopped
icing sugar, for dusting

Lift the bread pan out of the machine and fit the blade. Put the ingredients, except the chocolate and nuts, in the pan, following the order specified in the manual. Add the mashed banana with the milk.

Fit the pan into the machine and close the lid. Set to a 750 g (1¼ lb) loaf size on the fast/rapid bake programme. Add the chocolate and pecans when the machine beeps.

At the end of the programme lift the pan out of the machine and shake the bread out on to a wire rack to cool. Serve dusted with icing sugar.

For dark chocolate & ginger rolls, put the ingredients in the bread machine as above, replacing 25 g (1 oz) of the flour with 25 g (1 oz) cocoa powder. Reduce the yeast to 1½ teaspoons and add 3 pieces of stem ginger from a jar, finely chopped. Use chopped plain dark chocolate instead of the white. Set to the dough programme, adding the chocolate and nuts when the machine beeps. At the end of the programme turn out the dough and shape into 8 small balls. Space well apart on a greased baking sheet and cover loosely with oiled clingfilm. Leave in a warm place to rise until almost doubled in size. Bake in a preheated oven, 220°C (425°F), Gas Mark 7, for about 15 minutes until risen and lightly browned. Transfer to a wire rack to cool and serve dusted with icing sugar.

CINNAMON DOUGHNUTS

Makes **10 doughnuts**
Time 1½–2½ hours, depending on machine, plus
shaping, proving and cooking

Dough
1 large **egg**, beaten
225 ml (7½ fl oz) **milk**
2 teaspoons **vanilla extract**
25 g (1 oz) **unsalted butter**, softened
½ teaspoon **salt**
450 g (14½ oz) **strong white bread flour**
50 g (2 oz) **caster sugar**
1¼ teaspoons **fast-action dried yeast**

To finish
100 g (3½ oz) **caster sugar**
1 teaspoon **ground cinnamon**
oil, for deep frying

Lift the bread pan out of the machine and fit the blade. Put the dough ingredients in the pan, following the order specified in the manual.

Fit the pan into the machine and close the lid. Set to the dough programme.

At the end of the programme turn the dough out on to a floured surface and cut it into 10 equal pieces. Shape each into a ball and space them, well apart, on a large, greased baking sheet. Cover loosely with oiled clingfilm and leave to rise in a warm place for 30–40 minutes or until almost doubled in size.

Mix together the sugar and cinnamon on a plate. Put 8 cm (3 inches) oil in a large saucepan and heat it until a small piece of bread sizzles on the surface and turns pale golden in about 30 seconds.

Fry the doughnuts, 3–4 at a time, for about 3 minutes, turning them once until golden on both sides. Drain with a slotted spoon on to several sheets of kitchen paper. Cook the remainder. Roll the doughnuts in the cinnamon sugar while still warm.

For doughnuts with chocolate sauce, make the dough and leave to rise as above. Place 100 g (3½ oz) chopped plain chocolate in a heatproof bowl with 15 g (½ oz) butter, 4 tablespoons icing sugar and 2 tablespoons milk. Rest the bowl over a pan of gently simmering water and leave until melted, stirring frequently until smooth. Fry the doughnuts as above, draining them and rolling in the spiced sugar. Serve with little pots of the chocolate sauce.

TROPICAL FRUIT DRIZZLE CAKE

Makes **8–10 slices**
Time about 1¼ hours, depending on machine

125 g (4 oz) **semi-dried tropical fruits**, such as mango, papaya and pineapple
100 g (3½ oz) **creamed coconut**
150 g (5 oz) **unsalted butter**, softened
175 g (6 oz) **golden caster sugar**
3 **eggs**, beaten
finely grated rind of 3 **limes**, plus 4 tablespoons juice
225 g (7½ oz) **self-raising flour**
1 teaspoon **baking powder**
4 tablespoons **caster sugar**, for sprinkling

Roughly chop the tropical fruit mix if it is in large pieces. If the creamed coconut is in a solid block microwave on medium power for 2–3 minutes to make a soft paste.

Lift the bread pan out of the machine and fit the blade. Add half the chopped fruits, the creamed coconut, butter, 175 g (6 oz) caster sugar, eggs, lime rind, flour and baking powder to the pan.

Fit the pan into the machine and close the lid. Set to the cake programme. After about 5 minutes use a plastic spatula to scrape the mixture down from the sides and from the corners of the pan. Scatter in the remaining tropical fruit mixture.

Test the cake after 1¼ hours by inserting a skewer into the centre. If it comes out clean the cake is ready. If not, cook a little longer or complete the programme. Transfer the cake to a wire rack to cool.

While the cake is still warm, drizzle over the lime juice and then sprinkle over the sugar. Leave to cool.

For lemon & coconut drizzle cake, omit the tropical fruits and use the rind of 3 lemons instead of the lime, and use ordinary caster sugar instead of golden caster sugar. While the cake is cooking blend 4 tablespoons lemon juice with 4 tablespoons caster sugar. Transfer the cake to a wire rack and drizzle over the lemon syrup.

CHOCOLATE & RASPBERRY SOUFFLÉS

Serves **4**
Preparation time **10 minutes**
Cooking time **13–18 minutes**

100 g (3½ oz) **plain dark chocolate**
3 **eggs**, separated
50 g (2 oz) **self-raising flour**, sifted
40 g (1½ oz) **caster sugar**
150 g (5 oz) **raspberries**, plus extra to serve (optional)
icing sugar sifted, to decorate

Break the chocolate into squares and put them in a large heatproof bowl over a saucepan of simmering water. Leave until melted, then remove from the heat and allow to cool a little. Whisk in the egg yolks and fold in the flour.

Whisk the egg whites and caster sugar in a medium bowl until they form soft peaks. Beat a spoonful of the egg whites into the chocolate mixture to loosen it before gently folding in the rest.

Put the raspberries into 4 lightly greased ramekins, pour over the chocolate mixture and cook in a preheated oven, 190°C (375°F), Gas Mark 5, for 12–15 minutes until the soufflés have risen.

Sprinkle the soufflés with icing sugar and serve with extra raspberries, if liked.

For white chocolate & mango soufflés, substitute the plain dark chocolate with white chocolate and the raspberries with 1 mango, peeled, stoned, diced, and divided among the ramekins.

CHOCOLATE CHIP COOKIES

Makes **16**
Preparation time **10 minutes,** plus cooling
Cooking time **15 minutes**

125 g (4 oz) **unsalted butter**, diced and softened
175 g (6 oz) **soft light brown sugar**
1 teaspoon **vanilla extract**
1 **egg**, lightly beaten
1 tablespoon **milk**
200 g (7 oz) **plain flour**
1 teaspoon **baking powder**
250 g (8 oz) **plain dark chocolate chips**

Line a large baking sheet with nonstick baking paper. In a large bowl, beat the butter and sugar together until light and fluffy. Mix in the vanilla extract, then gradually beat in the egg, beating well after each addition. Stir in the milk.

Sift the flour and baking powder into a separate large bowl, then fold into the butter and egg mixture. Stir in the chocolate chips.

Drop level tablespoonfuls of the cookie mixture on to the prepared baking sheet, leaving about 3.5 cm (1½ inches) between each cookie, then lightly press with a floured fork. Bake in a preheated oven, 180°C (350°F), Gas Mark 4, for 15 minutes or until lightly golden. Transfer to a wire rack to cool.

For chocolate & mandarin log, drain a 300 g (10 oz) can mandarin segments and finely chop, reserving a few whole segments for decoration. In a bowl, whip 300 ml (½ pint) double cream with 25 g (1 oz) icing sugar until thick, then fold in the chopped mandarins. Sandwich the cooked chocolate chip cookies one on top of the other with half the mandarin cream, then carefully set the log on its side and wrap in foil. Chill in the refrigerator for at least 2–3 hours or overnight. Just before serving, put the log on a serving plate, cover with the remaining mandarin cream and decorate with the reserved mandarins. Serve in slices, cut on the diagonal.

OLIVE & TOMATO BREAD

Makes **1 large loaf**

Time **1½–2½ hours**, depending on machine, plus shaping, proving and baking

Dough

275 ml (9 fl oz) **water**

2 tablespoons **olive oil**

1 teaspoon **salt**

475 g (15 oz) **strong white bread flour**

1 teaspoon **caster sugar**

1¼ teaspoons **fast-action dried yeast**

To finish

125 g (4 oz) pitted or stuffed **green olives**, roughly chopped

40 g (1½ oz) **sun-dried tomatoes** (not in oil), roughly chopped

coarse sea salt and **paprika**, for sprinkling

Lift the bread pan out of the machine and fit the blade. Put the dough ingredients in the pan, following the order specified in the manual.

Fit the pan into the machine and close the lid. Set to the dough programme.

At the end of the programme lift the pan out of the machine and turn the dough out on to a floured surface. Gradually work in the chopped olives and tomatoes. Pat the dough into a circle about 20 cm (8 inches) across and use a floured knife to mark it into 8 wedges. Do not cut right through to the base.

Sprinkle the salt and paprika over the dough, transfer to a large, lightly greased backing sheet, cover loosely with oiled clingfilm and leave to rise in a warm place for 30 minutes until it is half as big again.

Bake in a preheated oven, 200°C (400°F), Gas Mark 6, for 30 minutes. Check after 15 minutes and cover with foil if over-browning. Transfer to a wire rack to cool.

For pancetta & Parmesan bread, finely chop 100 g (3½ oz) pancetta. Heat 1 tablespoon olive oil in a small frying pan and fry the pancetta with 1 chopped shallot for 5 minutes until it is beginning to colour. Leave to cool. Make the bread as above, adding the pancetta and shallot and 50 g (2 oz) grated Parmesan cheese to the dough instead of the olives and tomatoes. Finish as above.

SPEEDY SESAME BREAD

Makes **1 large loaf**

Time **1–2 hours**, depending on machine

275 ml (9 fl oz) warm **water**

2 tablespoons **sunflower oil**

1 teaspoon **salt**

2 tablespoons **milk powder**

2 tablespoons **sesame seeds**

475 g (15 oz) **strong white bread flour**

1 tablespoon **caster sugar**

2½ teaspoons **fast-action dried yeast**

To finish

melted **butter**, to brush

sesame seeds, for sprinkling

Lift the bread pan out of the machine and fit the blade. Put the dough ingredients in the pan, following the order specified in the manual.

Fit the pan into the machine and close the lid. Set to a 750 g (1½ lb) loaf size on the fast/rapid bake programme.

At the end of the programme lift the pan out of the machine and shake the bread out on to a wire rack. Brush the top of the loaf with the butter and sprinkle with a few extra sesame seeds. Brown under the grill, if liked.

For speedy three grain bread, omit the milk powder and sesame seeds from the above recipe and reduce the sugar to 1½ teaspoons. Replace 175 g (6 oz) of the white flour with malted bread flour and a further 50 g (2 oz) with purple wheat flakes. Just before baking begins lightly brush the top of the dough with milk and scatter with extra wheat flakes. Close the lid gently and complete the programme.

OLIVE OIL, ROSEMARY & RAISIN BREAD

Makes **1 large loaf**

Time **1½–2½ hours**, depending on machine, plus shaping, proving and baking

325 ml (11 fl oz) **water**
100 ml (3½ fl oz) extra-virgin **olive oil**
2 teaspoons **sea salt**, plus extra for sprinkling
2 tablespoons **milk powder**
2 teaspoons **fennel seeds**, lightly crushed
1 tablespoon chopped **rosemary**
600 g (1 lb 3 oz) **strong white bread flour**
1 tablespoon **caster sugar**
2 teaspoons **fast-action dried yeast**
100 g (3 oz) **raisins**
rosemary sprigs, to garnish

Lift the bread pan out of the machine and fit the blade. Put the ingredients, except the raisins, in the pan, following the order specified in the manual. Add the seeds and rosemary with the flour.

Fit the pan into the machine and close the lid. Set to the dough programme, adding the raisins when the machine beeps.

At the end of the programme turn the dough out on to a floured surface and shape it into a round. Make a hole through the centre of the loaf with your fingertips, then enlarge it with your hand until the dough is ring-shaped with a hole 10 cm (4 inches) in diameter in the middle. Put the dough on a large, greased baking sheet, cover loosely with oiled clingfilm and leave to rise in a warm place for about 45 minutes or until it has almost doubled in size.

Score the dough at intervals with a floured knife and scatter with rosemary sprigs and sea salt. Bake in a preheated oven, 220°C (425°F), Gas Mark 7, for 40 minutes until risen and golden. Cover the bread with foil and replace the rosemary sprigs if they start to over-brown.

For Mediterranean herb bread, make the dough as above using 2 teaspoons dried oregano instead of the rosemary and omitting the raisins. Add 25 g (1 oz) torn basil leaves and 3 tablespoons capers, drained and dried, when the machine beeps. Finish as above, without the rosemary sprigs.

BRIOCHE

Makes **1 loaf**

Time **1½–2½ hours**, depending on machine, plus shaping, proving and baking

3 **eggs**, beaten
75 g (3 oz) **unsalted butter**, softened
¼ teaspoon **salt**
250 g (8 oz) **strong white bread flour**
25 g (1 oz) **caster sugar**
1 teaspoon **fast-action dried yeast**
egg yolk, to glaze

Lift the bread pan out of the machine and fit the blade. Put the ingredients in the pan, following the order specified in the manual.

Fit the pan into the machine and close the lid. Set to the dough programme. Thoroughly butter a 750 ml (1¼ pint) brioche mould or a 1 kg (2 lb) loaf tin.

At the end of the programme turn the dough out on to a floured surface and cut off one quarter. Shape the larger piece into a ball and drop it into the brioche tin. Push a deep, wide hole into the dough with your fingers. Shape the remaining dough into a ball and press it gently into the indented top. (If you are using a loaf tin shape the dough into an oval and drop it into the tin.)

Cover loosely with oiled clingfilm and leave to rise in a warm place for 50–60 minutes or until almost doubled in size. Mix the egg yolk with 1 tablespoon water and gently brush over the dough. Bake in a preheated oven, 220°C (425°F), Gas Mark 7, for 20–25 minutes or until deep golden and firm. (Cover the loaf with foil if the crust starts to over-brown.)

After baking leave the bread in the tin for a few minutes, then shake out on to a wire rack to cool.

For baby chocolate brioche buns, make the dough as above and divide it into 8 pieces. Push 15 g (½ oz) plain dark chocolate into the centre of each piece and seal the dough around the chocolate. Space the buns well apart on a greased baking sheet. Cover loosely with oiled clingfilm and leave to rise in a warm place until almost doubled in size. Glaze and bake as above, reducing the cooking time to about 15 minutes.

BREAKFAST MUESLI BREAD

Makes **1 extra-large loaf**
Time **3–4 hours**, depending on machine

300 ml (½ pint) **apple juice**
1 large **egg**, beaten
25 g (1 oz) **unsalted butter**, softened
1½ teaspoons **salt**
2 tablespoons **milk powder**
1 teaspoon **ground mixed spice**
125 g (4 oz) **fruit muesli**, plus extra for sprinkling
425 g (13 oz) **strong white bread flour**
50 g (2 oz) **light muscovado sugar**
1¼ teaspoons **fast-action dried yeast**
50 g (2 oz) **raisins**
milk, to brush

Lift the bread pan out of the machine and fit the blade. Put the ingredients, except the raisins, in the pan following the order specified in the manual.

Fit the pan into the machine and close the lid. Set to a 1 kg (2 lb) loaf size on the basic white programme. Select your preferred crust setting. Add the raisins when the machine beeps.

Just before baking begins brush the top of the dough lightly with milk and sprinkle with a little muesli. Close the lid gently.

At the end of the programme lift the pan out of the machine, loosen the bread with a spatula if necessary and shake it out on to a wire rack to cool.

For fresh blueberry conserve, to accompany the bread, blend 1 teaspoon cornflour with 1 tablespoon water in a small saucepan. Add 100 ml (3½ fl oz) apple or orange juice, 3 tablespoons caster sugar and ½ teaspoon vanilla extract. Heat gently, stirring, until slightly thickened. Tip in 200 g (7 oz) fresh or frozen blueberries and cook gently for 1–2 minutes until the blueberries soften and start to burst. Serve warm or cold, spooned over the bread and topped with Greek yogurt.

RICH FRUIT TEABREAD

Makes **1 extra-large loaf**

Time **1½–2½ hours**, depending on machine, plus shaping, proving and baking

175 ml (6 fl oz) strong **black tea**, cooled

1 **egg**, beaten

50 g (2 oz) **unsalted butter**, softened

½ teaspoon **salt**

finely grated rind of 1 **orange**

1 tablespoon **ground mixed spice**

375 g (12 oz) **strong white bread flour**

75 g (3 oz) **dark muscovado sugar**

1½ teaspoons **fast-action dried yeast**

200 g (7 oz) luxury **mixed dried fruit**

100 g (3½ oz) ready-to-eat **dried apricots**, roughly chopped

100 g (3½ oz) **Brazil nuts**, chopped

demerara sugar, for sprinkling

Lift the bread pan out of the machine and fit the blade. Put the ingredients, except the dried fruit and nuts, in the pan, following the order specified in the manual. Add the spice with the flour.

Fit the pan in the machine and close the lid. Set to the dough programme, adding the dried fruits and nuts when the machine beeps.

At the end of the programme turn the dough out on to a floured surface and shape it into an oval. Grease a 1 kg (2 lb) loaf tin and drop the dough into the tin. Cover loosely with oiled clingfilm and leave to rise in a warm place for 50–60 minutes or until almost doubled in size.

Sprinkle generously with demerara sugar and bake in a preheated oven, 220°C (425°F), Gas Mark 7, for 35–40 minutes until risen and golden. Cover the top with foil if the surface starts to over-brown. Turn out of the tin and tap the base: it should sound hollow. If necessary, return to the oven (out of the tin) for a little longer.

For chunky fruit & nut loaf, put 1 egg, 175 ml (6 fl oz) milk, 50 g (2 oz) very soft butter, 1 tablespoon black treacle, ½ teaspoon salt, 375 g (12 oz) strong white bread flour, 1 tablespoon ground mixed spice, 50 g (2 oz) dark muscovado sugar and 1¼ teaspoons fast-action dried yeast in the bread pan, following the order specified in the manual. Set to the sweet programme. Add 150 g (5 oz) luxury mixed dried fruit and 75 g (3 oz) roughly chopped almonds when the machine beeps. At the end of the programme shake the bread out on to a wire rack to cool.

351

WARM SEEDY ROLLS

Makes 12
Preparation time **1 hour 40 minutes**, including resting time
Cooking time **15–20 minutes**

5 g (¼ oz) active **dried yeast**
300 ml (½ pint) **warm water** (not hot)
500 g (1 lb) **strong plain flour**, plus extra for dusting
1 teaspoon **salt**, plus a pinch
25 g (1 oz) **butter**, cut into cubes, plus extra for greasing
4 tablespoons **sunflower seeds**
2 tablespoons **poppy seeds**
2 tablespoons **pumpkin seeds**
1 **egg yolk**
1 tablespoon **water**

Sprinkle the yeast over the measured warm water, stir well and set aside for 10 minutes until it goes frothy. Sift the flour and salt into a large bowl and add the butter. Rub the butter into the flour until the mixture resembles fine breadcrumbs. Add all the seeds and stir. Make a well in the centre and add the yeast mixture. Stir well with a wooden spoon, then use your hands to mix to a firm dough.

Knead for 5 minutes until the dough feels firm, elastic and no longer sticky. Return to the bowl, cover with clingfilm and set aside in a warm place for 30 minutes until the dough has doubled in size.

Turn out the dough and knead again to knock out the air, then divide into 12 pieces. Knead each piece briefly, then form into a roll shape, or roll each piece into a long sausage shape and form into a loose knot. Place the rolls on a lightly greased baking sheet, cover with a clean tea towel and set aside in a warm place for 30 minutes until almost doubled in size.

Mix the egg yolk in a small bowl with a pinch of salt and the measured water and brush over the rolls to glaze. Bake in a preheated oven, 200°C (400°F), Gas Mark 6, for 15–20 minutes until golden and sounding hollow when tapped lightly on the base. Remove from the oven and allow to cool a little. Serve warm with soup.

For cheesy onion rolls, replace the seeds with 5 spring onions, finely chopped and lightly cooked for just 1 minute in 1 tablespoon olive oil. Once glazed, sprinkle with 3 tablespoons freshly grated Parmesan cheese.

WALNUT & HONEY BREAD

Makes 1 large loaf
Time **3½–5 hours**, depending on machine

100 g (3½ oz) **walnut pieces**
350 ml (12 fl oz) **water**
3 tablespoons **clear honey**, plus extra to drizzle
40 g (1½ oz) **unsalted butter**, softened
1½ teaspoons **salt**
350 g (11½ oz) **strong wholemeal bread flour**
150 g (5 oz) **strong white bread flour**
1¼ teaspoons **fast-action dried yeast**

Lightly toast the walnuts either in a frying pan over a gentle heat or under the grill.

Lift the bread pan out of the machine and fit the blade. Put the ingredients, except the walnuts, in the pan, following the order specified in the manual.

Fit the pan into the machine and close the lid. Set to a 750 g (1½ lb) loaf size on the wholemeal programme. Select your preferred crust setting. Add the walnuts when the machine beeps.

At the end of the programme lift the pan out of the machine and shake the bread out on to a wire rack to cool. Serve drizzled with extra honey.

For mini pecan & maple loaves, lightly toast 100 g (3½ oz) roughly chopped pecan nuts. Make the bread as above, using the pecans instead of the walnuts and replacing the honey with 3 tablespoons maple syrup. Use the dough programme, cut the dough into 8 pieces and press into 8 greased 200 ml (7 fl oz) individual loaf tins. Cover loosely with oiled clingfilm and leave to rise in a warm place for 30 minutes. Brush with a little maple syrup and bake in a preheated oven, 220°C (425°F), Gas Mark 7, for about 20 minutes until well risen and golden. Serve drizzled with extra maple syrup.

GRANDMA'S COURGETTE LOAF

Serves **8–10**
Preparation time **30 minutes**
Cooking time **about 1 hour 15 minutes**

275 g (9 oz) **self-raising flour**
1 teaspoon **baking powder**
2 teaspoons **mixed spice**
2 **courgettes**, grated
125 g (4 oz) **soft brown sugar**
1 **egg**
75 ml (3 fl oz) **milk**
75 g (3 oz) **butter**, plus extra for greasing
75 g (3 oz) **raisins**
75 g (3 oz) **walnuts**, chopped

Topping
50 g (2 oz) **plain flour**
25 g (1 oz) **soft brown sugar**
½ teaspoon **mixed spice**
50 g (2 oz) chilled **butter**, cut into cubes
50 g (2 oz) **walnuts**, finely chopped

Grease a 1 kg (2 lb) loaf tin lightly with butter and line the base with nonstick baking paper. Sift the flour, baking powder and mixed spice into a large bowl and add the courgettes and sugar. Stir well.

Beat the egg and milk together in a jug. Melt the butter in a small pan, then add the raisins and stir well over a gentle heat for a few seconds to help plump them up. Pour the melted butter and milk and egg mixture into the dry ingredients and stir until well combined. Add the walnuts and stir again. Transfer to the prepared tin and level.

Make the streusel topping: mix the flour with the sugar and mixed spice, then rub the butter into the dry ingredients until the mixture resembles fine breadcrumbs. Stir in the walnuts, then scatter over the cake.

Bake the loaf in a preheated oven, 180°C (350°F), Gas Mark 4, for 1 hour to 1 hour 10 minutes until well risen and firm to the touch and a skewer inserted comes out clean. Allow it to cool for 10 minutes in the tin before turning out on to a wire rack to cool completely.

For moist mango loaf, replace the courgettes, raisins and walnuts with 200 ml (7 fl oz) mango purée, 1 teaspoon vanilla essence and ½ mango, roughly chopped, all folded into the wet mixture. Use the same streusel topping as above, but bake for 40–45 minutes until firm and well risen.

COFFEE & WALNUT BREAD

Makes **1 large loaf**
Time **2¾–3½ hours**, depending on machine

2 tablespoons **espresso coffee powder**
1 large **egg**, beaten
50 g (2 oz) **unsalted butter**, melted
¼ teaspoon **salt**
350 g (11½ oz) **strong white bread flour**
50 g (2 oz) **light muscovado sugar**
1¼ teaspoons **fast-action dried yeast**
75 g (3 oz) **walnut pieces**, lightly toasted

Blend the coffee with 150 ml (¼ pint) boiling water and leave to cool. Lift the bread pan out of the machine and fit the blade. Put the ingredients, except the walnuts, in the pan, following the order specified in the manual.

Fit the pan into the machine and close the lid. Set to a 750 g (1½ lb) loaf size on the sweet programme (or basic if the machine doesn't have a sweet setting). Add the walnuts to the pan when the machine beeps.

At the end of the programme lift the pan out of the machine and shake the bread out on to a wire rack to cool.

For maple butter, to spread over the freshly baked bread, whisk together 100 g (3½ oz) soft unsalted butter, 4 tablespoons icing sugar and 1 teaspoon vanilla bean paste or vanilla extract until completely smooth. Beat in 5 tablespoons maple syrup until combined. Turn into a small serving dish and chill until ready to serve.

ASIAN-STYLE FLATBREADS

Makes **8 breads**

Time **1½–2½ hours**, depending on machine,
plus shaping, proving
and cooking

50 g (2 oz) **sesame seeds**
225 ml (7½ fl oz) **water**
1 **garlic clove**, chopped
25 g (1 oz) **fresh root ginger**, grated
25 g (1 oz) roughly chopped **fresh coriander**
2 tablespoons **sesame oil**
2 teaspoons **salt**
450 g (14½ oz) **strong white bread flour**
1 tablespoon **caster sugar**
1¼ teaspoons **fast-action dried yeast**

Put the sesame seeds in a food processor and grind until broken up.
(The seeds won't grind to a powder.)

Lift the bread pan out of the machine and fit the blade. Put the
ingredients in the pan, following the order specified in the manual.
Add the seeds, garlic, ginger and coriander with the water.

Fit the pan into the machine and close the lid. Set to the dough programme.

At the end of the programme turn the dough out on to a floured surface
and divide it into 8 equal pieces. Roll out each piece to a circle 20 cm
(8 inches) across. Leave the rounds on the floured surface, covered with
a clean, dry tea towel, for 15 minutes.

Heat a large frying pan or griddle, then reduce to the lowest setting.
Place a piece of dough in the pan and cook for 3–4 minutes, turning
once, until golden brown in places. Slide the bread on to a plate and
cover with a clean, damp tea towel while you cook the rest.

For spicy chicken wraps, diagonally slice 1 bunch of spring onions.
Thinly slice 2 celery sticks. Heat 3 tablespoons vegetable oil in a large
frying pan and fry the onions and celery for 2 minutes. Drain to a plate.
Add 3 thinly sliced chicken breast fillets to the pan and fry quickly,
stirring, for about 5 minutes or until cooked through. Add 4 tablespoons
sweet chilli sauce and 2 teaspoons rice wine vinegar. Return the onions
and celery to the pan and stir to mix. Spoon the filling across 4 of the
wraps (the remainder can be chilled or frozen for another time) and
scatter with pea shoots or sprouting beans. Roll up and serve warm.

TOMATO FOCACCIA

Makes 2 loaves

Time **1½–2½ hours**, depending on machine, plus
shaping, proving and baking

Dough

475 g (15 oz) **strong white bread flour**

1 teaspoon **caster sugar**

1 teaspoon **salt**

1½ teaspoons **fast-action dried yeast**

3 tablespoons **olive oil**

275 ml (9 fl oz) **water**

To finish

200 g (7 oz) **cherry tomatoes**

a few **rosemary sprigs**

a few **black olives**

1 teaspoon **salt flakes**

3 tablespoons **olive oil**

Lift the bread pan out of the machine and fit the blade. Put the dough ingredients in the pan, following the order specified in the manual.

Fit the pan into the machine and close the lid. Set to the dough programme.

At the end of the programme turn the dough out on to a floured surface and cut it in half. Press each into a rough oval a little larger than your hand.

Transfer the loaves to 2 greased baking sheets and use the end of a wooden spoon to make indentations over the surface. Press the tomatoes into some of the indentations, add small sprigs of rosemary and olives into some of the others. Sprinkle with salt flakes and leave, uncovered, for 20 minutes.

Drizzle the loaves with a little of the oil and bake in a preheated oven, 200°C (400°F), Gas Mark 6, for 15 minutes. Swap the shelf positions during cooking so that both loaves brown evenly. Drizzle with the remaining oil and serve warm or cold, torn into pieces.

For onion, sage & gorgonzola focaccia, make the dough as above, adding 1 tablespoon chopped sage with the flour. After shaping and making indentations, scatter the loaves with ½ small red onion, very finely sliced, and 75 g (3 oz) crumbled Gorgonzola. Drizzle with olive oil as above and scatter with small sage leaves halfway through baking.

CLASSIC
PUDDINGS

RAINBOW TART

Serves **8**
Preparation time **25 minutes**
Cooking time **30 minutes**

375 g (12 oz) packet **sweet pastry**
2 **egg yolks**
3 tablespoons **cornflour**
3 tablespoons **caster sugar**
300 ml (½ pint) **milk**
1 teaspoon **vanilla essence**
1 large **orange**, segmented
175 g (6 oz) **strawberries**, halved
125 g (4 oz) **blueberries**
2 thick fresh **pineapple** rings, cut into bite-sized chunks
2 **kiwifruits**, sliced
icing sugar, to dust
crème fraîche or **natural yogurt**, to serve

Line a 23 cm (9 inch) fluted flan tin with the pastry. Trim the edges, then press the pastry firmly into the grooves so the rim sits a little higher than the tin. Fill with scrunched-up nonstick baking paper and baking beans, then bake in a preheated oven, 180°C (350°F), Gas Mark 4, for 15 minutes. Remove the paper and beans and bake for a further 5 minutes. Set aside to cool.

Mix the egg yolks, cornflour and sugar in a bowl. Put the milk in a heavy-based nonstick pan and bring to the boil. Pour over the egg mixture and blend well using a balloon whisk. Add the vanilla essence, then return to the rinsed-out pan and bring to the boil, whisking continuously until boiled and thickened. Transfer to a bowl to cool, stirring occasionally. Cover with clingfilm to prevent a skin forming.

Place the cooled pastry case on a serving plate and fill with the custard using a metal spoon to swirl up to the rim. Put the fruit in a bowl and toss to mix, then loosely arrange over the top of the custard. Dust with icing sugar and serve in wedges with spoonfuls of crème fraîche or yogurt.

For sunshine tart, mix 2 segmented oranges, 3 thick slices fresh pineapple, cut into chunks, 2 bananas, cut into chunks and tossed in 2 tablespoons lemon or lime juice, and 1 small mango, cut into chunks. Toss together and use to fill as above.

FIG & HONEY POTS

Serves **4**
Preparation time **10 minutes**, plus chilling

6 **ripe fresh figs**, thinly sliced, plus 2 extra, cut into wedges, to decorate (optional)
450 ml (¾ pint) **Greek yogurt**
4 tablespoons **clear honey**
2 tablespoons chopped **pistachio nuts**

Arrange the fig slices snugly in the bottom of 4 glasses or glass bowls. Spoon the yogurt over the figs and chill in the refrigerator for 10–15 minutes.

Just before serving, drizzle 1 tablespoon honey over each dessert and sprinkle the pistachio nuts on top. Decorate with the wedges of fig, if liked.

For hot figs with honey, heat a griddle pan, add 8 whole ripe fresh figs and cook for 8 minutes, turning occasionally, until charred on the outside. Alternatively, cook under a preheated grill. Remove and cut in half. Divide between 4 plates, top each with a tablespoonful of Greek yogurt and drizzle with a little clear honey.

CHOCOLATE, DATE & ALMOND PANINI

Serves **4**
Preparation time **10 minutes**, plus cooling
Cooking time **26–28 minutes**

25 g (1 oz) whole **blanched almonds**
2 tablespoons **icing sugar**
75 g (3 oz) **white chocolate**, finely grated
8 soft **dates**, pitted and chopped
25 g (1 oz) **flaked almonds**, lightly toasted
8 slices **brioche**, buttered on both sides
50 ml (2 fl oz) **double cream**, whipped

Put the blanched almonds in a colander and sprinkle with a little cold water. Shake off any excess water and place the almonds on a nonstick baking sheet. Sift the icing sugar over the top and bake in a preheated oven, 180°C (350°F), Gas Mark 4, for about 20 minutes until they have crystallized.

Remove the almonds from the oven and set aside to cool, then put them in a freezer bag and tap lightly with a rolling pin until they are crushed but not powdery.

Mix together the grated chocolate, dates and almonds. Spoon the mixture on to 4 slices of the buttered brioche and top with the remaining slices to make 4 sandwiches.

Heat a griddle over a medium heat and cook the brioche sandwiches for 3–4 minutes. Turn them over and cook the other side for another 3–4 minutes to make a panini.

Cut the panini in half diagonally and serve immediately with whipped cream and sprinkled with crushed almonds.

For eggy bread, substitute the brioche for sweet French toasts. Dip each French toast in a mixture of 2 eggs lightly beaten with 4 tablespoons milk. Fry in butter, turning, until golden both sides. Omit the nuts and cream and serve with honey or syrup.

360

CLASSIC PUDDINGS

FIGS WITH YOGURT & HONEY

Serves **4**
Preparation time **5 minutes**
Cooking time **10 minutes**

8 ripe **figs**
4 tablespoons **natural yogurt**
2 tablespoons **clear honey**

Slice the figs in half and place on a hot griddle pan, skin-side down. Sear for 10 minutes until the skins begin to blacken, then remove.

Arrange the figs on 4 plates and serve with a spoonful of yogurt and some honey spooned over the top.

For brioche French toasts with figs, yogurt & honey, brush 4 slices brioche with a mixture of 50 g (2 oz) melted butter and 50 ml (2 fl oz) cream and toast under a grill. Top with figs, as above.

361

STRAWBERRY JELLIES

Serves **6**
Preparation time **10 minutes**, plus standing and chilling
Cooking time **5 minutes**

450 g (14½ oz) **strawberries**, hulled
100 g (3½ oz) **caster sugar**
500 ml (17 fl oz) **white grape juice**
2 sachets of **powdered gelatine** or 6 **gelatine leaves**
75 ml (3 fl oz) **crème de cassis** (optional)

Roughly chop three-quarters of the strawberries and put them in a food processor or blender with 300 ml (½ pint) boiling water and the sugar. Blend until smooth, then pour the mixture into a sieve set over a bowl and stir to allow the liquid to drip through.

Pour 200 ml (7 fl oz) of the grape juice into a heatproof bowl, sprinkle over the gelatine and allow to stand for 10 minutes. Place the bowl over a saucepan of simmering water and stir until the gelatine has dissolved. Leave to cool, then stir in the cassis (if used), strawberry liquid and the remaining grape juice.

Arrange the remaining strawberries in 6 large wine glasses, pour over the liquid and chill until the jelly has set.

For raspberry champagne jellies, substitute the strawberries for raspberries and omit the cassis. Dissolve the gelatine in only 100 ml (3½ fl oz) grape juice and, when cool, stir in 400 ml (14 fl oz) sparkling white wine. Finish as above.

MELON & PINEAPPLE SALAD

Serves **4**
Preparation time **10 minutes**

½ **cantaloupe melon**, peeled, deseeded and diced
½ small **pineapple**, peeled and diced
finely grated rind of 1 **lime**
2 teaspoons **fructose**
quarter slices of **lime**, to decorate

Put the melon and pineapple in a bowl or plastic storage box.

Mix together the lime rind and fructose until well combined. Sprinkle over the fruit and mix together well – in 1 hour or so the fructose will have dissolved.

Decorate with the lime slices and serve.

For watermelon, pear & strawberry salad, cut ½ small watermelon into cubes and place in a plastic storage box. Toss with 2 peeled, cored and sliced pears and 175 g (6 oz) hulled and halved small strawberries. Mix with 3 tablespoons orange juice and decorate with orange or clementine slices.

MULTICOLOURED FRESH FRUIT LOLLIES

Serves **8**
Preparation time **20 minutes**, plus freezing
Cooking time **15 minutes**

300 g (10 oz) fresh **raspberries**
25 g (1 oz) **caster sugar**
150 ml (¼ pint) **water**, plus
  4 tablespoons
400 g (13 oz) can **peaches** in natural juice

Place the raspberries and sugar in a small pan with 4 tablespoons of the measured water and bring to the boil, stirring well until the sugar dissolves. Add the remaining measured water.

Put the raspberry liquid through a sieve, pressing down well with a metal spoon to make as much of the pulp go through as possible, only discarding the seeds.

Pour the mixture into 8 lolly moulds, filling just the base of each. (Try using 8 rinsed yogurt pots placed in a roasting tin. Cover with foil and push lolly sticks through the foil into the centre of each pot. The foil will help secure the stick in the centre.) Freeze for 1–2 hours until firm.

Meanwhile, put the peaches and juice into a food processor and whiz until smooth. Once the raspberry base is firm, pour the peach liquid over the top of the raspberry mixture and freeze for a further 1–2 hours or overnight until firm.

For yogurt peach melba lollies, omit the sugar and water and whiz together the raspberries, peaches and 150 ml (¼ pint) raspberry-flavoured drinking yogurt in a food processor. Divide between 8 lolly moulds and freeze for 4–5 hours until firm.

PEACH & BLUEBERRY CRUNCH

Serves **4**
Preparation time **8 minutes**
Cooking time **8–10 minutes**

25 g (1 oz) **ground hazelnuts**
25 g (1 oz) **ground almonds**
25 g (1 oz) **caster sugar**
25 g (1 oz) **breadcrumbs**
410 g (13½ oz) can **peaches in natural juice**
125 g (4 oz) **blueberries**
150 ml (¼ pint) **double cream**
seeds from 1 **vanilla pod**
1 tablespoon **icing sugar**, sifted

Gently cook the ground nuts in a large frying pan with the sugar and breadcrumbs, stirring constantly until golden. Remove from the heat and leave to cool.

Put the peaches in a food processor or blender and blend with enough of the peach juice to make a thick, smooth purée.

Fold the blueberries gently into the purée and spoon into 4 glasses or individual serving dishes. Set aside some of the blueberries to decorate.

Whip the cream with the vanilla seeds and icing sugar until thick but not stiff and spoon evenly over the peach purée. When the crunchy topping is cool, sprinkle it over the blueberry mixture, top with the remaining blueberries and serve.

For apple & blackberry biscuit crunch, peel 450 g (14½ oz) cooking apples and cook with 2–3 tablespoons sugar and 2 tablespoons water. Fold 125 g (4 oz) blackberries into the apple purée and continue as above, but instead of breadcrumbs, use crushed digestive biscuits. Use the same amount and toast in the same way, but reduce the sugar to 1 tablespoon.

MANGO & PASSION FRUIT FOOL

Serves **4**
Preparation time **15 minutes**, plus chilling

2 ripe **mangoes**, peeled
  and stoned
1 tablespoon chopped **mint**
juice of ½ **lime**
250 ml (8 fl oz) **double cream**
250 ml (8 fl oz) **Greek yogurt**
2 **passion fruit**

Dice 1 mango and combine with the mint. Divide almost half the mango mixture between 4 small bowls, reserving a little for the topping.

Purée the remaining mango with the lime juice in a food processor or blender.

Beat the cream in a bowl until just holding soft peaks, then stir in the yogurt. Fold the cream mixture into the mango purée and swirl to marble.

Divide the cream mixture between the bowls and top with the reserved diced mango. Halve each passion fruit, then scoop the seeds of each half over each fool. Chill in the refrigerator until ready to serve.

For peach & amaretti fool, use a 400 g (13 oz) can peach halves, drained and diced, in place of the mango, mix with 2 tablespoons toasted flaked almonds and divide between 4 small bowls. Follow the recipe as above until the final stage. Then omit the passion fruit and instead top each dessert with a roughly crushed amaretti biscuit.

STRAWBERRY CHEESECAKE POTS

Serves **4**
Preparation time **15 minutes**, plus cooling and chilling
Cooking time **5 minutes**

25 g (1 oz) **butter**
5 **digestive biscuits**
175 g (6 oz) **strawberries**
2 tablespoons **caster sugar**
250 g (8 oz) **mascarpone cheese**
4 tablespoons **double cream**
4 tablespoons **icing sugar**
grated rind and juice of 1 **lemon**

Melt the butter in a small saucepan, then transfer to a food processor with the digestive biscuits and process to fine crumbs. Divide the mixture between 4 glasses and press into the base of each. Chill in the refrigerator.

Meanwhile, put the strawberries and caster sugar in a saucepan and cook, stirring, for 2–3 minutes, then leave to cool. In a bowl, mix together the mascarpone, cream, icing sugar and lemon rind and juice.

Fill the glasses with the mascarpone mixture and top each with the strawberries. Chill for 2–3 hours before serving.

For ginger raspberry cheesecake pots, follow the recipe above, but use gingernut biscuits in place of the digestive biscuits, raspberries instead of strawberries and Greek yogurt in place of the mascarpone. Sprinkle the top of each dessert with 1 teaspoon chopped stem ginger.

PINEAPPLE WITH LIME & CHILLI SYRUP

Serves **4**
Preparation time **10 minutes**, plus cooling
Cooking time **10 minutes**

100 g (3½ oz) **caster sugar**
100 ml (3½ fl oz) **water**
3 **red chillies**
grated rind and juice of 1 **lime**
1 **baby pineapple**, halved or quartered, cored and cut
   into wafer-thin slices
ice cream (optional)

Put the sugar in a saucepan with the water. Heat slowly until the sugar has dissolved, then add the chillies, bring to the boil and boil rapidly until the liquid becomes syrupy. Leave to cool.

Stir the lime rind and juice into the cooled syrup. Lay the pineapple slices on a plate and drizzle the syrup over. Serve chilled with a dollop of ice cream, if liked.

For pears with cinnamon syrup, peel 4 ripe pears, cut into quarters and remove the cores. Put in a saucepan, pour over water to cover and add the caster sugar as above, together with the grated rind and juice of 1 lemon, 1 cinnamon stick and 6 cloves. Simmer, turning occasionally, for 10 minutes or until tender. Remove the pears with a slotted spoon and set aside. Bring the liquid to the boil and boil rapidly until the liquid becomes syrupy. Leave to cool, then pour over the pears.

HOT PEACH & CINNAMON PANCAKES

Makes **8**
Preparation time **10 minutes**
Cooking time **20 minutes**

3 small ripe **peaches**
1 teaspoon **ground cinnamon**
6 tablespoons **maple syrup**
125 g (4 oz) **self-raising flour**
2 tablespoons **golden caster sugar**
1 **egg**
150 ml (¼ pint) **milk**
little **oil**, for greasing

Halve and stone the peaches. Roughly chop 1 of them and set it aside, then cut the remaining 2 into wedges and toss with a small pinch of the ground cinnamon and all the maple syrup in a small bowl and set aside.

Sift the flour and remaining cinnamon into a bowl and add the caster sugar. Make a well in the centre and set aside. Beat the egg and milk together well in a jug, then pour into the centre of the flour mixture. Mix quickly and as lightly as possible to make a batter the consistency of thick cream. Stir in the chopped peaches.

Lightly oil a heavy-based frying pan or flat griddle pan. Drop heaped tablespoons of the batter on to the pan surface and cook over a steady, moderate heat for 1–2 minutes until bubbles rise to the surface and burst. Turn the pancake over and cook for a further 1–2 minutes. Remove from the pan and keep warm while making the remaining pancakes.

Serve the pancakes warm, with a large spoonful of the peach and maple syrup mixture over the top of each.

For creamy banana pancakes, make the batter as above, replacing the peaches with 1 small banana, roughly chopped. Cook for 1 minute on each side until golden, and serve with 1 thinly sliced banana tossed with 2 tablespoons maple syrup over the top.

LEMON & ORANGE MOUSSE

Serves **4**

Preparation time **15 minutes**, plus chilling

300 ml (½ pint) **double cream**

grated rind and juice of **1 lemon**, plus extra finely pared strips of rind to decorate

grated rind and juice of ½ **orange**, plus extra finely pared strips of rind to decorate

65 g (2½ oz) **caster sugar**

2 **egg whites**

Whip together the cream, grated lemon and orange rinds and sugar in a large bowl until the mixture starts to thicken. Add the lemon and orange juices and whisk again until the mixture thickens.

Whip, in a separate large, perfectly clean bowl, the egg whites until soft peaks form, then fold into the citrus mixture. Spoon the mousse into 4 glasses and chill in the refrigerator. Decorate with lemon and orange rind strips.

For raspberry mousse, purée 200 g (7 oz) raspberries in a food processor or blender, then pass through a fine sieve. In a large bowl, whip together the cream and sugar as above until the mixture starts to thicken, then add the sieved raspberry purée and whip again until thickened. Continue with the recipe as above, but decorate with whole raspberries and plain dark chocolate shavings, shaved from a bar using a swivel-bladed vegetable peeler.

368

SOFT-COOKED BANANAS & YOGURT ICE

Serves **4**

Preparation time **20 minutes**, plus freezing

Cooking time **10 minutes**

3 tablespoons **caster sugar**

150 ml (¼ pint) **water**

2 x 500 ml (17 fl oz) pots **natural yogurt**

3 teaspoons **vanilla essence**

15 g (½ oz) **butter**, softened

4 ripe **bananas**

½ teaspoon **ground cinnamon** or **nutmeg** (optional)

To serve

4 tablespoons **maple syrup**

50 g (2 oz) broken **pecan nuts**

Place the sugar and measured water in a heavy-based saucepan and bring to the boil. Continue to boil for 3–5 minutes until the syrup has reduced by half. Remove from the heat and stir in the yogurt and vanilla essence. Transfer to a freezerproof container and freeze for 3 hours.

Remove the ice from the freezer and beat with a wooden spoon until slushy. Freeze for a further 4 hours, or overnight, until firm.

Heat the butter in a large nonstick frying pan. Halve the bananas lengthways, then cut each of the halves in half again across its width. Sprinkle the bananas, cut side up, with the spice, if using, and cook in the hot butter for 30–60 seconds on each side until golden. Remove from the pan using a slotted spoon.

Pile the bananas on to serving plates in a lattice pattern, then drizzle with the maple syrup and scatter with the pecans. Serve with scoops of the vanilla yogurt ice on top.

For strawberry yogurt ice, to serve as an alternative accompaniment, make as above, replacing the natural yogurt with a strawberry yogurt. Cook 375 g (12 oz) halved strawberries with ½ teaspoon freshly grated orange rind and 1 tablespoon maple syrup in the butter for 2–3 minutes until soft yet retaining their shape. Serve the warm strawberries with the strawberry yogurt ice.

COCONUT SYLLABUB & ALMOND BRITTLE

Serves **4**
Preparation time **15 minutes**, plus cooling and chilling
Cooking time **about 10 minutes**

100 g (3½ oz) **granulated sugar**
50 g (2 oz) **flaked almonds**, toasted

For the syllabub
200 ml (7 fl oz) **coconut cream**
300 ml (½ pint) **double cream**
15 **cardamom seeds**, lightly crushed
2 tablespoons **caster sugar**

To make the brittle, put the granulated sugar and almonds in a saucepan over a low heat. While the sugar melts, lightly oil a baking sheet. When the sugar has melted and turned golden, pour the mixture on to the baking sheet and leave to cool.

To make the syllabub, pour the coconut cream and double cream into a large bowl. Add the crushed cardamom seeds and caster sugar, then lightly whip until just holding soft peaks.

Spoon the syllabub into 4 glasses and chill in the refrigerator. Meanwhile, lightly crack the brittle into irregular shards. When ready to serve, top the syllabub with some of the brittle and serve the remainder separately on the side.

For lemon syllabub, put the grated rind and juice of 1 lemon in a bowl with 125 ml (4 fl oz) white wine and 40 g (1½ oz) caster sugar. Cover and leave to soak for about 1 hour. Whip 300 ml (½ pint) double cream until it forms soft peaks, then gradually add the wine mixture and continue whipping until it holds its shape. In a separate, perfectly clean bowl, whisk 1 egg white until stiff, then whisk in 40 g (1½ oz) caster sugar. Carefully fold into the cream mixture and spoon into 4 glasses. Chill in the refrigerator before serving.

SPIDER'S WEB PANCAKES

Serves **8**
Preparation time **15 minutes**
Cooking time **15–20 minutes**

2 **eggs**
150 g (5 oz) **plain flour**
1 teaspoon **caster sugar**
300 ml (½ pint) **milk**
15 g (½ oz) **butter**, melted
300 ml (½ pint) **double cream**
3 teaspoons **clear honey**
250 g (8 oz) **raspberries**
vegetable oil, for frying
icing sugar, to dust

Whisk the eggs, flour and sugar in a bowl until well combined, then whisk in the milk until you have a smooth batter. Whisk in the melted butter, then set the batter aside.

Whip the cream very lightly until just beginning to peak, then fold in the honey and raspberries and chill whilst making the pancakes.

Heat a few drops of oil in a small, nonstick frying pan. Transfer the batter to a jug with a narrow spout, and pour a very thin stream of the batter, starting in the centre of the pan and continuing in continuous circles around, then across the pan to form a small web pattern about 15 cm (6 inches) in diameter. Cook for about 1 minute until set, then, using a fish slice, flip the pancake over and cook the other side for 30 seconds. Repeat to make 8 pancakes, stacking them between sheets of nonstick baking paper to keep warm.

Serve the warm pancakes filled with a little raspberry cream and dusted with icing sugar.

For apple & cinnamon spider's web pancakes, place 2 large peeled, cored and roughly chopped cooking apples in a pan with 3 tablespoons sultanas, 3 tablespoons water, ½ teaspoon ground cinnamon and 2 tablespoons soft brown sugar. Cook over a gentle heat for 3–5 minutes, stirring continuously until soft and pulpy. Remove from the heat and allow to cool. Serve folded into the cream as above, replacing the raspberries, or fill the pancakes with the apple mixture alone and serve with yogurt.

QUICK WHITE CHOCOLATE MOUSSE

Serves **4**
Preparation time **5 minutes**, plus chilling
Cooking time **10 minutes**

125 g (4 oz) **caster sugar**
50 g (2 oz) **shelled pistachios**
200 g (7 oz) **white chocolate**, chopped
280 ml (9½ fl oz) **double cream**

Dissolve the sugar with 4 tablespoons water in a small pan over a low heat. Increase the heat and boil until it begins to caramelize. Tip in the pistachios and stir, then pour the mixture on to some greaseproof paper on a baking sheet and leave to set.

Put the chocolate in a heatproof bowl. Heat the cream in a pan until it reaches boiling point, then remove from the heat and pour directly over the chocolate, stirring constantly until it has melted. Refrigerate until cold, then beat with a hand-held electric whisk until thick.

Spoon the cold chocolate into serving dishes, decorate with broken shards of the pistachio praline and serve.

For dark chocolate & orange mousse, substitute the white chocolate for plain dark chocolate, add ¼ teaspoon orange essence to the melted chocolate and use chopped walnuts instead of pistachios in the praline.

STAR-OF-THE-DAY DESSERT

Serves **6**
Preparation time **20 minutes**, plus chilling
Cooking time **3 minutes**

125 g (4 oz) ready-to-eat **dried prunes**, roughly
   chopped
150 ml (¼ pint) **water**
125 g (4 oz) **plain dark chocolate** (70% cocoa solids),
   broken into pieces
500 ml (17 fl oz) **natural yogurt**
25 g (1 oz) **milk or plain dark chocolate**, made into
   shavings, to decorate

Place the prunes in a pan with the measured water and bring to the boil. Immediately remove from the heat, transfer to a food processor and whiz until completely smooth.

Return the prunes to the pan with the chocolate pieces and heat over a very gentle heat, stirring continuously until the chocolate has melted. Remove from the heat and beat in the yogurt. Allow to cool.

Divide the dessert between 4 serving glasses and decorate with the chocolate shavings. Chill for about 30 minutes and serve.

For minted chocolate star-of-the-day dessert, use a mint-flavoured chocolate (70% cocoa solids), dust the tops with a little organic cocoa powder and serve with mint-chocolate sticks for a real treat.

BLUEBERRY & PEACH PUDDING

Serves **4**
Preparation time **20 minutes**
Cooking time **40 minutes**

3 **eggs**
150 g (5 oz) **plain flour**
125 g (4 oz) **icing sugar**, plus extra to dust
300 ml (½ pint) **milk**
1 teaspoon **vanilla essence**
15 g (½ oz) **butter**, softened
2 **peaches**, halved, stoned and cut into wedges
125 g (4 oz) **blueberries**
finely grated rind of 1 **lemon**

Beat the eggs, flour, sugar, milk and vanilla essence in a bowl until thick and creamy. Heavily grease a 20 cm (8 inch) round tin or ovenproof dish with the butter and arrange the peaches and blueberries inside. Sprinkle over the lemon rind.

Pour the batter over the fruit and bake in a preheated oven, 190°C (375°F), Gas Mark 5, for 35 minutes until the batter is firm.

Dust with icing sugar and serve warm in wedges.

For strawberry, banana & cherry pudding, replace the peaches and blueberries with 1 large banana, sliced into chunks, 175 g (6 oz) strawberries and 125 g (4 oz) fresh pitted cherries. Try adding 1 teaspoon of ground cinnamon to the fruit and toss if liked.

CLASSIC PUDDINGS

BERRIED TREASURES

Serves **4**
Preparation time **15 minutes**
Cooking time **2 minutes**

125 g (4 oz) **white chocolate**, at room temperature
2 tablespoons **milk**
150 ml (¼ pint) **double cream**
150 g (5 oz) **blackberries**
1 tablespoon **clear honey**
1 **egg white**

Break off a quarter of the white chocolate. Using a potato peeler, shave off some chocolate curls to decorate the desserts.

Place the remaining pieces of chocolate in a small heatproof bowl. Add the milk and microwave on full power for 2 minutes. Leave to stand for 1 minute then stir. If lumps remain in the chocolate, microwave again for a further 30 seconds until melted. (Alternatively, put the chocolate and milk in a small heatproof bowl and rest it over a small saucepan of gently simmering water.) Stir in the cream and pour into a cool bowl, allow to cool completely, then put in the freezer for 5 minutes.

Reserve 4 blackberries and blend the remainder in a food processor with the honey until puréed. Turn into a fine-meshed sieve over a bowl and press the purée through with the back of a dessertspoon to extract the seeds.

Whisk the egg white until it stands in soft peaks when the whisk is lifted from the bowl.

Remove the chocolate cream from the freezer and whisk until it starts to thicken. This might take a few minutes. Gently stir in the egg white.

Spoon half the chocolate mixture into 4 small serving dishes or cups and spoon over the fruit purée. Top with the remaining chocolate mixture and give each a light stir with the handle end of a teaspoon so you can see a swirl of the blackberry purée. Decorate with the reserved berries and chocolate curls and chill until ready to serve.

TOFFEE PEACHES

Serves **4**
Preparation time **10 minutes**
Cooking time **15 minutes**

4 **peaches**, halved and stoned
50 g (2 oz) **ground almonds**

Sauce
125 (4 oz) **soft light brown sugar**
5 tablespoons **maple syrup**
25 g (1 oz) **butter**
150 ml (¼ pint) **single cream**

Cut 4 x 20 cm (8 inch) square pieces of foil and place 2 peach halves in each. Sprinkle over the ground almonds. Scrunch up the foil to form 4 parcels and place under a preheated medium grill or 5–8 minutes, turning once or twice during cooking until the peaches are soft.

Meanwhile, make the sauce. Place the sugar, maple syrup and butter in a nonstick saucepan over a moderately low heat until the sugar dissolves. Stir continuously until the sauce boils and thickens, which should take about 3 minutes. Add the cream and return to the boil, then immediately remove from the heat.

Drizzle the sauce over the peaches, and serve.

For toffee apples, place 4 halved apples in sheets of foil and divide 15 g (½ oz) butter between them in cubes, dotting over the top. Sprinkle with a little ground cinnamon and grill for 10–12 minutes until the apples have softened, yet still retain their shape. Serve with the sauce as above.

374

DRUNKEN ORANGE SLICES

Serves **4**
Preparation time **10 minutes**
Cooking time **12 minutes**

4 large sweet **oranges**
50 g (2 oz) **soft brown sugar**
3 tablespoons **Cointreau**
2 tablespoons **whisky**
juice of 1 small **orange**
1 **vanilla pod**, split
1 **cinnamon stick**
4 **cloves**
2–3 blades of **mace** (optional)
ginger ice cream, to serve

Cut off the base and the top of the oranges. Cut down around the curve of the orange to remove all the rind and pith, leaving just the orange flesh. Cut the flesh horizontally into 5 mm (½ inch) slices and set aside.

Heat 50 ml (2 fl oz) water gently with the sugar, 2 tablespoons of the Cointreau, the whisky, orange juice, vanilla pod, cinnamon stick, cloves and mace (if used) until the sugar has dissolved. Increase the heat and boil rapidly for 5 minutes. Allow to cool slightly, but keep warm.

Heat a griddle pan over a high heat and quickly cook the orange slices for about 1 minute on each side until caramelized. Top with the remaining Cointreau and set alight. Once the flames have died down, arrange the orange slices on serving dishes and drizzle with the orange syrup.

Serve the orange slices immediately with some ginger ice cream.

For non-alcoholic orange slices, slice 6 oranges as above and arrange them in a dish. Cut away the pith from the rind and finely slice the rind. Put it in a saucepan with just enough water to cover. Bring to the boil then immediately refresh in cold water. Place the rind in a clean pan, cover with water and simmer for 25 minutes. Dissolve 175 g (6 oz) caster sugar in 150 ml (¼ pint) water, boil for a few minutes and stir in 2 tablespoons lemon juice. Add the drained rind and pour over the sliced oranges. Chill, then serve with ice cream.

SUGARED FRUIT PANCAKES

Makes **20–24**
Preparation time **15 minutes**
Cooking time **10 minutes**

2 **eggs**
25 g (1 oz) **unsalted butter**
100 ml (3½ fl oz) **milk**
100 g (3½ oz) **plain flour**
1 teaspoon **baking powder**
2 tablespoons **vanilla** or **caster sugar**
125 g (4 oz) **blueberries**
cooking oil, for frying

Separate the eggs into 2 bowls, egg yolks in one and egg whites in another. Put the butter in a heatproof bowl and heat in the microwave for 30 seconds until melted. Add the milk and pour the mixture over the egg yolks, stirring well.

Put the flour, baking powder and 1 tablespoon of the sugar in a large bowl. Add the milk mixture and whisk well to make a smooth batter. Stir in the blueberries.

Whisk the egg whites until they form firm peaks. Using a large metal spoon, gently fold the whites into the batter until well mixed.

Heat a little oil in a large frying pan for 1 minute. Add a dessertspoonful of the batter to one side of the pan so it spreads to make a little cake. Add 2–3 more spoonfuls, depending on the size of the pan, so the pancakes can cook without touching. When the pancakes are golden on the underside (check by lifting with a palette knife or fish slice), flip them over and cook again until golden. Remove the pancakes from the pan and transfer to a serving plate, then keep them warm while you cook the remainder.

Sprinkle with the remaining sugar and serve.

For vanilla & fig pancakes, add 1 teaspoon vanilla essence to the milk in the pancakes, omit the blueberries and make as above. Cut 3 small figs into wedges and place into a pan with 15 g (½ oz) unsalted butter and 3 tablespoons maple syrup and heat for 2 minutes, stirring until soft. Spoon over the warm pancakes and serve with the yogurt.

PAPAYA & LIME SALAD

Serves **4**
Preparation time **15 minutes**
Cooking time **3–5 minutes**

3 firm, ripe **papayas**
2 **limes**
2 teaspoons **light brown sugar**
50 g (2 oz) **blanched almonds**, toasted
lime wedges, to garnish

Cut the papayas in half, scoop out the seeds and discard. Peel the halves, roughly dice the flesh and place in a bowl.

Finely grate the rind of both limes, then squeeze one of the limes and reserve the juice. Cut the pith off the second lime and segment the flesh over the bowl of diced papaya to catch the juice. Add the lime segments and grated rind to the papaya.

Pour the lime juice into a small saucepan with the sugar and heat gently until the sugar has dissolved. Remove from the heat and leave to cool.

Pour the cooled lime juice over the fruit and toss thoroughly. Add the toasted almonds and serve with lime wedges.

For papaya & lime yogurt, use 1 papaya and 1 lime. Prepare the papaya as above, omitting the segments and syrup. Chop the almonds. Mix with 400 g (13 oz) thick Greek yogurt and serve for breakfast with muesli or as a simple pudding, topped with granola. It is also very good as a topping for waffles.

ICED CHOCOLATE MOUSSES

Serves **6**
Preparation time **30 minutes**, plus cooling and freezing
Cooking time **10 minutes**

250 g (8 oz) **plain dark chocolate**
15 g (½ oz) **unsalted butter**
2 tablespoons **liquid glucose**
3 tablespoons **fresh orange juice**
3 **eggs**, separated
200 ml (7 fl oz) **double cream**

Make chocolate curls by paring the underside of the block of chocolate with a swivel-bladed vegetable peeler. If the curls are very small, microwave the chocolate in 10-second bursts on full power (or place in a warm oven) until the chocolate is soft enough to shape. When you have enough curls to decorate 6 mousses, break the remainder into pieces – you should have 200 g (7 oz) – and melt.

Stir the butter and glucose into the chocolate, then mix in the orange juice. Stir the egg yolks one by one into the mixture until smooth. Take off the heat and leave to cool.

Whisk the egg whites until softly peaking. Whip the cream until it forms soft swirls. Fold the cream, then the egg whites, into the chocolate mix. Pour the mixture into 6 coffee cups or ramekin dishes.

Freeze for 4 hours or overnight until firm. Decorate the tops with chocolate curls.

For chilled chocolate & coffee mousses, omit the chocolate curls and instead melt 200 g (7 oz) plain dark chocolate, then add 15 g (½ oz) butter (omit the liquid glucose), 3 tablespoons strong black coffee and 3 egg yolks. Fold in 3 whisked egg whites, then pour the mixture into 4 small dishes or glasses and chill in the refrigerator for 4 hours until set. Whip 125 ml (4 fl oz) double cream until it forms soft swirls, then fold in 2 tablespoons coffee cream liqueur, if liked. Spoon on to the top of the mousses and decorate with a little sifted cocoa powder.

BAKED LEMON CUSTARDS

Serves **4**
Preparation time **10 minutes**, plus infusing
Cooking time **about 1 hour**

12 **bay leaves**, bruised
2 tablespoons finely grated **lemon rind**
100 ml (3½ fl oz) **double cream**
4 **eggs**, plus 1 **egg yolk**
150 g (5 oz) **caster sugar**
100 ml (3½ fl oz) **lemon juice**

Put the bay leaves, lemon rind and cream in a small saucepan and heat gently until it reaches boiling point. Remove immediately from the heat and set aside for 2 hours to infuse.

Whisk together the eggs, egg yolk and sugar until the mixture is pale and creamy, then whisk in the lemon juice. Strain the cream mixture through a fine sieve into the egg mixture and stir until combined. Set aside 4 bay leaves for decoration.

Pour the custard into 4 individual ramekins and place on a baking sheet. Cook in a preheated oven, 120°C (250°F), Gas Mark ½, for 50 minutes or until the custards are almost set in the middle. Leave to stand until cold, then chill until required. Allow to return to room temperature before serving, decorated with the reserved bay leaves.

For plain baked custard, mix 1 tablespoon caster sugar with 1 egg, 150 ml (¼ pint) warm milk and a pinch of salt. Use the mixture to fill 1 flan case or 12 small pastry cases made from 250 g (8 oz) shortcrust pastry, pricked and baked blind in a preheated oven, 200°C (400°F), Gas Mark 6, for 20–25 minutes. Sprinkle over grated nutmeg and bake in a preheated oven, 200°C (400°F), Gas Mark 6, for about 20 minutes.

CHOCOLATE OVERLOAD

Serves **4**
Preparation time **8 minutes**

8 **chocolate cream sandwich biscuits**, crushed
25 g (1 oz) **butter**, melted
500 ml (17 fl oz) tub softened **chocolate cookie ice cream**
2 tablespoons **runny caramel** or **dulce de leche** (optional)
white chocolate shavings, to decorate
milk chocolate shavings, to decorate

Mix the crushed biscuits with the melted butter and press firmly into the base of 4 dessert dishes.

Scoop the ice cream over the top of the biscuit base. Drizzle with the caramel or spoon over the dulce de leche (if used) and decorate with white and milk chocolate shavings. Serve immediately.

For chocolate sundaes with raspberries, replace the biscuits with 20 mini meringues and omit the butter. Layer the ice cream, meringues and 200 g (7 oz) raspberries in glasses. Drizzle with single cream and top with grated chocolate.

HOT CARIBBEAN FRUIT SALAD

Serves **4**
Preparation time **15 minutes**
Cooking time **6–7 minutes**

50 g (2 oz) **unsalted butter**
50 g (2 oz) **light muscovado sugar**
1 large **papaya**, halved, deseeded, peeled and sliced
1 large **mango**, pitted, peeled and sliced
½ **pineapple**, cored, peeled and cut into chunks
400 ml (14 fl oz) can **full-fat coconut milk**
grated rind and juice of 1 **lime**

Heat the butter in a large frying pan, add the sugar and heat gently until just dissolved. Add all the fruit and cook for 2 minutes, then pour in the coconut milk, half the lime rind and all the juice.

Heat gently for 4–5 minutes, then serve warm in shallow bowls, sprinkled with the remaining lime rind.

For flamed Caribbean fruit salad, omit the coconut milk and add 3 tablespoons dark or white rum. When the rum is bubbling, flame with a long match and stand well back. When the flames have subsided, add the lime rind and juice and serve with scoops of vanilla ice cream.

CROISSANTS WITH CHESTNUT CREAM

Serves **4**
Preparation time **15 minutes**
Cooking time **2–3 minutes**

75 g (3 oz) **unsalted butter**, melted
4 day-old **croissants**, split in half horizontally
4 teaspoons **muscovado sugar**
125 ml (4 fl oz) **sweetened chestnut purée**
125 ml (4 fl oz) **mascarpone cheese**
2 tablespoons **natural yogurt**
1 tablespoon **clear honey**, plus extra for drizzling

To serve
chopped **marrons glacés** (optional)
crushed **chocolate-covered coffee beans** (optional)

Brush the melted butter over the cut sides of the croissants, then sprinkle them with the sugar. Set aside.

Beat the chestnut purée with the mascarpone, yogurt and honey until smooth.

Heat a griddle pan over a low heat and cook the croissants gently, cut-side down, for 2–3 minutes until hot and golden.

Transfer the croissants to serving plates, top with some of the chestnut cream and drizzle with a little extra honey. Sprinkle with a few chopped marrons glacés or crushed chocolate coffee beans, if liked, and serve immediately.

For chocolate cream to serve as an alternative to chestnut cream, substitute the chestnut purée for 4 tablespoons chocolate spread and mix with the mascarpone and yogurt. Omit the honey. After cooking the croissants, spread them with apricot conserve and then with the chocolate cream.

WHITE CHOC & RASPBERRY TIRAMISU

Serves **6**
Preparation time **20 minutes**

3 level teaspoons **instant coffee**
7 tablespoons **icing sugar**
250 ml (8 fl oz) **boiling water**
12 **sponge finger biscuits**, about 100 g (3½ oz)
250 g (8 oz) **mascarpone cheese**
150 ml (¼ pint) **double cream**
3 tablespoons **kirsch** (optional)
250 g (8 oz) **fresh raspberries**
75 g (3 oz) **white chocolate**, diced

Put the coffee and 4 tablespoons of the icing sugar into a shallow dish, then pour on the measured boiling water and mix until dissolved. Dip 6 biscuits, one at a time, into the coffee mixture, then crumble into the bases of 6 glass tumblers.

Put the mascarpone into a bowl with the remaining icing sugar, then gradually whisk in the cream until smooth. Stir in the kirsch, if using, then divide half the mixture between the glasses.

Crumble half the raspberries over the top of the mascarpone in the glasses, then sprinkle with half the chocolate. Dip the remaining biscuits in the coffee mix, crumble and add to the glasses. Then add the rest of the mascarpone and the remaining raspberries, this time left whole, finishing with a sprinkling of the chocolate. Serve immediately or chill until required.

For classic tiramisu, omit the raspberries and white chocolate from the layers. Mix the mascarpone with the cream and 3 tablespoons Kahlua coffee liqueur or brandy, then layer in one large glass dish with the coffee-dipped sponge finger biscuits and 75 g (3 oz) diced plain dark chocolate.

BLOOD-ORANGE SORBET

Serves **4–6**
Preparation time **25 minutes**, plus chilling and freezing
Cooking time **about 20 minutes**

250 g (8 oz) **caster sugar**
pared rind of 2 **blood oranges**
300 ml (½ pint) **blood orange juice**
chilled **Campari** (optional)
orange rind, to decorate

Heat the sugar over a low heat in a small saucepan with 250 ml (8 fl oz) water, stirring occasionally until completely dissolved.

Add the orange rind and increase the heat. Without stirring, boil the syrup for about 12 minutes and then set aside to cool completely.

When it is cold, strain the sugar syrup over the orange juice and stir together. Refrigerate for about 2 hours until really cold.

Pour the chilled orange syrup into an ice cream machine and churn for about 10 minutes. When the sorbet is almost frozen, scrape it into a plastic container and put it in the freezer compartment for a further hour until completely frozen. Alternatively, pour the chilled orange syrup into a shallow metal container and put it in the freezer for 2 hours. Remove and whisk with a hand-held electric whisk or balloon whisk, breaking up all the ice crystals. Return it to the freezer and repeat this process every hour or so until frozen.

Serve scoops of sorbet with a splash of chilled Campari, if liked, and decorate with thin strips of orange rind.

For papaya & lime sorbet, dissolve 125 g (4 oz) caster sugar in 150 ml (¼ pint) water. Boil for 5 minutes, then set aside to cool. Deseed, peel and dice the flesh of 1 ripe papaya. Process the papaya with the cooled sugar syrup. Stir in the grated rind and juice of 2 limes, chill and proceed as above.

380

CLASSIC PUDDINGS

SUMMER FRUIT CRUNCH

Serves **4–6**
Preparation time **10 minutes**
Cooking time **20 minutes**

50 g (2 oz) **rolled oats**
½ teaspoon **ground cinnamon**
½ teaspoon **mixed spice**
pinch of **ground ginger**
15 g (½ oz) **butter**, melted
1 tablespoon **clear honey**
2 tablespoons **sultanas**
400 g (13 oz) mixed fresh or frozen **summer fruits**
50 g (2 oz) **icing sugar**, plus extra to garnish
2 tablespoons **crème de cassis**
½ teaspoon **vanilla extract**
1 tablespoon **flaked almonds**, toasted, to garnish

Mix the oats and spices with the melted butter and honey until well combined.

Press on to a baking sheet and cook in a preheated oven, 180°C (350°F), Gas Mark 4, for 20 minutes, turning once. Remove and leave to cool before mixing in the sultanas.

Meanwhile, put the summer fruits in a pan with the icing sugar and 1 tablespoon water. Warm over a medium-low heat, stirring occasionally, until the fruit begins to collapse. Remove from the heat and stir in the crème de cassis and vanilla extract.

Spoon the fruit into dishes and sprinkle over the crunchy topping. Garnish with the toasted almonds and a sprinkling of icing sugar. Serve immediately.

For autumn plum crunch, stone and quarter 500 g (1 lb) plums and use instead of the summer fruits. Cook the plums in 100 ml (3½ fl oz) apple juice until just tender. Substitute the crème de cassis for sloe gin. Spoon into the dishes and finish as above.

MUFFIN TRIFLE WITH BOOZY BERRIES

Serves **4**

Preparation time **15 minutes**

400 g (13 oz) fresh **mixed berries**, such as strawberries, redcurrants and raspberries, plus extra to decorate

3 tablespoons **crème de cerises** or **cherry brandy**

1 tablespoon **maple syrup**

2 large **blueberry muffins**, sliced

150 ml (¼ pint) **double cream**, whipped to soft peaks

Put the fruit in a bowl and use the back of a fork to crush it with the cherry liqueur or brandy and maple syrup until well combined.

Arrange the sliced muffins in the bottom of a glass dish. Spoon over the fruit and top with the whipped cream. Decorate with the extra berries and serve.

For Black Forest trifle, slice 1 chocolate Swiss roll and arrange in the bottom of a glass dish. Substitute the mixed berries for stoned black cherries. Scrape the seeds of a vanilla pod into the double cream before whipping. Finish as above.

APPLE & SULTANA POT

Serves **4**

Preparation time **15 minutes**

Cooking time **15–23 minutes**

2 **lapsang souchong tea bags**

1 tablespoon **clear honey**

3 tablespoons **sultanas**

3 dessert or cooking **apples**, peeled, cored and diced

½ teaspoon **mixed spice**

25 g (1 oz) **dark brown sugar**

25 g (1 oz) **unsalted butter**

150 g (5 oz) **double cream**, whipped to soft peaks

caster sugar, as required

ginger snaps, to serve

Make a strong infusion of tea using the tea bags in 100 ml (3½ fl oz) boiling water. Stir in the honey and sultanas and set aside to infuse.

Put the apples in a saucepan with the mixed spice, brown sugar and butter. Remove the teabags from the infusion and pour the liquid over the apples.

Cover and cook over a medium-low heat, stirring frequently, for 15–20 minutes until the apples start to collapse. Crush to a chunky purée.

Stir the double cream into the apple purée until well combine, then spoon the mixture into 4 individual ovenproof dishes.

Sprinkle the surface generously with caster sugar, then place the dishes under a hot grill until the sugar begins to caramelize. Serve warm or cold with ginger snaps.

For raspberry & rosewater pots with ground almonds, use the back of a fork to lightly crush 250 g (8 oz) fresh raspberries with 2 tablespoons honey. Stir in 1 tablespoon rosewater and 3 tablespoons ground almonds. Spoon into 4 ramekin dishes and top each one with a generous tablespoon whipped cream before sprinkling with caster sugar and caramelizing as above.

CHOCOLATE ICE CREAM

Serves **4**
Preparation time **20 minutes**, plus cooling and freezing
Cooking time **10 minutes**

300 ml (½ pint) **double cream**
2 tablespoons **milk**
50 g (2 oz) **icing sugar**, sifted
½ teaspoon **vanilla essence**
125 g (4 oz) good-quality **plain dark chocolate**, broken
   into pieces
2 tablespoons **single cream**

Chocolate sauce (optional)
150 ml (¼ pint) **water**
3 tablespoons **caster sugar**
150 g (5 oz) **plain dark chocolate**, broken into pieces

Put the double cream and milk in a bowl and whisk until just stiff. Stir in the icing sugar and vanilla essence. Pour the mixture into a shallow freezer container and freeze for 30 minutes or until the ice cream begins to set around the edges. (This ice cream cannot be made in an ice-cream machine.)

Melt the chocolate together with the single cream, over a pan of gently simmering water. Stir until smooth, then set aside to cool.

Remove the ice cream from the freezer and spoon into a bowl. Add the melted chocolate and quickly stir it through the ice cream with a fork. Return the ice cream to the freezer container, cover and freeze until set. Transfer the ice cream to the refrigerator 30 minutes before serving, to soften slightly.

Heat all the ingredients for the chocolate sauce, if making, gently in a saucepan, stirring until melted. Serve immediately with scoops of the ice cream.

For chocolate double mint ice cream, make the ice cream as above, adding 2 tablespoons chopped fresh mint and 20 g (¾ oz) crushed peppermint sweets to the whipped cream and milk. Freeze as above, then stir in the melted dark chocolate mix.

FRESH MELON SORBET

Serves **4–6**
Preparation time **15 minutes**, plus freezing

1 **cantaloupe melon**, weighing 1 kg (2 lb)
50 g (2 oz) **icing sugar**
juice of 1 **lime** or small **lemon**
1 **egg white**

Cut the melon in half and scoop out and discard the seeds. Scoop out the melon flesh with a spoon and discard the shells.

Place the flesh in a food processor or blender with the icing sugar and lime or lemon juice and process to a purée. (Alternatively, rub through a sieve.) Pour into a freezer container, cover and freeze for 2–3 hours. If using an ice-cream machine, purée then pour into the machine, churn and freeze until half-frozen.

Whisk the melon mixture to break up the ice crystals. Then whisk the egg white until stiff and whisk it into the half-frozen melon mixture. Return to the freezer until firm. Alternatively, add whisked egg white to the ice-cream machine and churn until very thick.

Transfer the sorbet to the fridge 20 minutes before serving to soften slightly or scoop straight from the ice-cream machine. Scoop the sorbet into glass dishes to serve. To make differently coloured sorbet, make up three batches of sorbet using a cantaloupe melon in one and honeydew and watermelon in the others.

For gingered melon sorbet, peel and finely grate a 2.5 cm (1 inch) piece of root ginger, then stir into the melon purée. Scoop into small glasses and drizzle each glass with 1 tablespoon ginger wine.

PISTACHIO & YOGURT SEMIFREDDO

Serves **6**
Preparation time **40 minutes**, plus cooling and freezing
Cooking time **10–15 minutes**

4 **eggs**, separated
175 g (6 oz) **caster sugar**
grated rind of **1 lemon**
1½ teaspoons **rose water** (optional)
200 g (7 oz) **Greek yogurt**
½ **fresh pineapple**, sliced, halved and cored

Pistachio brittle
150 g (5 oz) **granulated sugar**
6 tablespoons **water**
100 g (3½ oz) **pistachio nuts**, roughly chopped

Make the brittle. Heat the sugar and measured water in a frying pan until it dissolves, stirring gently from time to time. Add the nuts, then increase the heat and boil the syrup for 5 minutes, without stirring, until pale golden. Quickly tip the mixture on to a greased baking sheet and leave to cool. Break the brittle in half, then crush half in a plastic bag with a rolling pin.

Whisk the egg whites until very stiff, then gradually whisk in half the sugar until thick and glossy. Whisk the egg yolks in a second bowl with the remaining sugar until very thick and pale and the mixture leaves a trail. Fold in the lemon rind and rose water, if using, then the yogurt and crushed brittle, then the egg whites. Pour into a plastic box and freeze for 4–5 hours until semi-frozen and firm enough to scoop.

Cook the pineapple slices on a hot barbecue or preheated griddle pan for 6–8 minutes, turning once or twice until browned. Divide between the serving plates, top with spoonfuls of semifreddo and decorate with broken pieces of the remaining brittle.

For rocky road ice cream, make the brittle with almonds, hazelnuts and pecan nuts instead of pistachios. Whisk the egg whites, then the eggs and sugar, as for the semifreddo, then fold 135 g (4½ oz) ready-made custard and 150 ml (¼ pint) whipped double cream into the yolks with the crushed brittle. Fold in the egg whites as above, then freeze. Serve scooped into glasses with wafer biscuits.

NUTTY CINNAMON RISOTTO

Serves **4**
Preparation time **5 minutes**
Cooking time **25 minutes**

50 g (2 oz) **pecan nuts**
50 g (2 oz) **hazelnuts**
50 g (2 oz) **butter**
125 g (4 oz) **risotto rice**
5 teaspoons **soft brown sugar**
1 teaspoon **ground cinnamon**
600 ml (1 pint) hot **milk**

Heat a frying pan over a medium heat and dry-fry the nuts until golden. Remove and set aside.

Melt the butter in a medium saucepan, add the rice and cook, stirring, for 1 minute.

Stir 4 teaspoons of the sugar and the cinnamon into the hot milk, then start adding the milk to the rice, adding a little more once each addition has been absorbed. This should take about 20 minutes, when the rice should be soft but still with a little bite.

Spoon the risotto into serving bowls.

Blitz the nuts in a food processor with the remaining teaspoon of sugar, then sprinkle the mix over the top of risotto. Serve immediately.

For apricot, citrus & almond risotto, replace the pecan nuts with 100 g (3½ oz) chopped ready-to-eat dried apricots, and the hazelnuts with 100 g (3½ oz) toasted almonds and 2 tablespoons chopped Italian mixed peel.

HONEYED BANANA ICE CREAM

Serves **4–6**
Preparation time **15 minutes**, plus freezing and setting

500 g (1 lb) **bananas**
2 tablespoons **lemon juice**
3 tablespoons **thick honey**
150 g (5 oz) **natural yogurt**
100 g (3½ oz) **chopped nuts**
150 ml (¼ pint) **double cream**
2 **egg whites**

Praline
50 ml (2 fl oz) **water**
170 g (6 oz) **caster sugar**
2 tablespoons **golden syrup**
175 g (6 oz) **toasted almonds**

Put the bananas in a bowl with the lemon juice and mash until smooth. Stir in the honey, followed by the yogurt and nuts, and beat well. Place the banana mix and the cream in an ice-cream machine. Churn and freeze following the manufacturer's instructions until half frozen. Alternatively, whisk the cream until it forms soft swirls, then fold into the banana mix and freeze in a plastic container for 3–4 hours until partially frozen.

Whisk the egg whites lightly until they form soft peaks. Add to the ice-cream machine and continue to churn and freeze until completely frozen. Alternatively, break up the ice cream in the plastic container with a fork, then fold in the whisked egg white and freeze until firm.

Make the praline. Pour the measured water into a heavy saucepan and add the sugar and golden syrup. Simmer gently until the sugar has dissolved, then cook to a caramel-coloured syrup. Place the toasted almonds on a lightly greased piece of foil and pour the syrup over. Leave to set for 1 hour. Once set, break up into irregular pieces and serve with the ice cream.

For honeyed banana ice cream with sticky glazed bananas, make the ice cream as above. When ready to serve, heat 25 g (1 oz) unsalted butter in a frying pan, add 3 thickly sliced bananas and fry until just beginning to soften. Sprinkle over 3 tablespoons light muscovado sugar and cook until dissolved and the bananas are browning around the edges. Add the grated rind and juice of 1 lime, cook for 1 minute, then serve with the ice cream.

PINK GRAPEFRUIT PARFAIT

Serves **4**
Preparation time **15 minutes**

2 **pink grapefruit**
5 tablespoons **dark brown sugar**, plus extra for sprinkling
250 ml (8 fl oz) **double cream**
175 ml (6 fl oz) **Greek yogurt**
3 tablespoons **elderflower cordial**
½ teaspoon **ground ginger**
½ teaspoon **ground cinnamon**
brandy snaps (optional)

Finely grate the rind of 1 grapefruit, making sure you don't get any of the bitter white pith. Cut the skin and the white membrane off both grapefruit and cut between the membranes to remove the segments. Put them in a large dish, sprinkle with 2 tablespoons of the sugar and set aside.

Whisk together the cream and yogurt until thick but not stiff.

Fold in the elderflower cordial, spices, grapefruit rind and remaining sugar until smooth. Pour the mixture into attractive glasses, arranging the grapefruit segments between layers of parfait.

Sprinkle the top with sugar and serve immediately with brandy snaps, if liked.

For orange & blackcurrant parfait, replace the grapefruit with segments from 3 oranges and the elderflower cordial with blackcurrant cordial. Omit the ground ginger and serve sprinkled with chocolate shavings.

CHERRY ALMOND ICE CREAM

Serves **6**
Preparation time **20 minutes**, plus cooling and freezing
Cooking time **20 minutes**

150 ml (¼ pint) **milk**
50 g (2 oz) **ground almonds**
1 **egg**
1 **egg yolk**
75 g (3 oz) **caster sugar**
2–3 drops **almond essence**
500 g (1 lb) **red cherries**, pitted, or **cherry compôte**
25 g (1 oz) **slivered almonds**
150 ml (¼ pint) **double cream**

Pour the milk into a small saucepan and stir in the ground almonds. Bring to the boil, then set aside.

Put the egg and the yolk into a heatproof bowl with the sugar and beat until pale and thick. Pour on the milk and almond mixture. Place the bowl over a pan of gently simmering water and stir until thick. Stir in the almond essence and leave to cool.

Purée the cherries in a food processor or blender (or use cherry compôte), then stir into the custard.

Toss the slivered almonds in a heavy pan over a low heat to toast them. Leave to cool.

Whip the cream until it forms soft peaks. Fold the whipped cream into the cherry mixture.

Transfer the mixture to a freezer container, cover and freeze until firm, beating twice at hourly intervals. Stir the slivered almonds into the mixture at the last beating. (If using an ice-cream machine, pour the cherry mixture into the machine, add the cream, churn and freeze. Once frozen, fold through the slivered almonds.) Serve the ice cream in individual glasses.

For strawberry & coconut ice cream, soak 50 g (2 oz) desiccated coconut in 150 ml (¼ pint) hot milk. Mix egg and egg yolk with sugar and make into custard as above, omitting the almond essence. When cold, fold in 500 g (1 lb) puréed strawberries and 150 ml (¼ pint) whipped double cream. Freeze as above. Serve with extra strawberries.

SWEET CHESTNUT MESS

Serves **4**
Preparation time **15 minutes**

250 g (8 oz) **fromage frais**
1 tablespoon **icing sugar**, sifted
100 g (3½ oz) **sweetened chestnut purée**
100 g (3½ oz) **meringues**, crushed
dark chocolate shards cut from a bar, to decorate

Beat the fromage frais with the icing sugar. Stir in half the chestnut purée and the crushed meringues.

Spoon the remaining chestnut purée into individual serving dishes and top with the meringue mess. Decorate with the dark chocolate shards and serve.

For sweet chestnut pancakes, stir the chestnut purée into the fromage frais. Heat 8 ready-made pancakes according to the instructions on the packet and spread them with the chestnut purée mix. Roll them up and sprinkle with cocoa and icing sugar .

ORCHARD FRUIT CRUMBLE

Serves **6**
Preparation time **20 minutes**
Cooking time **30–35 minutes**

2 **dessert apples**
2 **pears**
400 g (13 oz) **red plums**, quartered and pitted
2 tablespoons **water**
75 g (3 oz) **caster sugar**
100 g (3½ oz) **plain flour**
50 g (2 oz) **unsalted butter**, diced
50 g (2 oz) **desiccated coconut**
50 g (2 oz) **milk chocolate chips**

Quarter, core and peel the apples and pears. Slice the quarters and add the slices to a 1.2 litre (2 pint) pie dish. Add the plums and the water, then sprinkle with 25 g (1 oz) of the sugar. Cover the dish with foil and bake in a preheated oven, 180°C (350°F), Gas Mark 4, for 10 minutes.

Put the remaining sugar in a bowl with the flour and butter, then rub the butter in with your fingertips or an electric mixer until the mixture resembles fine crumbs. Stir in the coconut and chocolate chips.

Remove the foil from the fruit and spoon the crumble over the top. Bake for 20–25 minutes until golden brown and the fruit is tender. Serve warm with custard or cream.

For plum & orange crumble, put 750 g (1½ lb) plums, quartered and pitted, into a 1.2 litre (2 pint) pie dish with 50 g (2 oz) caster sugar. Make the crumble as above, adding the grated rind of 1 small orange and 50 g (2 oz) ground almonds instead of the coconut and chocolate chips. Bake as above.

PASSION FRUIT YOGURT FOOL

Serves **4**
Preparation time **8 minutes**

6 **passion fruit**, halved, flesh and seeds removed
300 ml (½ pint) **Greek yogurt**
1 tablespoon **clear honey**
200 ml (7 fl oz) **whipping cream**, whipped to soft peaks
4 pieces of **shortbread**, to serve

Stir the passion fruit flesh and seeds into the yogurt with the honey.

Fold the cream into the yogurt. Spoon into tall glasses and serve with the shortbread.

For mango & lime yogurt fool, omit the passion fruit, instead puréeing 1 large ripe peeled and stoned mango with the rind of 1 lime and icing sugar to taste. Mix into the yogurt and fold in the cream. Omit the honey.

JAM ROLY-POLY

Serves **6**
Preparation time **25 minutes**
Cooking time **2 hours**

300 g (10 oz) **self-raising flour**
1 teaspoon **baking powder**
150 g (5 oz) **shredded vegetable suet**
75 g (3 oz) **caster sugar**
50 g (2 oz) **fresh breadcrumbs**
finely grated rind of 1 **lemon**
finely grated rind of 1 **orange**
1 **egg**, beaten
175–200 ml (6–7 fl oz) **milk**
6 tablespoons **raspberry jam**
150 g (5 oz) **frozen raspberries**, just defrosted

Put the flour, baking powder, suet and sugar in a bowl, then stir in the breadcrumbs and fruit rinds. Add the egg, then gradually mix in enough milk to make a soft but not sticky dough.

Knead lightly, then roll out to a 30 cm (12 inch) square. Spread with the jam, leaving a 2.5 cm (1 inch) border, then sprinkle the raspberries on top. Brush the border with a little milk, then roll up the pastry. Wrap loosely in a large piece of nonstick baking paper, twisting the edges together and leaving a little space for the pudding to rise, then wrap loosely in foil.

Put on a roasting rack set over a large roasting tin, then pour boiling water into the tin but not over the roasting rack. Cover the tin with foil and twist over the edges to seal well, then bake in a preheated oven, 150°C (300°F), Gas Mark 2, for 2 hours until the pudding is well risen. Check once or twice during baking and top up the water level if needed.

Transfer the pudding to a chopping board using a teacloth. Unwrap, cut into thick slices and serve with hot custard.

For spotted dick, warm 3 tablespoons orange juice or rum in a small saucepan, add 150 g (5 oz) raisins, 1 teaspoon ground ginger and ¼ teaspoon grated nutmeg and leave to soak for 1 hour or longer. Add to the flour mix just before adding the egg and milk. Shape into a long sausage, wrap in paper and foil and steam in the oven as above. Serve sliced with custard flavoured with a little extra rum, if liked.

SUMMER BERRY SPONGE

Serves **6–8**
Preparation time **30 minutes**, plus cooling
Cooking time **10–12 minutes**

4 **eggs**
100 g (3½ oz) **caster sugar**
100 g (3½ oz) **plain flour**
finely grated rind and 2 tablespoons juice of 1 **lemon**
150 ml (¼ pint) **double cream**
150 g (5 oz) **fromage frais**
3 tablespoons **lemon curd**
500 g (1 lb) small **strawberries**, halved
150 g (5 oz) **blueberries**
4 tablespoons **redcurrant jelly**
1 tablespoon **water** (or **lemon juice**)

Whisk the eggs and caster sugar in a large bowl until very thick and the mixture leaves a trail when lifted. Sift the flour over the surface of the eggs, then fold in very gently. Add the lemon rind and juice and fold in until just mixed. Pour the mixture into a greased, floured 25 cm (10 inch) sponge flan tin, tilting the tin to ease into an even layer.

Bake in a preheated oven, 180°C (350°F), Gas Mark 4, for 10–12 minutes until the top of the sponge is golden and the centre springs back when lightly pressed. Cool the sponge in the tin for 5–10 minutes, then carefully turn it out on to a wire rack to cool.

Whip the cream until it forms soft swirls, then fold in the fromage frais and lemon curd. Transfer the sponge to a serving plate, spoon the cream into the centre, spread into an even layer, then top with the strawberries and blueberries. Warm the redcurrant jelly in a small saucepan with the measured water (or lemon juice), then brush over the fruit.

For strawberry sponge flan with Pimm's, make the sponge flan as above, then fill with 300 ml (½ pint) whipped cream flavoured with the grated rind of ½ orange. Top with 500 g (1 lb) sliced strawberries and 150 g (5 oz) raspberries that have been soaked in 3 tablespoons undiluted Pimm's and 2 tablespoons caster sugar for 30 minutes.

CHOCO BREAD & BUTTER PUDDING

Serves **4**
Preparation time **20 minutes**, plus standing
Cooking time **25 minutes**

4 **chocolate croissants**
50 g (2 oz) **unsalted butter**
50 g (2 oz) **caster sugar**
¼ teaspoon **ground mixed spice**
300 ml (½ pint) **milk**
4 **eggs**
1 teaspoon **vanilla essence**
icing sugar, to decorate

Grease a 1.2 litre (2 pint) shallow, round, ovenproof pie dish. Slice the croissants thickly and spread the butter over one side of each cut face of croissant. Stand the croissant slices upright and close together in the dish to completely fill it.

Mix the sugar and spice together, then spoon over the croissants and between the gaps. Stand the dish in a large roasting tin.

Beat the milk, eggs and vanilla essence together, then strain into the dish. Leave to stand for 15 minutes.

Pour hot water from the tap into the roasting tin to come halfway up the sides of the pie dish. Bake in a preheated oven, 180°C (350°F), Gas Mark 4, for about 25 minutes until the pudding is golden and the custard just set.

Lift the dish out of the roasting tin, dust with sifted icing sugar and serve the pudding warm with a little pouring cream.

For fruited bread & butter pudding, lightly butter 8 slices of white bread, cut into triangles and arrange in slightly overlapping layers in the dish, sprinkling with 75 g (3 oz) luxury dried fruit between the layers. Add the sugar as above, but omit the mixed spice. Mix the eggs, milk and vanilla, pour over the bread, then continue as above.

VANILLA CRÈME BRÛLÉE

Serves **6**
Preparation time **20 minutes**, plus standing and chilling
Cooking time **25–30 minutes**

1 **vanilla pod**
600 ml (1 pint) **double cream**
8 **egg yolks**
65 g (2½ oz) **caster sugar**
3 tablespoons **icing sugar**

Slit the vanilla pod lengthways and place it in a saucepan. Pour the cream into the pan, then bring almost to the boil. Take off the heat and allow to stand for 15 minutes. Lift the pod out of the cream and, holding it against the side of the saucepan, scrape the black seeds into the cream. Discard the rest of the pod.

Use a fork to mix together the egg yolks and caster sugar in a bowl. Reheat the cream, then gradually mix it into the eggs and sugar. Strain the mixture back into the saucepan.

Place 6 ovenproof ramekins in a roasting tin, then divide the custard between them. Pour warm water around the dishes to come halfway up the sides, then bake in a preheated oven, 180°C (350°F), Gas Mark 4, for 20–25 minutes until the custard is just set with a slight softness at the centre.

Leave the dishes to cool in the water, then lift them out and chill in the refrigerator for 3–4 hours. About 25 minutes before serving, sprinkle with the icing sugar and caramelize using a blowtorch (or under a hot grill), then leave at room temperature.

For Amaretto brûlée, omit the vanilla pod. Mix the egg yolks and sugar as above, bring the cream almost to the boil, then immediately mix into the egg yolks adding 125 ml (4 fl oz) Amaretto di Saronno liqueur. Strain and continue as above. When chilled, sprinkle with 6 teaspoons flaked almonds, then the sugar, and caramelize as above.

STICKY TOFFEE PUDDINGS

Makes **8**
Preparation time **20 minutes**
Cooking time **45–50 minutes**

125 g (4 oz) pitted chopped **dried dates**
150 ml (¼ pint) **water**
125 g (4 oz) **unsalted butter**, softened
125 g (4 oz) **caster sugar**
1 teaspoon **vanilla essence**
3 **eggs**
175 g (6 oz) **self-raising flour**
1 teaspoon **baking powder**

Toffee sauce
300 ml (½ pint) **double cream**
125 g (4 oz) **light brown sugar**
50 g (2 oz) **unsalted butter**

Put the dates in a small pan with the measured water and simmer gently for 5 minutes until the dates are soft and pulpy. Blend to a purée, then allow to cool.

Make the sauce. Heat half the cream in a small, heavy-bottomed pan with the sugar and butter until the sugar dissolves. Bring to the boil, then let the sauce bubble for about 5 minutes until a rich, dark caramel. Stir in the remaining cream and set aside.

Grease 8 metal 200 ml (7 fl oz) pudding moulds and line the bottoms with nonstick baking paper. Beat the butter, sugar, vanilla essence, eggs, flour and baking powder in a bowl for 1–2 minutes until pale and creamy. Stir the date purée into the pudding mixture.

Divide the mixture among the moulds. Level the tops and place in a roasting tin. Pour boiling water to a depth of 1.5 cm (³/₄ inch) in the tin and cover with foil. Bake in a preheated oven, 180°C (350°F), Gas Mark 4, for 35–40 minutes or until risen and firm to the touch.

Leave the puddings in the moulds while you reheat the sauce, then loosen the edges of the moulds and invert the puddings on to serving plates. Cover with sauce and serve with cream or ice cream, if liked.

For gingered figgy puddings, cook 125 g (4 oz) diced dried figs in the water in place of the dates. Make the sauce and puddings as above, adding 2 tablespoons chopped glacé ginger to the beaten pudding mix.

TUILE BASKETS & STRAWBERRY CREAM

Serves **6**
Preparation time **40 minutes**
Cooking time **15–18 minutes**

2 **egg whites**
100 g (3½ oz) **caster sugar**
50 g (2 oz) **unsalted butter**, melted
few drops **vanilla essence**
50 g (2 oz) **plain flour**

Strawberry cream
250 ml (8 fl oz) **double cream**
4 tablespoons **icing sugar**, plus extra for dusting
2 tablespoons chopped **fresh mint**, plus extra leaves to decorate
250 g (8 oz) **strawberries**, halved or sliced, depending on size

Put the egg whites in a bowl and break up with a fork. Stir in the caster sugar, then the butter and vanilla essence. Sift in the flour and mix until smooth.

Drop 1 heaped tablespoon of the mixture on to a baking sheet lined with nonstick baking paper. Drop a second spoonful well apart from the first, then spread each into a thin circle about 13 cm (5 inches) in diameter. Bake in a preheated oven, 190°C (375°F), Gas Mark 5, for 5–6 minutes until just beginning to brown around the edges.

Add 2 more spoonfuls to a second paper-lined baking sheet and spread thinly. Remove the baked tuiles from the oven and put the second tray in. Allow the cooked tuiles to firm up for 5–10 seconds, then carefully lift them off the paper one at a time and drape each over an orange. Pinch the edges into pleats and leave to harden for 2–3 minutes, then carefully ease off the oranges. Repeat until 6 tuiles have been made.

Whip the cream lightly, then fold in half the sugar, the mint and the strawberries, reserving 6 strawberry halves for decoration. Spoon into the tuiles, then top with the mint leaves and the strawberry halves. Dust with sifted icing sugar.

For fruit salad baskets, make the tuiles as above and fill with 200 g (7 oz) sliced strawberries, 150 g (5 oz) halved seedless ruby grapes, 2 kiwifruits, peeled, halved and sliced, and 2 small ripe peaches. Top with Greek yogurt and a drizzle of honey.

CRANBERRY EVE'S PUDDING

Serves **6**
Preparation time **25 minutes**
Cooking time **40–50 minutes**

750 g (1½ lb) **cooking apples**, quartered, cored,
 peeled and thickly sliced
125 g (4 oz) **frozen cranberries**
75 g (3 oz) **caster sugar**
1 tablespoon **water**
icing sugar, for dusting

Topping
125 g (4 oz) **unsalted butter**, at room temperature,
 or **soft margarine**
125 g (4 oz) **caster sugar**
125 g (4 oz) **self-raising flour**
2 **eggs**
grated rind of 1 small **orange**, plus 2 tablespoons
 of the juice

Put the apples and cranberries into a 1.5 litre (2½ pint), 5 cm (2 inch) deep ovenproof dish and sprinkle over the sugar and water. Cook, uncovered, in a preheated oven, 180°C (350°F), Gas Mark 4, for 10 minutes.

Put the butter, sugar, flour and eggs for the topping in a bowl, and beat together until smooth. Stir in the orange rind and juice.

Spoon the mixture over the partially cooked fruit and spread into an even layer. Return to the oven and cook for 30–40 minutes until the topping is golden and the centre springs back when pressed with a fingertip. Dust with sifted icing sugar and serve warm with custard or cream.

For apple & blackberry pudding, omit the cranberries and add 125 g (4 oz) frozen blackberries. Make the topping as above, but add the grated rind of 1 lemon and 2 tablespoons of the juice instead of the orange rind and juice.

GINGERED PINEAPPLE TRIFLE

Serves **4–5**
Preparation time **20 minutes**

200 g (7 oz) **Jamaican gingercake**, diced
½ **fresh pineapple**, sliced, cored, peeled and diced
grated rind and segmented flesh of 1 **orange**
2 **kiwifruits**, peeled, halved and sliced
3 tablespoons **rum**
425 g (14 oz) can or carton **custard**
300 ml (½ pint) **double cream**
grated rind of 1 **lime**

Arrange the gingercake in an even layer in the base of a 1.2 litre (2 pint) glass serving dish. Spoon the pineapple, orange segments and kiwifruits on top and drizzle with the rum. Pour the custard over the fruit and spread into an even layer.

Whip the cream in a bowl until it forms soft swirls, then fold in half the orange rind and half the lime rind. Spoon the cream over the custard, then sprinkle with the remaining fruit rinds. Chill until ready to serve.

For raspberry & peach trifle, dice 4 trifle sponges and sprinkle in the base of a glass dish instead of the gingercake. Add 150 g (5 oz) fresh raspberries and the diced flesh of 2 ripe peaches. Drizzle with 3 tablespoons dry sherry, then cover with custard as above. Whip the cream and flavour with the grated rind of 1 lemon, spoon it over the custard and sprinkle with 2 tablespoons toasted flaked almonds.

DOUBLE CHOCOLATE PUDDINGS

Serves **6**
Preparation time **25 minutes**
Cooking time **18–20 minutes**

125 g (4 oz) **unsalted butter**, at room temperature, or
  soft margarine
125 g (4 oz) **light muscovado sugar**
100 g (3½ oz) **self-raising flour**
15 g (½ oz) **cocoa powder**
2 **eggs**
75 g (3 oz) or 12 squares **plain dark chocolate**
100 g (3½ oz) **white chocolate**, broken into pieces
150 ml (¼ pint) **double cream**
¼ teaspoon **vanilla essence**

Put the butter or margarine, sugar, flour, cocoa and eggs into a mixing bowl or food processor and beat together until smooth. Divide the mixture between 6 greased sections of a deep muffin tin, then press 2 squares of dark chocolate into each and cover with the pudding mixture.

Bake in a preheated oven, 180°C (350°F), Gas Mark 4, for 18–20 minutes until well risen, slightly crusty around the edges and the centre springs back when pressed with a fingertip.

Meanwhile, warm the white chocolate, cream and vanilla essence together in a small saucepan, stirring until the chocolate has completely melted.

Loosen the edges of the baked puddings with a round-bladed knife, then turn out and transfer to shallow serving bowls. Drizzle with the white chocolate cream and serve immediately.

For walnut & chocolate puddings, omit the cocoa powder from the puddings and mix the butter, sugar and eggs with 125 g (4 oz) self-raising flour, 50 g (2 oz) roughly chopped walnuts and 2 level teaspoons instant coffee dissolved in 3 teaspoons boiling water. Spoon into the muffin tin and press the chocolate squares into the centre of each one as above. Bake as above and serve with pouring cream.

HOT BRIOCHE WITH CHOCOLATE SAUCE

Serves **4**
Preparation time **5 minutes**
Cooking time **12 minutes**

100 g (3½ oz) **plain dark chocolate**
1 tablespoon **golden syrup**
125 g (4 oz) **butter**
4 tablespoons **double cream**
4 thick slices **brioche**
100 g (3½ oz) **demerara sugar**
4 scoops **vanilla** or **praline ice cream**
2 tablespoons **flaked almonds**, lightly toasted

Put the chocolate in a small saucepan with the golden syrup, 25 g (1 oz) of the butter and the cream and heat, stirring occasionally, until shiny and melted.

Meanwhile, melt the remaining butter and brush it over the brioche slices. Sprinkle over the sugar.

Heat a large frying pan over a low heat and cook the brioche slices in the pan for 3–4 minutes on each side until golden and crispy.

Serve hot, with a scoop of ice cream, the warm chocolate sauce and a scattering of nuts.

For quick ice cream brioche, serve 4 individual brioches cut in half and arranged on 4 dessert plates with a scoop of chocolate ice cream, whipped cream and a scattering of roughly chopped chocolate chips.

INDEX

398

INDEX

ACKNOWLEDGEMENTS

Picture acknowledgements

Octopus Publishing Group/Stephen Conroy 2-3, 4-5, 23, 24, 25, 33, 35, 35, 37, 41, 43, 56, 61, 63, 67, 68, 75, 84, 93, 96-97, 109, 111, 129, 133, 135, 182-183, 185, 186, 195, 196, 197, 199, 200, 201, 203, 207, 208, 209, 213, 214, 215, 218, 219, 222, 223, 229, 230, 231, 235, 239, 244, 245, 256, 257, 315, 319, 320, 333, 338, 355, 356-357, 365, 366, 371, 383, 385; /Vanessa Davies 307, 326; /Gus Filgate 57, 60, 248; /Will Heap 312-313, 377, 384, 388, 393; /William Lingwood 40; /David Munns 17, 19, 85, 116, 117, 191; /Lis Parsons 1, 8-9, 11, 12, 18, 27, 28, 29, 52-53, 55, 64, 65, 69, 71, 79, 81, 88, 89, 99, 105, 106, 110, 121, 124, 125, 134, 139, 142-143, 145, 149, 154, 155, 157, 158, 159, 162, 163, 165, 166, 167, 171, 175, 179, 187, 226-227, 238, 243, 253, 259, 263, 264, 265, 267, 268-269, 271, 272, 273, 277, 278, 279, 283, 284, 285, 289, 290, 291, 295, 296, 297, 300, 301, 303, 308, 309, 325, 327, 331, 332, 359, 367, 372, 373; /Gareth Sambidge 13, 107, 249, 360, 361, 392; /William Shaw 48, 49, 337, 339, 342, 343, 345, 349, 350, 351, 354; /Ian Wallace 321.

Executive Editor Eleanor Maxfield
Managing Editor Clare Churly
Creative Director Tracy Killick
Design Janis Utton
Picture Library Manager Jennifer Veall
Senior Production Controller Carolin Stransky